Tokyo

"All you've got to do is decide to go and the hardest part is over.

So go!"

TONY WHEELER, COFOUNDER – LONELY PLANET

REBECCA MILNER & SIMON RICHMOND

Contents

COVID-19

We have re-checked every business in this book before publication to ensure that it is still open following the COVID-19 outbreak. However, the economic and social impacts of COVID-19 will continue to be felt long after the outbreak has been contained, and many businesses, services and events referenced in this guide may experience ongoing restrictions. Some businesses may be temporarily closed, have changed their opening hours and services, or require bookings; some unfortunately could have closed permanently. We suggest you check with venues before visiting for the latest information.

Sensō-ji p156
The city's oldest temple.

Rikugi-en p144
Tokyo's most beautiful formal gardens.

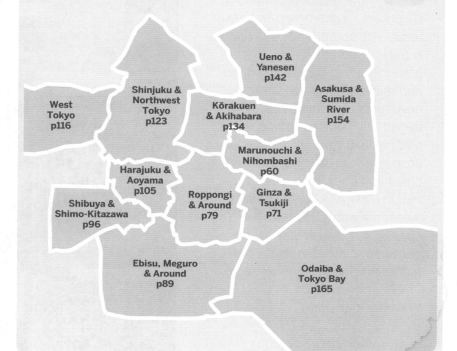

Right: Bentō box
display

WELCOME TO
Tokyo

I've lived in Tokyo for almost two decades now and am continually surprised – sometimes on a daily basis – by something new. Such is the joy of living in a city that prides itself on constant renewal and reinvention; it seriously never gets old. Tokyo has everything you can ask of a city, and has it in spades: a dynamic, cosmopolitan dining scene, more cafes and bars than you could visit in a lifetime, plenty of parks, awesome public transport and such a high level of safety and convenience that makes it hard to imagine living anywhere else.

By Rebecca Milner, Writer
For more about our writers, see p288

Tokyo's Top Experiences

1 CITY LIGHTS, CITY NIGHTS

With neon signs towering over alley-side *yakitori* (grilled chicken) stalls with their telltale red *chōchin* (lanterns), Tokyo's visual signature is distinct and highly photogenic. There's nothing quite like seeing the city from high in the air, cocktail in hand. By night, Tokyo appears truly beautiful, as if the sky were inverted with the glittering stars below.

Left: Kabukichō, Shinjuku-ku (p123)
Right: Omoide-Yokochō, Shinjuku-ku (p130)

Shibuya Crossing

This is the Tokyo you've dreamed about and seen in movies: the frenetic pace and dense crowds, the glowing lights and the giant video screens beaming larger-than-life celebrities over the streets. At Shibuya's famous 'scramble' crossing, all of this comes together every time the light changes. p98

Above: Shibuya Crossing

Shinjuku Nightlife

Shinjuku is the biggest nightlife area in the land of the rising neon sun. Here you'll find the anachronistic shanty bars of Golden Gai, a favourite haunt of writers and artists; the camp dance bars of Shinjuku-nichōme; and karaoke boxes, live music venues and sky-high cocktail bars. The options are dizzying, the lights spellbinding and the whole show continues past dawn. p130

Above: Karaoke singers

2 SUSHI, SAKE & NOODLES

One of the joys of visiting Tokyo is experiencing the true breadth of Japanese cuisine. It's all here: sushi, ramen, soba, *tonkatsu* (deep-fried pork cutlet), *okonomiyaki* (savoury pancake) and much, much more. There are restaurants that make tofu from scratch just as they have for centuries, plus innovative, owner/chef-led restaurants and many that specialise in regional Japanese dishes.

LOREANTO/SHUTTERSTOCK ©

JONATHON STOKES/LONELY PLANET ©

REBECCA MILNER/LONELY PLANET ©

Ramen

Tokyo-style ramen is thin, wavy noodles in a chicken and fish broth seasoned with soy sauce. But you can find everything from light *shio* (salt-flavoured) ramen to rich *tonkotsu* ramen (in a creamy pork-bone broth), as well as more experimental flavours like those at Mensho Tokyo. p138

Above: Lunchtime ramen bowl

Izakaya

At a classic *izakaya* – the Japanese equivalent of a pub – the food is designed to pair with the nation's signature tipple: sake. Many also offer tasting sets, which is an excellent way to sample the flavours of different regional sakes and styles. p42

Top: Glass of sake

Toyosu Market

Tokyo is known as the best place in the world to get sushi: the highest quality fresh ingredients arrive daily at the city's wholesale market. Going for a sushi breakfast at the fish market has long been a traveller tradition. p168

Bottom: Daiwa Sushi (p169), Toyosu Market

3 SHRINES & TEMPLES

Pass through *torii* (shrine gates) to enter sacred grounds. Clap your hands to summon the gods. Write your wishes on a prayer plaque. Let the incense wash over you. Tokyo's Shintō shrines and Buddhist temples are places of worship and age-old rituals. They're also fascinating repositories of ancient art, architecture and landscape design.

Meiji-jingū

Tokyo's largest and most famous Shintō shrine feels a world away from the city. The grounds are vast, enveloping the classic wooden shrine buildings and a landscaped garden in a thick coat of green. p107

Above: Meiji-jingū
Left: *Ema* (prayer plaques), Meiji-jingū

Sensō-ji

This Buddhist temple was founded over 1000 years before the city got its start. Today it retains an alluring, lively atmosphere redolent of Edo (old Tokyo) and the merchant quarters of yesteryear. p156

Top left: Sensō-ji

Nikkō

Nikkō, in the mountains north of Tokyo, is one of Japan's major attractions, with Shintō shrines and Buddhist temples enveloped in cedar forest – their artistic splendour reflective of the awesome power of the Tokugawa shogunate. p174

Left: Kanman-Ga-Fuchi Abyss (p176), Nikkō

4 TOKYO POP!

From Godzilla to the animated films of Miyazaki Hayao, Hello Kitty to Pokémon, Japanese pop culture has captivated the world for generations. Tokyo offers many ways to engage with your favourite characters and immerse yourself in their fantasy worlds. (And if you're not already a fan of Japanese pop culture, the city might just turn you).

Unicorn Gundam

Gundam is a widely popular Japanese anime series, and this 1:1 scale model of an RX-0 Unicorn Gundam is a photo op of the first degree. p168

Top left: Unicorn Gundam statue

Ghibli Museum, Mitaka

Enter the magical world of master animator Miyazaki Hayao. Designed by Miyazaki himself, this enchanting space is filled with whirring steampunk-esque machines and fairy-tale structures. p118

Bottom left: Ghibli Museum, Mitaka

Akihabara

'Akiba' is Tokyo's famous pop culture district, filled with shops selling anime, manga (Japanese comics) and gaming merch, neon-bright electronics stores, retro arcades, cosplay cafes and *gashapon* (capsule toy vending machines). p139

Above: Akihabara

5 SEASONAL SPECTACLES

© MARCO BOTTIGELLI/GETTY IMAGES ©

TIPHAINE BRYDNIAK / 500PX/GETTY IMAGES ©

UINO/SHUTTERSTOCK ©

Plum blossoms. Cherry blossoms. Lively traditional festivals. Spectacular displays of fireworks. The sunset shades of fall foliage. Sparkling winter illuminations. Whether this is your first visit to Tokyo or your tenth, there is always something new to experience – depending on the time of year. Whenever you visit, make sure to make the most of the season.

Cherry Blossoms

Hanami is a centuries-old tradition, a celebration of the fleeting beauty of life symbolised by the blossoms, which last only a week or two. It's the one time of year you'll see Tokyoites let their hair down en masse as a carnivalesque spirit envelopes the city. Yoyogi-kōen is where you'll find some of the most spirited and elaborate bacchanals – complete with barbecues and turntables. Many revellers stay long past dark for *yozakura* (night blossoms). p34

Top left: Cherry blossoms, Yoyogi-kōen (p108)

Traditional Festivals

Tokyo's *matsuri* (festivals) are carried out much like they have for centuries, with rollicking parades of portable shrines or folk dancing through the streets. Most take place during the summer months. p28

Bottom left: Illuminated paper lanterns, Mitama Matsuri festival (p29)

6 THE SHOGUN'S CITY

Before Tokyo became Tokyo, it was Edo, the city built by the powerful Tokugawa shoguns who reigned throughout the 17th and 18th centuries and into the 19th century. A lot of what we think of today as quintessentially Japanese – like kabuki theatre, sumo wrestling and woodblock prints – are rooted in the culture of Edo. And fortunately for visitors, traces of the old city remain to this day.

Kabuki at Kabukiza

Dramatic, intensely visual kabuki is Japan's most recognised art form. An afternoon at the theatre is a local tradition, and descendants of the great actors of Edo still appear on Tokyo stages. Kabukiza is Tokyo's dedicated kabuki theatre. p74

Below: Theatre poster, Kabukiza

J. HENNING BUCHHOLZ/SHUTTERSTOCK ©

Sumo

Purifying salt sails into the air; a flurry of slapping and heaving ensues before the shoving begins. From the ancient rituals to the thrill of the quick bouts, sumo is a fascinating spectacle. Tournaments are held at Ryōgoku Kokugi-kan in January, May and September. p158

Above: Sumo wrestlers

Tokyo National Museum

The Tokyo National Museum houses the world's largest collection of Japanese art, including samurai swords, colourful *ukiyo-e* (woodblock prints), gorgeous kimonos and much, much more. p145

Right: Buddha statue, Tokyo National Museum

7 OUTDOOR ADVENTURES

MARCO BOTTIGELLI/GETTY IMAGES ©

MATT MUNRO/LONELY PLANET ©

LEO DAPHNE/ALAMY STOCK PHOTO ©

Stretch your legs in one of Tokyo's many parks and gardens. Go for a jog along the popular circuit around the Imperial Palace moats. Book a cycling or kayaking tour – yes, kayaking in Tokyo's canals. There are lots of adventures to be had in the city. Just outside the city, within two hours by public transport, are opportunities for hiking and soaking in outdoor onsen (hot springs).

Mt Fuji

Mt Fuji (3776m) is one of Japan's most enduring icons. Hundreds of thousands of people climb 'Fuji-san' every year, continuing a centuries-old tradition of pilgrimages up the sacred volcano. Dawn from the summit is pure magic (even when it's cloudy). p172

Above: Mt Fuji behind Kawaguchi-ko lake

Hakone

Hakone is the collective name for several onsen resorts nestled in the mountains southwest of Tokyo. It's a favourite spot for locals looking to get away to relax. There are excellent day spas here, plus a pretty lake, a steaming volcano and hiking trails. p177

8 SHOPPING SPREES

Tokyo is the trendsetter for all of Japan, and fashion born here has set off waves across the globe. But the city also has a strong artisan tradition and a passion for *monozukuri* ('the art of making things'). Whether you are looking for a one-of-a-kind fashion piece, a hand-forged chef's knife or just inspiration, Tokyo has something for you.

Harajuku

The backstreets of Harajuku form Tokyo's street-fashion lab: the trendsetters, the peacocks and the photographers who chronicle it all. Nearby Aoyama is where many Japanese labels have their flagship stores. p114

Top left: Cosplay, Harajuku

Ginza

Ginza is Tokyo's classic, central shopping district, anchored by famous department stores like Mitsukoshi. Also here: pedigreed specialty shops, designer malls and high-concept boutiques. p77

Bottom left: Ginza Six (p77)

Asakusa

Asakusa is full of traditional craft shops – think pretty, dyed textiles and handmade paper – which makes it perfect for souvenir hunting. Meanwhile, Tokyo's kitchenware district, Kappabashi-dōri, is a short walk away. p161

Above: Traditional rice bowls, Asakusa

9 CONTEMPORARY STYLINGS

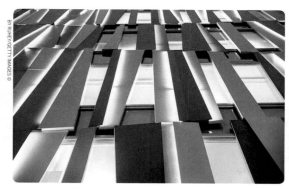

BY RUHEY/GETTY IMAGES ©

MARIO SERRANO/SHUTTERSTOCK ©

EXHIBITION VIEW OF MORI BUILDING DIGITAL ART MUSEUM: TEAMLAB BORDERLESS, 2018, ODAIBA, TOKYO © TEAMLAB. TEAMLAB IS REPRESENTED BY PACE GALLERY.

Omote-sandō

This broad, tree-lined boulevard is lined with boutiques from the top European fashion houses. But it's the buildings themselves that steal the show: many are designed by some of the biggest names in Japanese architecture. There's no better (or more convenient) place to gain an overview of Japan's current sense of design.

Top left: Omote-sandō architecture

teamLab Borderless

teamLab is Japan's most prominent digital-art collective, whose installations have appeared all over the world. At this museum, the first devoted solely to their work, they've gathered many of these installations (and added some new ones) to create a totally immersive, interactive art experience unlike anything else. Weaving together several worlds, it's full of surprises and makes for some great photos. p167

Bottom left: Exhibit, teamLab Borderless

Japan's architects are among the most celebrated in the world and Tokyo is a showcase for their works. The city is also the centre of Japan's contemporary art scene, with outstanding museums, galleries and public artworks. Tokyo has long been a source of inspiration for creators around the world; perhaps it will be for you, too.

What's New

In the build-up to the 2020 (turned 2021) Summer Olympics, Tokyo has been hard at work making itself more attractive to overseas visitors. This includes new developments and renovations, improved English signage and accessibility, and more bars and restaurants incorporating global trends like plant-based foods and non-alcoholic cocktails.

Shibuya Reimagined

Shibuya, a long-time favourite traveller destination, is two-thirds through a massive redevelopment that is transforming the station area. The newest additions: Shibuya Scramble Square, a huge glass tower with a rooftop observatory and floors of shops and restaurants; Shibuya Stream (p99), which has restaurants, a hotel and a riverside terrace – part of a movement to revitalise the city's waterways; and Miyashita Park, a (controversial) redevelopment of a public park into a multi-use complex with restaurants, cafes, a rooftop skate park and, yes, some public green space.

New Openings

Noteworthy new openings in Tokyo include: the Yayoi Kusama Museum (p126), devoted to one of Japan's most prominent contemporary artists; teamLab Borderless (p167), an immersive, interactive art experience created by Japan's leading digital-art collective, teamLab; and Toyosu Market (p168), which replaces Tsukiji Market (p73) as the city's central wholesale market (the 'outer' dry market at Tsukiji is still in place).

And for the first time in nearly 50 year, the city's iconic Yamanote line got a new station: Takanawa Gateway, designed by Kuma Kengo.

LOCAL KNOWLEDGE

WHAT'S HAPPENING IN TOKYO

Rebecca Milner, Lonely Planet writer

For near on a decade – since the successful bid was announced in 2013 – Tokyo has been on Olympics watch. Initially there was general enthusiasm, and a flurry of redevelopment projects intended to turn Tokyo into a model, contemporary city for international audiences. Then came the spiralling costs (to be shouldered by taxpayers). By 2021, after the COVID-19 pandemic had already postponed the Olympics by a year, public opinion polls were in favour of cancelling the event entirely.

Tokyo was the epicentre of Japan's COVID-19 outbreak, though fortunately the city (and Japan as a whole) did not experience the same devastating losses of life recorded elsewhere. But it was far from business as usual, and the hospitality industry in particular took a serious hit. Locals were torn between following government guidelines to refrain from dining out and flouting them in order to support their beloved, struggling neighbourhood spots. Meanwhile, many office workers were given the opportunity to work from home – revolutionary in a country with a rigid office culture – which has led to discussions about what the future of work–life in Tokyo could look like.

Neo Yokochō

'Yokochō' are side streets with small restaurants, bars and food stalls and they've been a part of Tokyo's dining culture for decades. While new developments are constantly altering the cityscape, some are adding 'neo yokochō' – purpose-built with gourmet offerings and a retro design flair – in a nod to the city's roots. Shibuya Yokochō, on the ground floor of the new Miyashita Park complex, has 19 options with outdoor seating. See also Toranomon Yokochō inside Toranomon Hills (p82), which is accessed via the new Hibiya line station Toranomon Hills.

Sake, Tea & Mocktails

Japan went all-in on the recent craft beer and third-wave coffee trends, but now we're seeing that same spirit of innovation and attention to detail being poured into two distinctly Japanese drinks: tea and sake. This means craft sake bars, like Gem by Moto (p94) and Another 8 (p95), and third-wave-style teahouses, like Sakurai Japanese Tea Experience (p112).

Non-alcoholic options are also getting more interesting, with more bars making original mocktails with the same enthusiasm they typically reserve for cocktails.

Stylish Accommodation

The build-up to the Tokyo Olympics has seen a flurry of new hotels and hostels go up, including some with cool interiors, boutique amenities and fun vibes. Check out Mustard Hotel (p191), Turntable (p191) and Millennials (p191).

Restorations & Reopenings

Following more than two decades of work, the restoration process of Nikkō's spectacular shrines and temples is nearly complete. A few structures (none of the major ones) may still be under wraps, but the rest gleam anew with brilliant colour (created using historical materials and techniques).

Restoration work on Tokyo's signature shrine, Meiji-jingū (p107), was completed in 2020 in time for its centennial; note

the new wooden *torii* (shrine gates) and copper plated roof. In spring 2021, Mori Art Museum (p81) reopened with refurbished gallery spaces, a new gift shop and timed admissions scheme.

Smoking Ban

Long considered a smoker's paradise, Tokyo introduced laws to make bars and restaurants (with some exceptions) smoke-free in 2020.

Cannabis remains very, very illegal – with more police crackdowns than ever (don't risk it).

LISTEN, WATCH AND FOLLOW

For inspiration and up-to-date news, visit www.lonelyplanet.com/japan/tokyo/articles.

Go Tokyo (www.gotokyo.org) The city's official website has information, events and trip planning tools.

The Japan Times (www.japantimes.co.jp) Japan's long-running, English-language newspaper.

Tokyo Art Beat (www.tokyoartbeat.com) Listings and reviews for museum and gallery shows.

Tokyo Cheapo (www.tokyocheapo.com) Hints on how to do Tokyo on the cheap.

FAST FACTS

Food Trend Vegan ramen

Number of convenience stores 7785

Tallest building Tokyo Skytree (634m)

Population 13.96 million

JAPAN   TOKYO

≈ 350 people per sq km

Need to Know

For more information, see Survival Guide (p229)

Currency
Japanese yen (¥)

Language
Japanese

Visas
Visas are generally not required for stays of up to 90 days.

Money
Convenience stores and post offices have international ATMs. Credit cards are widely accepted, though it's still best to keep some cash on hand.

Mobile Phones
Prepaid data-only SIM cards (for unlocked smartphones only) are widely available at the airports and electronics stores. Many hotels now offer Handy phone service.

Time
Japan Standard Time (GMT/UTC plus nine hours)

Tourist Information
Tokyo Metropolitan Government Building Tourist Information Center (p243) has English-language information and publications. There are additional branches in Keisei Ueno Station (p243), Haneda Airport (p243) and Shinjuku Bus Terminal (p243).

Daily Costs

Budget:
Less than ¥8000

➡ Dorm bed: ¥3000

➡ Free sights such as temples and markets

➡ Bowl of noodles: ¥800

➡ Happy-hour drink: ¥500

➡ 24-hour subway pass: ¥600

Midrange:
¥8000–20,000

➡ Double room at a business hotel: ¥15,000

➡ Museum entry: ¥1000

➡ Dinner for two at an *izakaya* (Japanese pub-eatery): ¥6000

➡ Live music show: ¥3000

Top End:
More than ¥20,000

➡ Double room in a four-star hotel: from ¥35,000

➡ Private cooking class: ¥10,000

➡ Sushi-tasting menu: ¥15,000

➡ Taxi ride back to the hotel: ¥3000

Advance Planning

Three months before Purchase tickets for the Ghibli Museum, Mitaka; book a table at a top restaurant.

One month before Book tickets online for theatre and sporting events, activities, courses and tours of the Imperial Palace.

When you arrive Look for discount coupons for attractions at airports and hotels; have your accommodation help you reserve seats at popular *izakaya*.

Useful Websites

Go Tokyo (www.gotokyo. org) The city's official website includes information on sights, events and suggested itineraries.

Lonely Planet (www.lonely planet.com/tokyo) Destination information, hotel reviews, traveller forum and more.

Spoon & Tamago (www. spoon-tamago.com) Japanese arts and culture blog with great suggestions for cool spots and events.

Tokyo Cheapo (https://tokyo cheapo.com) Hints on how to do Tokyo on the cheap.

Time Out Tokyo (www.timeout. jp) Arts and entertainment listings.

WHEN TO GO

Spring and autumn have mild weather; spring has cherry blossoms. Mid-June to mid-July is the rainy season. August is hot and humid, but also has festivals.

Tokyo

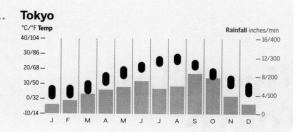

Arriving in Tokyo

Narita Airport An express train or highway bus to central Tokyo costs around ¥3000 (one to two hours). Both run frequently from 6am to 10.30pm; pick up tickets at kiosks inside the arrivals hall (no advance reservations required). Taxis start at ¥20,000.

Haneda Airport Frequent trains and buses (¥400 to ¥1200, 30 to 45 minutes) to central Tokyo run from 5.30am to midnight; times and costs depend on your destination in the city. There are only a couple of night buses. For a taxi, budget between ¥5000 and ¥8000.

Tokyo Station Connect from the *shinkansen* (bullet train) terminal here to the Japan Railways (JR) Yamanote line or the Marunouchi subway for destinations around central Tokyo.

For much more on **arrival** see p230

Language

Tokyo is making strides to provide more English on the ground for travellers. TICs have English-speaking staff (and plenty of English-language info). Most centrally located hotels, department stores and electronics emporiums also have staff who can speak some English. Train and subway stations have English signage; announcements are usually made in English (station staff rarely speak English). More and more restaurants in well-touristed areas are making an effort with English menus.

Inconsistency, though, is still common, with some cultural attractions (like museums) making a better effort than others. In general, English ability varies widely among Tokyoites. Asking for directions on the street is hit-or-miss.

For much more on **getting around** see p232

Sleeping

As in any major city, accommodation will take up a major chunk of your Tokyo budget. But here's the good news: there are plenty of attractive budget and midrange options, and levels of cleanliness and service are generally high everywhere. You can play it safe with a standard hotel or change it up with a more local option, like a ryokan (traditional inn with Japanese-style bedding) or a capsule hotel.

Marunouchi (Tokyo Station), Shinjuku, Shibuya and Ikebukuro all have direct access to Narita Airport on the Narita Express; Ueno has its own direct line to Narita, the Skyliner. In general, neighbourhoods on the east side of town, like Ueno and Asakusa, have cheaper sleeping options; however, many travellers opt for one of the west-side hubs, Shinjuku or Shibuya, which have more nightlife.

For much more on **sleeping** see p185

First Time Tokyo

For more information, see Survival Guide (p229)

Checklist

➡ Purchase any of the Japan Rail Passes (www.japanrailpass.net) if you plan to travel extensively around the country.

➡ Get an international licence if you want to experience go-karting; car rental isn't necessary for day trips, but does mean you have more flexibility.

What to Pack

➡ Tokyo hotels tend to be tiny, so bring as small a suitcase as possible.

➡ Japanese pharmacies don't carry foreign medications; local substitutes can be found in a pinch, but it's a good idea to have some stuff from home on hand.

➡ Certain medications that are legal in your home country may be illegal in Japan or require paperwork to import (see p236).

Top Tips for Your Trip

➡ Pick just a couple of proximate neighbourhoods to explore in a day. Tokyo is huge, and while public transport is effortlessly smooth, you don't want to spend half the day on it.

➡ Splurge at lunch. Many restaurants – including those in notoriously pricey districts like Ginza – offer midday meals that cost half (or less!) of what you'd find at dinner, and often for a meal that is not significantly smaller or lower in quality.

➡ Rent a pocket wi-fi device. Tokyo has free wi-fi in spots, but it's frustratingly clunky. Having constant internet access means you can use navigation apps to help you get around (as Tokyo's address system is famously confusing).

➡ Walk: in the city centre the distance between two subway stations is rarely more than 10 minutes – you'll save a little yen and see a more local side of the city.

What to Wear

Tokyoites are smart dressers – preferring to look as neat, tidy and on-trend as possible – but are never overly fancy. That said, expectations for foreign tourists are pretty low. Tracksuits are generally fine, although would, ideally, be of the latest brand-name style.

Only the highest-end restaurants and bars have enforced dress codes, and even that usually just means no sleeveless shirts or sandals for men. Religious sites (Buddhist temples and Shintō shrines) do not have dress codes.

Do keep in mind that you may be taking your shoes on and off a lot so it helps to have footwear that doesn't need lacing up. You may also find yourself sitting on the floor, which can be tricky in short or tight clothing.

Be Forewarned

The biggest threat to travellers in Tokyo is the city's general aura of safety; keep up the same level of caution and common sense that you would back home. For more, see p241.

Credit Cards

Once uncommon in Japan, most businesses in Tokyo now accept credit cards, usually displaying the logo for the cards they accept on the cash register. If a restaurant, bar or shop is particularly small or old-looking (and you don't see any signage), it's wise to ask upfront.

Taxes & Refunds

Japan's consumption tax is 8% (with a planned rise to 10% in October 2019). Many retailers (often noted by a sticker in English on the window) offer duty-free shopping for purchases of more than ¥5000. Only visitors on tourist visas are eligible; you'll need to show your passport. For more, see p241.

Tipping

Tipping There is no custom of tipping in Japan, although if you hire a private guide a small gratuity for excellent service is appreciated.

Service fee In lieu of a tip, high-end restaurants, bars and hotels often add a 10% to 15% service fee to the bill.

Groups Some restaurants, no matter the price point, may levy a service charge on larger groups; a party as small as six may be deemed large, but it varies.

Language

Is there a Western-/Japanese-style room?
洋室/和室はありますか?
yō·shi·tsu/wa·shi·tsu wa a·ri·mas ka

Some lodgings have only Japanese-style rooms, or a mix of Western and Japanese – ask if you have a preference.

Please bring a (spoon/knife/fork).
(スプーン/ナイフ/フォーク)をください。
(spūn/nai·fu/fō·ku) o ku·da·sai

If you haven't quite mastered the art of eating with chopsticks, don't be afraid to ask for cutlery at a restaurant.

How do I get to ...?
…へはどう行けばいいですか?
... e wa dō i·ke·ba ī des ka

Finding a place from its address can be difficult in Japan. Addresses usually give an area (not a street) and numbers aren't always consecutive. Practise asking for directions.

I'd like a nonsmoking seat, please.
禁煙席をお願いします。
kin·en·se·ki o o·ne·gai shi·mas

There are smoking seats in many restaurants and on bullet trains so be sure to specify if you want to be smoke-free.

What's the local speciality?
地元料理は何がありますか?
ji·mo·to·ryō·ri wa na·ni ga a·ri·mas ka

Throughout Japan most areas have a speciality dish and locals usually love to talk food.

Etiquette

Japan is famous for its etiquette, though it's not as strict (or consistent) as you may think.

Greetings Japanese typically greet each other with a slight bow, but may greet foreigners with a handshake; hugging and cheek-kissing would be considered alarming.

Queueing Tokyoites are famous queuers, forming neat lines in front of subway doors, ramen shops and more.

Eating & drinking Japanese frown upon eating and drinking on streets and on public transport; beverages in resealable containers are an exception.

Shoes off Many lodgings and restaurants request you leave your shoes at the door. Take a quick look around for a sign – or slippers in the foyer – to see if this rule applies. Shoes should never be worn on tatami mats.

Escalators Stand to the left on escalators.

Getting Around

For more information, see Transport (p230)

Efficient, clean and generally safe, Tokyo's public transport system is the envy of the world. Of most use to travellers is the train and subway system, which is easy to navigate thanks to English signage.

Subway
The quickest and easiest way to get around central Tokyo. Runs 5am to midnight.

Train
Japan Railways (JR) Yamanote (loop) and Chūō-Sōbu (central) lines service major stations. Run from 5am to midnight.

Taxi
A pricey option, but the only one that runs all night; easy to hail.

Bicycle
A fun way to get around, though traffic can be intense. Rentals available; some hostels and ryokan (traditional inns) lend bicycles.

Walking
Subway stations are close to each other in the city centre; save cash by walking if you only need to go one stop.

Key Phrases

Chikatetsu (地下鉄) Japanese for subway.

JR Short for Japan Railways, which runs the useful Yamanote, Sōbu and Chūō Tokyo train lines as well as the Narita Express and the national *shinkansen* (bullet train) network.

Midori-no-madoguchi (緑の 窓口; green window) Found in larger JR train stations, these are ticket counters for purchasing long-distance (including bullet train) tickets. Credit cards accepted.

Pasmo (パスモ) Prepaid rechargeable train pass, good on all city subways, trains and buses. Also works on vending machines and kiosks in stations and at some convenience stores. Sold at subway and commuter line stations.

Suica (スイカ) JR's version of Pasmo, which functions exactly the same.

Tokkyū (特急) Limited express trains; includes both commuter trains that make limited stops and reserved-seat resort liners that require a surcharge to ride.

Key Routes

Ginza subway line Shibuya to Asakusa, via Ginza and Ueno. Colour-coded orange.

Hibiya subway line Naka-Meguro to Ebisu, Roppongi, Ginza, Akihabara and Ueno. Colour-coded grey.

JR Yamanote line Loop line stopping at many sightseeing destinations, such as Shibuya, Harajuku, Shinjuku, Tokyo and Ueno. Colour-coded light green.

JR Chūō line Express between Tokyo Station and Shinjuku, and onwards to points west. Colour-coded reddish-orange.

JR Sōbu line Runs across the city centre connecting Shinjuku with Iidabashi, Ryōgoku and Akihabara. Colour-coded yellow.

Yurikamome line Elevated train running from Shimbashi to points around Tokyo Bay.

How to Hail a Taxi

➡ Train stations and hotels have designated taxi stands.

➡ If there's no stand, hail a cab from the street by standing on the curb and sticking your arm out, though it may be quicker to walk to the nearest stand.

➡ Red characters on the digital sign in the front window indicate a cab is free.

➡ All cabs run by the meter.

➡ Step back from the door; they open and close automatically.

TOP TIPS

➡ Figure out the best route to your destination with the Japan Travel app (https://navitimejapan.com).

➡ Most train and subway stations have several different exits. Try to get your bearings and decide where to exit while still on the platform; look for the yellow signs that indicate which stairs lead to which exits.

➡ If you're not sure which exit to take, look for street maps of the area, usually posted near the ticket gates, which show the locations of the exits.

➡ Taxi drivers almost never speak English; be prepared to show the name of your destination in Japanese.

When to Travel

➡ Trains and subways run 5am to midnight.

➡ The morning rush (7am to 9.30am) for trains going towards central Tokyo (from all directions) is the worst, with some lines running at 200% capacity.

➡ Until 9.30am women (and children) can ride in women-only cars, which tend to be less crowded.

➡ The evening rush (around 5pm to 8pm) hits trains going out of central Tokyo – though as many people work late or stay out, it's not as bad as the morning commute.

➡ The last train of the night heading out of the city (around midnight) is also usually packed – with drunk people. Friday night is the worst.

➡ Trains going the opposite directions during peak hours (towards central Tokyo in the evening, for example) are uncrowded, as are trains in the middle of the day.

Etiquette

➡ Have your train pass or ticket in hand when approaching the ticket gates, especially during rush hour, to avoid creating a jam.

➡ You will get dirty looks for getting on rush-hour trains with large luggage.

➡ When the platform is crowded, Tokyoites will form neat lines on either side of where the doors will be when the train pulls up (though once the train pulls up this falls apart a bit).

➡ It's considered bad form to eat or drink on the train (long-distance trains are an exception). Talking on the phone or having a loud conversation is also frowned upon.

➡ Stand to the left on escalators.

➡ Seats at the end of train cars are set aside as 'priority seats' for elderly, disabled or pregnant passengers (though Tokyoites are known to ignore this).

Tickets & Passes

➡ Prepaid rechargeable Suica and Pasmo cards (they're interchangeable) work on all city trains, subways and buses.

➡ Purchase from any touch-screen ticket-vending machine in Tokyo (including those at Haneda and Narita Airports); most have an English option. JR stations sell Suica; subway and independent lines sell Pasmo.

➡ Both require a ¥500 deposit, which is refunded (along with any remaining charge) when you return the pass to any ticket window.

➡ Passes can be topped-up at any touch-screen ticket-vending machine (not just, for example, at JR stations for Suica passes) in increments of ¥1000.

➡ To use the cards, just run them over the card readers at the ticket gates upon entering and exiting.

➡ If you somehow manage to invalidate your card, take it to the station window and staff will sort it out.

➡ Bonus: fares for pass users are slightly less (a few yen per journey) than for paper-ticket holders.

For much more on **getting around** see p232

Perfect Days

Day One

Harajuku & Aoyama (p105)

 Start with a visit to **Meiji-jingū**, Tokyo's signature Shintō shrine. Then walk down **Omote-sandō** to check out the stunning contemporary architecture along this stylish boulevard. Spend some time shopping in Harajuku's trendsetting boutiques, or check out a museum like the **Ukiyo-e Ōta Memorial Museum of Art**.

> **Lunch** Stop for dumplings at local fave Harajuku Gyōza-rō (p109).

Shibuya & Shimo-Kitazawa (p96)

 Head next to Shibuya (you can walk) where the main attraction is Tokyo's most photogenic (and chaotic) intersection, **Shibuya Crossing**. Shibuya is a youthful district, which you can get a feel for by wandering around the main drag, **Shibuya Center-gai**. At the end is supreme souvenir hunting ground, the variety store **Tokyu Hands**.

> **Dinner** At *izakaya* Donjaca (p130) or *yakitori* in Omoide-yokochō (p130).

Shinjuku & Northwest Tokyo (p123)

Take the train to Shinjuku and immerse yourself in the swarming crowds and neon lights of this famous nightlife district. The **Tokyo Metropolitan Government Building** observatories stay open until 11pm for free night views. From around 9pm the shanty bars of **Golden Gai** come to life; take your pick from the eccentric offerings and finish up with a time-honoured Tokyo tradition: a late-night bowl of noodles at **Nagi**.

Day Two

Ginza & Tsukiji (p69)

 Skip breakfast and head to **Tsukiji Market**, where you can cobble together a morning meal from the food vendors here. There are also stalls selling kitchen tools, tea and more. From Tsukiji it's an easy walk to the landscape garden **Hama-rikyū Onshi-teien**, where you can stop for tea in the teahouse, **Nakajima no Ochaya**.

> **Lunch** Go for broke at Ginza sushi counter Kyūbey (p75); book ahead.

Odaiba & Tokyo Bay (p169)

Take an after-lunch stroll around Ginza, with its art galleries and luxury boutique windows. Then from nearby Shimbashi Station, take the meandering above-ground Yurikamome line to Tokyo Bay. Spend a couple of hours exploring the fascinating new digital-art museum, **team-Lab Borderless**, and stick around until dark to see **Unicorn Gundam** all lit up.

> **Dinner** Sample *anago* (seafaring eel) at Nihonbashi Tamai (p68).

Marunouchi & Nihombashi (p58)

 There's not much to do by the bay at night, so return to the centre city for some classic Japanese food and maybe a nightcap at a posh hotel bar, like **Peter: the Bar**, or see traditional performing arts at dinner theatre **Suigian**.

Ameya-Yokochō (p151)

Hama-rikyū Onshi-teien (p7.

Day Three

Asakusa & Sumida River (p154)

 Get an early start on the crowds at Tokyo's top temple **Sensō-ji**; see the shrine **Asakusa-jinja** here, too, and the maze of narrow lanes that surrounds the whole complex, where there are lots of shops selling traditional crafts and foodstuffs. Then take the subway to nearby Ueno.

Lunch Go for classic Japanese cuisine in the park at Innsyoutei (p149).

Ueno & Yanesen (p142)

 Spend the afternoon exploring the many attractions of **Ueno-kōen**, home to the **Tokyo National Museum** and centuries-old temples and shrines. Then take a stroll through the old-fashioned, open-air market, **Ameya-yokochō**, and the historical neighbourhood of **Yanaka**; in the latter you'll find art galleries and studios.

Dinner Eat at iconic *izakaya* (Japanese pub-eatery) Shinsuke (p150).

Asakusa & Sumida River (p154)

 The east side of the city is quieter at night than the west side, but you can come back to Asakusa in the evening to see Sensō-ji lit up (and deserted) and catch a folk-music show at **Oiwake**, or dig into Japan's craft-beer scene at legendary Ryōgoku beer bar **Popeye**, further south down the river.

Day Four

West Tokyo (p116)

 Take the Chūō line west to the magical **Ghibli Museum, Mitaka** (reservations necessary; we recommend getting in early at 10am). Afterwards, walk through woodsy **Inokashira-kōen** (stopping at **Inokashira Benzaiten**) to Kichijōji, which has some good homewares boutiques and an old market, **Harmonica-yokochō**.

Lunch Stop off in Kōenji for amazing tempura at Tensuke (p120).

Kōrakuen & Akihabara (p134)

 After lunch, take the Chūō line back east to **Akihabara**, where you can visit manga and anime superstore **Mandarake** and ride go-karts through the streets with **MariCAR** (reserve ahead; international driving licence necessary). If you haven't yet worked in an onsen dip, visit nearby **Spa LaQua**.

Dinner Get the nouveau ramen experience at Mensho Tokyo (p138).

Roppongi & Around (p79)

 For your last night, head to Roppongi to check out **Roppongi Hills**, the first of Tokyo's new breed of live-work-and-play megamalls. On the top floor of a tower here is the excellent **Mori Art Museum**, which stays open until 10pm. Then head out into the wilds of Roppongi's infamous nightlife. Make sure to fit in a round of karaoke.

Month by Month

January

Tokyo is eerily quiet for Shōgatsu, the first three days of the new year set aside for family and rest; most places close, sometimes for the whole week. Things stay pretty quiet all month, actually.

Hatsu-mōde

Hatsu-mōde, the first shrine visit of the new year, starts just after midnight on 1 January and continues through Shōgatsu. Meiji-jingū (p109) is the most popular spot in Tokyo; it can get very, very crowded, but that's part of the experience.

February

February is the coldest month, crisp and clear with only the rare dusting of snow. It's not a popular time of year to visit (except over Chinese New Year), which means sights are less crowded.

Setsubun

The first day of spring *(setsubun)* on the traditional lunar calendar, 3 February, signals a shift once believed to bode evil. People visit Buddhist temples, toss roasted beans and shout *'Oni wa soto! Fuku wa uchi!'* (Devil out! Fortune in!).

Plum Blossoms

Plum *(ume)* blossoms, which appear towards the end of the month, are the first sign that winter is ending. Popular viewing spots include Koishikawa Kōrakuen (p136).

March

Spring begins in fits and starts. The Japanese have a saying: *sankan-shion* – three days cold, four days warm; pack accordingly.

Tokyo Marathon

Tokyo's biggest running event happens on the first Sunday of March. Competition for slots is fierce; sign up the summer before via www.marathon.tokyo/en.

☆ Tokyo Haru-sai

Month-long classical-music festival Tokyo Haru-sai (www.tokyo-harusai.com) is held annually over March and April at venues around Ueno-kōen. Look out for the occasional performance in unconventional spaces like the Gallery of Hōryū-ji Treasures and the National Museum of Nature & Science. Buy tickets online.

April

Warmer weather and spring blooms make this quite simply the best month to be in Tokyo.

Cherry Blossoms

For two weeks, usually late March and early April, Tokyoites toast spring in spirited parties called *hanami* under the blooming cherry trees. Top spots include the parks Ueno-kōen (p148), Yoyogi-kōen (p108), Shinjuku-gyoen (p126) and Inokashira-kōen (p119); and the strolling paths alongside the canals Meguro-gawa (p93) and Chidori-ga-fuchi (p63).

Azalea Blossoms

Sakura (cherries) are not the only things blooming

in April. From mid-April to early May the city's azaleas bloom bold shades of pink. Nezu-jinja (p149) is the place to see them, but they're actually everywhere: much of Tokyo's ornamental shrubbery is made up of azalea bushes.

May

There's a string of national holidays between 29 April and 5 May known as Golden Week, which means lots of events (but also crowds and accommodation price hikes). Weather-wise, May is blissfully warm and sunny.

✈️ Tokyo Rainbow Pride

A week of events over Golden Week culminates with a two-day festival at Yoyogi-kōen (p108) over the first weekend of May, which includes a parade. It's no London- or Sydney-style affair, but Tokyo Rainbow Pride (http://tokyo rainbowpride.com) gets bigger and prouder with every year.

✈️ Kanda Matsuri

Kanda Matsuri, put on by Kanda Myōjin (p136), was historically one of Tokyo's most important festivals – and it still puts on a good show, with a parade of *mikoshi* (portable shrines) around Kanda and Akihabara. It's held on the weekend closest to 15 May on odd-numbered years.

◉ Design Festa

Weekend-long Design Festa (www.designfesta.com), held at Tokyo Big Sight in mid-May, is Asia's largest

art festival, featuring performances and thousands of exhibitors. It takes place again in November.

✈️ Sanja Matsuri

Tokyo's biggest festival is held over the third weekend of May and attracts about 1.5 million spectators to Asakusa-jinja (p157). The highlight is the rowdy parade of *mikoshi* carried by men and women in traditional dress, with the grandest floats making the rounds on Sunday.

◉ Roppongi Art Night

Held in late May, this weekend-long (literally, venues stay open all night) arts event (www.roppongi artnight.com) sees large-scale installations and performances taking over the museums, galleries and streets of Roppongi. The vibe is more party than highbrow.

June

Early June is lovely, though by the end of the month *tsuyu* (the rainy season) sets in.

🍷 BeerFes Tokyo

Sample over 100 different craft beers from around Japan and the world – as much as you want for 3½ hours! – over the first weekend of June at Yebisu Garden Place (p91). Tickets often sell out; get them early at www.beerfes.jp.

July

When the rainy season passes in mid-July, suddenly it's summer

– the season for lively street fairs, *hanabi taikai* (fireworks shows) and persistent humidity.

🏃 Mt Fuji Climbing

The most popular hiking route up Mt Fuji, the Yoshida Trail, opens 1 July; other trails open 10 July. All remain open until 10 September.

✈️ Tanabata

On 7 July, the day the stars Vega and Altar (stand-ins for star-crossed lovers, a princess and cowherd) meet across the Milky Way, children tie strips of coloured paper bearing wishes around bamboo branches. Colourful lanterns are strung up at the entrance to Shibuya Center-gai (p98).

📷 Mitama Matsuri

Yasukuni-jinja (p136) celebrates O-Bon early (according to the solar calendar): from 13 to 16 July, the shrine holds a festival of remembrance for the dead featuring 30,000 illuminated *bonbori* (paper lanterns).

✈️ Sumida-gawa Fireworks

The grandest of the summer fireworks shows, held the last Saturday in July, sees an incredible 20,000 pyrotechnic wonders explode over the Sumida-gawa in Asakusa. The show starts around 7pm, but you'll have to arrive way earlier to secure a good spot.

✈️ Shinjuku Eisa Matsuri

A parade of drumming and folk dancing in the Okinawan tradition takes over the streets of Shinjuku on the last Saturday of July (www.shinjuku-eisa.com).

August

This is the height of Japan's sticky, hot summer (which locals love to bemoan). School holidays mean attractions popular with students and families will be crowded.

O-Bon

Three days in mid-August are set aside to honour the dead, when their spirits are said to return to the earth. Graves are swept, offerings are made and *bon-odori* (folk dances) take place. Many Tokyo residents return to their home towns; some shops may close too.

☆ Summer Sonic

The Tokyo area's biggest music festival (www.summersonic.com) is this part-indoor, part-outdoor weekend-long bash held in mid-August at Makuhari Messe, in neighbouring Chiba Prefecture.

Kōenji Awa Odori

Kōenji Awa Odori (www.koenji-awaodori.com) is Tokyo's biggest outdoor dance party – of the traditional kind (*awa odori* is a folk dance associated with O-Bon). Over 10,000 dancers parade through the streets, drawing upwards of a million spectators, over the last weekend in August.

September

Days are still warm, hot even – though typhoons roll through this time of year.

Top: Performer at Kōenji Awa Odori

Bottom: Autumn foliage, Koishikawa Kōrakuen (p136)

CANYALCIN/SHUTTERSTOCK ©

CHEN MIN CHUN/SHUTTERSTOCK ©

◉ Moon Viewing

Full moons in September and October call for *tsukimi* (moon-viewing gatherings). People eat *tsukimi dango – mochi*, pounded rice dumplings that are round like the moon.

☆ Tokyo Jazz Festival

Tokyo's biggest jazz festival (www.tokyo-jazz.com) is held over the first weekend of September at NHK Hall, near Yoyogi-kōen (p108). The line-up includes international superstars and local talent. New sister event **Tokyo Jazz X** (www.tokyo -jazz.com/x), at Shibuya's WWW (p103), has more ewxperimental artists.

October

Pleasantly warm days and cool evenings make this an excellent time to be in Tokyo.

☆ Festival/Tokyo

Tokyo's annual performing arts festival, Festival/Tokyo (p48) is held over a month from mid-October to mid-November at venues around the city. Works include theatre and dance, by Japanese and international artists (and especially emerging ones from Asia). Some are performed with English subtitles of synopses.

☆ Tokyo International Film Festival

During the last week in October, the Tokyo International Film Festival (www. tiff-jp.net) screens works from international and Japanese directors – the latter usually with English

subtitles. The main venue is Toho Cinemas Roppongi Hills (p87).

🎎 Halloween

Tokyo has gone mad for Halloween recently. Thousands of costumed merry-makers now converge on Shibuya Crossing (p98) for one big, chaotic street party over the last weekend in October. Shinjuku Ni-chōme and Roppongi are two other popular destinations, where many bars and clubs host Halloween events.

November

November: A quieter month; days are cooler but comfortable.

🎎 Tori-no-ichi

On 'rooster' *(tori)* days in November, *O-tori* shrines such as Hanazono-jinja (p126) hold fairs called Tori-no-ichi where vendors sell *kumade* – rakes that literally symbolise 'raking in the wealth'. The days are set according to an old calendar that marks days by the zodiac.

☆ Tokyo Filmex

Tokyo Filmex (https:// filmex.jp), held over a week in late November, focuses on emerging directors in Asia and screens many films with English subtitles.

◉ Autumn Leaves

The city's trees undergo magnificent seasonal transformations during *kōyō* (autumn foliage season); Rikugi-en (p144), Koishikawa Kōrakuen (p136) and Hama-rikyū Onshi-teien (p73) are three favourite local viewing spots.

December

The first half of the month is a little-known sweet time to visit. Later in the month the chill sets in and restaurants, filled with Tokyoites hosting *bōnenkai* (end-of-the-year parties), are harder to book.

◉ Golden Gingkos

Tokyo's official tree, the *ichō* (gingko), turns a glorious shade of gold in late autumn, usually around the first week of December; Ichō-namiki – Gingko Ave – in Gaienmae (near Aoyama) is the top viewing spot.

🎎 Ako Gishi-sai

On 14 December Sengakuji (p94) hosts a memorial service honouring the 47 *rōnin* (masterless samurai) who famously avenged their fallen master. The same number of volunteers dress as the samurai and parade through the nearby streets.

◉ Winter Illuminations

Tokyo loves its winter illuminations, and commercial districts like Ginza outdo themselves with extravagant displays throughout December. Keiyaki-zaka at Roppongi Hills (p81) is particularly magical.

🎎 Joya-no-kane

Temple bells around Japan ring 108 times at midnight on 31 December, a purifying ritual called *joya-no-kane*. Sensō-ji (p156) is Tokyo's most popular spot for this.

With Kids

Tokyo is a parent's dream: clean, safe and with every mod con. Crowds can be overwhelming and many top attractions won't appeal to younger ones, but plenty of sights and activities will. Odaiba (p165) and Tokyo Dome City (p141) are two areas designed especially for families.

Pop Culture

Kids (and kids at heart) will get a kick out of Tokyo's pop culture.

Ghibli Museum, Mitaka (p118) A portal to the magical world of famed animator Miyazaki Hayao (*Ponyo, Spirited Away*).

Unicorn Gundam (p168) Enormous illuminated robot statue from the popular anime.

Godzilla (p126) A huge replica of the famous monster of Japanese cinema.

Sakurazaka-kōen (p82) Neighbourhood park with robot-themed play equipment.

NI-Tele Really Big Clock (p74) Animated time-piece designed in collaboration with Miyazaki in the middle of downtown.

Amusement Parks

The last two are indoors and connected to big malls – good for rainy days.

Tokyo Disney Resort (p170) An obvious kid-pleaser, but be prepared for long lines.

Tokyo Dome City Attractions (p141) In the city centre, with thrill rides (plus more sedate rides for little ones), a Ferris wheel with karaoke-equipped gondolas and a baseball stadium (p139).

Sky Circus (p133) Get virtually shot out of a cannon over Tokyo.

Tokyo Joypolis (p170) Virtually enhanced video games and rides.

Hands-on Culture

Mokuhankan (p1684) Young artists can learn the Japanese art of making woodblock prints.

Toyokuni Atelier Gallery (p140) Try *sumie*, the art of ink brush painting.

Outdoors

Book a cycling (p70) or kayaking (p164) tour, or just enjoy one of Tokyo's great parks: Inokashira-kōen (p119) and Yoyogi-kōen (p108) are two family favourites.

Interactive Museums

teamLab Borderless (p167) Kids of all ages can engage with digital artworks and create their own.

National Museum of Emerging Science & Innovation (Miraikan) (p168) See humanoid robot ASIMO in action.

TeNQ (p136) All about outer space.

Need to Know

Nappy changing and nursing

Department stores and shopping malls always have nappy-changing facilities; newer ones have nursing rooms.

Transport

Avoid trains during the morning rush (7am to 9.30am); prams won't fit and small children may feel overwhelmed. Major stations (and many smaller ones, too) have elevators.

Like a Local

To get to know Tokyo is to enjoy it as the locals do: by hanging out in cafes, hitting the shops, going for beers and yakitori (and 'just one round' of karaoke) or taking it easy in one of the city's chiller neighbourhoods.

URAWONS/SHUTTERSTOCK ©

'akitori restaurant, Omoide-yokochō (p130)

Local Hang-Outs

Spend too much time in one of Tokyo's heaving districts, like Shinjuku or Shibuya, and it's hard to imagine how anyone could possibly live full-time in a city like this. But tucked away here and there are many low-key neighbourhoods where locals gather. Here are five to get you started:

Shimo-Kitazawa (p96) Long-time favourite of artists and students, with eccentric bars and a bohemian vibe.

Naka-Meguro (p92) Fashionable boutiques and canalside strolls.

Kōenji (p116) Street art, punk rock and second-hand clothing shops.

Tomigaya (p102) Hipster 'hood with indie cafes, neo-bistros and boutiques, right down the street from Shibuya.

Kiyosumi (p162) A creative hot spot east of the Sumida-gawa.

Have Breakfast at a Kissaten

Kissaten (喫茶店) – or *'kissa'* for short – is the old word for coffee shop, the one used before chains like Starbucks arrived in Japan and changed the game. Today the word is used to describe independently run coffee shops that either date from the early or mid-20th century – when Japan's coffee first wave hit – or at least look like they do. In addition to pour-over or siphon-brewed coffee (you'll get no espresso drinks here), most *kissa* serve a 'morning set' (モーニ ング セット; *mōningu setto*), until around 11am, that includes thick, buttery toast and a hard-boiled egg for little more than the original price of a cup of coffee. Iconic Tokyo *kissa* include Berg (p127), Sabōru (p138) and Kayaba Coffee (p151).

Go for Drinks in a Nomiyagai

A *nomiyagai* (飲み屋街) is literally a bar strip, but more specifically an alleyway (or cluster of alleys) lined with tiny bars, *izakaya* (Japanese pub-eateries) and *yakitori-ya* (restaurants specialising in grilled chicken skewers), often with no more than a few seats – sometimes with makeshift tables outside – and a cacophony of colourful signs, *chōchin* (paper lanterns) and *noren* (door curtains). Tokyo's most famous *nomiyagai* is Shinjuku's Golden Gai (p125); there's also Omoide-yokochō (p130) (*yokochō*, by the way, means 'alley'). If you want to really dig deep, head out on the Chūō line to the neighbourhoods in western Tokyo, where there are several lively *nomiyagai* loved by locals. Two to check out: Yanagi-kōji (p120), in Nishi-Ogikubo, and Kōenji Gādo-shita (p120), under the train tracks in Kōenji.

Sing Your Heart out at Karaoke

Karaoke (カラオケ; pronounced kah-rah-oh-kay) isn't just about singing: it's an excuse to let loose, a bonding ritual, a reason to keep the party going past the last train and a way to kill time until the first one starts in the morning. When words fail, it's a way to express yourself: are you the type to sing the latest J-pop hit (dance moves included) or do you go for an Okinawan folk ballad? It doesn't matter if you're a good singer, so long as you've got heart.

In Japan, karaoke is sung in a private room among friends. Admission is usually charged per person per half-hour. Food and drinks (ordered by phone) are brought to the room. To choose a song, use the touch screen to search by artist or title; most have an English function and plenty of English songs to choose from. Karaoke is dominated by a few major chains, which include Karaoke-kan (カラオケ館), Pasela (パセラ), Big Echo (ビッグエコー) and Uta Hiroba (歌広場). They're always brightly lit and easy to spot; look for them in entertainment districts like Shinjuku, Shibuya and Roppongi.

Visit a Shōtengai

Shōtengai (商店街, market streets), have traditionally been the lifeblood of Japanese neighbourhoods. Most residential neighbourhoods have one, usually near the train station. Often pedestrian-only, they're lined with sundry shops – butchers, produce stalls, rice sellers and tea merchants – and takeaway food counters. Their supremacy has been challenged (often successfully) in the past few decades by supermarkets and big-box stores but *shōtengai* loyalists remain. There are also market streets that have transcended local status to become popular attractions, such as the vintage, mid-20th-century Yanaka Ginza (p149).

Hit up a Convenience Store

Konbini (コンビニ; convenience stores) are a way of life for many Tokyoites. Indeed, there seems to be a Lawson, 7-Eleven or Family Mart on just about every corner. They offer a bounty of budget eats, particularly *onigiri* (rice balls), *nikuman* (stuffed buns) and curiously crustless *sando* (sandwiches); the egg salad sandwiches in particular are a beloved convenience store treat. You can also buy pretty much anything you need here; use the ATM; ship your luggage to the airport; buy concert tickets and more – Tokyo's convenience stores really are the definition of convenience.

How to Hanami

So you've planned your whole trip around the cherry blossoms, but how exactly is *hanami* (blossom-viewing) done? There are essentially two different styles: a picnic in a park under the flowering trees or a stroll along a path lined with them; the latter are often lantern-lit in the evening. Picnics usually start early and the most gung-ho *hanami*-goers will turn up very early to secure a prime spot with a plastic groundsheet; however, you can usually find a good sliver of ground whenever you turn up (unless you are a large group). You can buy a groundsheet, along with food and booze, at a convenience store – or go upscale and stock up on picnic supplies at a *depachika* (department store food floor).

While Yoyogi-kōen (p108) is an all-around favourite spot, another good picnicking spot is Shinjuku-gyoen (p126) – especially good for families as it closes at dusk and doesn't get too rowdy. For strolling, try Naka-Meguro's canal, Meguro-gawa (p93), and along the old castle moat at Chidori-ga-fuchi (p61).

For Free

Tokyo consistently lands near the top of the list of the world's most expensive cities. Yet many of the city's top sights cost nothing and free festivals take place year-round. Of course, the best way to enjoy Tokyo is to simply wander its colourful neighbourhoods – which doesn't cost a thing.

Free Sights

Shrines & Temples

With few exceptions, the city's shrines and temples are free to enter – meaning that two of the city's top sights, Meiji-jingū (p107) and Sensō-ji (p156), won't cost you a thing.

Parks & Gardens

Spend an afternoon picnicking in one of Tokyo's excellent public parks, like Yoyogi-kōen (p108) or Inokashira-kōen (p119).

City Views

Enjoy a view over the city for free from the observatories atop the Tokyo Metropolitan Government Building (p126) and the Asakusa Culture Tourist Information Center (p243).

Architecture

Japan's internationally renowned architects are behind the design of many museums (two-in-one sights) and fashion boutiques; see the latter along Omote-sandō (p108) in Harajuku.

Galleries

Take the pulse of the city's art scene in its free galleries; you'll find the best collection in Ginza, including Ginza Maison Hermès Le Forum (p73), Shiseido Gallery (p73) and the cluster inside the Okuno Building (p77).

Markets

Peek inside the new wholesale market at Toyosu (p168), soak up the vibes of historic Tsukiji Market (p73) or stroll through the old-fashioned, open-air Ameya-yokochō (p151).

Free Festivals

Throughout the year, traditional festivals (free to observe) are held at shrines and temples; check listings at Go Tokyo (www.gotokyo.org).

In the warmer months, festivals and markets of the more modern variety – celebrating Pride, Earth Day or Tokyo's Thai community, for example – set up most weekends in the plaza adjacent Yoyogi-kōen (p108). And festivals always mean cheap street-food vendors.

Money-Saving Tips

Sightseeing on a budget

National museums, like the Tokyo National Museum (p145), are the best value for money. If you plan to visit several museums, invest in a Grutto Pass (p236).

Tokyo Metro Pass

Pack a lot in one day and save money with Tokyo Metro's 24-hour unlimited travel pass (adult/child ¥600/300).

Lunchtime deals

Restaurants that charge several thousand yen per person for dinner often serve lunch for just ¥1000.

¥100 Stores

Stock up on sundries (even food and souvenirs) at these budget emporiums.

Under the Radar

In a city this enormous, there is always, always something new to discover. Go beyond the top sights to find low-key (and secretly happening) neighbourhoods and overlooked (but excellent) sights, support local businesses and help keep overtourism in check.

Rikugi-en (p144)

Tokyo & Tourism

Tokyo being huge and, by nature, already crowded, it hasn't felt the strain of over-tourism to the extent of many other cities (in Japan, the city most struggling with this is Kyoto). The people most likely to feel the effects of the increased number of visitors are other tourists. Major sights like Meiji-jingū (p107), Sensō-ji (p156), Hama-rikyū Onshi-teien (p73) and Tsukiji Market (p73) are routinely crowded. The best advice is simply to try to get to these as early in the day as possible.

Some popular attractions, including Ghibli Museum, Mitaka (p118), Yayoi Kusama Museum (p126), Mori Art Museum (p81), teamLab Borderless (p167) and the tuna auction at Toyosu Market (p168) have timed or limited entry. This makes for a more pleasant visiting experience, but also means you'll need to plan ahead to reserve an entry time.

One thing that does make locals cranky is the added strain on public transportation. If you need to take commuter trains (ie not the Narita Express or the Skyliner) or the subway on your journey to or from the airport or onwards to other destinations in Japan, consider having your luggage shipped to your accommodation (this is what most Tokyoites do) or taking a taxi. There are several courier services in the arrivals lobbies of both Narita and Haneda airports and also at the tourism information centre at the Shinjuku Bus Terminal. For travel onwards, note that the *shinkansen* (bullet train) now requires that you book space for large suitcases.

Outside of Tokyo, both Nikkō and Kamakura can get very crowded with day trippers. If you plan to visit, consider making an overnight trip out of it: local businesses will appreciate it and you'll be able to get an earlier start on the sights.

Mt Fuji, too: most climbers attempt to summit it in one go, overnight, with the aim of catching sunrise from the top. If you climb during the day, or break up the hike with a stay in a mountain hut, you can avoid the worst crowds. Also be sure to carry cash to pay the voluntary donation of ¥1000, which helps cover maintenance of the trails, and the toilet fees (typically ¥200, which also goes towards facility maintenance).

East of the Sumida

The Sumida-gawa was long thought of as Tokyo's central waterway; however, development throughout the 20th century – of Shinjuku and the western suburbs – pulled the city centre westward. Nowadays the river almost feels like the eastern edge of the city, but there is actually much more to discover further east still.

There are historic neighbourhoods at the mouth of the river, like Fukagawa, which was a typical merchant district in the Edo period (1603–1868). Learn about this history at the Fukagawa Edo Museum (p162), a small museum with a full-scale recreation of a townscape from this era. Fun fact: the famous haiku poet Matsuo Bashō (1644–94) lived for a time in Fukagawa. Nearby is the excellent Museum of Contemporary Art, Tokyo (MOT) (p162) and the landscape garden, Kiyosumi-teien (p162); both are usually uncrowded.

Kiyosumi-Shirakawa (p162) is another historic neighbourhood but one that has been adopted by young creatives. There are cafes here as well as canal-side strolls. Neighbouring Monzen-Nakachō, meanwhile, is known for its old-school *izakaya* (Japanese-style pub eateries).

Further north, and right across the river from Asakusa, Mukōjima is another old Tokyo neighbourhood (and a great place to escape Asakusa's crowds). There is an attractive (and little-visited) garden, Mukōjima Hyakka-en, as well as long-running restaurants, cafes and sweets shops.

Few overseas travellers spend much, if any, time east of the river. This means restaurants are less likely to have English menus or English-speaking staff; however, this also means you might get a warmer (if a little surprised) welcome for making the journey.

While most visitors choose to stay in the city centre or westside hubs like Shinjuku, there are a few convenient eastside hubs where accommodations are likely to be less expensive. These include Kinshichō, on the JR Chūō-Sōbu line and Hanzōmon subway line, and Kita-Senju, on the Chiyoda and Hibiya subway lines. Both have big station complexes with shops and restaurants.

Tokyo's Last Streetcar

Given Tokyo's tangled streets, it's hard to imagine that streetcars were common here until the 1960s. Tokyo Sakura Tram (originally the Toden Arakawa line) is the only one left within central Tokyo; the oldest section dates back to 1913. It was due to be demolished along with the other streetcar lines, but public outcry preserved it.

The route arcs across the north of the city, starting at Minowa (north of Asakusa) in the east and ending at Waseda (north of Shinjuku) in the west. The complete journey takes 50 minutes. Along the way, you'll pass plenty of the sort of everyday street life that most visitors miss.

Notable stops are Arakawa-Shakomae, where some vintage street cars are parked in a depot (open only on weekends); Ōji, for Ōji Inari-jinja, a local shrine famous for its fox legend, and Asukayama-kōen, an excellent *hanami* (cherry blossom viewing) spot; and Kōshinzuka for Sugamo, a neighbourhood known as 'Harajuku for grannies' as it's filled with shops aimed at seniors. Waseda, meanwhile, is home to Waseda University (one of Tokyo's top schools) and is full of student haunts. Purchase the Toden 1Day Pass (adult/child ¥400/200), good for unlimited rides, at either terminus; otherwise, a single trip costs ¥170.

BEST UNDER-THE-RADAR ATTRACTIONS

Rikugi-en (p144) A scenic landscape garden in a sleepy north Tokyo neighbourhood.

Edo-Tokyo Open Air Architecture Museum (p120) Historic buildings (you can enter) in the western suburbs.

Institute for Nature Study (p91) A park (with limited entry) that's as close to Tokyo *au natural* as you can get.

Japan Folk Crafts Museum (p99) Artisan crafts in a quietly sophisticated residential district.

Nihombashi Cruise (p70) City canals hiding in plain sight that can be explored in an open-top barge.

Tonkatsu at Tonki (p94)

 # Dining Out

As visitors to Tokyo quickly discover, the people here are absolutely obsessed with food. The city has a vibrant and cosmopolitan dining scene and a strong culture of eating out – popular restaurants are packed most nights of the week. Best of all, you can get superlative meals on any budget.

Sushi restaurant

Tokyo Food Scene

Tokyo foodies take pride in what they like to think of as their 'boutique' dining scene. Rather than offering long menus of elaborate dishes, many of the best restaurants make just a few things – and sometimes even just one! Sushi shops make sushi; tempura shops make tempura. A restaurant that does too much might be suspect: how can it compare to a speciality shop that has been honing its craft for three generations?

Tokyo has very few actual local specialities; its strength lies in its variety. You can find anything here, and get it done to perfection: all the Japanese staples, like tempura, *tonkatsu* (deep-fried pork cutlets), *yakitori* (chicken grilled on skewers), soba (buckwheat noodles) and *okonomiyaki* (savoury pancake); regional dishes from all over Japan, including Kyoto-style *kaiseki* (Japanese haute cuisine); and a wide spread of international cuisines.

But if there is one dish that Tokyo can truly claim, it's *nigiri-zushi,* the style of sushi most popular around the world today: those bite-sized slivers of seafood hand-pressed onto pedestals of rice. It's a dish that originated in the urban culture of Edo (the old name for Tokyo) and is sometimes still called 'Edo-mae' sushi (as in the style of Edo). Unless you have dietary restrictions, a good sushi meal should be at the top of your Tokyo bucket list.

Tokyoites twin passions for novelty and eating out means that the city is also a hotbed for experimentation. Trends come and go, but one that has stuck around – and spread roots – is the city's home-grown

farm-to-table movement. Increasingly, owner-chefs are working directly with rural producers to source ingredients, which might be used in orthodox-style Japanese cooking or creatively, to add a new twist to a classic dish or a fresh take on an imported one.

NEED TO KNOW

Opening Hours

Most restaurants open roughly 11.30am to 2.30pm for lunch and 6pm to 10pm for dinner. Chains usually stay open through the afternoon. *Izakaya* (pub-eateries) open around 5pm and run until 10pm or 11pm (sometimes later). Last order is usually 30 minutes before closing.

Price Ranges

The following price ranges represent the cost of a meal for one person.

¥ less than ¥2000

¥¥ ¥2000–¥5000

¥¥¥ more than ¥5000

Reservations

Reservations are expected at high-end places and recommended at popular midrange places and for groups of five or more.

Extra Charges

Izakaya often levy a small cover charge, called *otoshi* (お通し), of a few hundred yen per person. In exchange, you'll be served a small dish of food to snack on until the kitchen can prepare your order. But no, you can't pass it up even if you don't want to eat it.

Etiquette

Don't stick your chopsticks upright in your rice or pass food from one pair of chopsticks to another – both are reminiscent of funeral rites.

Useful Resources

Ramen Adventures (www.ramenadventures.com) Low-down on Tokyo's ramen scene.

Tokyo Food Page (www.bento.com) Extensive database of restaurant and bar info in English.

Above: Small eatery, Omoide-yokochō (p130)

Left: *Okonomiyaki* (savoury pancake)

Which brings us to Tokyo's two hottest dining trends right now: nouveau ramen, creativity distilled in a bowl of noodles and the best budget gourmet experience around; and neo-bistros, a format that has afforded chefs more leeway for innovation than classic Japanese cooking allows (or at least that's their current feeling). Increasingly, Japanese cuisine is a global one – borrowing this and contributing that – and Tokyo, naturally, is at the forefront.

Dining Out Like a Local

When you enter a restaurant in Japan, the staff will likely all greet you with a hearty *'Irasshai!'* (Welcome!). In all but the most casual places, where you seat yourself, the waitstaff will next ask you *'Nan-mei sama?'* (How many people?). Indicate the answer with your fingers, which is what the Japanese do. You may also be asked if you would like to sit at a *zashiki* (low table on the tatami), at a *tēburu* (table) or the *kauntā* (counter). Once seated, you will be given an *o-shibori* (hot towel), a cup of tea or water (this is free) and a menu.

There are two ways to order: *omakase* (chef's choice) and *okonomi* (your choice). It's common for high-end restaurants to offer nothing but *omakase* – the equivalent of a chef's tasting course, usually two or three options of different value. (Pricier doesn't necessarily mean more food; it often means more luxurious ingredients.) Most other restaurants will hand you a menu and expect you to choose what you like. If there's no English menu (and you're game), you can ask for the server's recommendation *(O-susume wa nan desu ka?)* and give the OK to whatever he or she suggests.

When your food arrives, it's the custom to say *'Itadakimasu'* (literally 'I will receive', but closer to 'bon appétit' in meaning) before digging in. All but the most extreme type-A chefs will say they'd rather have foreign visitors enjoy their meal than agonise over getting the etiquette right. Still, there's nothing that makes a Japanese chef grimace more than out-of-towners who over-season their food – a little soy sauce and wasabi go a long way.

Often a bill is placed discreetly on your table after your food has been delivered. If not, catch your server's eye with a *sumimasen* (excuse me) and ask for the cheque by saying *'O-kaikei kudasai'*. Payment, even at high-end places, is often settled at a counter near the entrance, rather than at the table. On your way out, it's polite to say *'Gochisō-sama deshita'* (literally 'It was a feast'; a respectful way of saying you enjoyed the meal) to the staff.

A FOODIE'S DAY IN TOKYO

Start with a trip to Toyosu Market (p168), arriving by 6am to watch the tuna auction, then head to Sushi Dai (p169) for a decadent sushi breakfast (prepare to queue). From here, a bus goes direct to Tsukiji Market (p73), where the wholesale market used to be and many old stalls remain. (You're probably still too full to indulge, so soak up the atmosphere instead.)

Work off breakfast with a walk to Ginza (15 minutes). Have a wander through the basement food hall at Mitsukoshi (p77). Nearby Akomeya (p77) is a beautiful foodstuffs boutique that stocks packaged foods from around Japan. Both are fantastic for gifts.

Hungry again yet? Head to Tempura Kondō (p75), one of the city's most acclaimed restaurants, for delicately fried vegetables and seafood. (Reservations essential.) After lunch, walk (10 minutes) to Marunouchi's Chashitsu Kaboku (p68), a teahouse run by famed Kyoto tea shop Ippōdō.

From here you could keep walking (20 minutes) to Nihombashi to explore the gourmet stores inside Coredo Muromachi (p70). Then hop on the Ginza line for Kappabashi-dōri, Tokyo's kitchen supply strip and home to excellent kitchenware and knife specialist Kama-asa (p161).

In the late afternoon, take the subway to Ueno. Stroll through the old-fashioned outdoor market, Ameya-yokochō (p151), on your way to Shinsuke (p150), one of Tokyo's best *izakaya* (Japanese pub-eatery). Order dishes one or two at a time, paired with Shinsuke's excellent sake. If you have the energy to make it back across town, end with a nightcap at BenFiddich (p130) in Shinjuku, Tokyo's most inventive cocktail bar.

Where to Eat

IZAKAYA

Izakaya (居酒屋) translates as 'drinking house'; it's the Japanese equivalent of a pub. An evening at an *izakaya* is dinner and drinks all in one: food is ordered for the table a few dishes at a time along with rounds of beer, sake or *shōchū* (strong distilled alcohol often made from potatoes). While the vibe is lively and social, it's perfectly acceptable to go by yourself and sit at the counter. If you don't want alcohol, it's fine to order a soft drink instead, but it would be strange to not order at least one drink.

An orthodox *izakaya* is family-run, with menu items like *shio-yaki-zakana* (塩焼魚; a whole fish grilled with salt) designed to go with sake. They might look a bit weathered – but that's often a good sign. There are also large, cheap chains, popular with students, that often have some Western pub-style dishes (like chips), and stylish chef-driven *izakaya* with creative menus.

Classic starters to get you going that most *izakaya* will have include: *sashimi moriawase* (刺身盛り合わせ; a selection of sliced sashimi), *edamame* (枝豆; salted and boiled fresh soy beans) and *moro-kyū* (もろきゅう; sliced cucumbers and chunky barley miso).

Some *izakaya,* and especially chains, offer course menus that may or may not include unlimited drinks for a limited amount of time, which makes ordering simple.

Even if they don't, you can often order *omakase* anyway – especially if you're sitting at the counter (the best place to sit at an *izakaya*). Tell the server or chef '*Omakase shimasu*' (please decide for me) and they'll most likely bring you a succession of the restaurant's greatest hits and some seasonal specialities. It's probably a good idea to set a price cap, like: '*Hitori de san-zen-en*' (one person for ¥3000).

A night out at an average *izakaya* should run from ¥3000 to ¥5000 per person, depending on how much you drink; a bit more for a more gourmet one.

SHOKUDŌ

Shokudō (食堂) are casual, inexpensive eateries that serve homey meals – similar to what might be called a greasy spoon cafe or diner in the United States. Some are scruffy and some are well-scrubbed, but appearance has little to do with the food.

One thing to order here is a *teishoku* (定食), a set meal with one main dish (such as grilled fish), rice, miso soup and pickles.

An izakaya in Ueno

Other likely menu items include various *donburi* (どんぶり or 丼; large bowls of rice with meat or fish piled on top) and *katsu* (カツ) dishes, where the main is crumbed and deep fried, as in *tonkatsu* (豚カツ or とんかつ; deep-fried pork cutlets) and *ebi-katsu* (海老カツ; breaded and fried prawns).

Tokyo's working and student population take a significant number of their meals at *shokudō;* you'll find them around every train station, and also in popular tourist areas. Meals typically cost ¥800 to ¥1500 per person. Many have plastic food displays in the windows, which of course makes ordering simple.

STREET FOOD

Street-food stands, called *yatai* (屋台), don't have the same ubiquitous presence in Tokyo as they do in other Asian cities. However, you can find them in markets, including Tsukiji Market (p73) or Ameya-yokochō (p151); heavily touristed areas, such as Asakusa and Ueno-kōen (p152); and always at festivals. Typical *yatai* food includes *okonomiyaki* (お好み焼き; savoury pancakes), *yaki-soba* (焼きそば; stir-fried noodles) and *tai-yaki* (たい焼き; fish-shaped cakes stuffed with bean paste).

Food trucks are popular with the downtown office crowd, gathering daily around the Tokyo International Forum (p64) at lunchtime; they also make the weekend rounds of farmers markets. And keep an eye out for Tokyo's original food trucks: *Yaki-imo* (roasted whole sweet potato) carts that rove the city from October to March, the sellers crooning *'yaki-imohhhhh...!'*.

FARMERS MARKETS

On weekends, farmers markets take place around the city and are good options for fresh fruit and bread, plus packaged goods (such as miso and pickles) to take home. The biggest is the Farmer's Market @UNU, held every weekend in Aoyama. Check out the blog Japan Farmers Markets (www.japanfarmersmarkets.com) to see what else is happening where.

What to Eat
SUSHI

Sushi (寿司 or 鮨; a combination of raw fish and rice seasoned with vinegar) is actually a very broad category, but in Tokyo it's near-synonymous with *nigiri-zushi* (hand-pressed sushi). The toppings are called *neta* (the rice part is called *shari*)

COOKING COURSES & FOOD TOURS

Tsukiji Soba Academy (p78) Soba-making lessons from a seasoned pro.

Kitchen Kujo Tokyo (p153) Make curry rice (and more) with the Curryman.

Buddha Bellies (p153) Small chef-led courses on sushi and *bentō*-making.

Tokyo Cook (p88) Learn to make *shōjin ryōri* (vegetarian temple food).

Tokyo Kitchen (p164) Japanese standards; can do vegetarian and gluten-free.

and common ones include *aji* (horse mackerel), *ama-ebi* (sweet shrimp), *hamachi* (yellow tail), *ika* (squid), *katsuo* (bonito), *maguro* (tuna) and *toro* (fatty tuna belly meat). In truth, not all *neta* are raw fish: you many encounter *anago* (seafaring eel) that has been grilled and lacquered in a sweet soy sauce glaze; *tako* (octopus) that has been boiled; or *hotate* (scallops) that have been seared – among others. Delicacies like *ikura* (salmon roe) and *uni* (sea urchin roe) are served as *gunkan-maki* ('battleship rolls' wrapped in laver; it will make sense when you it!).

Most sushi restaurants offer set meals – say 10 or 12 pieces of sushi – of varying price (somewhere between ¥1500 and ¥5000, depending on the ingredients rather than portion size). These are always the most economical way to go (à la carte can add up quickly, and prices may not be posted). Truly high-end places, where the *omakase* course consists of a procession of some 20 dishes, will set you back a minimum of ¥10,000 per person for dinner (and possibly much, much more). At the other end of the spectrum are cheap *kaiten-sushi* (回転寿司), where ready-made plates of sushi are sent around the restaurant on a conveyor belt. The best thing about these restaurants is that you don't have to worry about ordering: just grab whatever looks good as it goes by; the plates are colour-coded according to cost.

A few sushi etiquette notes: sometimes (and often at higher-end places) the chef has already seasoned the sushi and thus it does not go in soy sauce (staff will note this). Also, it's totally fine to eat it with your hands. The pickled ginger (called *gari*) served with sushi is to cleanse your palate between pieces.

RAMEN

Ramen may have been imported from China, but in Tokyo it has developed into a legitimate passion: the subject of profuse blogs, a reason to stand in line for over an hour, and a dream for many to master – in the form of their own shop. By conservative estimates there are over 3000 ramen shops in the capital (some say 4000).

Your basic ramen is a big bowl of crinkly egg noodles in broth, served with toppings such as *chāshū* (sliced roast pork), *moyashi* (bean sprouts) and *menma* (pickled bamboo sprouts). Ramen should be eaten at whip speed, before the noodles become soggy; that's why you'll hear diners slurping, sucking in air to cool their mouths. Many shops also sell *tsukemen,* noodles that come with a dipping sauce (like a really condensed broth) on the side.

The broth can be made from pork or chicken bones or dried seafood; usually it's a top-secret combination of some or all of the above. It's typically seasoned with *shio* (salt), *shōyu* (soy sauce) or hearty miso – though at less orthodox places, anything goes. Tokyo's classic style is a *shōyu*-flavoured broth with a subtle bitter smokiness that comes from *niboshi* (dried young sardines).

Ramen restaurants (and sometimes udon and soba restaurants, too) often use a unique ordering system: a vending machine. Insert your money and select the button with your desired dish; you'll get a coupon from the machine, which you should hand to the cooks behind the counter.

Dietary Restrictions

Most Tokyo restaurants are small, so dietary restrictions can be hard to accommodate. They'll try, but in many cases your options will be defined by how strictly you adhere to restrictions; for example, unless noted otherwise, your vegetable tempura is going to be fried in the same oil as the prawns.

Dishes can also be deceiving: many that look ostensibly vegetarian are prepared with *dashi* (fish stock); pork is often used in curry roux. Always state your restrictions up front when making a reservation to give the restaurant more time to prepare.

Happy Cow (www.happycow.net) is a great resource for restaurants that prepare strictly vegetarian and vegan dishes; also check TICs for the Tokyo VegeMap (vegemap.org). For certified halal restaurants, see Halal Gourmet Japan (www.halalgourmet.jp); the

Top: Seafood stall, Tsukiji Market (p73)
Middle: Ramen
Bottom: *Nigiri-zushi* (hand-pressed sushi)

Soba noodles with prawn and vegetable tempura

city also publishes a travel guide for Muslims, which lists restaurants and is available at most Tourist Information Centers (TICs).

Many chain restaurants and deli counters label their dishes with icons indicating potential allergens (such as dairy, eggs, peanuts, wheat and shellfish), but otherwise this can be tricky. Have on hand a list of allergens written in Japanese.

Gluten-free is particularly challenging, as there is little awareness of coeliac disease in Japan and many kitchen staples, such as soy sauce, contain wheat (and even restaurant staff may not be aware of this). The Gluten-Free Expats Japan! Facebook group is a good resource.

Eating by Neighbourhood

Marunouchi & Nihombashi (p65) Midrange options for the local office crowd in Marunouchi; classic Japanese in Nihombashi.

Ginza & Tsukiji (p74) Upscale restaurants and great sushi.

Roppongi & Around (p83) Both break-the-bank and midrange options, with a good selection of international cuisines.

Ebisu, Meguro & Around (p91) Cosmopolitan and hip, with excellent dining options in all price ranges.

Shibuya & Shimo-Kitazawa (p99) Lively, inexpensive restaurants that cater to a young crowd, and some stylish, upmarket options on the fringes.

Harajuku & Aoyama (p109) Fashionable midrange restaurants and excellent lunch options aimed at shoppers.

West Tokyo (p119) Nothing fancy, but lots of local faves doing Japanese classics.

Shinjuku & Northwest Tokyo (p127) High-end restaurants, under-the-tracks dives and everything in between; great for ramen.

Kōrakuen & Akihabara (p137) Famous for historic eateries in Kanda, comfort food in Akihabara.

Ueno & Yanesen (p149) Classic Japanese restaurants, mostly midrange and budget.

Asakusa & Sumida River (p158) Unpretentious Japanese fare, old-school charm and modest prices.

Odaiba & Tokyo Bay (p169) Family-friendly restaurants, mall food courts and chains in Odaiba; sushi in Toyosu.

Lonely Planet's Top Choices

Kizushi (p68) Carrying the torch for Edo-mae (Tokyo-style) sushi, with techniques unchanged for nearly a century.

Tempura Kondō (p75) Works of batter-fried art from master chef and tempura-whisperer Kondo Fumiō.

Mensho Tokyo (p138) Leading light of the nouveau ramen movement.

Tonki (p94) Iconic *tonkatsu* restaurant, beloved by generations of Tokyoites.

Best by Budget

¥

Commune 2nd (p112) Hip outdoor space with vendors serving all kinds of dishes.

Misojyu (p158) Trendy new spot for miso soup and creative *onigiri*.

Delifucious (p94) Fish burgers from a former sushi chef.

¥¥

Sushi Dai (p169) The best-value sushi set in the city, but you'll have to queue.

Steak House Satou (p121) Reasonably priced *wagyū* (Japanese beef) steaks.

Innsyoutei (p149) Elegant, but affordable, traditional Japanese in a beautiful wooden building.

¥¥¥

Kikunoi (p86) Tokyo branch of legendary Kyoto *kaiseki* restaurant.

Asakusa Imahan (p159) Historic restaurant for top-class

sukiyaki (sautéed beef dipped in raw egg).

Kozue (p130) Exquisite classic-meets-modern Japanese dishes, with distractingly good views over the city.

Best by Cuisine

Sushi

Sushi Dai (p169) The spot for sushi breakfast inside Toyosu Market.

Kyūbey (p75) Rarefied Ginza sushi at its finest.

Nemuro Hanamaru (p65) One of the city's best *kaiten-sushi*.

Ramen

Harukiya (p120) The definitive Tokyo ramen, since 1949.

Afuri (p93) Light citrus-y broth and contemporary cool.

Nagi (p127) Smoky *niboshi* ramen in late-night haunt, Golden Gai.

Japanese Classics

Kanda Yabu Soba (p137) Specialising in soba since 1880.

Maisen (p112) Long-time favourite for *tonkatsu*, in a former bathhouse.

Bird Land (p75) Upscale *yakitori* from free-range heirloom birds.

Nihonbashi Tamai (p68) *Anago* served grilled in a lacquered box.

Regional Japanese

Ginza Sato Yosuke (p74) Serves *inaniwa udon* (delicate wheat noodles) from Akita, in northern Japan.

Aoyama Kawakami-an (p112) Tokyo outpost of a famous soba (buckwheat noodles) restaurant in Nagano.

Shimanto-gawa (p74) *Izakaya* specialising in *Tosa-ryōri* (the cuisine of Shikoku's Kōchi Prefecture).

d47 Shokudō (p100) Regional dishes from around Japan.

Best Izakaya

Narukiyo (p101) Cult-fave spot on the fringes of Shibuya.

Shinsuke (p150) Century-old local institution adored by sake aficionados.

Kanae (p130) Classic *izakaya* dishes, beautifully presented.

Donjaca (p130) Vintage mid-20th-century vibe and homestyle food.

Best Vegetarian & Vegan

Ain Soph (p75) Pretty vegan spreads and a chic cafe vibe; more branches around the city.

Mominoki House (p109) Long-running macrobiotic restaurant with many vegan options.

Nagi Shokudō (p100) Hip (and hidden) vegan hang-out.

Falafel Brothers (p86) Falafel sandwiches made to order, with your choice of toppings.

Best Brunch

Bricolage Bread & Co (p86) Chic space with excellent coffee and tartines.

Iki Espresso (p162) Get your avocado toast fix in up-and-coming Kiyosumi.

Bar Open

Make like Lady Gaga in a karaoke box; sip sake with an increasingly rosy salaryman in a tiny postwar bar; or dance under the rays of the rising sun at an enormous bayside club: that's nightlife, Tokyo style. The city's drinking culture embraces everything from refined teahouses and indie coffee shops to craft-beer pubs and maid cafes.

Where to Drink

Roppongi has the lion's share of foreigner-friendly bars, while Shinjuku offers the retro warren Golden Gai and the LGBT-friendly bar district Ni-chōme.

Other top party districts include youthful Shibuya and Harajuku; Shimbashi and Yūrakuchō, which teem with salarymen; and Ebisu and nearby Daikanyama, both of which have some excellent bars. Asakusa's Hoppy-dōri (p158) is a fun, retro-style hang-out.

BARS & IZAKAYA

Places selling alcohol run the gamut from *tachinomi-ya* (standing-only bars) to ritzy cocktail lounges. A staple is the humble *nomiya* (bar), patronised by businesspeople and regular customers. Some will demur at serving foreigners who don't speak or read Japanese.

Izakaya (Japanese pub-eateries) can be cheap places for beer and food in a casual atmosphere resembling that of a pub; more upmarket ones are wonderful places to sample premium sake and the distilled spirit *shōchū*.

In summer, beer gardens open up on department-store roofs, and in hotel grounds and gardens. Many of these places offer all-you-can-eat-and-drink specials for around ¥4000 per person.

KARAOKE & CLUBS

If you've never tried a karaoke box (a small room rented by you and a few of your friends), it's definitely less embarrassing than singing in a bar in front of strangers. With booze and food brought directly to your room, it can easily become a guilty pleasure; rooms generally cost around ¥700 per person per hour.

Top international DJs and domestic artists do regular sets at club venues with body-shaking sound systems. EDM rules, but as with anything in Tokyo, variety is key, so you're likely to find a club playing your kind of music if you hunt around. Most clubs kick off after 10pm or so and continue until dawn (or later).

CAFES & TEAHOUSES

Chain cafes such as Doutor, Tully's and Starbucks (a nonsmoking oasis with free wi-fi) are common. But don't miss the opportunity to explore Tokyo's vast range of *kissa* (short for *kissaten,* coffee shops) and tearooms – many are gems of retro or contemporary design, sport art galleries or are showcases for a proprietor's beloved collection, such as vintage jazz records or model trains.

What to Drink

SAKE & SHŌCHŪ

Japan's national beverage is sake, aka *nihonshū* (酒 or 日本酒). Made from rice, it comes in a wide variety of grades, flavours and regions of origin. According to personal preference, sake can be served hot *(atsu-kan),* but premium sake is normally served well chilled *(reishu)* in a small jug *(tokkuri)* and poured into tiny cups known as *o-choko* or *sakazuki.*

NEED TO KNOW

Opening Hours

Tokyo's nightspots stay open from 5pm well into the wee hours.

Prices

To avoid a nasty shock when the bill comes, check prices and cover charges before sitting down. If you are served a small snack (o-tsumami) with your first round, you'll usually be paying a cover charge of a few hundred yen or more.

Cheers

Don't forget to say (or yell, depending on the venue) 'Kampai!' when toasting your drinking buddies.

Etiquette & Tipping

It's customary to pour for others and wait for them to refill your glass. At smaller bars, male bartenders are often called 'master' and their female counterparts are 'mama-san'. There's no need to tip in bars.

Beware

Avoid sunakku (snack bars), cheap hostess bars that charge hefty sums, and kyabakura (cabaret clubs), exorbitant hostess clubs that are often fronts for prostitution. These are concentrated in Shinjuku's Kabukichō and Roppongi.

Useful Websites

Japan Beer Times (http://japanbeertimes.com) Print and online magazine about local craft-beer industry.

Tokyo Beer Drinker (http://tokyobeerdrinker.blogspot.co.uk) Reviews of craft-beer bars across the city.

Nonjatta (www.nonjatta.com) Comprehensive source on Japanese whisky.

Sake World (http://sake-world.com) Site of leading non-Japanese sake authority John Gauntner.

Good Coffee (https://en.goodcoffee.me) Comprehensive listings covering Tokyo's coffee scene.

Tokyo Coffee (https://tokyocoffee.org) Reviews cafes across the city.

Tokyo Cheapo (http://tokyocheapo.com) Where to drink if you're short on cash.

More popular than sake, the clear spirit shōchū (焼酎) is made from a variety of raw materials, including potato and barley. Because of its potency (alcohol content of around 30%), shōchū is usually served diluted with hot water (oyu-wari) or in a chūhai (shōchū highball) cocktail with soft drinks or tea.

BEER

Biiru (beer; ビール) is by far Japan's favourite tipple. Lager reigns supreme, although several breweries also offer darker beers, including the top four – Kirin, Asahi, Sapporo and Suntory. The craft-beer scene, however, is booming and at specialist pubs and microbreweries you can happily work your way through a bewildering range of ales from across Japan.

In bars you can order either nama biiru (draught beer) or bin biiru (bottled beer) in many varieties. Hoppy, a cheap, low-alcohol mix of carbonated malt and hops that debuted in 1948, is also found on the menus of some retro izakaya and bars.

WHISKY

Japan produces some of the finest whiskies in the world and Tokyo now has a growing number of dedicated whisky and Scotch bars where travellers can sample the best of the major makers Suntory and Nikka, as well as products from several other active single malt distilleries in Japan and abroad.

COFFEE & TEA

Third-wave cafes, where passionate baristas coax the best from roasted coffee beans, are increasingly common. At a growing number of specialist tea houses, you will find local varieties of tea that you may not be so familiar with. Green tea is the default, coming in a variety of forms. Matcha, powdered green tea, features in the traditional tea ceremony and has a high caffeine kick. Sencha is medium-grade green tea, while o-cha and the brownish bancha are the regular stuff. You may also come across mugicha (roasted barley tea) and hōjicha (roasted green tea).

Lonely Planet's Top Choices

Popeye (p160) Get very merry working your way through the most beers on tap in Tokyo.

BenFiddich (p130) Original cocktails made using freshly ground spices and herbs.

Sakurai Japanese Tea Experience (p112) Enjoy a contemporary take on the tea ceremony.

Dandelion Chocolate (p160) Swoon over the luscious drinks and sweets at this small-batch chocolate factory.

Lonely (p125) Classic Golden Gai bar run by the same guy for over 50 years.

Best for Beer

Beer-Ma Kanda (p138) Beer heaven with hundreds of different brands available.

Two Dogs Taproom (p86) Great range of craft beer and decent pizza in Roppongi.

Yanaka Beer Hall (p151) Microbrew ales in a charming complex of old wooden buildings.

Best for Cocktails & Spirits

Gen Yamamoto (p86) Savour superior fruit cocktails at this Zen teahouse-like bar.

Zoetrope (p131) Sample premium whiskies at a Shinjuku hole-in-the-wall.

Bar Trench (p95) Ebisu-based pioneer in Tokyo's new cocktail scene.

Fuglen Tokyo (p103) Aeropress coffee by day and creative cocktails by night.

Best Bars with a View

New York Bar (p131) Make like Bill Murray in the Park Hyatt's starry jazz bar.

Two Rooms (p114) Cool views and a cool crowd, plus an outdoor terrace.

Jicoo the Floating Bar (p169) See Tokyo illuminated as you cruise the bay.

Asahi Sky Room (p160) Spectacular sunset views over the Sumida-gawa.

Best Clubs

Contact (p103) Sign up online to get into Tokyo's coolest members-only club.

Ageha (p170) One of Asia's largest clubs, set on Tokyo Bay.

Circus Tokyo (p101) Underground venue focusing on experimental music.

Ele Tokyo (p87) Join the smart set for a night out in Roppongi.

Best Teahouses

Cha Ginza (p75) Stylish modern version of a teahouse in the heart of Ginza.

Chashitsu Kaboku (p68) A chance to sample super viscous *koicha* green tea.

Jugetsudo (p76) Kabukiza branch of this venerable tea merchant.

Best Indie Coffee

Toranomon Koffee (p87) Baristas in white lab coats operating a sleek coffee bar.

Cafe de l'Ambre (p76) Ginza institution specialising in aged beans from around the world.

Turret Coffee (p75) Ideal for an early morning espresso en route to or from Tsukiji.

Blue Sky Coffee (p121) Tiny wooden cottage concealing a shiny, state-of-the-art coffee roaster.

Onibus Coffee (p95) Third-wave coffee in a converted former tofu shop.

Best Karaoke

Karaoke Rainbow (p101) Shibuya's most popular karaoke spot, free for the first hour.

'Cuzn Homeground (p160) Offering a wild night of warbling in Asakusa.

Pasela Resorts (p87) Six floors of rooms in Roppongi.

Best Gay & Lesbian Venues

Eagle (p131) Pose in front of manga artist Inuyoshi's great mural of beefy guys.

Aiiro Cafe (p131) Start your Ni-chōme night at this popular corner bar.

Bar Goldfinger (p131) Friendly vibe at this lesbian bar designed to look like a '70s motel.

Best Unique Atmosphere

Samurai (p131) Classic jazz at this *kissa* stacked with 2500 *maneki-neko* (beckoning cats).

Aoyama Flower Market Teahouse (p112) Sip your tea surrounded by colourful blooms.

Ginza Lion (p75) Traditional beer hall with a gorgeous art deco design.

Showtime

Tokyo's range of entertainment is impressive. Take your pick from smoky jazz bars, grand theatres, rockin' live houses, comedy shows and major sports events. And don't be afraid to sample the traditional performing arts: the major venues that stage these shows will offer earphones or subtitles with an English translation of the plots and dramatic dialogue.

Traditional Performing Arts

Little can prepare the uninitiated for the lavish costumes, sets, make-up and acting of a classic kabuki play. This highly dramatic, visually arresting form of theatre, with all male performers, is the best known of Japan's traditional performing arts, but there are other forms you can readily view in Tokyo, too, including the stately, slow-moving drama of *nō*, and bunraku plays with large puppets expertly manipulated by up to three black-robed puppeteers.

Contemporary Theatre

Language can be a barrier to the contemporary theatre scene, as nearly all productions are in Japanese. Sometimes, though, a show's visual creativity compensates, such as with the camp, colourful musical review shows of Takarazuka (p76). The long-running Tokyo International Players (www.tokyoplayers. org) regularly performs English-language theatre, as does Black Stripe Theater (http://blackstripetheater.com). You can also catch English and other language shows at Festival/Tokyo (フェスティバル/トーsキョー, F/T; www.festival-tokyo.jp), usually held each November.

Dance

While Tokyo has Western dance performances, including shows by Tokyo Ballet (http://thetokyoballet.com), it's the home-grown forms of movement that are likely to be of more interest. Keep an eye out for special dance shows in Asakusa and elsewhere by Tokyo's geisha: there are groups representing the six main traditional entertainment areas of the city – Akasaka, Asakusa, Kagurazaka, Mukojima, Shimbashi and Yoshichō (present-day Nihombashi and Ningyōchō).

Top troupes specialising in the avant-garde genre *butō*, in which dancers use their naked or seminaked bodies to express the most elemental human emotions, include Sankai Juku (www.sankaijuku.com) and Dairakudakan Kochūten (www.dairakudakan.com), based in Kichijōji.

Live Music

All kinds of live music, including rock, blues, jazz, classical and electronica, can be seen performed live in Tokyo. Big international acts often appear at major venues such as Nippon Budōkan (p69) or Tokyo Dome (p139). There are also many good small live houses for intimate shows.

Sport

Sports fans are well served with baseball matches held at Tokyo Dome (p139) and Jingū Baseball Stadium (p114) during the April to October season. Even if you're not in town for one of the year's big sumo tournaments (in January, May and September), it's still possible to watch wrestlers training daily at their stables.

Lonely Planet's Top Choices

National Theatre (p87) Top-notch *nō*, bunraku and other drama in a grand setting.

Kabukiza (p74) A visual and dramatic feast of traditional theatre awaits inside and out.

Setagaya Public Theatre (p104) Renowned for contemporary drama and dance.

Ryōgoku Kokugikan (p158) Clash of sumo titans at the city's three big tournaments.

Suigian (p69) Enjoy up-close and personal tasters of traditional Japanese performing arts in a chic bar venue in Nihombashi.

Best Traditional Arts

National Nō Theatre (p114) Watch dramas unfold slowly on an elegant cypress stage.

Oiwake (p160) Listen to indigenous tunes at this rare *minyō izakaya* (pub where traditional folk music is performed).

Kanze Nōgakudō (p76) *Nō* theatre in the bowls of the Ginza Six complex.

Best Classical Music Venues

Suntory Hall (p87) Gorgeous 2000-seat hall hosting major international performers.

Tokyo International Forum (p64) Location for the La Folle Journée au Japon classical-music festival.

Tokyo Bunka Kaikan (p151) Great acoustics and interiors at this Ueno-kōen venue.

Tokyo Opera City Concert Hall (p132) With legendary acoustics, this hall hosts the Tokyo Philharmonic Orchestra and other famed ensembles.

Tokyo University of the Arts Performing Arts Center (p151) Intimate hall that's ideal for a classical concert.

Best Live Houses

Unit (p95) Offering both live gigs and DJs to a stylish crowd.

Club Quattro (p104) Slick venue with an emphasis on rock and roll and world music.

WWW (p103) Great views of the stage for all at this happening Shibuya live house.

Shimo-Kitazawa Three (p103) Making live music more accessible through its free events.

Best Jazz Clubs

Shinjuku Pit Inn (p132) Tokyo jazz-scene institution for serious devotees.

Cotton Club (p69) Centrally located venue for high-pedigree performers.

Best Spectator Sports

Ryōgoku Kokugikan (p158) Location of the three annual Tokyo *bashō* (sumo-wrestling tournaments).

Tokyo Dome (p139) Home to the Yomiuri Giants, Japan's top baseball team.

Jingū Baseball Stadium (p114) The base of Tokyo underdogs Yakult Swallows.

NEED TO KNOW

Cinemas

The best time to go to the movies in Tokyo is Cinema Day (generally the first day of the month), when all tickets cost ¥1100 instead of the regular price of ¥1800.

Tickets

The easiest way to get tickets for many live shows and events is at one of the Ticket Pia kiosks scattered across Tokyo. Its online booking site (http://t.pia.jp) is in Japanese only.

Useful Websites

Tokyo Time Out (http://www.timeout.com/tokyo) Sign up for regular bulletins on what's happening.

Kabuki Web (www.kabukiweb.net) Book tickets online for Shōchiku's theatres, including Kabukiza (p74).

Japan Times (www.japantimes.co.jp/events) Listings from the daily English-language newspaper.

Creativeman (http://creativeman.co.jp) Tickets for some theatre and music shows.

Tokyo Dross (http://tokyodross.blogspot.co.uk) Listings for live music and other events.

Tokyo Jazz (http://tokyojazzsite.com) Low-down on the jazz scene.

Ginza Six (p77)

Treasure Hunt

Since the Edo era, when courtesans set the day's trends in towering geta *(traditional wooden sandals), Tokyoites have lusted after both the novel and the outstanding. The city remains the trendsetter for the rest of Japan, and its residents shop – economy be damned – with an infectious enthusiasm. Join them in the hunt for the cutest fashions, the latest gadgets or the perfect teacup.*

Fashion

For most of the 20th century, Tokyo's grand *depāto* (department stores) were the great arbitrators of style. The oldest and most famous ones are in Nihombashi. While department stores are still popular with shoppers of a certain age, in the new century fashion cred has shifted to the boutiques on the west side of town, in neighbourhoods like Shibuya, Harajuku, Aoyama, Ebisu, Daikanyama and Naka-Meguro.

Tokyoites make a sport of tracking down the latest hot boutique, and you can too. But if you want to spend more time shopping and less time looking for shops, hit one of the malls. Far from unfashionable, Tokyo's malls pull together popular national and international chains and branches of trendsetting boutiques, plus homewares shops. The best malls are in Ginza (in some cases on sites that once held department stores).

For good secondhand and vintage shops, head to Harajuku (the backstreets; not the main drags), Shimo-Kitazawa (north side) or Kōenji (everywhere around the station). You'll find merchandise to be expensive but of excellent quality.

Crafts

Trendy Tokyo still has a strong artisan tradition. Older neighbourhoods on the east side of town such as Asakusa and Ningyōchō have shops that sell woven bamboo boxes, hog's hair brushes and indigo-dyed *noren* (cloths hung as a sunshade, typically carrying the name of the shop or premises) – much like they did 100 (or more) years ago.

There's also a new generation of craftspeople who are no less devoted to *monozukuri* (the art of making things), but who are channelling more contemporary needs and tastes. They too are drawn to east Tokyo (largely by cheap rent) and are breathing new life into districts formerly known for small-scale manufacturing, turning old warehouses into ateliers, shops and galleries. Some areas to explore include Kuramae (p161), Bakurochō (p69) and the 2k540 Aki-Oka Artisan (p139) mall under the elevated tracks between Akihabara and Okachi-machi.

Gourmet & Kitchenware

Kappabashi-dōri (p161) is Tokyo's professional kitchenware district – a great place to source chef's knives and other tools of the Japanese kitchen (like bamboo mats for rolling sushi), plus ceramic and lacquer serving wares. Tokyo's original market district was Nihombashi, and you'll still find many foodstuffs shops here (including some with impressive lineages); many have outlets in the Coredo Muromachi (p70) complex. The new Toyosu Market (p168) also has gourmet shops on the upper floors.

Department store basement food floors (called *depachika*) stock all sorts of gourmet items, including tea, *wagashi* (traditional sweets) and sake; look to the upper floors for traditional-style homewares, like cast-iron teapots and delicate sake glasses.

Kimonos

New kimonos are generally expensive, on par with couture. Secondhand kimonos, on the other hand, can be found for as little as ¥1000 – though one in decent shape will cost more like ¥10,000 (and up). In addition to speciality shops, you can also find racks of used kimonos at flea markets. It takes a lot of practice to master the art of tying an obi (sash or belt) properly, so it's a good idea to ask shop staff to help you (though there's no reason you can't just wear one

NEED TO KNOW

Opening Hours
Department stores 10am to 8pm daily

Electronics stores 10am to 10pm daily

Boutiques Noon to 8pm, closed irregularly

Paying
It's rare to find a shop in Tokyo that doesn't accept credit cards; very small or very old shops might be an exception.

Service
Service is attentive, increasingly so at more expensive stores, where sales staff will carry your purchase to the door and send you off with a bow.

Sales
Major sales happen, sadly, just twice a year in Japan: at the beginning of January (after the New Year's holiday) and again at the beginning of July.

Sizes
All sorts of sizing systems are used and often you'll find only a 'medium', which is meant to fit everyone, but is smaller than a 'medium' in a Western country.

Useful Phrases
➡ *Fukuro ha irimasen* (I don't need a bag)

➡ *Kore o shichaku dekimasu ka?* (Can I try this on?)

➡ *Mitteiru dake desu* (I'm just looking)

Useful Websites
Tax Free Japan (https://tax-freeshop.jnto. go.jp/eng/index.php) Details on how to shop duty-free in Japan.

Tokyo Fashion (http://tokyofashion. com) Info on the latest trends, brands and boutiques.

like a dressing gown and forgo the sash entirely).

A more affordable and practical option is a *yukata,* a lightweight, cotton kimono that's easier to wear – if you hit a summer *matsuri* (festival), you'll see loads of Tokyoites wearing them. In season, department stores hold *yukata* fairs, with a variety of styles to choose from in both traditional

Shopping by Neighbourhood

Ueno & Yanesen
Art galleries and an old-time open-air market (p151)
Shinjuku & Northwest Tokyo
Major shopping hub with everything (p132)
Kōrakuen & Akihabara
Electronics, manga and contemporary crafts (p139)
West Tokyo
Homewares, vintage and collectables (p122)
Asakusa & Sumida River
Traditional crafts and artisan workshops (p161)
Marunouchi & Nihombashi
Classic department stores and gourmet foodstuffs (p69)
Harajuku & Aoyama
High-street brands, street fashion and designer labels (p114)
Ginza & Tsukiji
Luxury boutiques and high-end malls (p77)
Roppongi & Around
Designer homewares and contemporary malls (p88)
Shibuya & Shimo-Kitazawa
Trendy youth fashion and second-hand shops (p104)
Ebisu, Meguro & Around
Style-setting boutiques (p95)
Tokyo Bay

and contemporary designs; prices range from around ¥15,000 to ¥30,000, plus more for the obi and accessories. But you can also find cheaper ones (under ¥10,000) at shops like Uniqlo.

There are also some interesting fashion brands riffing on kimono silhouettes and motifs or using traditional textiles in contemporary looks.

Flea Markets & Antique Fairs

Pretty much every weekend there is a flea market happening somewhere: larger ones take place at plazas in parks like Yoyogi-kōen and Shinjuku Chūō-kōen. Many smaller ones are held on the grounds of Shintō shrines, like the Sunday market at Shinjuku's Hanazono-jinja (p126).

On the first weekend of the month, **Raw Tokyo** (Map p276; www.rawtokyo.jp; 5-53-7 Jingūmae, Shibuya-ku; ⏲11am-5pm; [S]Ginza line to Omote-sandō, exit B2) is a contemporary-style flea market – the kind that has a DJ booth, live painting and food trucks. The long-running, twice-monthly Ōedo Antique Market (p70) draws hundreds of dealers selling all kinds of vintage items.

For an updated schedule of all the city's flea markets, see www.frma.jp (in Japanese). Although bargaining is permitted, it is considered bad form to drive too hard a bargain.

Lonely Planet's Top Choices

Tokyu Hands (p104) Fascinating emporium of miscellaneous oddities.

Okuno Building (p77) Dozens of tiny galleries and boutiques inside a vintage 1930s Ginza apartment building.

Beams Japan (p132) Floors of cool Japanese labels, original artwork and contemporary crafts.

Japan Traditional Crafts Aoyama Square (p88) Collection of high-end Japanese artisan work.

Isetan (p132) Fashion-forward department store with a great basement food floor.

Best for Fashion

Kapital (p95) Denim woven on vintage looms and lush, hand-dyed textiles.

House @Mikiri Hassin (p114) Hidden spot for under-the-radar local brands.

Babaghuri (p162) Earthy looks made from recycled or renewable materials.

Dover Street Market Ginza (p77) Comme des Garçons and other avant-garde labels.

Arts & Science (p114) Vintage-inspired elegance from celebrity stylist Sonya Park.

Okura (p92) Beautiful indigo-dyed clothing and accessories.

Best for Arts & Crafts

Takumi (p77) One-stop shop for earthy traditional crafts from all over Japan.

Itōya (p77) Ginza institution for stationery and art supplies.

Bengara (p161) Natural-dyed *noren* and other traditional textile items.

Geidai Art Plaza (p153) Gallery attached to Tokyo's top art school, with student works.

Best for Kimonos

Y. & Sons (p139) Custom kimonos and *yukata* for the modern urban dandy.

Sou-Sou (p115) Traditional Japanese clothing with contemporary panache.

Tsukikageya (p102) *Yukata* in punk-rock prints.

Best for Antiques & Vintage

Ōedo Antique Market (p70) Quality vendors twice a month at Tokyo International Forum.

Tokyo Hotarudo (p163) Treasure trove of early-20th-century accessories and homewares.

Ohya Shobō (p140) Stacks of woodblock prints and antique maps.

PukuPuku (p122) Hundred-year-old ceramics.

Best for Design

d47 design travel store (p104) Showcase for regional Japanese product design trends and traditions.

Good Design Store Tokyo by Nohara (p70) Goods that have earned Japan's official 'Good Design' stamp of approval.

Souvenir from Tokyo (p88) Curated collection of covetable items from local designers.

Best for Books & Music

Daikanyama T-Site (p92) Designer digs for art and travel tomes.

Kinokuniya (p133) The city's best selection of books on Japan in English.

Union Record Shinjuku (p133) Crates and crates of vinyl, with lots of local stuff.

Best for Home & Kitchen

Kama-asa (p161) Hand-forged kitchen knives.

Yanaka Matsunoya (p153) Handmade household staples, such as brooms and baskets.

Muji (p70) Minimalist, utilitarian and utterly indispensable homewares at reasonable prices.

Best for Food & Drink

Akomeya (p77) Beautifully packaged, traditional artisanal foodstuffs.

Toraya (p88) Centuries-old purveyor of sweets to the imperial household.

Chabara (p140) Miso, soy sauce and more from top regional producers.

Best Malls

Coredo Muromachi (p70) Top-class, made-in-Japan fashion and food items.

Ginza Six (p77) High-fashion mall with fantastic art installations.

KITTE (p69) Full of on-trend fashion and homewares boutiques.

Explore Tokyo

TOKYO'S
TOP EXPERIENCES

Tokyo Sky Tree (p157)

Neighbourhoods at a Glance

1 Marunouchi & Nihombashi p60

Marunouchi is a high-powered business district. Its top draw is the Imperial Palace, Tokyo's symbolic centre. Neighbouring Nihombashi is a historic district with shops and restaurants that date to the era of the shogun.

2 Ginza & Tsukiji p71

Ginza is Tokyo's most polished neighbourhood, a luxury fashion centre resplendent with department stores, art galleries and exclusive restaurants. Tsukiji is no longer home to the central wholesale market but still has great food, shops and atmosphere.

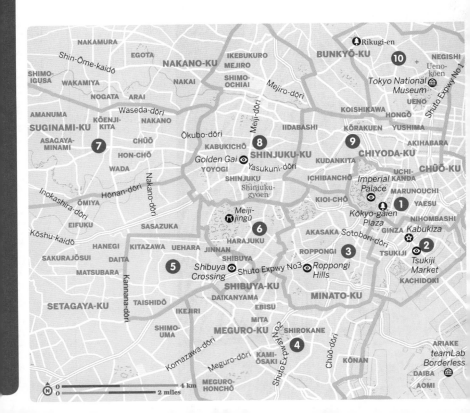

3 Roppongi & Around p79

Legendary for its nightlife, Roppongi offers the chic Roppongi Hills and Tokyo Midtown complexes ousing excellent art museums.

4 Ebisu, Meguro & Around p89

This broad collection of hip neighbourhoods has art museums, fashionable boutiques, (relatively) quiet streets and few tourists by day. Ebisu has a dynamic dining and bar scene.

5 Shibuya & Shimo-Kitazawa p96

Shibuya, the heart of Tokyo's youth culture, impresses with its sheer presence: the continuous flow of people, the glowing video screens and the buzz. Shimo-Kitazawa offers an alternative vision of Tokyo: what it might look like if hippies ran the city.

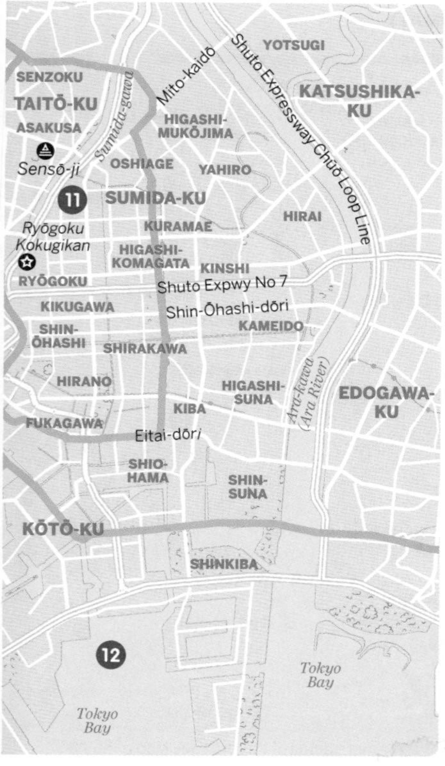

6 Harajuku & Aoyama p105

Harajuku is one of Tokyo's biggest draws thanks to grand Meiji-jingū, street fashion, contemporary architecture and art museums. Neighbouring Aoyama is a shopping and dining district for the fashionable elite.

7 West Tokyo p116

Ghibli Museum, Mitaka is the top sight, but locals love neighbourhoods Nakano and Kōenji for their vintage mid-20th-century look and bohemian spirit, and Kichijōji for its park.

8 Shinjuku & Northwest Tokyo p123

Shinjuku is a city within a city, with soaring skyscrapers and Tokyo's largest entertainment district North of here, Ikebukuro, also feels as if it contains a whole world within.

9 Kōrakuen & Akihabara p134

This swath of Tokyo runs alongside the former outer moat of Edo Castle and the Kanda-gawa, from the dazzling traditional garden Koishikawa Kōrakuen to the electronic and pop culture emporiums of Akihabara.

10 Ueno & Yanesen p142

Ueno is the cultural heart of Tokyo, with the highest concentration of museums. Yanesen is a charming part of Tokyo that feels like time stopped several decades ago.

11 Asakusa & Sumida River p154

Tokyo's eastern neighbourhoods, on the banks of Sumida-gawa, have an old-Tokyo feel, with temples and shrines, gardens, traditional restaurants and artisan shops.

12 Odaiba & Tokyo Bay p165

Odaiba, a collection of islands on Tokyo Bay, is a family-oriented leisure district, with interactive museums and pop culture attractions. The new wholesale market is on Toyosu island.

Marunouchi & Nihombashi

IMPERIAL PALACE | KITANOMARU-KŌEN | MARUNOUCHI | NIHOMBASHI

Neighbourhood Top Five

1 Imperial Palace (p62) Strolling through the manicured gardens that were once only for the emperor and his family, and climbing the base of the keep that was at the centre of Edo Castle.

2 Intermediatheque (p64) Being blown away by the beautiful displays at this fascinating museum crafted from the eclectic collection of Tokyo University.

3 Tokyo International Forum (p64) Gazing up at the vast atrium of this convention and arts centre, which also hosts a great antiques market twice a month.

4 National Museum of Modern Art (MOMAT) (p64) Browsing the impressive collection of artworks by both Japanese and international artists.

5 Nihombashi (p64) Eyeballing the sculpted dragons on Tokyo's most famous bridge, then sailing underneath it on a river cruise.

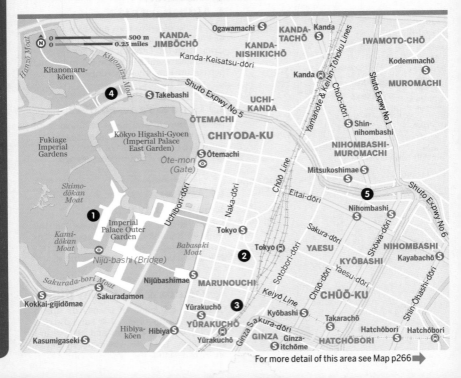

For more detail of this area see Map p266

Explore Marunouchi & Nihombashi

At the city's geographic centre, the Imperial Palace (p62) is the home of Japan's emperor and a natural draw. Most of the palace's inner grounds are off limits; see some of it on a tour or visit the Imperial Palace East Garden (p63), which includes some of the remains of the mammoth stone walls of the castle that once stood here. The outer grounds are open to the public, including woodsy Kitanomaru-kōen, north of the main palace area. The National Museum of Modern Art (MOMAT; p64) and other museums are here.

Immediately east of the palace, the business stronghold of Marunouchi has blossomed in recent years with a slew of new and revamped buildings, including high-end hotels, shops and restaurants. Highlights here include Intermediatheque (p64).

Adjacent to Marunouchi, and just east, is the historic district of Nihombashi (also spelled Nihonbashi). Tokyo's first fish market was here (before Tsukiji) and there are still many venerable food-related businesses in the area, including some great places to eat and shop. The city's grandest and oldest department store, Mitsukoshi (p70), is here. Neither Marunouchi or Nihombashi are known nightlife centres, but for top-grade cocktails zone in on the five-star hotels clustered in these neighbourhoods.

Local Life

→ **Eating** Food trucks serving bargain meals and drinks to local office workers gather at lunch Monday to Friday at Tokyo International Forum (p64).

→ **Shopping** Browse high-end boutiques along Marunouchi's Naka-dōri (p69).

→ **Jogging** Tokyo's favourite jogging course is around the Imperial Palace (p62).

Getting There & Away

→ **Train** The Yamanote and other JR lines, including the Narita Express and *shinkansen* (bullet train) services, stop at Tokyo Station. Yūrakuchō Station, one stop south, is also convenient for the area.

→ **Subway** The Marunouchi line stops at Tokyo Station and Ōtemachi; the Chiyoda Hanzōmon and Tōzai line also stop at Ōtemachi, a major subway hub. The Ginza line stops at Nihombashi and Mitsukoshimae.

→ **Bus** The free Marunouchi Shuttle runs on a circular route through Marunouchi and Nihombashi every 15 minutes from 10am to 8pm.

Lonely Planet's Top Tip

East of Nihombashi, towards the Sumida-gawa, is Ningyōchō (人形町), named after the dolls (*ningyō*) and puppets that were made here. It's a neighbourhood that has a definite 'old Tokyo' vibe and is known to harbour some long-running businesses. Two established restaurants to seek out here are Tamahide (p68) and Kizushi (p68).

Best Places to Eat

→ Kizushi (p68)

→ Nihonbashi Tamai (p66)

→ Dhaba India (p65)

→ Tamahide (p68)

→ Taimeiken (p65)

For reviews, see p65.

Best Places to Drink

→ Toyama Bar (p68)

→ Chashitsu Kaboku (p68)

→ Bridge Coffee & Icecream (p69)

→ (marunouchi) House (p68)

For reviews, see p68.

Best Places to Shop

→ Mitsukoshi (p70)

→ KITTE (p69)

→ Muji (p70)

→ Ōedo Antique Market (p70)

For reviews, see p69.

JANKEN/SHUTTERSTOCK ©

DISCOVER IMPERIAL PALACE & ITS GROUNDS

The Imperial Palace, sitting where the Tokugawa shogunate's castle, Edo-jō, once stood, is the residence of Japan's emperor and empress. The innermost area of the palace compound, which includes the imperial residence, is closed to the public – though a tour can get you close. Surrounding the palace is Kōkyo-gaien, a 115-hectare national garden with public green spaces.

Imperial Palace

In its heyday, Edo-jō was the largest fortress in the world. When the shogunate fell and the emperor moved to Tokyo, the castle became the imperial residence – Kōkyo. Much of it was destroyed by fires in 1873 and construction on a new palace was finished in 1888.

WWII air raids levelled most of the palace and the current ferro-concrete buildings, done in Japanese modernist style, were completed in the 1960s. The central building, which contains the throne room, Matsu-no-Ma (Pine Chamber), is called the **Kyūden** (宮殿; Map p266). The low-slung structure is surprisingly modest – at least from what can be seen on public tours.

The moats and imposing stone walls around the perimeter of the palace grounds belonged to the original castle.

Palace Tours

The only way to see the palace's inner compound is as part of an official tour organised by the Imperial Household Agency. Tours (lasting around 1¼ hours) run at 10am and 1.30pm usually on Tuesday through to Saturday, but not on public holidays or on afternoons from late July through to the end of August. Tours are also not held at all from 28 December to 4 January or when Imperial Court functions are scheduled.

DON'T MISS

→ Imperial Palace East Garden
→ Fushimi-yagura
→ Nijū-bashi
→ Chidori-ga-fuchi

PRACTICALITIES

→ 皇居, Kōkyo
→ Map p266, B4
→ ☎ 03-5223-8071
→ http://sankan.kunai cho.go.jp
→ 1 Chiyoda, Chiyoda-ku
→ admission free
→ ⏱ tours usually 10am & 1.30pm Tue-Sat
→ Ⓢ Chiyoda line to Ōtemachi, exits C13b & C10

Arrive no later than 10 minutes before the scheduled departure time at **Kikyō-mon** (桔梗門; Map p266; 🕐tour bookings 8.45am-noon & 1-5pm), the starting and ending point. Bring photo ID.

Reservations are taken – via the website, phone or by post – up to a month in advance (and no later than four days in advance via the website). Alternatively, go to the office at Kikyō-mon from 8.30am (for the morning tour) or noon (for the afternoon tour) – if there is space available you'll be able to register.

The tour will give you a glimpse of the outside of the Kyūden, a few other statehouses, and two watchtowers, Fujimi-yagura and Fushimi-yagura, that date to the days of Edo-jō. The tour doesn't enter any of the palace buildings.

Explanations on palace tours are given only in Japanese; download the free app (www.kunaicho.go.jp/e-event/app.html) for explanations in English, Chinese, Korean, French or Spanish.

Imperial Palace East Garden

Crafted from part of the original castle compound, the **Imperial Palace East Garden** (東御苑; Kōkyo Higashi-gyoen; Map p266; 🕐9am-4pm Nov-Feb, to 4.30pm Mar–mid-Apr, Sep & Oct, to 5pm mid-Apr–Aug, closed Mon & Fri year-round) [FREE] has been open to the public since 1968. Here you can get up-close views of the massive stones used to build the castle walls, and even climb the ruins of one of the *donjons* (main keeps), off the upper lawn. The large lawn is where the Honmaru (central part of the castle) was once located.

Don't miss the Ninomaru Grove, a woodland area that is one of the prettiest parts of the garden, with a pond and the elegant teahouse, Suwa-no-chaya.

Entry is free, but the number of visitors at any one time is limited, so it never feels crowded. Most people enter through **Ōte-mon** (大手門; Map p266), the closest gate to Tokyo Station.

Kōkyo-gaien Plaza

Kōkyo-gaien (皇居外苑広場, Kōkyo-gaien Hiroba, Map p266; www.env.go.jp/garden/kokyogaien; b Hibiya line to Hibiya, exit B6) is a grassy expanse southeast of the palace compound, which is planted with roughly 2000 immaculately maintained Japanese black pine trees.

This is the closest you can get to the Imperial Palace without taking the palace tour. There is a famous view from here of two of the palace bridges, stone **Megane-bashi** (眼鏡橋; Map p266) and iron **Nijū-bashi** (二重橋; Map p266), with the watchtower Fushimi-yagura rising behind them. Megane-bashi is nicknamed Eyeglass Bridge because its support arches reflected in the water create the appearance of spectacles; both bridges date to the 1880s.

CHERRY-BLOSSOM VIEWING

The moat, **Chidori-ga-fuchi** (千鳥ヶ淵; Map p266; ☎03-3234-1948; www.city.chiyoda.lg.jp/shisetsu/koen/073.html; Kudan-minami, Chiyoda-ku; boat rental per 30min ¥500; 🕐boat rental 11am-4.30pm Tue-Sun; [S]Hanzōmon line to Hanzōmon, exit 5 or Kudanshita, exit 2), on the western edge of the palace grounds, is one of the city's most popular *hanami* (cherry-blossom viewing) spots. There's a 700m-long pedestrian path (for strolling, not picnicking) alongside the water that's especially pretty when the blossoms are lit up at night. Between March and November, you can rent row boats to take out on the water from the small pier here.

WALKING TOURS

Free two-hour guided walking tours of the east garden are led every Wednesday, Saturday and Sunday in English by volunteer members of the Tokyo Systematized Goodwill Guide (SGG) Club; meet at the JNTO Tourist Information Center (p243) before 1pm.

SIGHTS

Imperial Palace & Kitanomaru-kōen

IMPERIAL PALACE PALACE

See p60.

KŌKYO-GAIEN PLAZA PARK

See p61.

★NATIONAL MUSEUM OF MODERN ART (MOMAT) MUSEUM

Map p266 (国立近代美術館, Kokuritsu Kindai Bijutsukan; ☎03-5777-8600; www.momat.go.jp; 3-1 Kitanomaru-kōen, Chiyoda-ku; adult/child ¥500/free, 1st Sun of month free; ⏲10am-5pm Tue-Thu & Sun, to 8pm Fri & Sat; [S]Tōzai line to Takebashi, exit 1b) Regularly changing displays from the museum's superb collection of more than 12,000 works, by both local and international artists, are shown over floors 2 to 4; special exhibitions are mounted on the ground floor. All pieces date from the Meiji period onward and impart a sense of how modern Japan has developed through portraits, photography, contemporary sculptures and video works. The museum closes in between exhibitions, so first check the schedule online.

Don't miss the 'Room with a View' for a panorama of the Imperial Palace East Garden. The museum also hosts excellent special exhibitions, which cost extra.

CRAFTS GALLERY MUSEUM

Map p266 (東京国立近代美術館 工芸館; www.momat.go.jp; 1 Kitanomaru-kōen, Chiyoda-ku; adult/child ¥250/free, 1st Sun of month free; ⏲10am-5pm Tue-Sun; [S]Tōzai line to Takebashi, exit 1b) Housed in a vintage red-brick building, this MOMAT annex stages excellent changing exhibitions of *mingei* (folk crafts): ceramics, lacquerware, bamboo, textiles, dolls and more. Some exhibits feature works by contemporary artisans, including Japan's official 'living national treasures'.

Marunouchi

★INTERMEDIATHEQUE MUSEUM

Map p266 (インターメディアテク; ☎03-5777-8600; www.intermediatheque.jp; 2nd & 3rd fl, JP Tower, 2-7-2 Marunouchi, Chiyoda-ku; ⏲11am-6pm, to 8pm Fri & Sat, usually closed Sun & Mon; 🚉JR Yamanote line to Tokyo, Marunouchi exit) [FREE] Dedicated to interdisciplinary experimentation, Intermediatheque cherry-picks from the vast collection of the University of Tokyo (Tōdai) to craft a fascinating, contemporary museum experience. Go from viewing the best ornithological taxidermy collection in Japan to a giant pop art print or the beautifully encased skeleton of a dinosaur. A handsome Tōdai lecture hall is reconstituted as a forum for events, including playing 1920s' jazz recordings on a gramophone or old movie screenings.

TOKYO STATION LANDMARK

Map p266 (東京駅; www.tokyostationcity.com; 1-9 Marunouchi, Chiyoda-ku; 🚉JR lines to Tokyo Station) Tokyo Station celebrated its centenary in 2014 with a major renovation and expansion. Kingo Tatsuno's original elegant brick building on the Marunouchi side includes domes faithful to the original design, decorated inside with relief sculptures. It's best viewed straight on from the plaza on Miyuki-dōri.

TOKYO INTERNATIONAL FORUM ARCHITECTURE

Map p266 (東京国際フォーラム; ☎03-5221-9000; www.t-i-forum.co.jp; 3-5-1 Marunouchi, Chiyoda-ku; ⏲7am-11.30pm; 🚉JR Yamanote line to Yūrakuchō, central exit) [FREE] This architectural marvel by Rafael Viñoly houses a convention and arts centre, with eight auditoriums and a spacious courtyard in which concerts and events are held. The eastern wing looks like a glass ship; you can access the catwalks from the 7th floor (take the lift).

Nihombashi

NIHOMBASHI BRIDGE

Map p266 (日本橋, Nihonbashi; 1 Nihombashi, Chūō-ku; [S]Ginza line to Mitsukoshimae, exits B5 & B6) Guarded by bronze lions and dragons, this handsome 1911-vintage granite bridge over Nihombashi-gawa is partly obscured by the overhead expressway. During the Edo period, this was the beginning of the great trunk roads (Tōkaidō, Nikkō Kaidō etc) that took *daimyō* (domain lords) between the capital and their home provinces. Distances to Tokyo are still measured from here.

MITSUI MEMORIAL MUSEUM MUSEUM

Map p266 (三井記念美術館; ☎03-5777-8600; www.mitsui-museum.jp; 7th fl, Mitsui Main Bldg, 2-1-1 Nihombashi-Muromachi, Chūō-ku; adult/student ¥1000/500; ⏲10am-5pm Tue-Sun; [S]Ginza line to Mitsukoshimae, exit A7) Stately wood panelling surrounds a small collection of traditional Japanese art and artefacts, including ceramics, paintings and *nō* (stylised dance-drama) masks, amassed over three centuries by the families behind today's Mitsui conglomerate. On permanent display is a reconstruction of the interior of the Jo-an tea-ceremony room; the original National Treasure is in Inuyama.

 EATING

★DHABA INDIA
SOUTH INDIAN ¥

Map p266 (ダバ インディア; ☎03-3272-7160; www.dhabaindia.com; 2-7-9 Yaesu, Chūō-ku; lunch/mains from ¥850/1370; ⊙11.15am-3pm & 5-11pm Mon-Fri, noon-3pm & 5-10pm Sat & Sun; ⓓ; ⓢGinza line to Kyōbashi, exit 5) Indian meals in Tokyo don't come much better than those served at this long-established restaurant with deep-indigo plaster walls. The food is very authentic, particularly the curries served with basmati rice, naan or crispy *dosa* (giant lentil-flour pancakes). Set lunches are spectacularly good value.

NIHONBASHI DASHI BAR HANARE
JAPANESE ¥

Map p266 (日本橋だし場はなれ; ☎03-5205-8704; www.ninben.co.jp/hanare; 1st fl, Coredo Muromachi 2, 2-3-1 Nihombashi-Muromachi, Chūō-ku; set meals ¥1025-1950, dishes ¥650-1300; ⊙11am-2pm & 5-11pm; ⊝ⓓ; ⓢGinza line to Mitsukoshimae, exit A6) This casual restaurant from long-time producer (300-plus years!) of *katsuo-bushi* (dried bonito flakes), Ninben, naturally serves dishes that make use of the umami-rich ingredient. Set meals, with dishes such as hearty miso soups and *dashi takikokomi gohan* (rice steamed in stock), are good value, and healthy to boot.

TAIMEIKEN
JAPANESE ¥

Map p266 (たいめいけん; ☎03-3271-2463; www.taimeiken.co.jp; 1-12-10 Nihombashi, Chūō-ku; mains ¥750-2650; ⊙11am-8.30pm Mon-Sat, to 8pm Sun; ⓓ; ⓢGinza line to Nihombashi, exit C5) This classic restaurant, open since 1931, specialises in *yōshoku* – Western cuisine adapted to the Japanese palate. Its signature dish is *omuraisu* (an omelette stuffed with ketchup-flavoured fried rice), to which you can add a side of borscht and coleslaw for the very retro price of ¥50 each.

It's easier to get a seat on the 2nd floor, where the prices are higher, but the old-school atmosphere on the 1st floor is worth the queuing for.

EASY DINING & DRINKING

The major shopping centres in Marunouchi and Nihombashi, such as KITTE (p69) and Coredo Muromachi (p70), have lots of actually good (not just compromise) eating options, as well as plenty of cafes. The Shin-Maru Building has a whole floor of restaurants, *izakaya* (Japanese pub-eateries) and bars at (marunouchi) House (p68). With millions of travellers passing through, Tokyo Station (p64) offers all kinds of meals, including the collection of ramen vendors, **Tokyo Ramen Street** (東京ラーメンストリート; Map p266; www.tokyoeki-1bangai.co.jp/ramenstreet; basement, First Avenue, Tokyo Station, 1-9-1 Marunouchi, Chiyoda-ku; ramen from ¥800; ⊙7.30am-11.30pm; ⓡJR lines to Tokyo, Yaesu south exit).

NEMURO HANAMARU
SUSHI ¥

Map p266 (根室花まる; ☎03-6269-9026; www.sushi-hanamaru.com; 4th fl, KITTE, 2-7-2 Marunouchi, Chiyoda-ku; sushi per plate ¥140-540; ⊙11am-10pm, until 9pm Sun; ⓡJR lines to Tokyo, Marunouchi south exit) The port of Nemuro in northern Hokkaidō is where this popular sushi operation first started. At this branch, on the 4th floor of the KITTE mall, it's a self-serve *kaiten-sushi* where the vinegared rice bites are delivered by rotating conveyor belt. The line here can often be very long but quality and price make up for the wait.

MEAL MUJI YŪRAKUCHŌ
DELI ¥

Map p266 (MealMUJI有楽町; ☎03-5208-8245; http://cafemeal.muji.com/jp; 2nd fl, 3-8-3 Marunouchi, Chiyoda-ku; meals ¥500-1200; ⊙10am-9pm; ⊝ⓔⓓ; ⓡJR Yamanote line to Yūrakuchō, Kyōbashi exit) Those who subscribe to the Muji lifestyle will be delighted to know that the 'no name brand' experience goes beyond neutral-toned notebooks and linens. Meal MUJI follows the 'simpler is better' mantra with fresh deli fare uncluttered by chemicals and unpronounceable ingredients.

POKÉMON CAFE
CAFE ¥

Map p266 (ポケモンカフェ; ☎03-6262-3439; www.pokemoncenter-online.com/cafe; 5th fl, Nihombashi Takashimaya Tōkan, 2-11-2 Nihombashi, Chūō-ku; meals from ¥1600, drinks from ¥650; ⊙10.30am-10pm; ⊝ⓔⓓⓗ; ⓢGinza line to Nihombashi, exit B2) Pokémon fans will find it hard to pass on this chance to sample

1. Nihombashi (p64)
A 1911 bridge guarded by bronze dragons.

2. Tokyo International Forum (p64)
An architectural marvel by Rafael Viñoly.

3. KITTE (p69)
This elegant shopping mall also contains a
fascinating interdisciplinary museum.

4. Imperial Palace (p62)
The residence of Japan's emperor and empress.

Pikachu-themed food and drink, made with classic *kyara-ben* (character *bentō*) techniques (like using thinly sliced *daikon* (radish) and *nori* (seaweed) to make round anime eyes). While it's predictably overpriced, the food isn't bad for a theme cafe. Seating is by reservation only.

★NIHONBASHI TAMAI JAPANESE ¥¥

Map p266 (玉ゐ　本店; ☎03-3272-3227; www.anago-tamai.com; 2-9-9 Nihombashi, Chūō-ku; mains from ¥1450; 🕐11am-2.30pm & 5-9.30pm Mon-Fri, 11.30am-3.30pm & 4.30-9pm Sat & Sun; 📋; [S]Ginza line to Nihombashi, exit C4) This Nihombashi stalwart specialises in *anago* (seafaring eel), which is cheaper and not endangered like its freshwater cousin *unagi*. The eels are prepared to perfection here, laid out in lacquerware boxes (a style known as *hakomeshi*) and served either grilled or boiled – you can sample both cooking styles by asking for half and half.

It's based in a charming 1950s wooden shop and there's often a line outside.

★KIZUSHI SUSHI ¥¥¥

Map p266 (喜寿司; ☎03-3666-1682; 2-7-13 Nihombashi-Ningyōchō, Chūō-ku; course from ¥3500-10,000; 🕐11.45am-2.30pm Mon-Sat, 5-9.30pm Mon-Fri, to 9pm Sat; 🚭📋; [S]Hibiya line to Ningyōchō, exit A3) While sushi has moved in the direction of faster and fresher, Kizushi, in business since 1923, is keeping it old school. Third-generation chef Yui Ryuichi uses traditional techniques, such as marinating the fish in salt or vinegar, from back when sushi was more about preservation than instant gratification. The shop is in a lovely old timber-frame house.

Reservations are required for dinner and we recommend to choose a course of ¥5000 or above to truly sample the range of food that is served here.

TAMAHIDE JAPANESE ¥¥¥

Map p266 (玉ひで; ☎03-3668-7651; www.tamahide.co.jp; 1-17-1 Nihombashi-Ningyōchō, Chūō-ku; lunch from ¥1500, dinner set course from ¥6800; 🕐11.30am-1.30pm & 5-10pm Mon-Sat; 🚭; [S]Hibiya line to Ningyōchō, exit A1) For generations, people have been lining up outside this restaurant – in business since 1760 – to try its signature dish *oyakodon,* a sweet-savoury mix of chicken, soy broth and lightly cooked egg, served over a bowl of rice. It also has dishes using minced chicken or duck and they're all delicious and filling. Pay before you sit down at lunch.

DRINKING & NIGHTLIFE

★CHASHITSU KABOKU TEAHOUSE

Map p266 (茶室　嘉木; ☎03-6212-0202; www.ippodo-tea.co.jp; 3-1-1 Marunouchi, Chiyoda-ku; tea set ¥1080-2600; 🕐11am-7pm; 🚭📋; 🚆JR Yamanote line to Yurakuchō, Tokyo International Forum exit) Run by famed Kyoto tea producer Ippōdō – which celebrated 300 years of business in 2017 – this teahouse is a fantastic place to experience the pleasures of *ocha* (green tea). It's one of the few places that serves *koicha* (thick tea), which is even thicker than ordinary *matcha* (powdered green tea). Sets are accompanied by a pretty, seasonal *wagashi.*

★TOYAMA BAR BAR

Map p266 (トヤマバー; ☎03-6262-2723; www.toyamakan.jp; 1-2-6 Nihombashi-muromachi, Chūō-ku; 🕐11am-9pm; 📋; [S]Ginza line to Mitsukoshimae, exit B5) This slick counter bar offers a selection of sakes from 17 different Toyama breweries. A set of three 30mL cups costs only ¥700 (90mL cups from ¥700 each). English tasting notes are available. It's part of the Nihonbashi Toyama-kan (日本橋とやま館), which promotes goods produced in Japan's northern Toyama Prefecture. Pick up a bottle of anything you like at the attached shop.

PETER: THE BAR COCKTAIL BAR

Map p266 (☎03-6270-2763; http://tokyo.peninsula.com/en/fine-dining/peter-lounge-bar; 24th fl, 1-8-1 Yūrakuchō, Chiyoda-ku; 🕐noon-midnight, to 1am Fri & Sat; [S]Hibiya line to Hibiya, exits A6 & A7) The Peninsula Tokyo (p189) hotel's 24th-floor bar has dress-circle views across the Imperial Palace, Hibiya Park and Ginza and a generous happy hour (5pm to 8pm Sunday to Thursday), when drinks – including the bar's signature 'Tokyo Joe' cocktail (gin, *ume* (plum) liqueur, Drambuie and cranberry juice) – and snacks are all ¥800. There's a 15% service charge, but no cover charge.

(MARUNOUCHI) HOUSE BAR

Map p266 (丸の内ハウス; ☎03-5218-5100; www.marunouchi-house.com; 7th fl, Shin-Maru Bldg, 1-5-1 Marunouchi, Chiyoda-ku; 🕐11am-4am Mon-Sat, to 11pm Sun; 📶📋; 🚆JR lines to Tokyo, Marunouchi north exit) On the 7th floor of the Shin-Maru Building, this collection of nine bars and pubs is a popular after-work gathering spot. There's a wraparound terrace, so many spots have outdoor seating. The views aren't sky-high; instead you feel curiously suspended among the office towers, hovering over Tokyo Station below. The bars often come together to hold joint events.

ENTERTAINMENT

SUIGIAN PERFORMING ARTS

Map p266 (水戯庵; ☎03-3527-9378; https://suigian.jp; basement, 2-5-10 Nihombashi-Muromachi, Chūō-ku; seating charge from ¥3800 plus 1 drink or food; ⏲11am-11.30pm, until 9pm Sun; [S] Ginza line to Mitsukoshimae, exit A6) If you would like an up-close and personal taster of traditional Japanese performing arts, including *nō*, *kyōgen* (comic drama) and courtly dances, make a reservation for one of three 40-minute performances that take place here. The small stage is backed by a beautiful painting of a pine tree, and surrounded by an intimate, sophisticated restaurant and bar.

From 8.30pm (except Sunday) the space becomes the Momokawa Lounge with dance performances on its stage. The easiest way to find Suigian, which is beneath the Coredo Muromachi 2 building, is to locate the steps down from ground level beside the Fukutoku shrine.

ARASHIO STABLE SPECTATOR SPORT

Map p266 (荒汐部屋, Arashio-beya; ☎03-3666-7646; www.arashio.net; 2-47-2 Hama-chō, Nihombashi, Chūō-ku; ⏲7.30am-10am; [S] Toei Shinjuku line to Hamachō, exit A2) [FREE] Watch the wrestlers practise through the window between 7.30am and 10am at this friendly sumo stable. Call the day before to double-check that practice *(keiko)* is on – they take breaks during the March, July and September tournaments; more info is on the English website.

NIPPON BUDŌKAN LIVE MUSIC

Map p266 (日本武道館; ☎03-3216-5100; www.nipponbudokan.or.jp; 2-3 Kitanomaru-kōen, Chiyoda-ku; [S] Hanzōmon line to Kudanshita, exit 2) The 14,000-plus-seat Budōkan was built for the judo competition of the 1964 Olympics (*budō* means 'martial arts') and will be pressed into service again for the 2020 event. Martial-arts practice and contests are still held here, but the Budōkan is better known as a concert hall: lots of big names, from the Beatles to Beck, have played here.

COTTON CLUB JAZZ

Map p266 (コットンクラブ; ☎03-3215-1555; www.cottonclubjapan.co.jp; 2nd fl, Tokia, Tokyo Bldg, 2-7-3 Marunouchi, Chiyoda-ku; tickets ¥6000-10,000.; ⏲5-11pm Mon-Fri, 4-10.30pm Sat & Sun; [R] JR lines to Tokyo, Marunouchi south exit) You're more likely to hear contemporary international jazz stars here than musicians harking back to the 1920s New York club it honours. Also on the roster is a medley of interesting Japanese artists such as saxophonist Itō Takeshi. Check the website for schedules and ticket prices.

LOCAL KNOWLEDGE

BAKUROCHŌ

The wholesale district of Bakurochō (馬喰町) has morphed into a hub for small galleries and craft shops. Zone in on the Agata Takezawa Building, where you'll find **Gallery aM** (Map p266; ☎03-5829-9109; http://gallery-alpham.com; 1-2-11 Higashi-Kanda, Chiyoda-ku; ⏲11am-7pm Tue-Sat; [R] JR Sobu line to Bakurochō, exit 2). The area is awash with a number of hip hostels with attached cafe-bars, too, as well as stand-alone third-wave coffee shops such as **Bridge Coffee & Icecream** (Map p266; ☎03-3527-3399; www.facebook.com/Bridge.coffee; 1-13-9 Nihonbashi-Bakurochō, Chūō-ku; ⏲9am-7pm; 📶; [R] JR Sobu line to Asakusa-bashi, east exit).

SHOPPING

★KITTE MALL

Map p266 (☎03-3216-2811; www.jptower-kitte.jp; 2-7-2 Marunouchi, Chiyoda-ku; ⏲shops 11am-9pm Mon-Sat, to 8pm Sun, restaurants to 11pm, to 10pm Sun; [R] JR lines to Tokyo, Marunouchi south exit) This well-designed shopping mall at the foot of JP Tower incorporates the restored original facade of the Tokyo Central Post Office. It is notable for its atrium, around which is arrayed a quality selection of craft-oriented Japanese-brand shops selling homewares, fashion, accessories and lifestyle goods.

For a great selection of Japanese gifts and souvenirs drop by Good Design Store Tokyo by Nohara (p70), and – if there isn't a long line – grab some affordable, good-quality sushi at Nemuro Hanamaru (p65).

Also in the building is fascinating museum Intermediatheque (p64).

★ COREDO MUROMACHI   MALL

Map p266 (コレド室町; www.mitsui-shopping-park.com/urban/muromach; 2-2-1 Nihombashi-Muromachi, Chūō-ku; ⏰most shops 10am-9pm; SGinza line to Mitsukoshimae, exit A4) Spread over three buildings, this stylish development houses many shops from famous gourmet food purveyors, as well as reliable places to eat and drink. In Coredo Muromachi 3 are elegant fashion and homewares boutiques, including a branch of Muji.

★ MITSUKOSHI   DEPARTMENT STORE

Map p266 (三越; ☏03-3241-3311; www.mitsu koshi.co.jp; 1-4-1 Nihombashi-Muromachi, Chūō-ku; ⏰10am-7pm; SGinza line to Mitsukoshimae, exit A2) Mitsukoshi's venerable Nihombashi branch was Japan's first department store. It's a grand affair with an entrance guarded by bronze lions and a magnificent statue of Magokoro, the goddess of sincerity, rising up from the centre of the ground floor. For the full effect, arrive at 10am for the bells and bows that accompany each day's opening.

GOOD DESIGN STORE TOKYO BY NOHARA   GIFTS & SOUVENIRS

Map p266 (☏03-5220-1007; http://gdst.nohara-inc.co.jp; 3rd fl, KITTE, 2-7-2 Marunouchi, Chiyoda-ku; ⏰11am-9pm, until 8pm Sun; ⅢJR lines to Tokyo, Marunouchi south exit) A fab selection of products that have gained Japan's Good Design Award are showcased at this lifestyle boutique. It's divided into sections – the front garden, the living, dining and hobby rooms – with nifty, desirable buys throughout.

ŌEDO ANTIQUE MARKET   ANTIQUES

Map p266 (大江戸骨董市; ☏03-6407-6011; www.antique-market.jp; 3-5-1 Marunouchi, Chiyoda-ku; ⏰9am-4pm 1st & 3rd Sun of month; ⅢJR Yamanote line to Yūrakuchō, Kokusai Forum exit) Held in the courtyard of Tokyo International Forum (p64; check the website for exact dates), this is a brilliantly colourful event with hundreds of dealers in retro and antique Japanese goods, from old ceramics and kimono to kitsch plastic figurines and vintage movie posters.

MUJI   HOMEWARES

Map p266 (無印良品; ☏03-5208-8241; www.muji.com/jp/flagship/yurakucho/en; 3-8-3 Marunouchi, Chiyoda-ku; ⏰10am-9pm; ⅢJR Yamanote line to Yūrakuchō, Kyōbashi exit) The flagship store of the famously understated brand sells elegant, simple clothing, accessories, homewares and food. There are scores of outlets across Tokyo, but the Yūrakuchō store, renovated in 2017, is the largest with the biggest range. It also offers tax-free shopping, bicycle rental (¥1080 per day from 10am to 8pm; passport required) and a great cafeteria (p65).

🏃 SPORTS & ACTIVITIES

★ TOKYO GREAT CYCLING TOUR   CYCLING

Map p266 (☏03-4590-2995; www.tokyocycling. jp; 1-3-2 Shinkawa, Chūō-ku; tours ¥3000-10,000; SHibiya line to Kayabachō, exit 3) There's a fine variety of routes and themes offered here to suit everyone from casual pedallers to more serious cyclists. The English-speaking staff and guides are very friendly and professional. You can also rent bikes from ¥2500 a day.

The same company also offers excellent kayaking tours (the longest route takes you on a fascinating 10km circuit including the Sumida, Kanda and Nihombashi Rivers) and running tours around the palace and along the Sumida-gawa.

TIME TO GEISHA   CULTURAL

Map p266 (☏03-3242-2334; www.nihonbashi-in fo.jp/omotenashi/geisha.html; Coredo Muromachi 3, 3rd flr, 1-5-5 Nihombashi-Muromachi, Chūō-ku; adult/child ¥5500/3500; ⏰1pm Sat; SGinza line to Mitsukoshimae, Mitsukoshi gate) This is your chance to spend an hour in the company of a couple of Nihombashi's few remaining geisha. These fabled entertainers will dance, play *shamisen* (three-stringed instrument resembling a lute or a banjo) and school you in the ways of *ozashiki* drinking games. You'll also get to sample tea and sweets in Kyoraku-tei, a traditional tatami event space, and its teahouse, Meguria-an. It's recommended to reserve at least a day before.

NIHOMBASHI CRUISE   CRUISE

Map p266 (日本橋クルーズ; ☏03-5679-7311; http://ss3.jp/nihonbashi-cruise; 1 Nihombashi, Chūō-ku; 45/60/90min cruises ¥1500/2000/2500; SGinza line to Mitsukoshimae, exits B5 & B6) For a unique perspective on Tokyo, hop aboard one of these daily river cruises. They proceed along Nihombashi-gawa towards Sumida-gawa, or make a loop around Nihombashi-gawa to Kanda-gawa. The landing stage is next to Nihombashi. You'll get to see beneath many historic bridges as well as the expressway built above the river.

Ginza & Tsukiji

Neighbourhood Top Five

❶ Tsukiji Market (p73) Sampling a delicious array of seafood and other delicious eats at this bustling market area next to the old wholesale market.

❷ Kabukiza (p74) Lining up for a one-act ticket and being entertained by the Technicolor spectacle of kabuki drama.

❸ Hama-rikyū Onshi-teien (p73) Strolling past immaculately manicured trees, some hundreds of years old, and sipping green tea in this beautiful bayside garden.

❹ Tsukiji Soba Academy (p78) Learning to make soba noodles with an English-speaking expert who has taught Michelin-starred chefs.

❺ Okuno Building (p77) Exploring this handsome 1932 apartment block crammed with tiny galleries hosting mini-exhibitions that change week by week.

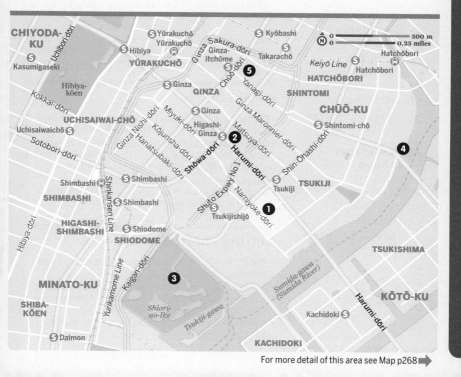

For more detail of this area see Map p268

Lonely Planet's Top Tip

Unpretentious bars and eateries, many specialising in *yakitori* (chicken, and other meats or vegetables, grilled on skewers) can be found clustered under the arches of the swath of railway tracks and the raised expressway running from Yūrakuchō to Shimbashi. They are among some of Tokyo's most atmospheric places to grab a quick meal and frothy beer.

 ### Best Places to Eat

➡ Kyūbey (p75)

➡ Tempura Kondō (p75)

➡ Apollo (p74)

➡ Ginza Sato Yosuke (p74)

For reviews, see p74.

Best Places to Drink

➡ Ginza Lion (p75)

➡ Cha Ginza (p75)

➡ Ginza Music Bar (p75)

➡ Turret Coffee (p75)

For reviews, see p75. ➡

 ### Best Places to Shop

➡ Takumi (p77)

➡ Itōya (p77)

➡ Okuno Building (p77)

➡ Akomeya (p77)

For reviews, see p77. ➡

Explore Ginza & Tsukiji

Proudly ranking alongside Fifth Avenue and the Champs-Élysées, Ginza is one of the world's most famous shopping districts. It's a compact area but you could easily spend a day sashaying from the likes of Mikimoto Pearls and Louis Vuitton to Uniqlo (p78). There's also some interesting architecture and art to be found at Ginza Maison Hermès Le Forum (p73), Shiseido Gallery (p73) and the 1932 Okuno Building (p77).

The famous wholesale seafood and produce market at nearby Tsukiji moved across Tokyo Bay to a new home in Toyosu in 2018. Still, the area remains well worth visiting: Tsukiji Market (p73), which made up the unofficial 'outer market' of the old wholesale market, remains and is still home to a mouth-watering array of food-related businesses. Enjoy breakfast or lunch here and combine them with a stroll around Hama-rikyū Onshi-teien (p73), a gorgeous bayside garden that's home to a serene traditional teahouse.

Providing a 21st-century backdrop to the manicured greenery of Hama-rikyū Onshi-teien are the skyscrapers of Shiodome. Top sights here include the small Advertising Museum Tokyo (p73) and the charming NI-Tele Really Big Clock (p74), partly designed by Studio Ghibli's Miyazaki Hayao.

Ginza has some of Tokyo's finest restaurants, where reservations are pretty much mandatory. But modestly priced meals can be found; check the top levels of the many department stores and malls. For casual spots with lots of atmosphere, try neighbouring Shimbashi and Yūrakuchō (especially under the elevated railroad tracks).

Local Life

➡ **Eating** Browse the *depachika* (department store food floor) at Mitsukoshi (p77) for trending gourmet items.

➡ **Promenading** Go for a stroll along Chūō-dōri each weekend, when a long section of the road is traffic-free from noon to 5pm (until 6pm, April to September).

➡ **People-watching** In the evenings, spot high-class hostesses, clad in kimonos, greeting customers (the moneyed elite) on Ginza streets.

Getting There & Away

➡ **Train** The JR Yamanote line stops at Shimbashi and Yūrakuchō Stations.

➡ **Subway** The Ginza, Hibiya and Marunouchi lines stop at Ginza. For Tsukiji, take either the Hibiya line to Tsukiji or the Ōedo line to Tsukijishijō.

➡ **Water Bus** Hama-rikyū Onshi-teien has a dock for Tokyo Cruise (p232) boats.

SIGHTS

★ TSUKIJI MARKET MARKET

(場外市場, Jōgai Shijō; www.tsukiji.or.jp; 6-chōme Tsukiji, Chūō-ku; ⊙5am-2pm, closed irregularly; ⓢHibiya line to Tsukiji, exit 1) Tokyo's main wholesale market may have moved to Toyosu (p168), but there are many reasons to visit its old home. The tightly packed rows of vendors (which once formed the Outer Market) hawk market and culinary goods, such as dried fish, seaweed, kitchen knives, rubber boots and crockery. It's also a fantastic place to eat, with great street food and a huge concentration of small restaurants and cafes, most specialising in seafood.

The area can get very crowded – avoid the narrow lanes if you're pushing a stroller or pulling luggage. Come early as most shops close by 2pm. Some shops are closed on Sundays and Wednesdays.

★ HAMA-RIKYŪ ONSHI-TEIEN GARDENS

(浜離宮恩賜庭園, Detached Palace Garden; ☑03-3541-0200; www.tokyo-park.or.jp/teien; 1-1 Hama-rikyū-teien, Chūō-ku; adult/child ¥300/ free; ⊙9am-5pm; ⓢŌedo line to Shiodome, exit A1) This beautiful garden, one of Tokyo's finest, is all that remains of a shogunate summer villa next to Tokyo Bay. There's a large pond with an island, connected by a causeway, upon which sits the teahouse Nakajima no Ochaya (p212), where you can sip matcha (¥740, traditional sweet included). Don't miss the spectacularly manicured 300-year-old black pine tree near the Otemon entrance.

There are free guided tours of the garden in English at 11am on Saturdays and Mondays (except during August). A great way to access or depart from the garden is via Tokyo Cruise (p232), which runs water buses from Asakusa, via the Sumida-gawa (Sumida River), to a pier on the garden's edge.

ADVERTISING MUSEUM TOKYO MUSEUM

(アド・ミュージアム東京; ☑03-6218-2500; www.admt.jp; basement, Caretta Bldg, 1-8-2 Higashi-Shimbashi, Minato-ku; ⊙11am-6pm Tue-Sat; ⓢŌedo line to Shiodome, Shimbashi exit) FREE If you see advertising as art, this museum is a spectacle. Run by Dentsu, Japan's largest advertising agency, this fine collection runs from woodblock-printed handbills from the Edo period via sumptuous art nouveau and art deco Taishō-era works to the best of today. There's English signage throughout, and touch screens to view classic TV ads.

NAKAGIN CAPSULE TOWER ARCHITECTURE

(中銀カプセルタワー; www.nakagincapsuletower .com/nakagincapsuletour; 8-16-10 Ginza, Chūō-ku; tours in Japanese/English ¥3000/4000; ⓢŌedo line to Tsukijishijō, exit A3) This early-1970s building by Kurokawa Kishō is a seminal work of Metabolism, an experimental architecture movement to create fluid, more organic structures. The tower is made up of self-contained pods around a central core that are meant to be replaced every 20 years. Long story short: they were never replaced and the building is just shy of being condemned, though remaining residents (and many more fans) have been campaigning to save it. Entry is by tour only.

Tours run a few times a month, usually on Saturday or Sunday (in Japanese), with an English tour on Thursday at noon. The schedule is posted monthly on the website. To reserve, send an email in simple English with your name, party size and requested tour date. Given the condition of the building, it's not a good idea to bring small children.

GINZA MAISON
HERMÈS LE FORUM GALLERY

(☑03-3569-3300; www.maisonhermes.jp; 8F Maison Hermès, 5-4-1 Ginza, Chūō-ku; ⊙11am-8pm, until 7pm Sun; ⓢGinza, Hibiya, Marunouchi lines to Ginza, exit B9) FREE On the 8th floor of the French luxury goods boutique is a spacious, light-filled gallery that hosts around three different contemporary art shows per year, usually showcasing works by French artists. Renzo Piano was the architect of the skinny building constructed from specially made glass blocks – it looks like a giant lantern at night.

Also check if anything is on at the building's second exhibition and events space **Le Studio**, where free foreign movies are screened every weekend – details are on the website.

SHISEIDO GALLERY GALLERY

(資生堂ギャラリー; ☑03-3572-3901; www. shiseidogroup.com/gallery; basement, 8-8-3 Ginza, Chūō-ku; ⊙11am-7pm Tue-Sat, to 6pm Sun; ⓢGinza line to Shimbashi, exit 1 or 3) FREE The cosmetics company Shiseido runs its experimental art space out of the basement of its Shiseido Parlour complex of cafes and restaurants.

An ever-changing selection, particularly of installation pieces, lends itself well to the gallery's high ceiling.

NI-TELE REALLY BIG CLOCK — PUBLIC ART

(日テレ大時計; 1-6-1 Higashi-Shimbashi, Minato-ku; ⏰operates at noon, 3pm, 6pm & 8pm, also 10am Sat & Sun; 🚊JR services to Shimbashi, Shiodome exit) **FREE** Studio Ghibli's animation director Miyazaki Hayao collaborated with sculptor Kunio Shachimaru on this fantastic, steampunk-style timepiece beside the entrance to Nippon Television Tower. Four times daily (with an extra morning show on weekends) various automaton elements spring to life as the clock strikes the hour and plays a jolly tune.

🍴 EATING

GINZA SATO YOSUKE — NOODLES ¥¥

(銀座佐藤養助; 📞03-6215-6211; www.sato-yoske.co.jp/en/shop/ginza; 6-4-17 Ginza, Chūō-ku; noodles from ¥1300; ⏰11.30am-3pm & 5-10pm; Ⓢ Marunouchi line to Ginza, exit C2) A speciality of Akita Prefecture, *inaniwa* wheat noodles have been made by seven generations of the Sato family.

As you'll be able to tell from the glossy, silky-textured results, they've pretty much got it down to perfection. Sample the noo-dles in a hot chicken broth or cold dipping sauces such as sesame and miso or green curry.

SHIMANTO-GAWA — IZAKAYA ¥¥

(四万十川; 📞03-3591-5202; www.dd-holdings.jp/shops/shimantogawa/yurakucho; 2-1-21 Yūrakuchō, Chiyoda-ku; cover charge per person ¥500, dishes ¥530-3800; ⏰4-11.30pm; 🚭; Ⓢ Ginza line to Hibiya, exit A4) This beneath-the-train-tracks *izakaya* (Japanese pub/eatery) takes its theme literally by creating a dining area of wooden booths built beside and over a flowing stream – the Shimanto-gawa is a river in Shikoku – and serving *Tosa-ryōri* (the specialist cuisine of Shikoku's Kōchi Prefecture). Try the seared bonito grilled on straw-fed fires.

AIN SOPH — VEGAN ¥¥

(📞03-6228-4241; www.ain-soph.jp; 4-12-1 Ginza, Chūō-ku; mains from ¥1680, bentō boxes & set menus lunch/dinner from ¥2480/3250; ⏰11.30am-10pm Wed-Mon; 🚭; Ⓢ Asakusa or Hibiya line to Higashi-Ginza, exit A7) Truly vegan restaurants are few and far between in Tokyo and ones that make so much effort over their food as Ain Soph are even rarer. Thank heavens then for this stylish place

---

◉ TOP EXPERIENCE
CATCH A KABUKI PERFORMANCE

The flamboyant facade of the Kabukiza theatre (established in 1889 and renovated in 2013) is fitting for the extravagant dramatic flourishes that are integral to kabuki, Japan's signature performing art.

A full kabuki performance comprises three or four acts (usually from different plays) over an afternoon or an evening (typically 11am to 3.30pm or 4.30pm to 9pm), with long intervals between the acts. Be sure to rent a headset (single act/full program ¥500/1000) for blow-by-blow explanations in English.

It's tradition to eat a *bentō* (boxed meal) at the theatre during the intermission. Purchase one (around ¥1000) inside the theatre, at stalls in the subway station or in the food hall of nearby Mitsukoshi (p77).

If four-plus hours sounds too long, 90 sitting and 60 standing tickets are sold on the day for each single act. You'll be at the back of the auditorium, but the views are still good. Some acts tend to be more popular than others, so ask ahead as to which to catch, and arrive at least 1½ hours before the start of the performance. Learn more about kabuki on p217.

DID YOU KNOW?

➡ Only men appear in kabuki; actors who specialise in portraying women are called *onnagata*.

PRACTICALITIES

➡ 歌舞伎座
➡ 📞03-3545-6800
➡ www.kabukiweb.net
➡ 4-12-15 Ginza, Chūō-ku
➡ tickets ¥4000-20,000, single-act tickets ¥800-2000
➡ 🚊Hibiya line to Higashi-Ginza, exit 3

(bookings are essential for dinner) that serves delicious *bentō* box meals, vegan-cheese fondue, smoothies and fluffy US-style pancakes.

Ginza is the main branch but check its website for details of other ones in Shinjuku and Ikebukuro.

★KYŪBEY
SUSHI ¥¥¥

(久兵衛; ☎03-3571-6523; www.kyubey.jp; 8-7-6 Ginza, Chūo-ku; lunch/dinner courses from ¥8250/11,000; ⏰11.30am-2pm & 5-10pm Mon-Sat; 🌐📵; Ⓢ Ginza line to Shimbashi, exit 3) Kyūbey, running since 1935 is one of Tokyo's prestige sushi restaurants, where each piece of *nigiri-zushi* (hand-pressed sushi) is made and delivered one at a time. But there's no snobbery here: staff speak English (and deliver no side eyes) and the prices are very reasonable for Ginza. Reservations must be made through your accommodation. There's a 10% service charge.

★TEMPURA KONDŌ
TEMPURA ¥¥¥

(てんぷら近藤; ☎03-5568-0923; 9th fl, Sakaguchi Bldg, 5-5-13 Ginza, Chūo-ku; lunch/dinner course from ¥8800/14,300; ⏰noon-3pm & 5-10pm Mon-Sat; 🌐📵; Ⓢ Ginza line to Ginza, exit B5) Nobody in Tokyo does tempura vegetables like chef Kondō Fumio. The carrots are julienned to a fine floss; the corn is pert and juicy; and the sweet potato is comfort food at its finest. Courses include seafood, too. Lunch servce is at noon or 1.30pm; last dinner booking is at 8pm. Reserve through your accommodation.

APOLLO
GREEK ¥¥¥

(☎03-6264-5220; www.theapollo.jp; 11th fl, Tōkyū Plaza Ginza, 5-2-1 Ginza, Chūo-ku; small dishes ¥660-2860, mains ¥2090-6820; ⏰11am-11pm; 🌐📵; Ⓢ Ginza line to Ginza, exits C2 & C3) We know you didn't come to Tokyo to eat Greek food but hear us out: this Sydney import nails dishes like grilled octopus and fennel salad, taramasalata, and lamb shoulder with lemon and Greek yoghurt. The wine list is deep, the original cocktails excellent and, oh, you also get views over Ginza from the floor-to-ceiling windows.

BIRD LAND
YAKITORI ¥¥¥

(バードランド; ☎03-5250-1081; www.ginza-birdland.sakura.ne.jp; 4-2-15 Ginza, Chūo-ku; course ¥6800-9240; ⏰5-9.30pm, closed Sun & Mon; 🌐📵; Ⓢ Ginza line to Ginza, exit C6) This is as suave as it gets for gourmet grilled chicken. Chefs in whites behind a U-shaped counter dispense *yakitori* (chicken, and other meats or vegetables, grilled on skewers) in all shapes, sizes, colours and organs – don't pass up the dainty serves of liver pâté or the tiny cup of chicken soup. Pair it with wine from the extensive list. Enter beneath Suit Company. Reservations recommended.

DRINKING & NIGHTLIFE

★CHA GINZA
TEAHOUSE

(茶・銀座; ☎03-3571-1211; www.uogashi-meicha.co.jp; 5-5-6 Ginza, Chūo-ku; ⏰teahouse noon-5pm Tue-Sat, shop 11am-6pm Tue-Sat; Ⓢ Ginza line to Ginza, exit B3) Take a pause for afternoon tea (¥700 to ¥1400) at this slick contemporary tea salon. The menu is seasonal, but will likely include a cup of perfectly prepared *matcha* (powdered green tea) and a small sweet or two, or a choice of *sencha* (premium green tea).

The ground-floor shop sells top-quality teas from various different growing regions in Japan.

★GINZA MUSIC BAR
COCKTAIL BAR

(☎03-3572-3666; www.ginzamusicbar.com; 4F Brownplace, 7-8-13 Ginza, Chūo-ku; cover charge after midnight ¥1000; ⏰6pm-4am Mon-Sat; Ⓢ Ginza line to Shimbashi, exits 1 & 3) A superb sound system showcases the 3000-plus vinyl collection that ranges from the likes of cool classic jazz to contemporary electronica. There are deep-blue walls and comfy seats in which to enjoy inventive cocktails (starting from ¥1400), such as the *matcha* and wasabi martini.

GINZA LION
BEER HALL

(銀座ライオン; ☎050-5269-7095; https://ginzalion.net; 7-9-20 Ginza, Chūo-ku; ⏰11.30am-11pm, until 10.30pm Sun; Ⓢ Ginza line to Ginza, exit A2) So what if Sapporo's beers are not among the best you can quaff in Tokyo? Dating to 1934, the gorgeous art deco design at Japan's oldest beer hall – including glass mosaic murals – is to die for. The oompah-pah atmosphere, with waiters ferrying frothy mugs and plates of Bavarian-style sausages to the tables, is also priceless.

TURRET COFFEE
CAFE

(2-12-6 Tsukiji, Chūo-ku; ⏰7am-6pm Mon-Sat, from noon Sun; 🌐📵; Ⓢ Hibiya line to Tsukiji, exit 2) Turret Coffee (right around the corner from Starbucks) makes some of Tokyo's best espresso drinks: the signature two-shot Turret latte (¥580) hits just the right balance and is photogenic to boot.

The shop is named for the three-wheeled delivery trucks that beetle around Tokyo's fish market – there's one on the premises. This place is ideal for an early-morning espresso en route to or from Tsukiji Market (p73).

JUGETSUDO TEAHOUSE

(寿月堂; ☎03-6278-7626; www.maruyamanori.com; 5th fl, Kabuki-za Tower, 4-12-15 Ginza, Chūō-ku; ⌚10am-7pm; 📋; [S]Hibiya line to Higashi-Ginza, exit 3) This venerable tea seller's main branch is closer to Tsukiji, but this classy outlet in the Kabuki-za Tower has a Kengo Kuma–designed cafe where you can sample the various Japanese green teas, including *matcha;* sets, which include *wagashi* (Japanese sweets), cost ¥1100 to ¥2200. Enter on Shōwa-dōri.

Book for its tea-tasting experience (¥3200; 11am to noon), which covers four different types of tea.

CAFE DE L'AMBRE CAFE

(カフェ・ド・ランブル; ☎03-3571-1551; www.cafedelambre.com; 8-10-15 Ginza, Chūō-ku; ⌚noon-10pm Mon-Sat, to 7pm Sun; 📋; 🚉Ginza line to Ginza, exit A4) The sign over the door here reads 'Coffee Only' but, oh, what a selection.

Local legend Sekiguchi Ichirō started the business in 1948, sourcing aged beans from all over the world and roasting them in-house long before it was trendy (and he did so every day until he passed away at the age of 103 in 2018).

A whole generation of cafe owners have trained here.

OLD IMPERIAL BAR BAR

(Mezzanine, Main Bldg, Imperial Hotel, 1-1-1 Uchisaiwai-chō, Chiyoda-ku; ⌚11.30am-midnight; 📋; [S]Hibiya line to Hibiya, exit A13) This is one of the few parts of the Imperial Hotel to feature some of the designs and materials used in the original 1923 Frank Lloyd Wright building (note the architectural drawing behind the cash desk). The vintage early 20th-century interior suits the menu of classic cocktails (around ¥1500, plust 10% service charge).

There's no seating charge, but 10% service is added to the bill.

BONGEN COFFEE COFFEE

(☎03-6264-3988; www.ginza-bongen.jp; 2-16-3 Ginza, Chūō-ku; ⌚10am-8pm; 📶📋; [S]Asakusa or Hibiya line to Higashi-Ginza, exit A7) Down a side street of Higashi-Ginza is this tiny third-wave coffee shop serving single-estate brews with side orders of *onigiri* (Japanese rice balls) or sandwiches of raisins and cream.

An elegant traditional Japanese design pervades with warm woods and a spotlit bonsai tree behind the espresso machine.

KARAT KARAOKE

(☎03-5537-3111; http://bankaratokyo.jp; 7-5-10 Ginza, Chūō-ku; per hr male/female from ¥1000/1500; ⌚8pm-4am; [S]Ginza line to Shinbashi, exits 1 & 3) If singing to a karaoke machine's tinny soundtrack isn't your cup of tea, how about having a live band strum along to your song of choice? Karat offers that option (along with tablet-style gizmos to provide the lyrics to hundreds of songs in English).

Perhaps don't get too carried away – after 10pm the charges go up to ¥2000 per hour and there's a 12% service charge plus 8% tax on top of everything else.

☆ ENTERTAINMENT

KABUKIZA THEATRE

See p74.

KANZE NŌGAKUDŌ PERFORMING ARTS

(観世能楽堂; ☎03-6274-6579; www.kanze.net; Ginza Six B3, 6-10-1 Ginza, Chūō-ku; [S]Ginza line to Ginza, exit A2) This venerable group specialising in *nō* dramas relocated to the bowels of the Ginza Six shopping complex in 2017. The theatre seats 48.

If you haven't booked in advance and would like a taster, you can check on the day for ¥3000 'happy hour' tickets; one of these gets you an unreserved seat for the performance's last act.

TOKYO TAKARAZUKA THEATRE THEATRE

(宝塚劇場; ☎0570-00-5100; http://kageki.hankyu.co.jp/english/index.html; 1-1-3 Yūrakuchō, Chiyoda-ku; tickets ¥3500-12,000; [S]Hibiya line to Hibiya, exits A5 & A13) If you love camp, this is for you. The all-female Takarazuka revue, going back to 1914, stages highly stylised musicals in Japanese (English synopses are available) where a mostly female audience swoons over actors, some of whom are in drag.

It's massively popular, so shows often sell out quickly. Fear not: back of the balcony seats (¥2500) with a slightly obscured view and *tachimi* (standing tickets; ¥1500) are reserved for sale on the day of the show – but get in line early.

SHOPPING

★TAKUMI — ARTS & CRAFTS

(たくみ; ☎03-3571-2017; www.ginza-takumi.co.jp; 8-4-2 Ginza, Chūō-ku; ⏲11am-7pm Mon-Sat; [S]Ginza line to Shimbashi, exit 5) You're unlikely to find a more elegant selection of traditional folk crafts, including toys, textiles and ceramics from around Japan. Ever thoughtful, this shop also encloses information detailing the origin and background of the pieces if you make a purchase.

★ITŌYA — ARTS & CRAFTS

(伊東屋; ☎03-3561-8311; www.ito-ya.co.jp; 2-7-15 Ginza, Chūō-ku; ⏲10am-8pm, to 7pm Sun; [S]Ginza line to Ginza, exit A13) Explore the nine floors (plus several more in the nearby annex) of stationery at this famed, century-old Ginza establishment.

There are everyday items (notebooks and greeting cards) and luxuries (fountain pens and leather agendas). Also: *washi* (handmade paper), *tenugui* (hand towels, traditionally hand dyed or printed) and *furoshiki* (wrapping cloths) in gorgeous colours and patterns.

OKUNO BUILDING — ARTS & CRAFTS

(奥野ビル; 1-9-8 Ginza, Chūō-ku; [S]Yūrakuchō line to Ginza-itchōme, exit 10) This 1932 apartment block (cutting-edge for its time) is a retro time capsule, its seven floors packed with a fascinating array of some 40 tiny boutiques and gallery spaces. Climbing up and down the Escher-like staircases, or using the antique elevator, you'll come across mini-exhibitions that change week by week.

If you'd like some direction, check Wakako Shibata's gallery **Ishi** (http://artgalleryishi.com) on the 2nd floor – she speaks English and French. On the ground floor look out for **Makoto Optical** (www.makotoweb.com) selling vintage and new spectacles, and **Union Works** shoe shop and repairs.

AKOMEYA — FOOD

(アコメヤ; ☎03-6758-0271; www.akomeya.jp; 2-2-6 Ginza, Chūō-ku; ⏲11am-8pm, to 9pm Fri & Sat; [S]Yūrakuchō line to Ginza-itchōme, exit 4) Rice is at the core of Japanese cuisine and drink. This stylish store sells not only many types of the grain but also products made from it (such as sake), a vast range of quality cooking ingredients, and a choice collection of kitchen, home and bath items.

There's also a good, casual restaurant here where rice, unsurprisingly, features heavily on the menu. There's a big branch in the Shinjuku NEWoMan mall (p133).

GINZA SIX — MALL

(☎03-6891-3390; http://ginza6.tokyo; 6-10-1 Ginza, Chūō-ku; ⏲10am-10pm; [S]Ginza line to Ginza, exit A4) This high-end mall was designed by architect Taniguchi Yoshio, who also did the Gallery of Hōryū-ji Treasures. Large-scale art installations are held in the atrium and there's a garden on the roof with city views. Shopping-wise, it's mostly international brands, but Japanese craftwork and design is well represented on the 4th floor.

MITSUKOSHI — DEPARTMENT STORE

(三越; ☎03-3562-1111; http://mitsukoshi.mistore.jp/store/ginza; 4-6-16 Ginza, Chūō-ku; ⏲10.30am-8pm Mon-Sat, to 7.30pm Sun; [S]Ginza line to Ginza, exits A7 & A11) Mitsukoshi is Ginza's most famous department store, anchoring one corner of the neighbourhood's main intersection. The fashion is mostly from international brands, but the 7th-floor homewares section has gallery-like displays of works by contemporary artisans, including ceramics and lacquerware (a good deal of it affordable). It also has an excellent gourmet food hall in the basement.

There's a roof garden on the 9th floor; the duty free counter is in the basement.

DOVER STREET MARKET GINZA — FASHION & ACCESSORIES

(☎03-6228-5080; http://ginza.doverstreetmarket.com; 6-9-5 Ginza, Chūō-ku; ⏲11am-8pm; [S]Ginza line to Ginza, exit A2) A department store as envisioned by Rei Kawakubo (of Comme des Garçons), DSM has seven floors of avant-garde brands, including several Japanese labels and everything in the Comme des Garçons line-up. The eccentric art installations alone make it worth the visit.

Inexplicably, it's connected via passageways to Uniqlo Ginza, opposite it.

MORIOKA SHOTEN & CO
BOOKS

(森岡書店; ☏03-3535-5020; Suzuki Bldg, 1–28–15 Ginza, Chūō-ku; ⏰1-8pm Tue-Sun; Ⓢ Asakusa or Hibiya line to Higashi-Ginza, exit A7) This tiny bookshop showcases a single title a week, be it a novel, a cook book or an art tome, alongside an exhibition. However, the real reason for coming here is to admire the wonderful art deco architecture of the 1929 Suzuki Building, with its warm red-brick and decorative tile facade.

UNIQLO GINZA
FASHION & ACCESSORIES

(ユニクロ銀座店; ☏03-6252-5181; www.uniqlo. com; 5-7-7 Ginza, Chūō-ku; ⏰11am-9pm; Ⓢ Ginza line to Ginza, exit A2) Stop any Tokyoite on the street and odds are they're wearing at least one thing from Uniqlo, the ubiquitous retailer of indispensible basics. There are branches all over the city but this is the largest, stocking everything in the current line-up (which usually includes some collaborations with designers and artists).

If you're overwhelmed, start on the top floor, which has all the top-sellers in one place. The floor below carries limited-edition T-shirts.

🏃 SPORTS & ACTIVITIES

★ TSUKIJI SOBA ACADEMY
COOKING

(築地そばアカデミー; https://soba.specialist. co.jp; Hins Minato #004, 3-18-14 Minato, Chūō-ku; up to 3 people from ¥30,000, per additional person ¥10,000; ♿; Ⓢ Yūrakuchō line to Shintomichō, exit 7) Genial English-speaking chef Inoue Akila is a master of soba – noodles made from nutty buckwheat flour. He has taught chefs who have gone on to win Michelin stars for their versions of this classic Tokyo dish. Classes are held in a compact kitchen overlooking the Sumida-gawa.

Additional vegetarian and gluten-free menus and longer courses aimed at professionals are available for an extra fee upon request.

KOMPARU-YU
BATHHOUSE

(金春湯; ☏03-3571-5469; www002.upp.so-net. ne.jp/konparu; 8-7-5 Ginza, Chūō-ku; adult/child ¥460/80; ⏰2-10pm Mon-Sat; Ⓡ Ginza line to Shimbashi, exit 1 or 3) Join women and salarymen freshening up at this simple bathhouse without stand-up showers that's been located here since 1863. Tile art includes old-school koi (carp) and the traditional Mt Fuji motifs.

Roppongi & Around

ROPPONGI | AKASAKA | SHIBA-KŌEN

Neighbourhood Top Five

❶ Mori Art Museum (p81) Enjoying contemporary art and Tokyo's urban panorama from this gallery that occupies the top of Mori Tower, along with the observatory Tokyo City View.

❷ 21_21 Design Sight (p82) Pondering cutting-edge art, architecture and design ideas at the Tadao Ando–designed building in the park behind Tokyo Midtown.

❸ Zōjō-ji (p83) Walking through the massive entrance gate to this venerable temple and seeing Tokyo Tower in the background.

❹ National Art Center Tokyo (p82) Digging the very curvy architecture and top-notch exhibitions at this Kurokawa Kishō–designed building.

❺ Hotel New Ōtani Japanese Garden (p82) Strolling around this serene 400-year-old Japanese garden that hides within the grounds of this 1960s hotel.

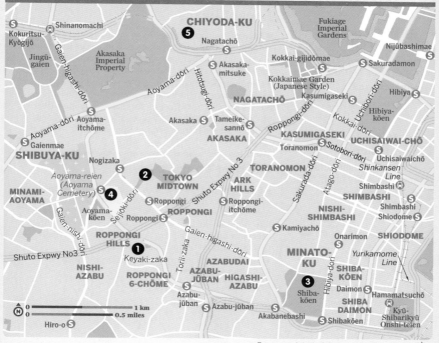

For more detail of this area see Map p270 ➡

Lonely Planet's Top Tip

Keep your ticket stub for Mori Art Museum (p81), Suntory Museum of Art (p82) or the National Art Center Tokyo (p82), and when you visit one of the other two galleries you'll be entitled to a discount on admission. At any of these venues, pick up the *Art Triangle Roppongi* walking map, which lists dozens of smaller galleries in the area.

Best Places to Eat

➡ Tofuya-Ukai (p86)

➡ Honmura-An (p83)

➡ Sougo (p83)

➡ Kikunoi (p86)

➡ Bricolage Bread & Co (p86)

For reviews, see p83.➡

Best Places to Drink

➡ Gen Yamamoto (p86)

➡ Two Dogs Taproom (p86)

➡ Brewdog (p87)

For reviews, see p86.➡

Best Places to Shop

➡ Japan Traditional Crafts Aoyama Square (p88)

➡ Souvenir From Tokyo (p88)

➡ Tolman Collection (p88)

For reviews, see p88.➡

Explore Roppongi & Around

Long one of Tokyo's prime nightlife districts, Roppongi has diversified over the past decade, adding arts, culture and high-end shopping to its menu of attractions. The successful mixed-use real-estate developments Roppongi Hills (p81) and Tokyo Midtown (p88) have transformed the area. Similar projects in neighbouring Akasaka and Toranomon are now putting the spotlight on those districts, too.

You can easily spend a day exploring the compact Roppongi Art Triangle, its points anchored by the lofty Mori Art Museum (p81) in Roppongi Hills, Suntory Museum of Art (p82) in Tokyo Midtown and the National Art Center Tokyo (p82). Strike out further, and you can visit the grand Buddhist temple Zōjō-ji (p83), in pleasant Shiba-kōen (Shiba Park); the beautiful, 400-year-old Hotel New Ōtani Japanese Garden (p82) in Akasaka; or the early-20th-century imperial palace turned State Guest House, Akasaka Palace (p83).

As night falls, Roppongi Crossing becomes a magnet for an international crowd of hedonistic party-goers and club touts; it generally isn't sophisticated, but remains a prime location for alcohol-fuelled nocturnal adventures. Head downhill towards either Nishi-Azabu or Azabu-Jūban for classier dining and drinking options.

Local Life

➡ **Events** Roppongi Hills, Tokyo Midtown and Toranomon Hills all have open public spaces that often host events (like outdoor yoga); check their respective websites. Also check out Nerd Nite Tokyo (p87).

➡ **Landmarks** Tokyo Tower, 333m tall and painted bright orange, might look like a knock-off Eiffel Tower but it's an object of affection for many Tokyoites; it's often lit up for special occasions. It's near Shiba-kōen, but you can see it from around Roppongi.

Getting There & Away

➡ **Subway** The Hibiya and Ōedo subway lines stop at Roppongi. Other useful Ōedo line stations include Azabu-jūban and Daimon (for Zōjō-ji). The Chiyoda line stops at Akasaka aGnd Nogizaka, which has direct access to the National Art Center Tokyo. This area is central and a lot of lines pass around here.

➡ **Bus** Bus 1 runs along Roppongi-dōri between Roppongi and Shibuya.

TOP EXPERIENCE

DO IT ALL AT ROPPONGI HILLS

This postmodern mall covers more than 11 hectares and is home to a contemporary art museum, a sky-high observatory, shops galore, dozens of restaurants and even a formal Japanese garden. It's imposing, upmarket and polarising – an architectural marvel, a grand vision realised or a crass shrine to conspicuous consumption? Explore this urban maze and decide for yourself.

Atop Mori Tower, **Mori Art Museum** (森美術館; Map p270; www.mori.art.museum; 52nd fl, 6-10-1 Roppongi, Minato-ku; adult/child ¥1800/600; 🕙10am-10pm Wed-Mon, to 5pm Tue, inside Sky Deck 10am-11pm), with high ceilings and broad views, hosts contemporary exhibitions that include superstars of the art world from both Japan and abroad. Unlike most museums, Mori Art Museum is open late – until 10pm daily except Tuesday.

Admission to the Mori Art Museum is shared with **Tokyo City View** (東京シティビュー; Map p270; ☎03-6406-6652; www.roppongihills.com; 6-10-1 Roppongi, Minato-ku; adult/child ¥1800/600; 🕙10am-11pm Mon-Thu & Sun, to 1am Fri & Sat), the observatory that wraps itself around the 52nd floor, 250m high. The view is particularly spectacular at night. Weather permitting, you can also pop out to the rooftop Sky Deck (additional adult/child ¥500/300; 11am to 8pm) for alfresco views.

The open-air plaza near the street entrance is home to Louise Bourgeois' giant **Maman spider sculpture** (Map p270). It has an amusing way of messing with the scale of the buildings, especially in photos. There are other sculptures, paintings and installations – including works by Miyajima Tatsuo and Cai Guo-Qiang – scattered around the complex, too.

Mohri Garden (毛利庭園, Mōri-teien; Map p270) is the mall's Edo-style strolling garden, complete with meandering paths and a central pond. When juxtaposed with the gleaming towers, the garden creates a fascinating study of luxury then and now.

DON'T MISS

- Mori Art Museum
- Tokyo City View
- *Maman* spider sculpture
- Mohri Garden
- Sakurazaka-kōen

PRACTICALITIES

- 六本木ヒルズ
- Map p270, B5
- ☎03-6406-6000
- www.roppongihills.com
- 6-chōme Roppongi, Minato-ku
- 🕙11am-11pm
- [S]Hibiya line to Roppongi, exit 1

Above: The TV Asahi building, beside Mohri Gardens

👁 SIGHTS

👁 Roppongi

ROPPONGI HILLS   LANDMARK
See p81.

21_21 DESIGN SIGHT   MUSEUM
Map p270 (21_21デザインサイト; ☎03-3475-2121; www.2121designsight.jp; Tokyo Midtown, 9-7-6 Akasaka, Minato-ku; adult/child ¥1100/free; ⊙11am-7pm Wed-Mon; ⓈŌedo line to Roppongi, exit 8) An exhibition and discussion space dedicated to all forms of design, the 21_21 Design Sight is a beacon for local art enthusiasts, whether they be designers or onlookers. The striking concrete and glass building, bursting out of the ground at sharp angles, was designed by Pritzker Prize–winning architect Tadao Ando.

NATIONAL ART CENTER TOKYO   MUSEUM
Map p270 (国立新美術館; ☎03-5777-8600; www.nact.jp; 7-22-1 Roppongi, Minato-ku; admission varies; ⊙10am-6pm Wed, Thu & Sun-Mon, to 8pm Fri & Sat; ⓈChiyoda line to Nogizaka, exit 6) Designed by Kurokawa Kishō, this architectural beauty has no permanent collection, but boasts the country's largest exhibition space for visiting shows, which have included Renoir and Modigliani. A visit here is recommended to admire the building's awesome undulating glass facade, its cafes atop giant inverted cones and the great gift shop, Souvenir from Tokyo (p88).

SUNTORY MUSEUM OF ART   MUSEUM
Map p270 (サントリー美術館; ☎03-3479-8600; www.suntory.co.jp/sma; 4th fl, Tokyo Midtown, 9-7-4 Akasaka, Minato-ku; admission varies, child free; ⊙10am-6pm Sun-Wed, to 8pm Fri & Sat; ⓈŌedo line to Roppongi, exit 8) Since its original 1961 opening, the Suntory Museum of Art has subscribed to an underlying philosophy of lifestyle art. Rotating exhibitions focus on the beauty of useful things: Japanese ceramics, lacquerware, glass, dyeing, weaving and such. Its current Tokyo Midtown (p88) digs, designed by architect Kengo Kuma, are both understated and breathtaking.

COMPLEX 665   GALLERY
Map p270 (6-5-24 Roppongi, Minato-ku; ⊙11am-7pm Tue-Sat; ⓈHibiya line to Roppongi, exit 1) Opened in 2016, this three-storey building tucked on a backstreet is the shared location of three leading commercial art galleries: Taka Ishii (www.takaishiigallery.com), ShugoArts (http://shugoarts.com) and Tomio Koyama Gallery (www.tomiokoyamagallery.com). The free shows cover a broad spectrum of Japanese contemporary works and are generally worth a look. Note that the galleries are closed in between exhibitions.

SAKURAZAKA-KŌEN   PARK
Map p270 (さくら坂公園; www.city.minato.tokyo.jp/shisetsu/koen/azabu/06.html; 6-16-46 Roppongi, Minato-ku; 🚻; ⓈHibiya line to Roppongi, exit 1) **FREE** South Korean artist Choi Jeong-Hwa designed the dazzlingly colourful robot-themed sculptures and play areas in this kids' park that's part of the Roppongi Hills complex. If you're travelling with young children they are sure to love it, and it's a pleasant splash of greenery in an otherwise fairly concrete area.

👁 Akasaka

HOTEL NEW ŌTANI JAPANESE GARDEN   GARDENS
(ホテルニューオータニ日本庭園; www.newotani.co.jp; 4-1 Kioi-chō, Chiyoda-ku; ⊙6am-10pm; ⓈGinza line to Akasaka-mitsuke, exit D) **FREE** Nonguests are welcome to visit Hotel New Ōtani's beautiful 400-year-old Japanese garden, which once belonged to a Tokugawa regent. Including vermilion arched bridges, koi (carp) ponds and a waterfall, it is one of Tokyo's most enchanting outdoor spaces. Return in the evening to see the garden illuminated with LED lights.

MUSÉE TOMO   MUSEUM
Map p270 (智美術館; ☎03-5733-5131; www.musee-tomo.or.jp; 4-1-35 Toranomon, Minato-ku; adult/student ¥1000/500; ⊙11am-6pm Tue-Sun; ⓈHibiya line to Kamiyachō, exit 4B) One of Tokyo's most elegant and tasteful museums is named after Kikuchi Tomo, whose collection of contemporary Japanese ceramics wowed them in Washington and London before finally being exhibited at home. Exhibitions change every few months but can be relied on to be atmospheric and beautiful.

TORANOMON HILLS   LANDMARK
Map p270 (http://toranomonhills.com; 1-23 Toranomon, Minato-ku; 📶; ⓈGinza line to Toranomon, exit 1) Opened in June 2014, the 52-storey, 247m Toranomon Hills mixed-

WORTH A DETOUR

STATE GUEST HOUSE, AKASAKA PALACE

Outside, **State Guest House, Akasaka Palace** (迎賓館, 赤坂離宮; ☎03-3478-1111; www.geihinkan.go.jp/en/akasaka; 2-1-1, Moto-Akasaka, Minato-ku; front & main garden ¥300, palace adult/child/student ¥1500/free/500; ⏲10am-5pm according to opening schedule; [R]JR lines to Yotsuya) is a dead ringer for London's Buckingham Palace. Inside, the tour route passes through four grandly decorated rooms – the most impressive being the Kacho-no-Ma (Room of Flowers and Birds), with Japanese ash panels inset with cloisonné panels – plus the entrance hall and main staircase.

Japan's only neo-baroque European-style palace was designed by Katayama Tōkuma, a pupil of British architect Josiah Conder, and completed in 1909. It serves as the State Guest House, providing accommodation and a diplomatic meeting space for visiting heads of state and other VIPs.

Check online for the opening schedule and somewhat complex admission details. If you haven't reserved an entry ticket online (which you will need to do around two months in advance), head to the front gate to get one of the timed entry tickets, which are made available from 8am. It's very popular with locals so you may have to wait anything up to an hour to get in when your time slot comes up.

Online reservation is essential for 10 daily guided tours (lasting 30 minutes) around Yushin-Tei, the Japanese-style annex building in a separate part of the grounds; the 3pm tour (the last of the day) is in English. The cost of this tour plus entry to the main palace for an adult is ¥2000.

use complex is crowned by the sleek hotel, **Andaz** (Map p270; ☎03-6830-1234; https://tokyo.andaz.hyatt.com; 1-23-4 Toranomon; r from ¥64,000; 🚭❄@📶🏊), with panoramic views from its bars and restaurants; there are also pleasant places to eat and drink at lower levels.

In the small public garden, you can see Jaume Plensa's *Roots*, which is a large figure incorporating the characters of eight languages.

◉ Shiba-kōen

ZŌJŌ-JI BUDDHIST TEMPLE

Map p270 (増上寺; ☎03-3432-1431; www.zojoji.or.jp/en/index.html; 4-7-35 Shiba-kōen, Minato-ku; ⏲dawn-dusk; [S]Ōedo line to Daimon, exit A3) [FREE] One of the most important temples of the Jōdō (Pure Land) sect of Buddhism, Zōjō-ji dates from 1393 and was the funerary temple of the Tokugawa regime. It's an impressive sight, particularly the main gate, **Sangedatsumon** (三解脱門; Map p270), constructed in 1605, with its three sections designed to symbolise the three stages one must pass through to achieve nirvana. The Daibonsho (Big Bell; 1673) is a 15-tonne whopper considered one of the great three bells of the Edo period.

🍴 EATING

Both the Roppongi Hills (p81) and Tokyo Midtown (p88) complexes have many affordable options to suit all tastes.

🍴 Roppongi & Akasaka

★**HONMURA-AN** SOBA ¥

Map p270 (本むら庵; ☎03-5772-6657; www.honmuraantokyo.com; 7-14-18 Roppongi, Minato-ku; noodles from ¥900, set meals lunch/dinner ¥1600/7400; ⏲noon-2.30pm & 5.30-10pm Tue-Sun, closed 1st & 3rd Tue of month; 🚭📶[menu]; [S]Hibiya line to Roppongi, exit 4) This fabled soba shop, once located in Manhattan, now serves its handmade buckwheat noodles at this rustically contemporary noodle shop on a Roppongi side street. The noodles' delicate flavour is best appreciated when served on a bamboo mat, with tempura or with dainty slices of *kamo* (duck).

SOUGO JAPANESE ¥

Map p270 (宗胡; ☎03-5414-1133; www.sougo.tokyo; 3rd fl, Roppongi Green Bldg, 6-1-8 Roppongi, Minato-ku; set meals lunch/dinner from ¥1500/6500; ⏲11.30am-3pm & 6-11pm Mon-Sat; 🚭🥕[menu]; [S]Hibiya line to Roppongi, exit 3) Sit at the long counter beside the open kitchen or in booths and watch the expert chefs

1. National Art Center Tokyo (p82)

An architectural beauty by Kurokawa Kishō, with the country's largest temporary exhibition space.

2. Zōjō-ji (p83)

A very important temple in the Jōdō (Pure Land) sect of Buddhism, with Tokyo Tower in the background.

3. 21_21 Design Sight (p82)

A beacon for local art enthusiasts, designed by Tadao Ando.

prepare delicious and beautifully presented *shōjin-ryōri* (mainly vegetarian cuisine as served at Buddhist temples – note some dishes use *dashi* stock, which contains fish). Lunch is a bargain. Reserve at least one day in advance if you want a vegan meal (lunch/dinner ¥7000/10,000) prepared.

FALAFEL BROTHERS VEGAN ¥

Map p270 (☎03-6459-2844; www.falafelbrothers.jp; 5-1-10 Roppongi, Minato-ku; half/full sandwich ¥500/900; 🕐11am-10pm Mon-Sat; ✍; [S]Hibiya line to Roppongi, exit 3) Mainly for takeaways, this cosy joint dedicated to crispy chickpea balls offers a couple of stools inside and out at which to get your chops around its pita pocket sandwiches packed with vegan goodness. There are salad bowls and rice plates too, as well as variations such as falafel styled as hot dogs and burgers.

BRICOLAGE BREAD & CO CAFE ¥¥

Map p270 (☎03-6804-3350; www.bricolagebread.com; 6-15-1 Roppongi, Minato-ku; mains ¥900-1600; 🕐9am-7.30pm Tue-Sun; 📖; [S]Hibiya line to Roppongi, exit 1) A collaboration between coffee shop Fuglen, Michelin-starred restaurant L'effervescence and Osaka-based bakery Le Sucré Coeur, this appealing spot is decorated like a chic country farmhouse, with an enormous flower display on its central table. Enjoy single-origin Aeropress coffee along with sweet and savoury *tartines* (open-faced sandwiches) on slices of delicious sourdough bread. The perfect spot for breakfast or lunch.

JŌMON IZAKAYA ¥¥

Map p270 (ジョウモン; ☎03-3405-2585; www.teyandei.com; 5-9-17 Roppongi, Minato-ku; skewers ¥250-500, dishes from ¥580; 🕐5.30-11.45pm Sun-Thu, until 5am Fri & Sat; ✍📖; [S]Hibiya line to Roppongi, exit 3) This cosy kitchen has bar seating, rows of ornate *shōchū* (liquor) jugs lining the wall and hundreds of freshly prepared skewers splayed in front of the patrons – don't miss the heavenly beef stick. Jōmon is almost directly across from the Family Mart – look for the name in Japanese on the door. Cover charge ¥300 per person.

KIKUNOI KAISEKI ¥¥¥

Map p270 (菊乃井; ☎03-3568-6055; www.kikunoi.jp; 6-13-8 Akasaka, Minato-ku; lunch/dinner course from ¥11,900/16,000; 🕐noon-12.30pm Tue-Sat, 5-7.30pm Mon-Sat; [S]Chiyoda line to Akasaka, exit 7) Exquisitely prepared seasonal dishes are as beautiful as they are delicious at this Tokyo outpost of one of Kyoto's most acclaimed *kaiseki* restaurants. Kikunoi's third-generation chef, Murata Yoshihiro, has written a book translated into English on *kaiseki* that the staff helpfully use to explain the dishes you are served, if you don't speak Japanese.

Reservations are necessary. There are two seatings at lunch (noon and 12.30pm) and last sitting in the evening is 7.30pm.

🍴 Shiba-kōen

★TOFUYA-UKAI KAISEKI ¥¥¥

Map p270 (とうふ屋うかい; ☎03-3436-1028; www.ukai.co.jp/english/shiba; 4-4-13 Shiba-kōen, Minato-ku; set meals lunch/dinner from ¥5940/10,800; 🕐11.45am-3pm & 5-7.30pm Mon-Fri, 11am-7.30pm Sat & Sun; 🚭✍📖; [S]Ōedo line to Akabanebashi, exit 8) One of Tokyo's most gracious restaurants is located in a former sake brewery (moved from northern Japan), with an exquisite traditional garden in the shadow of Tokyo Tower. Seasonal preparations of tofu and accompanying dishes are served in the refined *kaiseki* style. Make reservations well in advance. Vegetarians should advise staff when they book, and last orders for weekday lunch is 3pm, for dinner 7.30pm.

🍷 DRINKING & NIGHTLIFE

★GEN YAMAMOTO COCKTAIL BAR

Map p270 (ゲンヤマモト; ☎03-6434-0652; www.genyamamoto.jp; 1-6-4 Azabu-Jūban, Minato-ku; cover charge ¥1000, 4-/6-cocktail menu ¥4700/6700; 🕐3-11pm Tue-Sun; 📖; [S]Namboku line to Azabu-jūban, exit 7) The delicious fruit-based drinks served here use local seasonal ingredients. Yamamoto's tasting menus are design to be savoured, not to get you sozzled (servings are small), and the bar's ambience – eight seats around a bar made from 500-year-old Japanese oak – is reminiscent of a traditional teahouse. We highly recommend the six-cocktail menu.

★TWO DOGS TAPROOM CRAFT BEER

Map p270 (☎03-5413-0333; www.twodogs-tokyo.com; 3-15-24 Roppongi, Minato-ku; 🕐11.30am-2.30pm Mon-Fri, 5-11pm Sun & Mon, until midnight Tue & Wed, until 2am Thu-Sat; [S]Hibiya line to Roppongi, exit 3) There are 24 taps devoted to Japanese and international craft beers, including its own Roppongi Pale Ale, at this convivial pub just off the main Roppongi drag. Work your way through a few jars to wash down the tasty and decent-sized pizzas.

ELE TOKYO CLUB

Map p270 (☎03-5572-7535; www.eletokyo.com; Fukao Bldg, 1-4-5 Azabu-Jūban, Minato-ku; women free, men incl 1 drink Thu ¥2000, Fri & Sat ¥3000; ⏲10pm-5am Thu-Sat; [S]Ōedo line to Azabu-jūban, exit 7) Dress to impress to gain entry to this bling-tastic, two-level dance club that's one of the classier late-night joints around Roppongi. It's always free entry for women. You must be over 20 years old and have photo ID.

BREWDOG CRAFT BEER

Map p270 (☎03-6447-4160; http://brewdogbar.jp; 5-3-2 Roppongi, Minato-ku; ⏲5pm-midnight Mon-Fri, from 3pm Sat & Sun; 📶📋; [S]Hibiya line to Roppongi, exit 3) This Scottish craft brewery's Tokyo outpost is nestled off the main drag. Apart from its own brews, there's a great selection of other beers, including Japanese varieties on tap, mostly all served in small, regular or large (a full pint) portions. Tasty food plus computer and board games to while away the evening round out a class operation.

ŌIZUMI KŌJŌ CAFE

Map p270 (大泉工場; ☎03-6427-4749; http://oks-nishiazabu.com; 2 Chome-13-13 Nishi-Azabu, Minato-ku; kombucha ¥600; ⏲8am-10pm; [S]Hibiya line to Roppongi, exit 3) A feel-good alternative to Roppongi's bars, Ōizumi Kōjō specialises in kombucha, a fermented type of organic tea that has a natural fizz and many health benefits. The drink comes in a variety of flavours – all tasting pretty good and served in stylish wine glasses.

PASELA RESORTS KARAOKE

Map p270 (パセラリゾーツ; ☎0120-911-086; www.pasela.co.jp/shop/roppongi/karaoke; 5-16-3 Roppongi, Minato-ku; per hr per person Sun-Thu ¥1100, Fri & Sat ¥1300; ⏲noon-6am Sun-Thu, to 7am Fri & Sat; 📋; [S]Hibiya line to Roppongi, exit 3) With decor that is a cut above the other yodelling parlours, Pasela offers six floors of karaoke rooms (including swanky VIP suites), an extensive selection of Western songs, and wine, champagne and sweets on the menu. The two-hour *nomi-hōdai* (all-you-can-drink) package (¥3700 per person, ¥4200 on Friday; room rental included) is a good deal.

LOCAL KNOWLEDGE

NERD NITE TOKYO

Held monthly (usually on a Friday night) at the co-working space Nagatachō GRID, **Nerd Nite Tokyo** (☎03-5759-0300; www.facebook.com/nerdnitetokyo; Nagatachō GRID, 2-5-3 Hirakawachō, Chiyoda-ku; ¥1000; [S]Nanboku line to Nagatachō , exit 5) is a fun event billed as 'the Discovery Channel with beer'. Listen to up to three speakers present on anything from the process of animation to the latest on artificial intelligence.

☆ ENTERTAINMENT

NATIONAL THEATRE THEATRE

(国立劇場, Kokuritsu Gekijō; ☎03-3265-7411, box office 03-3230-3000; www.ntj.jac.go.jp; 4-1 Hayabusa-chō, Chiyoda-ku; tickets ¥1700-7000; [S]Hanzōmon line to Hanzōmon, exit 1) This is the capital's premier venue for traditional performing arts with 1600-seat and 590-seat auditoriums. Performances include kabuki (a form of stylised Japanese theatre), *gagaku* (music of the imperial court) and *bunraku* (classic puppet theatre). Earphones with English translation are available for hire (¥700, plus ¥1000 deposit). Check the website for performance schedules.

TOHO CINEMAS ROPPONGI HILLS CINEMA

Map p270 (TOHO; シネマズ 六本木ヒルズ; ☎10am-9pm 050-6868-5024; https://tohotheater.jp; Keyakizaka Complex, Roppongi Hills, 6-chōme Roppongi, Minato-ku; adult/student/senior/child ¥1800/1500/1100/1000; [S]Hibiya line to Roppongi, exit 1C) Besides being one of Tokyo's nicest and biggest cinemas (it has nine screens, some with 3D and 4D capability), Toho's Roppongi Hills theatre screens some popular Japanese new releases with English subtitles. The 3D and 4D screenings cost extra.

SUNTORY HALL CLASSICAL MUSIC

Map p270 (サントリーホール; ☎03-3505-1001, ticket centre 0570-55-0017; www.suntory.com/culture-sports/suntoryhall; Ark Hills, 1-13-1 Akasaka, Minato-ku; [S]Ginza line to Tameike-sannō, exit 13) This is one of Tokyo's best venues for classical concerts, with a busy schedule of accomplished musicians. Its 2000-seat main hall has one of the largest organs in the world, with seating arranged in the 'vineyard' style where all seats face the stage.

SHOPPING

★JAPAN TRADITIONAL CRAFTS AOYAMA SQUARE ARTS & CRAFTS

Map p270 (伝統工芸 青山スクエア; ☎03-5785-1301; www.kougeihin.jp; 8-1-22 Akasaka, Minato-ku; ⏲11am-7pm; [S]Ginza line to Aoyama-itchōme, exit 4) Supported by the Japanese Ministry of Economy, Trade and Industry, this is as much a showroom as a shop, exhibiting a broad range of traditional crafts from around Japan, including lacquerwork boxes, woodwork, cut glass, textiles and pottery. There are some exquisite heirloom pieces here, but also beautiful items at reasonable prices. Summon videos of the artisans at work from the touch screens in the front of the shop.

TORAYA FOOD & DRINKS

Map p270 (とらや; ☎03-3408-4121; https://global.toraya-group.co.jp; 4-9-22 Akasaka, Minato-ku; ⏲8.30am-7pm Mon-Fri, 9.30am-6pm Sat & Sun, tearoom 11am-6.30pm, to 5.30pm Sat & Sun) Founded in the 16th century in Kyoto, Toraya's traditional confectionary has long been patronised by the Imperial Court, giving it a cachet that other sweet-makers can only dream about. This is its impressive flagship store, reopened in 2018. It specialises in *yōkan,* a jelly made from red bean paste, but also sells other seasonal sweets, all beautifully packaged.

SOUVENIR FROM TOKYO GIFTS & SOUVENIRS

Map p270 (スーベニアフロムトーキョー; ☎03-6812 9933; www.souvenirfromtokyo.jp; basement, National Art Center Tokyo, 7-22-2 Roppongi, Minato-ku; ⏲10am-6pm Sat-Mon, Wed & Thu, to 8pm Fri; [S]Chiyoda line to Nogizaka, exit 6) There's always an expertly curated, and ever-changing, selection of home-grown design bits and bobs that make for unique souvenirs at this shop.

TOLMAN COLLECTION ARTS & CRAFTS

Map p270 (トールマンコレクション; ☎03-3434-1300; www.tolmantokyo.com; 2-2-18 Shiba-Daimon, Minato-ku; ⏲11am-7pm Wed-Sun; [S]Ōedo line to Daimon, exit A3) Expat and former US diplomat Norman Tolman has been collecting modern and contemporary Japanese print art for 50 years and has authored many books on the subject. His gallery, in a traditional wooden building, represents nearly 50 leading Japanese artists of printing, lithography, etching, woodblock and more. Prints start at around ¥10,000 and rise steeply from there; international shipping available.

TOKYO MIDTOWN MALL

Map p270 (東京ミッドタウン; www.tokyo-midtown.com; 9-7 Akasaka, Minato-ku; ⏲11am-9pm; [S]Ōedo line to Roppongi, exit 8) This sleek complex, where escalators ascend alongside waterfalls of rock and glass, brims with sophisticated shops. Most notable is the selection of homewares and lifestyle boutiques, including The Cover Nippon and Wise-Wise, which carry works by Japanese designers and artisans, on the 3rd floor of the Galleria section.

SPORTS & ACTIVITIES

TOKYO COOK COOKING

Map p270 (☎03-5414-2727; www.tokyo-cook.com; 3rd fl, Roppongi Green Bldg, 6-1-8 Roppongi, Minato-ku; classes from ¥8640; [S]Hibiya line to Roppongi, exit 3) Among the several types of cooking classes in English on offer here are ones focusing on making vegetarian dishes, *shōjin-ryōri* and soba noodles. Courses are led by professional chefs and are held inside the restaurant Sougo (p83).

SŌGETSU KAIKAN ARTS & CRAFTS

Map p270 (草月会館; ☎03-3408-1209; www.sogetsu.or.jp/e; 7-2-21 Akasaka, Minato-ku; Japanese/English lessons from ¥3240/4100; ⏲bldg hours 9.30am-5.30pm Mon-Fri; [S]Ginza line to Aoyama-itchōme, exit 4) Sōgetsu is one of Japan's leading schools of avant-garde ikebana – Japan's centuries-old art of flower arranging. Classes are held in English on Mondays from 10am to noon; book via the web before noon of the preceding Thursday. The class fee includes materials. Exhibitions are sometimes held in the lobby.

Ebisu, Meguro & Around

EBISU | MEGURO | DAIKANYAMA & NAKA-MEGURO

Neighbourhood Top Five

❶ **TOP Museum** (p91) Seeing an exhibition (or three!) at Tokyo's leading photography museum, where the collection includes both icons of Japanese photography and up-and-comers.

❷ **Daikanyama & Naka-Meguro** (p92) Shopping (or window-shopping) your way through these fashionable,

adjacent neighbourhoods full of one-of-a-kind shops.

❸ **Ebisu Bar Scene** Squeezing into a space at one of Ebisu's trendy (and typically small) bars, like sake specialist Gem by Moto (p94).

❹ **Beer Museum Yebisu** (p91) Learning about the history of beer in Japan

at the site of one of the country's first breweries (followed by a tasting flight, naturally).

❺ **Tokyo Metropolitan Teien Art Museum** (p91) Admiring one of Tokyo's few art deco buildings (and its decorative arts exhibitions).

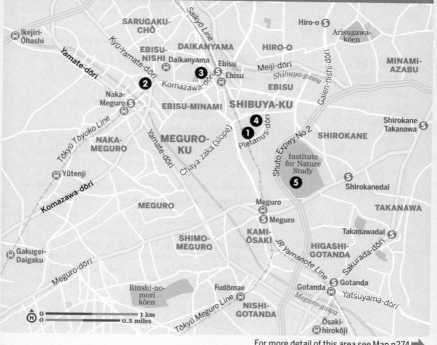

For more detail of this area see Map p274 ➡

Lonely Planet's Top Tip

Daikanyama and Naka-Meguro have a late start; don't expect cafes or boutiques to open before 11am (and sometimes not until noon). The exception is Daikanyama T-Site (p92), which opens from 7am.

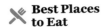 Best Places to Eat

➡ Tonki (p94)

➡ Yakiniku Champion (p93)

➡ Ippo (p94)

➡ Delifucious (p94)

For reviews, see p91.➡

Best Places to Drink

➡ Gem by Moto (p94)

➡ Another 8 (p95)

➡ Bar Trench (p95)

➡ Onibus Coffee (p95)

For reviews, see p94.➡

Best Places to Shop

➡ Okura (p92)

➡ Kapital (p95)

➡ Daikanyama T-Site (p92)

➡ Minä Perhonen (p92)

For reviews, see p95.➡

EBISU, MEGURO & AROUND

Explore Ebisu, Meguro & Around

Bookmark this area for a day when you're looking to take it easy. Though both are nodes on the Yamanote line, Ebisu and Meguro aren't frenetic hubs. The sights here are smaller and generally uncrowded.

Ebisu has the largest concentration of sights, including the Beer Museum Yebisu (p91) and the city's photography museum, TOP (p91). Both are part of Yebisu Garden Place (p91), the culture complex located where the original Yebisu brewery once stood. They also stay open relatively late, so you could leave them for later. Meguro, one train stop south of Ebisu, sees few tourists, despite having two excellent attractions: the Institute for Nature Study (p91), a rare pocket of raw Tokyo, and the Tokyo Metropolitan Teien Art Museum (p91) next to it. From here, you could take a detour to Sengaku-ji (p94), a historic temple with deep cultural significance.

Beyond Ebisu and Meguro, the adjacent residential enclaves Daikanyama and Naka-Meguro (p92) are favourite haunts of fashion, art and media types, whose tastes are reflected in the shops and cafes here. There's a leafy canal in Naka-Meguro that's perfect for an afternoon stroll. Both Daikanyama and Naka-Meguro are within walking distance of Ebisu.

Of all these neighbourhoods, Ebisu has the most dynamic eating and drinking scene. In fact, this is the one occasion where you may have to contend with crowds: popular restaurants and bars are packed most nights of the week.

Local Life

➡ **Hang-outs** Locals love retro arcade Ebisu-yokochō (p91); it's packed every night of the week.

➡ **Events** Yebisu Garden Place (p91), with its wide open plaza, hosts weekend events year-round.

➡ **Urban Oasis** Few locals know about the raw pocket of nature that is the Institute for Nature Study (p91); the Tokyo Metropolitan Teien Art Museum (p91) has a fantastic lawn perfect for post-exhibit lazing.

Getting There & Away

➡ **Train** The JR Yamanote line stops at Ebisu and Meguro Stations. The Tōkyū Tōyoko line runs from Shibuya to Daikanyama and Naka-Meguro; some Fukutoshin subway trains continue on the Tōyoko line.

➡ **Subway** The Hibiya line stops at Ebisu and Naka-Meguro. The Namboku and Mita lines stop at Meguro.

👁 SIGHTS

👁 Ebisu

TOP MUSEUM   MUSEUM

Map p274 (東京都写真美術館, Tokyo Photographic Arts Museum; 📞03-3280-0099; www.topmuseum.jp; 1-13-3 Mita, Meguro-ku; ¥500-1000; ⏱10am-6pm Tue, Wed, Sat & Sun, to 8pm Thu & Fri; 🚉JR Yamanote line to Ebisu, east exit) Tokyo's principal photography museum usually holds three different exhibitions at once, drawing on both its extensive collection of Japanese artists and images on loan. Shows may include the history of photography, retrospectives of major artists or surveys of up-and-coming ones.

The museum is at the far end of Yebisu Garden Place, on the right side of the complex if you're coming from Ebisu Station. There's a branch of the excellent art bookshop Nadiff here, too.

BEER MUSEUM YEBISU   MUSEUM

Map p274 (エビスビール記念館; 📞03-5423-7255; www.sapporoholdings.jp/english/guide/yebisu; 4-20-1 Ebisu, Shibuya-ku; ⏱11am-7pm Tue-Sun; 🚉JR Yamanote line to Ebisu, east exit) **FREE** Photos, vintage bottles and posters document the rise of the Yebisu brewery, and beer in general, in Japan at this small museum located where the actual Yebisu brewery stood from the late 19th century until 1988.

At the 'tasting salon' you can sample four kinds of Yebisu beer (¥400 each or three smaller glasses for ¥800). It's behind the Mitsukoshi department store at Yebisu Garden Place.

YEBISU GARDEN PLACE   PLAZA

Map p274 (恵比寿ガーデンプレイス; www.gardenplace.jp; 4-20 Ebisu, Shibuya-ku; 🚉JR Yamanote line to Ebisu, east exit) This shopping and cultural centre was built on the site of the original Yebisu Beer Brewery (1889) that gave the neighbourhood its name. Unlike most modern Tokyo malls, this one is short on shops and big on public space: the large central plaza regularly hosts events, including a farmers market on Sundays (11am to 5pm).

👁 Meguro

TOKYO METROPOLITAN TEIEN ART MUSEUM   MUSEUM

Map p274 (東京都庭園美術館; www.teien-art-museum.ne.jp; 5-21-9 Shirokanedai, Minato-ku; adult/child ¥1200/960; ⏱10am-6pm, closed 2nd & 4th Wed each month; 🚉JR Yamanote line to Meguro, east exit) Although the Teien museum often hosts excellent exhibitions – usually of decorative arts – its chief appeal lies in the building itself: it's an art deco structure, a former princely estate built in 1933, designed by French architect Henri Rapin, with much of the original interior intact. Tip: budget time to lounge around on the manicured lawn. A recent renovation saw the addition of a modern annex designed by artist Sugimoto Hiroshi. Note that the museum is closed between exhibitions.

INSTITUTE FOR NATURE STUDY   PARK

Map p274 (自然教育園, Shizen Kyōiku-en; 📞03-3441-7176; www.ins.kahaku.go.jp; 5-21-5 Shirokanedai, Meguro-ku; adult/child ¥310/free; ⏱9am-4.30pm Tue-Sun Sep-Apr, to 5pm Tue-Sun May-Aug, last entry 4pm; 🚉JR Yamanote line to Meguro, east exit) What would Tokyo look like were it left to its own natural devices? Since 1949 this park, affiliated with the Tokyo National Museum, has let the local flora go wild. There are wonderful walks through its groves, around ponds and on boardwalks over marshes. No more than 300 people are allowed in at a time, which makes for an even more peaceful setting.

🍴 EATING

🍴 Ebisu

EBISU-YOKOCHŌ   STREET FOOD ¥

Map p274 (恵比寿横町; www.ebisu-yokocho.com; 1-7-4 Ebisu, Shibuya-ku; dishes ¥500-1500; ⏱5pm-late; 🚉JR Yamanote line to Ebisu, east exit) Locals love this retro arcade chock-a-block with food stalls dishing up everything from humble *yaki-soba* (fried buckwheat noodles) to decadent *hotate-yaki* (grilled scallops). Seating is on stools; some of the tables are made from repurposed beer crates. It's

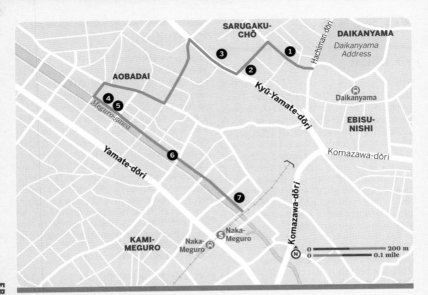

Local Life
Shopping in Daikanyama & Naka-Meguro

Many Japanese fashion brands – high-fashion and street; established and not (yet) – have boutiques in the neighbouring 'hoods of Daikanyama and Naka-Meguro. Both are great for scouting unique pieces and outside-the-mainstream looks. Though just one and two stops (respectively) removed from Shibuya, the pace here is noticeably unhurried, encouraged by outdoor cafes and leafy sidewalks.

❶ Okura

Okura (オクラ; Map p274; ☏03-3461-8511; www.hrm.co.jp; 20-11 Sarugaku-chō, Shibuya-ku; ⏰11.30am-8pm Mon-Fri, 11am-8.30pm Sat & Sun; 🚊Tōkyū Tōyoko line to Daikanyama) may seem out of place in trendy Daikanyama (the shop looks like a farmhouse), but it is actually a neighbourhood landmark. It's full of artsy original clothing items, almost all of which are made from natural textiles and dyed a deep indigo blue.

❷ Minä Perhonen

Minä Perhonen (Map p274; ☏03-6826-3770; www.mina-perhonen.jp; Daikanyama Hillside Terrace, 18-12 Sarugaku-chō, Shibuya-ku; ⏰11am-8pm; 🚊Tōkyū Tōyoko line to Daikanyama), from designer Minagawa Akira, is one of Japan's most successful womenswear labels, known for its instantly classic prints in soft, flattering colours; luxurious fabrics; and loose silhouettes that are both sufficiently sophisticated and easy to wear.

❸ Daikanyama T-Site

Locals love **Daikanyama T-Site** (代官山 T-SITE; Map p274; ☏03-3770-2525; http://real.tsite.jp/daikanyama/; 17-5 Sarugaku-chō, Shibuya-ku; ⏰7am-2am; 🚊Tōkyū Tōyoko line to Daikanyama). This stylish shrine to the printed word has fantastic books on travel, art, design and food (some in English). You can even sit at the in-house Starbucks and read all afternoon – if you can get a seat.

❹ Cow Books

Cow Books (Map p274; www.cowbooks.jp/english.html; 1-14-11 Aobadai, Meguro-ku; ⏰1-9pm Tue-Sun; 🚇Hibiya line to Naka-Meguro, main exit) is a Naka-Meguro institution, a secondhand bookstore specialising in counterculture works and small print runs. Most titles are in Japanese, but there is usually a small selection of English-language and art books; the atmosphere, on the other hand, is universal.

Cherry blossom over Meguro-gawa

❺ ...research General Store

This **shop** (Map p274; www.sett.co.jp; 1-14-11 Aobadai, Meguro-ku; ⏰noon-7pm; [S]Hibiya line to Naka-Meguro, main exit) sells original made-in-Japan outdoor wear and gear for stylish mountain hermits (or what designer Kobayashi Setsumasa calls 'anarcho-mountaineers' and 'saunter punks'). There's plenty in here or the more sedentary too, like T-shirts and tableware.

❻ Meguro-gawa

It's the **Meguro-gawa** (目黒川; Map p274; [S]Hibiya line to Naka-Meguro, main exit) – not so much a river as a canal – that gives Naka-Meguro its unlikely village vibe. On either side are walking paths lined with cherry trees – it is a great *hanami* (blossom-viewing) spot – plus shops, restaurants and cafes.

❼ Vase

One of Naka-Meguro's tiny, impeccably curated boutiques, **Vase** (Map p274; ☎03-5458-0337; www.vasenakameguro.com; 1-7-7 Kami-Meguro, Meguro-ku; ⏰noon-8pm; [S]Hibiya line to Naka-Meguro, main exit) stocks avant-garde designers and vintage pieces. It's in a little white house set back from Meguro-gawa.

loud and lively pretty much every night of the week; go early to get a table. Hours and prices vary by shop.

You won't find much English, but the adventurous can point at their fellow diners' dishes (you'll be sitting cheek-by-jowl with them). The entrance is marked with a rainbow-coloured sign.

AFURI — RAMEN ¥

Map p274 (あふり; www.afuri.com; 1-1-7 Ebisu, Shibuya-ku; ramen from ¥980; ⏰11am-5am; 🚭🌿📋; 🚉JR Yamanote line to Ebisu, east exit) Afuri has been a major player in the local ramen scene, making a strong case for a light touch with its signature *yuzu-shio* (a light, salty broth flavoured with *yuzu*, a type of citrus) ramen. It's since opened branches around the city, but this industrial-chic Ebisu shop is the original. It now does a vegan ramen. Order from the vending machine.

OUCA — ICE CREAM ¥

Map p274 (櫻花; www.ice-ouca.com; 1-6-6 Ebisu, Shibuya-ku; ice cream from ¥400; ⏰11am-11.30pm Mar-Oct, noon-11pm Nov-Feb; 📋; 🚉JR Yamanote line to Ebisu, east exit) Green tea isn't the only flavour Japan has contributed to the ice-cream playbook; other delicious innovations available (seasonally) at this famous Ebisu ice-cream stand include *kurogoma* (black sesame), *kinako kurosato* (roasted soybean flour and black sugar) and *beni imo* (purple sweet potato).

RANGMANG SHOKUDŌ — SHOKUDO ¥

Map p274 (らんまん食堂; ☎03-5489-4129; www.rangmang.com; 1-4-1 Ebisu-nishi, Shibuya-ku; dishes ¥460-660; ⏰11.30am-2.30pm & 6pm-midnight Mon-Fri, noon-2.30pm & 5-9.30pm Sat; 🚉JR Yamanote line to Ebisu) Fried chicken – which in Japan is lightly coated in a very fine starch – is having a moment and Rangmang Shokudō has a lot to do with that. Each order comes with four or five large bites, so you can eat light or go all out and sample several flavours. Staff recommend starting out with the classic *shio* (salt).

★YAKINIKU CHAMPION — BARBECUE ¥¥

Map p274 (焼肉チャンピオン; ☎03-5768-6922; www.yakiniku-champion.com; 1-2-8 Ebisu, Shibuya-ku; dishes ¥780-3300, course from ¥5600; ⏰5pm-midnight; 📋; 🚉JR Yamanote line to Ebisu, west exit) Champion is one of Tokyo's best spots for *yakiniku* – literally 'grilled meat' and the Japanese term for Korean barbecue. The menu runs the gamut from

WORTH A DETOUR

SENGAKU-JI

The story of the 47 *rōnin* (masterless samurai) is legend in Japan. Their master was Lord Asano of Akō domain (in present-day Hyōgo Prefecture), who was manipulated into pulling a sword on a rival, Lord Kira, inside the shogun's castle Edo-jō – an act for which he was punished with death. For over a year, Lord Asano's now masterless samurai laid low, plotting vengeance, eventually trapping Lord Kira and beheading him. On a winter day in 1702, they brought the head to the grave of their lord as an offering of fealty.

For their actions, the *rōnin* were sentenced to death; however, according to lore, so moved was the shogun by their display of loyalty that he allowed them to commit seppuku (ritual suicide), an honourable death for a samurai. Their ashes are interred, alongside their lord's, at the Zen temple, **Sengaku-ji** (泉岳寺; www.sengakuji.or.jp; 2-11-1 Takanawa, Minato-ku; ⏲7am-6pm Apr-Sep, to 5pm Oct-Mar; [S]Asakusa line to Sengaku-ji, exit A2). It's a story that resonates today: Sengaku-ji – out of the way in a residential neighbourhood – is never crowded, but it's never deserted either; it's common to see a visitor or two lighting incense at the graves.

Attached to the temple is a small museum with artefacts relating to the samurai, and also a video re-enactment of the fateful events (there's an English version). On the grounds is the well where the samurai washed the head of Lord Kira before presenting it to Lord Asano's grave.

It's easiest to reach Sengaku-ji via taxi (about ¥1500 and 15 minutes) from Meguro.

sweetbreads to the choicest cuts of grade A5 *wagyū;* there's a diagram of the cuts as well as descriptions. It's very popular; reservations recommended.

IPPO IZAKAYA ¥¥

Map p274 (一歩; ☎03-3445-8418; www.sakanabar-ippo.com; 2nd fl, 1-22-10 Ebisu, Shibuya-ku; cover charge ¥500, dishes ¥450-1700; ⏲6pm-3am; 📄; 🚆JR Yamanote line to Ebisu, east exit) This mellow little *izakaya* (Japanese pub-eatery) specialises in simple pleasures: fish and sake (there's an English sign out front that says just that). The friendly chefs speak some English and can help you decide what to have grilled, steamed, simmered or fried; if you can't decide, the ¥2500 set menu is great value. The entrance is up the wooden stairs.

🍴 Daikanyama & Naka-Meguro

DELIFUCIOUS BURGERS ¥

Map p274 (☎03-6874-0412; www.delifucious.com; 1-9-13 Higashiyama, Meguro-ku; burgers from ¥1000; ⏲noon-9pm Thu-Tue; 📄; [S]Hibiya line to Naka-Meguro, main exit) What happens when a former Ginza sushi chef turns his attention to – of all things – hamburgers? You get fish burgers and *anago* (seafaring eel) hot dogs prepared with the same attention to ingredients, preparation and presentation that you'd expect from a high-end sushi counter (but at a far more acceptable price).

🍴 Meguro

★**TONKI** TONKATSU ¥

Map p274 (とんき; ☎03-3491-9928; 1-2-1 Shimo-Meguro, Meguro-ku; meals ¥1800; ⏲4-10.45pm Wed-Mon, closed 3rd Mon of the month; 🚭📄; 🚆JR Yamanote line to Meguro, west exit) Tonki is a Tokyo *tonkatsu* (crumbed pork cutlet) legend, deep-frying with an unchanged recipe for nearly 80 years. The seats at the counter – where you can watch the perfectly choreographed chefs – are the most coveted, though there is usually a queue. There are tables upstairs.

🍷 DRINKING & NIGHTLIFE

★**GEM BY MOTO** BAR

Map p274 (ジェムバイモト; ☎03-6455-6998; 1-30-9 Ebisu, Shibuya-ku; ⏲5pm-midnight Tue-Fri, 1-9pm Sat & Sun; 🚭📄; 🚆JR Yamanote line to Ebisu, east exit) Tiny Gem has a seriously good selection of interesting sakes from ambitious brewers. Start with one of the Gem originals (brewed in collaboration with the bar) – or let owner Chiba-san select one for you. Sake by the glass runs from ¥650 to ¥5000 (but most are on the more reasonable end). Cover charge ¥800; reservations recommended.

ANOTHER 8 BAR

Map p274 (☎03-6417-9158; http://sakahachi.jp; 1-2-18 Shimo-Meguro, Meguro-ku; ⏰5pm-1am, closed irregularly; 🚭📋; 🚆JR Yamanote line to Meguro, west exit) Choose from a changing selection of over a dozen craft beers and sakes at this popular new hang-out in an old garage on a side street just south of Meguro-dōri. DJs spin here most Friday and Saturday evenings. Drinks from ¥750.

BAR TRENCH COCKTAIL BAR

Map p274 (バートレンチ; ☎03-3780-5291; www.small-axe.net; 1-5-8 Ebisu-nishi, Shibuya-ku; ⏰7pm-2am Mon-Sat, 6pm-1am Sun; 📋; 🚆JR Yamanote line to Ebisu, west exit) One of the pioneers of Tokyo's new cocktail scene, Trench (a suitable name for a bar hidden in a narrow alley) is a tiny place with an air of old-world bohemianism – but that might just be the absinthe talking. The always-changing original tipples are made with infusions, botanicals, herbs and spices. Drinks from ¥1500; cover ¥500. If it's full, ask the staff for direction to sister bar Tram, one block over.

ONIBUS COFFEE COFFEE

Map p274 (オニバスコーヒー; ☎03-6412-8683; www.onibuscoffee.com; 2-14-1 Kami-Meguro, Meguro-ku; ⏰9am-6pm; 📋; [S]Hibiya line to Naka-Meguro, south exit) Local hot spot Onibus Coffee perfectly nails two of Tokyo's current obsessions: third-wave coffee and restored heritage buildings. The beans here are roasted in-house and the cafe is set in a lightly renovated former tofu shop.

☆ ENTERTAINMENT

★UNIT LIVE MUSIC

Map p274 (ユニット; ☎03-5459-8630; www.unit-tokyo.com; 1-34-17 Ebisu-nishi, Shibuya-ku; ticket ¥2500-5000; 🚆Tōkyū Tōyoko line to Daikanyama) This subterranean club stages live music and DJ-hosted events (sometimes staggered on the same night). The solid line-up includes Japanese indie bands, veterans playing to a smaller crowd and overseas artists making their Japan debut. Unit has high ceilings and an intentionally industrial-cool interior (in addition to excellent sound), separating it from Tokyo's grungier live-music spots.

🛍 SHOPPING

★KAPITAL FASHION & ACCESSORIES

Map p274 (キャピタル; ☎03-5725-3923; www.kapital.jp; 2-20-2 Ebisu-Minami, Shibuya-ku; ⏰11am-8pm; 🚆JR Yamanote line to Ebisu, west exit) Cult brand Kapital is hard to pin down, but perhaps a deconstructed mash-up of the American West and the centuries-old Japanese aesthetic of *boro* (tatty) chic comes close. Almost no two items are alike; most are unisex. The shop itself is like an art installation. The staff, not snobby at all, can point you towards the other two shops nearby.

Shibuya & Shimo-Kitazawa

Neighbourhood Top Five

❶ Shibuya Crossing (p98) Losing yourself in the crowds at Japan's busiest intersection – and getting swept along in the beating heart of desire, aspiration and materialism that is Shibuya.

❷ Shibuya Center-gai (p98) Eating, drinking and shopping your way down the neighbourhood's always lively, neon-lit main drag.

❸ Shimo-Kitazawa (p101) Bar-hopping in this bohemian neighbourhood, beloved by generations of students, musicians and artists, starting at Mother.

❹ Tomigaya (p102) Checking out the hip hang-outs in this up-and-coming 'un-Shibuya'.

❺ Shibuya Stream (p99) Strolling along the Shibuya-gawa (yes, a river in Shibuya!) at this commercial complex with an outdoor terrace.

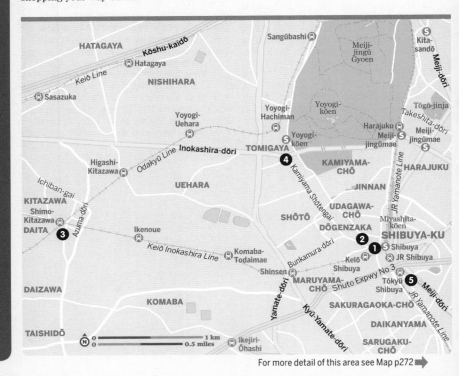

For more detail of this area see Map p272 ➡

Explore Shibuya & Shimo-Kitazawa

Shibuya is a neighbourhood that gets a late start – after all it was partying until the first trains started running in the morning. Come for lunch. Ease your way in by starting with the Shibuya of the future: the new riverside complex, Shibuya Stream (p99), south of the train station and part of the neighbourhood's massive redevelopment.

Then head into the thick of things to see the frenetic intersection that has become synonymous with Tokyo, Shibuya Crossing (p98). Shibuya Center-gai (p98) is the neighbourhood's lively main artery, lined with shops, eateries and bars. We don't quite understand it ourselves, but it is easy to lose hours here.

Shibuya is, above all, an entertainment district and it really comes alive at night. There are dance clubs, live-music venues, theatres and cinemas galore. While weekends are the busiest, you'll find people from all over Tokyo here any night of the week (and you may find yourself drawn back night after night). Bars and karaoke parlours stay open until dawn.

Shimo-Kitazawa, a short train ride away, offers an alternative scene, with secondhand clothing stores, scrappy bars and underground live-music venues and a streetscape like a doll's house version of Tokyo, barely passable by car. Tomigaya, too, has its hipster cafes, bistros and boutiques. Both are great places to explore in the late afternoon and evenings, when you're in the mood for a chiller scene.

Local Life

➜ **Nightclubs** Shibuya has the city's best club scene: check out Circus (p101) and Contact (p103).

➜ **Shopping** Both Shibuya and Shimo-Kitazawa are known for their record shops; Shimokita has lots of vintage-clothing shops, too.

Getting There & Away

➜ **Train** The JR Yamanote line stops at Shibuya Station. The Keiō Inokashira line departs from Keiō Shibuya Station for Shinsen, Komaba-Todaimae and Shimo-Kitazawa.

➜ **Subway** The Ginza, Hanzōmon and Fukutoshin lines stop in Shibuya. The Chiyoda line stops at Yoyogi-kōen (for Tomigaya); some Chiyoda line trains continue on the Odakyū line for Shimo-Kitazawa.

➜ **Bus** The useful bus 1 for Roppongi departs from **bus stand 51** (Map p272); it's signposted in English.

Lonely Planet's Top Tip

Missed the last train? You're not alone – or stuck for options. Shibuya has plenty for night crawlers who were lured out late by the neighbourhood's charms but who'd rather not fork over the yen for a taxi home. In addition to love hotels and *manga kissa* (comic book internet cafes), consider waiting for the first train at a karaoke parlour; most offer discounted all-night packages from midnight to 5am.

 Best Places to Eat

➜ Matsukiya (p100)
➜ Narukiyo (p101)
➜ Pignon (p103)
➜ Camelback (p102)

For reviews, see p99.

Best Places to Drink

➜ Circus Tokyo (p101)
➜ Ghetto (p101)
➜ Fuglen Tokyo (p103)
➜ Rhythm Cafe (p101)

For reviews, see p101.

Best Places to Shop

➜ Tokyu Hands (p104)
➜ d47 design travel store (p104)
➜ Tsukikageya (p102)

For reviews, see p104.

SHIBUYA & SHIMO-KITAZAWA

TOP EXPERIENCE
LOSE YOURSELF AT SHIBUYA CROSSING

Rumoured to be the busiest intersection in the world (and definitely in Japan), Shibuya Crossing, also known as Shibuya Scramble, is like a giant beating heart, sending people in all directions with every pulsing light change. Perhaps nowhere else says 'Welcome to Tokyo' better than this.

Hundreds of people – and at peak times upwards of 3000 people – cross at a time, coming from everywhere at once yet still managing to dodge each other with a practised, nonchalant agility. Then, in the time that it takes for the light to go from red to green again, all corners have replenished their stock of people – like a video on loop. All told, it's been estimated that on busy days, some 500,000 use the crossing – as many as some of Tokyo's busiest train stations.

Mag's Park (Map p272; 1-23-10 Jinnan, Shibuya-ku; ⊙11am-11pm), the rooftop of the Shibuya 109-2 department store, has the best views over the crossing. It's screened with plexiglass, but you can get good photos without having to worry about losing anything over the edge. The intersection is most impressive after dark on a Friday or Saturday night, when the crowds pouring out of the station are at their thickest and neon-lit by the signs above. (Rainy days have their own visual appeal, with all the colourful umbrellas.)

Coming from the station, follow the pedestrian traffic across to **Shibuya Center-gai** (渋谷センター街, Shibuya Sentā-gai; Map p272), Shibuya's main drag, which is closed to cars and chock-a-block with fast-food joints and high-street fashion shops. At night, lit bright as day, with a dozen competing soundtracks (coming from who knows where), wares spilling onto the streets and strutting teens, it feels like a block party.

DID YOU KNOW?

Shibuya Crossing sits over the confluence of two rivers, Shibuya-gawa and Uda-gawa, which were routed underground in the 1960s.

PRACTICALITIES

➡ 渋谷スクランブル交差点, Shibuya Scramble
➡ Map p272, E3
➡ 🚃JR Yamanote line to Shibuya, Hachikō exit

👁 SIGHTS

HACHIKŌ STATUE
STATUE

Map p272 (ハチ公像; Hachikō Plaza; 🚃 JR Yamanote line to Shibuya, Hachikō exit) Meet Tokyo's most famous pooch, Hachikō. This Akita dog came to Shibuya Station every day to meet his master, a professor, returning from work. After the professor died in 1925, Hachikō continued to come to the station daily until his own death nearly 10 years later. The story became legendary and a small statue was erected in the dog's memory in front of Shibuya Station.

Since Hachikō is a landmark everyone knows, it's Shibuya's de facto rendezvous point and the plaza around the statue is always buzzing.

MYTH OF TOMORROW
PUBLIC ART

Map p272 (明日の神話, Asu no Shinwa; 🚃 JR Yamanote line to Shibuya, Hachikō exit) Okamoto Tarō's mural, *Myth of Tomorrow* (1967), was commissioned by a Mexican luxury hotel but went missing two years later. It finally turned up in 2003 and, in 2008, the haunting 30m-long work, which depicts the atomic bomb exploding over Hiroshima, was installed inside Shibuya Station. It's on the 2nd floor, in the corridor leading to the Inokashira line.

D47 MUSEUM
MUSEUM

Map p272 (www.hikarie8.com; 8th fl, Shibuya Hikarie, 2-21-1 Shibuya, Shibuya-ku; ⏱11am-8pm; 🚃 JR Yamanote line to Shibuya, east exit) **FREE** Lifestyle brand D&Department combs the country for the platonic ideals of the utterly ordinary: the perfect broom, bottle opener or salt shaker (to name but a few). See rotating exhibitions of its latest finds from all 47 prefectures at this one-room museum. The excellent d47 design travel store (p104) is next door.

SHIBUYA STREAM
LANDMARK

Map p272 (渋谷ストリーム; https://shibuyastream.jp; 3-21-3 Shibuya, Shibuya-ku; 🚇Ginza, Hanzōmon & Fukutoshin lines to Shibuya, exit 16b; 🚃 JR Yamanote line to Shibuya, new south exit) Shibuya Crossing sits where two rivers meet, the Shibuya-gawa and the Uda-gawa, both diverted underground decades ago. Shibuya Stream, part of Shibuya's redevelopment, is a step towards bringing the city's waterways back. It's mostly a giant, glass multipurpose complex, but there's a lovely stretch of the newly liberated Shibuya-gawa flanked by terraces and some bars and restaurants.

WORTH A DETOUR

JAPAN FOLK CRAFTS MUSEUM

The *mingei* (folk crafts) movement was launched in the early 20th century to promote the works of artisans over cheaper, mass-produced goods. Central to the *mingei* philosophy is *yo no bi* (beauty through use). The **Japan Folk Crafts Museum** (日本民藝館, Mingeikan; Map p272; http://mingeikan.x0.com; 4-3-33 Komaba, Meguro-ku; adult/student/child ¥1100/600/200; ⏱10am-5pm Tue-Sun; 🚃 Keiō Inokashira line to Komaba-Todaimae, west exit) houses a collection of some 17,000 examples of craftwork from around Japan, in a farmhouse-like building designed by one of the movement's founders. Note that it closes between exhibitions (check the schedule online).

From Komaba-Tōdaima Station (two stops from Shibuya on the Keiō Inokashira line), walk with the train tracks on your left; when the road turns right (after about five minutes), the museum will be on your right.

🍴 EATING

Shibuya's dining scene is deceptive: hang out around Shibuya Center-gai and it's all fast-food joints, cheap *izakaya* (Japanese pub-eateries) and chain restaurants. But head towards the fringes and you'll find some seriously good restaurants frequented by locals in the know. In a pinch, the restaurant floors at Shibuya Hikarie (p104) and Shibuya Stream, both connected to Shibuya Station, have decent offerings.

GYŪKATSU MOTOMURA
TONKATSU ¥

Map p272 (牛かつ　もと村; ☎03-3797-3735; www.gyukatsu-motomura.com; basement fl, 3-18-10 Shibuya, Shibuya-ku; set meal from ¥1300; ⏱10am-10pm; 🈂🍴; 🚃 JR Yamanote line to Shibuya, east exit) You know *tonkatsu*, the deep-fried breaded pork cutlet that is a Japanese staple; meet *gyūkatsu*, the deep-fried breaded beef cutlet and currently much-hyped dish. At Motomura, diners get a small individual grill to cook the meat to their liking. Set meals include cabbage, rice and soup. It's just off Meiji-dōri, at the southern end of Shibuya Stream.

SAGATANI SOBA ¥

Map p272 (嵯峨谷; 2-25-7 Dōgenzaka, Shibuya-ku; noodles from ¥320; ⏲24hr; 🀫🀫; 🚃JR Yamanote line to Shibuya, Hachikō exit) Proving that Tokyo is only expensive for those who don't know better, this all-night joint serves up bamboo steamers of delicious noodles for just ¥320. You won't regret 'splurging' on the *goma-dare soba* (ごまだれそば; buckwheat noodles with sesame dipping sauce) for ¥450. Look for the stone mill in the window and order from the vending machine.

FOOD SHOW SUPERMARKET ¥

Map p272 (フードショー; basement fl, 2-24-1 Shibuya, Shibuya-ku; ⏲10am-9pm; 🀫; 🚃JR Yamanote line to Shibuya, Hachikō exit) A best friend to harried and hungry commuters, Food Show has steamers of dumplings, crisp *karaage* (deep-fried chicken), sushi sets and heaps of salads from which to choose, all packaged to go. It's in the basement of Shibuya Station; look for the green signs near Hachikō and in the station pointing downstairs.

D47 SHOKUDŌ JAPANESE ¥

Map p272 (d47食堂; www.hikarie8.com; 8th fl, Shibuya Hikarie, 2-21-1 Shibuya, Shibuya-ku; meals ¥1550-1780; ⏲11.30am-2.30pm & 6-10.30pm; 🀫🀫; 🚃JR Yamanote line to Shibuya, east exit) There are 47 prefectures in Japan and d47 serves a changing line-up of *teishoku* (set meals) that evoke the specialities of each, from the fermented tofu of Okinawa to the stuffed squid of Hokkaidō. A larger menu of small plates is available in the evening.

NAGI SHOKUDŌ VEGAN ¥

Map p272 (なぎ食堂; ☎03-3461-3280; http://nagi shokudo.com; 15-10 Uguisudani-chō, Shibuya-ku; meal from ¥1080; ⏲noon-4pm daily, 6-11pm Mon-Sat; 🀫🀫🀫🀫; 🚃JR Yamanote line to Shibuya, west exit) A vegan haven in fast-food-laced Shibuya, Nagi serves up dishes like falafel and coconut curry. The most popular thing on the menu is a set meal with three small dishes, miso soup and rice. It's a low-key, homely place with mismatched furniture, catty-corner from a post office and hidden behind a concrete wall; look for the red sign.

SHIRUBE IZAKAYA ¥

Map p272 (汁べゑ; ☎03-3413-3785; 2-18-2 Kitazawa, Setagaya-ku; dishes ¥620-1080; ⏲5.30pm-midnight; 🀫; 🚃Odakyū or Keiō Inokashira line to Shimo-Kitazawa, southwest exit) It's easy to see why everyone loves this *izakaya*:

the young chefs put on a dramatic show in the open kitchen and the creative takes on classics, while not exactly gourmet, are totally satisfying, especially the house speciality, *aburi saba* (blowtorch grilled mackerel). The two-hour all-you-can-drink course (¥4000), which comes with seven dishes, is great value. There is a ¥400 cover; reservations recommended.

It's down the alley from the corner with the Mr Donuts, on your right with white *noren* (doorway curtains).

KATSU MIDORI SUSHI ¥¥

Map p272 (活美登利; ☎03-5728-4282; www.ka tumidori.co.jp; 8th fl, Seibu Bldg A, 21-1 Udagawa-chō, Shibuya-ku; ⏲11am-11pm; 🀫🀫🀫; 🚃JR Yamanote line to Shibuya, Hachikō exit) There's nearly always a queue at this very popular *kaiten-sushi* (conveyor-belt sushi restaurant) inside Seibu department store, but it moves quickly. The menu is huge, including lots of nonseafood items; especially tasty is the sushi served *'aburi'* style – lightly seared with a blowtorch.

MARU BENGARA JAPANESE ¥¥

Map p272 (圓　弁柄; ☎03-6427-7700; www. maru-mayfont.jp; 3rd fl, Shibuya Stream, 3-21-3 Shibuya, Shibuya-ku; lunch set ¥1240-3760, dinner course from ¥6480, à la carte dishes ¥920-3565; ⏲11am-3pm & 5-11pm; 🀫🀫; 🚇Ginza, Hanzōmon & Fukutoshin lines to Shibuya, exit 16b, 🚃JR Yamanote line to Shibuya, new south exit) Maru is a meal made easy: at lunch the restaurant does really good grilled fish *teishoku;* in the evenings, courses with sashimi, seasonal sides and vegetables, a main of meat or fish and a choice of Japanese-style desserts. It's part of the new Shibuya Stream complex, so you can get here right from the subway.

⭐**MATSUKIYA** HOTPOT ¥¥¥

Map p272 (松木家; ☎03-3461-2651; 6-8 Maruyama-chō, Shibuya-ku; meals from ¥5400; ⏲5-11pm Mon-Sat; 🀫; 🚃JR Yamanote line to Shibuya, Hachikō exit) There are only two things on the menu at Matsukiya, established in 1890: *sukiyaki* (thinly sliced beef cooked in sake, soy and vinegar broth, and dipped in raw egg) and *shabu-shabu* (thin slices of beef or pork swished in hot broth and dipped in a citrusy soy or sesame sauce). The beef is top-grade *wagyū* from Ōmi. Meals include veggies and noodles cooked in the broths. There's a white sign out front and the entrance is up some stairs. Reservations recommended.

★ NARUKIYO IZAKAYA ¥¥¥

Map p272 (なるきよ; ☎03-5485-2223; 2-7-14 Shibuya, Shibuya-ku; dishes ¥700-4800; ☺6pm-12.30am; 🚉JR Yamanote line to Shibuya, east exit) Cult favourite *izakaya*, Narukiyo serves seasonal Japanese cuisine with creative panache. The menu, which changes daily, is handwritten on a scroll and totally undecipherable; say the magic word, *omakase* (chef's choice; and set a price cap, say ¥5000 or ¥7000 per person), and trust that you're in good hands. Reservations recommended.

DRINKING & NIGHTLIFE

Shibuya provides a fantastic night out. The streets are never quiet and there are tonnes of bars, nightclubs and karaoke parlours – all in a concentrated area, which makes hopping from one venue to the next easy work. The bars are good most any night of the week, though clubs only really get going on Friday and Saturday (and not until 11pm).

★ CIRCUS TOKYO CLUB

Map p272 (www.circus-tokyo.jp; 3-26-16 Shibuya, Shibuya-ku; ☻; 🚉JR Yamanote line to Shibuya, new south exit) Circus, the Tokyo offshoot of an Osaka club, is aggressively underground: small, out of the way, in a basement (of course), with no decor to speak of and all attention laser-focused on the often experimental music. It's open most Fridays and Saturdays from 11pm, and sometimes other nights; check the schedule online. Cover ¥2000 to ¥3000 and drinks ¥600; ID required. Wear your comfy shoes because there's nowhere to sit.

★ GHETTO BAR

Map p272 (月灯; 1-45-16 Daizawa, Setagaya-ku; ☺8.30pm-late; 🚉Keiō Inokashira line to Shimo-Kitazawa, north exit) Ghetto – the name comes from the characters for 'moon' *(ge)* and 'light' *(to)* – is one of the little bars inside Shimo-Kitazawa's iconic (and rickety) Suzunari theatre complex. Each night a different character is behind the counter; on the other side, a mix of local creatives and travellers. By open until late we mean very, very late. No cover charge; drinks from ¥600.

RHYTHM CAFE BAR

Map p272 (リズムカフェ; ☎03-3770-0244; http://rhythmcafe.jp; 11-1 Udagawa-chō, Shibuya-ku; ☺6pm-2am; 🚉JR Yamanote line to Shibuya, Hachikō exit) Rhythm Cafe is a fun little spot secreted among the windy streets of Udagawa-chō. It's run by a record label and known for having offbeat event nights, such as the retro Japanese pop night on the fourth Thursday of the month. Drinks start at ¥600; some events have a cover, but not usually more than ¥1000.

KARAOKE RAINBOW KARAOKE

Map p272 (☎03-6455-3240; www.karaoke-rainbow.com; 8th fl, Shibuya Modi, 1-21-3 Shibuya, Shibuya-ku; per 30min before/after 7pm ¥150/410; ☺11am-5am; ☻🖥; 🚉JR Yamanote line to Shibuya, Hachikō exit) This is Shibuya's most popular karaoke spot for two reasons: it doesn't have the same dated look as the generic chains and you get the first hour free (though, technically, you need to buy one drink; from ¥465). Staff speak some English and the English song list is extensive. It's on the 8th floor of the building with the Marui department store.

OATH BAR

Map p272 (www.djbar-oath.com; basement fl, 1-6-5 Dōgenzaka, Shibuya-ku; ☺8pm-5am Mon-Sat; 🚉JR Yamanote line to Shibuya, Hachikō exit) Oath is a tiny space covered in gilt and mirrors, dripping with chandeliers and absolutely not taking itself seriously. It's a very popular spot for pre-partying and after-partying, thanks to cheap drinks (¥500), fun DJs and a friendly crowd. Cover charge is ¥1000 (one drink included).

BEAT CAFE BAR

Map p272 (www.facebook.com/beatcafe; basement fl, 2-13-5 Dōgenzaka, Shibuya-ku; ☺8pm-5am; 🚉JR Yamanote line to Shibuya, Hachikō exit) Join an eclectic mix of local and international regulars at this comfortably shabby bar among the nightclubs and love hotels of Dōgenzaka. It's a known hang-out for musicians and music fans; check the website for info on parties (and after-parties). Look for Gateway Studio on the corner; the bar is in the basement. Drinks from ¥500.

MOTHER BAR

Map p272 (マザー; ☎03-3421-9519; www.rock-mother.com; 5-36-14 Daizawa, Setagaya-ku; ☺5pm-2am Sun-Thu, 5pm-5am Fri & Sat; 🖥; 🚉Odakyū or Keiō Inokashira line to Shimo-Kitazawa, southwest exit) Mother is a classic Shimo-Kitazawa bar with a soundtrack from the '60s and '70s and an undulating,

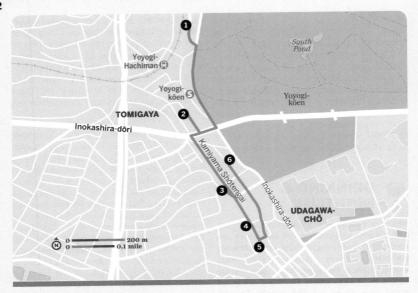

🏃 Local Life
Hanging out in Tomigaya

For years Tomigaya, a residential part of what's known as Oku-Shibuya ('deep Shibuya'), was a well-kept secret, but with more and more creative cafes, bistros and boutiques opening, the buzz is too great to contain. Take a break from the brashness of central Shibuya – just 15 minutes away on foot – to see what locals are so excited about.

❶ Little Nap Coffee Stand

On the western edge of Yoyogi-kōen, **Little Nap Coffee Stand** (リトルナップコーヒースタンド; www.littlenap.jp; 5-65-4 Yoyogi, Shibuya-ku; ⏱9am-7pm Tue-Sun; 🅿; Ⓢ Chiyoda line to Yoyogi-kōen, exit 3) is popular with local dog walkers and joggers. Which isn't to say that convenience is the only appeal here: the lattes and single-origin pour-overs (¥450; from beans roasted at Little Nap's roaster up the street) are excellent.

❷ Tsukikageya

Forget cute. Natsuki Shigeta designs *yukata* (light cotton kimonos) with a punk-rock slant that pair with wild accessories. Her studio and shop, **Tsukikageya** (月影屋; Map p272; www.tsukikageya.com; 1-9-19 Tomigaya, Shibuya-ku; ⏱noon-8pm Thu-Mon, closed irregularly; Ⓢ Chiyoda line to Yoyogi-kōen, exit 2), is all but hidden in the back of an apartment complex; enter from the alley behind, and look for the jewellery vending machine out front.

❸ Camelback

Sandwich counter **Camelback** (キャメルバック; Map p272; www.camelback.tokyo; 42-2 Kamiyama-chō, Shibuya-ku; sandwiches ¥450-900; ⏱8am-5pm Tue-Sun; 🍴🚲🅿; Ⓢ Chiyoda line to Yoyogi-kōen, exit 2) is an example of the creative new spots popping up in Tomigaya. It's run by a young and savvy English-speaking crew (among them a trained sushi chef). Order the omelette sandwich, made with the same kind of fluffy, rolled omelette served at sushi restaurants. Seating is on the bench outside.

❹ Shibuya Publishing & Booksellers

Come browse the selection of art, food and travel magazines and small-press offerings at indie bookshop **Shibuya Publishing & Booksellers** (SPBS; Map p272; ☎03-5465-0588; www.shibuyabooks.co.jp; 17-3 Kamiyama-chō, Shibuya-ku; ⏱11am-11pm Mon-Sat, to 10pm Sun; 🚃JR Yamanote line to Shibuya, Hachikō exit).

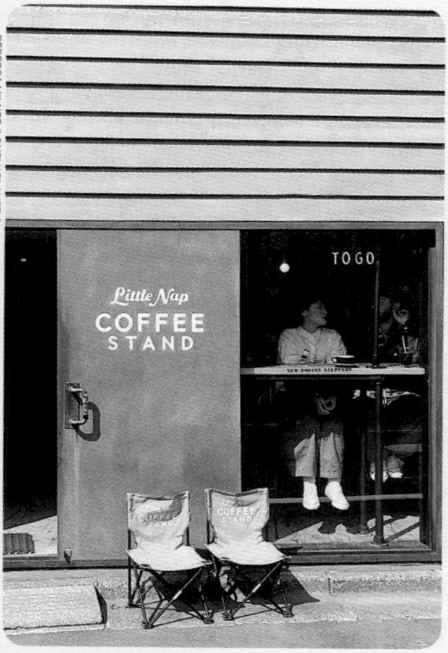

Little Nap Coffee Stand

There's a small selection of books in English, and also other items, like totes and accessories from Japanese designers.

❺ Pignon

Tomigaya is the centre of Tokyo's neo-bistro movement and **Pignon** (ピニョン; Map p272; ☎03-3468-2331; www.pignontokyo.jp; 16-3 Kamiyama-chō, Shibuya-ku; dishes ¥1700-4200; 🕐6.30-10.30pm Mon-Sat; 📋; 🚉JR Yamanote line to Shibuya, Hachikō exit) is a perfect example. It sources its ingredients directly from local producers, has a menu influenced by chef Yoshikawa Rimpei's travels and an affable coolness. Reservations recommended, but early in the week you can usually get a seat.

❻ Fuglen Tokyo

Fuglen Tokyo (Map p272; www.fuglen.no; 1-16-11 Tomigaya, Shibuya-ku; 🕐8am-10pm Mon & Tue, to 1am Wed & Thu, to 2am Fri, 9am-2am Sat, 9am-midnight Sun; 🚭📶📋; [S]Chiyoda line to Yoyogi-kōen, exit 2) – Tomigaya's principal gathering spot – does coffee by day and some of the city's most creative cocktails (from ¥1250) by night (Wednesday to Sunday). Check the calendar for special events, which happen several times a month.

womb-like interior covered in mosaic tile. It does cocktails (from ¥600) with in-house infusions – try the signature 'mori' liquor, served from a glass skull – and also Okinawan and Southeast Asian food.

CONTACT CLUB

Map p272 (コンタクト; ☎03-6427-8107; www.contacttokyo.com; basement, 2-10-12 Dōgenzaka, Shibuya-ku; 🕐Fri-Wed; 🚭; 🚉JR Yamanote line to Shibuya, Hachikō exit) Shibuya's most fashionable club at the time of research, Contact is several storeys under a parking garage. Come after 1am on a Friday or Saturday night to see it in top form. Music may be hip-hop, house or techno – it depends on the night. It has plenty of space for just lounging, too. To enter, you must first sign up for a membership. ID required. The cover is steep: ¥3500 on a Friday or Saturday (¥2000 for under 23s); it's cheaper if you purchase a ticket in advance (through the website).

GEN GEN AN TEAHOUSE

Map p272 (幻幻庵; https://en-tea.com; 4-8 Udagawa-chō, Shibuya-ku; 🕐11am-7pm Tue, Wed & Sun, to 11pm Thu-Sat; 🚭📋; 🚉JR Yamanote line to Shibuya, Hachikō exit) Your Shibuya pit stop for green-tea lattes, fresh-brewed ice teas, earthy *hōjicha* (roasted green tea) and more, all made from organic leaves harvested in Saga Prefecture.

☆ ENTERTAINMENT

Both Shibuya and Shimo-Kitazawa have several 'live houses' (small to medium-sized concert venues).

★SHIMO-KITAZAWA THREE LIVE MUSIC

Map p272 (下北沢Three; ☎03-5486-8804; https://shimokitazawathree.tumblr.com; basement fl, 5-18-1 Daizawa, Setagaya-ku; free-¥3500; 🚉Odakyū or Keiō Inokashira line to Shimo-Kitazawa, southwest exit) Three's mission is to make live music more accessible in Tokyo: it hosts 10 free events a month (otherwise they average around ¥2000). The line-up is pretty random, but the welcoming attitude means there's usually a good crowd, which doesn't take much – capacity is 170. Live shows start at 6pm or 7pm; club events from 11.30pm.

★WWW LIVE MUSIC

Map p272 (☎03-5458-7685; https://www-shibuya.jp; 13-17 Udagawa-chō, Shibuya-ku;

tickets ¥3000-5000; JR Yamanote line to Shibuya, Hachikō exit) In a former art-house cinema with the tell-tale tiered floor still intact, this is one of those rare venues where you could turn up just about any night and hear something good. The line-up varies from indie pop to hip-hop to electronica. Upstairs is WWW X, a bigger space.

Both spots also sometimes host late-night club events, in which case you'll need photo ID to enter.

CLUB QUATTRO LIVE MUSIC

Map p272 (クラブクアトロ; ☎03-3477-8750; www.club-quattro.com; 4th & 5th fl, 32-13-4 Udagawa-chō, Shibuya-ku; tickets ¥3000-4000; JR Yamanote line to Shibuya, Hachikō exit) This small venue attracts a more grown-up, artsy crowd than the club's location – near Shibuya Center-gai (p98) – might lead you to expect. There's no explicit musical focus, but the line-up leans towards indie rock and world music. One drink (¥600) minimum order.

**SETAGAYA
PUBLIC THEATRE** PERFORMING ARTS

Map p272 (世田谷パブリックシアター; ☎03-5432-1515; www.setagaya-pt.jp; 4-1-1 Taishidō, Setagaya-ku; tickets ¥5000-7500; Tōkyū Den-en-toshi line to Sangenjaya, Carrot Tower exit) Setagaya Public Theatre, comprising a main stage and the smaller, more experimental Theatre Tram, is the city's top venue for contemporary drama and dance. Particularly accessible to non-Japanese speakers is the theatre's series on modern *nō* (a stylised Japanese dance-drama performed on a bare stage); *butō* (an avant-garde form of dance) is also sometimes staged here.

Unless otherwise noted, productions are in Japanese. The theatre is inside the Carrot Tower building connected to Sangenjaya Station, a five-minute train ride from Shibuya.

 # SHOPPING

Shibuya is a popular shopping spot for teens and 20-somethings, but there are also branches of big-box electronics stores and department stores, too.

★ **TOKYU HANDS** DEPARTMENT STORE

Map p272 (東急ハンズ; http://shibuya.tokyu-hands.co.jp; 12-18 Udagawa-chō, Shibuya-ku; ⏱10am-9pm; JR Yamanote line to Shibuya,

Hachikō exit) This DIY and *zakka* (miscellaneous things) store has eight fascinating floors of everything you didn't know you needed – reflexology slippers, bee-venom face masks and cartoon-character-shaped rice-ball moulds, for example. Most is inexpensive, perfect for souvenir- and gift-hunting. Warning: you could lose hours in here. There's another branch in **Shinjuku** (東急ハンズ新宿店; Map p280; Takashimaya Times Sq, 5-24-2 Sendagaya, Shibuya-ku; ⏱10am-9pm; JR Yamanote line to Shinjuku, new south exit).

★ **D47 DESIGN TRAVEL STORE** DESIGN

Map p272 (☎03-6427-2301; 8th fl, Shibuya Hikarie, 2-21-1 Shibuya, Shibuya-ku; ⏱11am-8pm; JR Yamanote line to Shibuya, east exit) The folks behind the D&D Department lifestyle brand and magazine are expert scavengers, searching Japan for outstanding examples of artisanship – be it ceramics from Ishikawa or linens from Fukui. An ever-changing selection of finds are on sale.

MEGA DONKI VARIETY

Map p272 (MEGAドンキ; ☎03-5428-4086; 28-6 Udagawa-chō, Shibuya-ku; ⏱24hr; JR Yamanote line to Shibuya, Hachikō exit) You could show up in Tokyo completely empty-handed and this huge, new outpost of all-night, bargain retailer 'Don Quijote' would have you covered. There are groceries, toiletries, electronics and clothes – along with all sorts of random stuff, including the best selection of unusual flavoured Kit-Kat chocolates we've seen. Don't miss the giant moray eel in the tank at the entrance.

TOWER RECORDS MUSIC

Map p272 (タワーレコード; ☎03-3496-3661; http://tower.jp/store/Shibuya; 1-22-14 Jinnan, Shibuya-ku; ⏱10am-11pm; JR Yamanote line to Shibuya, Hachikō exit) Yes, Tower lives – in Japan at least! This eight-storey temple of music has a deep collection of Japanese and world music. Even if you're not into buying, it can be a great place to browse and discover local artists. There are lots of listening stations.

SHIBUYA HIKARIE MALL

Map p272 (渋谷ヒカリエ; www.hikarie.jp; 2-21-1 Shibuya, Shibuya-ku; ⏱10am-9pm; JR Yamanote line to Shibuya, east exit) The first five floors of this skyscraper are filled with fashion and lifestyle boutiques from international and domestic brands. In the basement levels are dozens of gourmet takeaway counters.

Harajuku & Aoyama

HARAJUKU | AOYAMA & GAIENMAE

Neighbourhood Top Five

❶ Meiji-jingū (p107) Leaving the city behind as you pass through the towering cedar *torii* (entrance gate), which marks the entrance to the abode of the gods, and following the wooded path to Tokyo's most impressive Shintō shrine.

❷ Omote-sandō (p108) Gawking at the contemporary architecture, the work of Japan's leading architects, along this wide, boutique-lined boulevard.

❸ Yoyogi-kōen (p108) Stretching out on the grassy lawn or catching a food festival at the city's most popular park, which buzzes with life on weekends.

❹ Harajuku Street Fashion (p108) Scouting new looks in this famously fashion-forward neighbourhood, starting with Harajuku landmark Takeshita-dōri.

❺ Nezu Museum (p108) Retreating into the calm galleries and gardens of this excellent antiquities museum.

For more detail of this area see Map p276 ➡

HARAJUKU & AOYAMA

Lonely Planet's Top Tip

Harajuku, and especially the boulevard Omote-sandō, can be extremely crowded – with foot traffic moving at a slow, platform-shoe shuffle. If you want to seriously shop or zip around to see the museums and architecture, then head over on a weekday. If you want to get caught up in it all, check out the markets and people-watch, then come on a Saturday or Sunday afternoon.

 Best Places to Eat

➡ Eatrip (p112)

➡ Maisen (p112)

➡ Mominoki House (p111)

➡ Gomaya Kuki (p111)

For reviews, see p111. ➡

 Best Places to Drink

➡ Sakurai Japanese Tea Experience (p112)

➡ Two Rooms (p114)

➡ Aoyama Flower Market Teahouse (p112)

For reviews, see p112. ➡

Best Places to Shop

➡ Arts & Science (p114)

➡ House @Mikiri Hassin (p114)

➡ Sou-Sou (p115)

➡ Pass the Baton (p115)

➡ Musubi (p115)

For reviews, see p114. ➡

Explore Harajuku & Aoyama

Harajuku is a neighbourhood that rewards an early start: Meiji-jingū can get very busy; the earlier you arrive, the more likely you are to experience the kind of serene atmosphere that does the shrine justice. From here, continue along Omote-sandō (p108), the boulevard that connects Harajuku and Aoyama, to see the contemporary architecture. This is a compact district, where much can be accomplished in a day – and on foot.

Shopping is, of course, a major attraction for many (locals included). But a day here needn't fall heavily on shopping: you could spend a whole afternoon exploring Harajuku and Aoyama's unsung cultural highlights, including the excellent Ukiyo-e Ōta Memorial Museum of Art (p108), for woodblock prints, and the Nezu Museum (p108), for antiquities. Or take a deep dive into the world of Japanese tea at the Sakurai Japanese Tea Experience (p112).

Harajuku and Aoyama have lots of great cafes and teahouses for leg-weary shoppers. Both neighbourhoods become pretty quiet after the shops close for the day; there are a handful of glowing windows after dark, but you have to know where to find them.

Local Life

➡ **Hang-outs** On sunny weekends, Yoyogi-kōen (p108) draws crowds of picnicking families, dog-walkers and amateur musicians and dancers using the grassy lawn as free practice space. During the warmer months, festivals take place on the plaza across from the park.

➡ **Shopping** 'Ura-Hara' (literally 'behind Harajuku') is the nickname for the maze of backstreets behind Omotesandō Hills, where you'll find the ever-changing tiny boutiques and secondhand stores.

➡ **Markets** On weekends the most popular lunch spot is Aoyama's farmers market (p111).

Getting There & Away

➡ **Train** The JR Yamanote loop line stops at Harajuku Station.

➡ **Subway** The two key subway stops for this area are at opposite ends of Omote-sandō: Meiji-jingūmae (Chiyoda and Fukutoshin lines), at the Harajuku end, and Omote-sandō (Chiyoda, Ginza and Hanzōmon lines), at the Aoyama end. Taking a Ginza line train from Shibuya, Omote-sandō is the first stop, followed by Gaienmae.

➡ **Walking** It's an easy walk between Shibuya and Harajuku.

◉ TOP EXPERIENCE
LEAVE THE CITY BEHIND AT MEIJI-JINGŪ

Tokyo's grandest Shintō shrine is dedicated to Emperor Meiji and Empress Shōken, whose reign (1868–1912) coincided with Japan's transformation from isolationist, feudal state to modern nation. Constructed in 1920, the shrine was destroyed in WWII air raids and rebuilt in 1958; however, unlike so many of Japan's postwar reconstructions, Meiji-jingū has atmosphere in spades.

The shrine is secreted in a wooded grove, accessed via a winding gravel path. At the entrance you'll pass through the first of several towering, wooden *torii* (gates). These mark the boundary between the mundane world and the sacred one; it's the custom to bow upon passing through a *torii*. In preparation for its centennial in 2020, Meiji-jingū is currently undergoing renovations. Some shrine structures may be under wraps, but the shrine as a whole will remain open.

In front of the final *torii* before the main shrine is the *temizu-ya* (font), where visitors purify themselves by pouring water over their hands (purity is a tenet of Shintoism). To do so, dip the ladle in the water and first rinse your left hand then your right. Pour some water into your left hand and rinse your mouth, then rinse your left hand again.

The main shrine is made of unpainted cypress wood with a copper-plated roof. To make an offering (and a wish), toss a coin (a ¥5 coin is believed lucky) into the box, bow twice, clap your hands twice and bow again. To the right are kiosks selling *ema* (wooden plaques with prayers) and *omamori* (charms).

The shrine itself occupies only a small fraction of the sprawling grounds, which contain some 120,000 trees donated from all over Japan. Only the strolling garden **Meiji-jingū Gyoen** (明治神宮御苑, Inner Garden; Map p276; ¥500; ⊙9am-4.30pm, to 4pm Nov-Feb) is accessible to the public. Here there are peaceful walks, a good dose of privacy at weekdays and spectacular irises in June. The entrance is halfway along the gravel path to the shrine.

DON'T MISS

➡ The gates
➡ The font
➡ Main shrine
➡ Meiji-jingū Gyoen

PRACTICALITIES

➡ 明治神宮
➡ Map p276, B2
➡ www.meijijingu.or.jp
➡ 1-1 Yoyogi Kamizono-chō, Shibuya-ku
➡ admission free
➡ ⊙dawn-dusk
➡ 🚇JR Yamanote line to Harajuku, Omote-sandō exit

SIGHTS

Harajuku

MEIJI-JINGŪ SHINTO SHRINE

See p107.

★OMOTE-SANDŌ STREET

Map p276 (表参道; [S]Ginza line to Omote-sandō, exits A3 & B4, [R]JR Yamanote line to Harajuku, Omote-sandō exit) This broad, tree-lined boulevard is lined with boutiques from the top European fashion houses. More interesting are the buildings themselves, designed by some of the biggest names in Japanese architecture. There's no better (or more convenient) place to gain an overview of Japan's current sense of design. See the highlights along our walking tour (p113).

★YOYOGI-KŌEN PARK

Map p276 (代々木公園; www.yoyogipark.info; Yoyogi-kamizono-chō, Shibuya-ku; [R]JR Yamanote line to Harajuku, Omote-sandō exit) If it's a sunny and warm weekend afternoon, you can count on there being a crowd lazing around the large grassy expanse that is Yoyogi-kōen. You'll usually find revellers and noisemakers of all stripes, from hula-hoopers to African drum circles to retro greasers dancing around a boom box. It's an excellent place for a picnic and probably the only place in the city where you can reasonably toss a Frisbee without fear of hitting someone.

★UKIYO-E ŌTA MEMORIAL MUSEUM OF ART MUSEUM

Map p276 (浮世絵太田記念美術館; ☎03-3403-0880; www.ukiyoe-ota-muse.jp; 1-10-10 Jingūmae, Shibuya-ku; adult ¥700-1000, child free; 🕒10.30am-5.30pm Tue-Sun; [R]JR Yamanote line to Harajuku, Omote-sandō exit) This small museum (where you swap your shoes for slippers) is the best place in Tokyo to see *ukiyo-e*. Each month it presents a seasonal, thematic exhibition (with English curation notes), drawing from the truly impressive collection of Ōta Seizo, the former head of the Toho Life Insurance Company. Most exhibitions include a few works by masters such as Hokusai and Hiroshige. The museum closes the last few days of the month (between exhibitions).

The shop in the basement sells beautifully printed *tenugui* (traditional hand-dyed, thin cotton towels).

YOYOGI NATIONAL STADIUM ARCHITECTURE

Map p276 (国立代々木競技場, Kokuritsu Yoyogi Kyōgi-jō; 2-1-1 Jinnan, Shibuya-ku; [R]JR Yamanote line to Harajuku, Omote-sandō exit) This early masterpiece by architect Tange Kenzō was built for the 1964 Olympics (and will be used again in the latest games for the handball event). The stadium, which looks vaguely like a samurai helmet, uses suspension-bridge technology – rather than beams – to support the roof.

TAKESHITA-DŌRI STREET

Map p276 (竹下通り; Jingūmae, Shibuya-ku; [R]JR Yamanote line to Harajuku, Takeshita exit) This is Tokyo's famous fashion bazaar. It's an oddly mixed bag: newer shops selling trendy, youthful styles alongside stores still invested in the trappings of decades of subcultures past (plaid and safety pins for the punks; colourful tutus for the *decora;* Victorian dresses for the Gothic Lolitas). Be warned: this pedestrian alley is a pilgrimage site for teens from all over Japan, which means it can be packed.

DESIGN FESTA GALLERY

Map p276 (デザインフェスタ; ☎03-3479-1442; www.designfestagallery.com; 3-20-2 Jingūmae, Shibuya-ku; 🕒11am-8pm; 📶; [R]JR Yamanote line to Harajuku, Takeshita exit) [FREE] Design Festa has long been a champion of Tokyo's DIY art scene and its maze-like building is a Harajuku landmark. Inside there are dozens of small galleries rented by the day. More often than not, the artists themselves are hanging around, too.

Aoyama & Gaienmae

★NEZU MUSEUM MUSEUM

Map p276 (根津美術館; ☎03-3400-2536; www.nezu-muse.or.jp; 6-5-1 Minami-Aoyama, Minato-ku; adult/child ¥1100/free, special exhibitions extra ¥200; 🕒10am-5pm Tue-Sun; [S]Ginza line to Omote-sandō, exit A5) Nezu Museum offers a striking blend of old and new: a renowned collection of Japanese, Chinese and Korean antiquities in a gallery space designed by contemporary architect Kengo Kuma. Select items from the extensive collection are displayed in seasonal exhibitions. The English explanations are usually pretty good. Behind the galleries is a woodsy strolling garden laced with stone paths and studded with teahouses and sculptures.

TARO OKAMOTO MEMORIAL MUSEUM MUSEUM

Map p276 (岡本太郎記念館; ☎03-3406-0801; http://taro-okamoto.or.jp; 6-1-19 Minami-Aoyama, Minato-ku; adult/child ¥620/310; ⏲10am-6pm Wed-Mon; [S]Ginza line to Omote-sandō, exit A5) A painter and sculptor, Okamoto Tarō was Japan's most recognised artist from the post-WWII period, a rare avant-garde figure with mass appeal. His works are both playful and sinister, life-affirming and chaotic. This small museum, which includes a sculpture garden, is inside the artist's home.

EATING

As befitting a shopping district, Harajuku and Aoyama have lots of great, inexpensive lunch spots. Harajuku is famous for being the place that foreign franchises drop their first Tokyo outlet, which attracts buzz (and some huge lines – in case you were wondering what those were about). In the evening, after the shopping day trippers recede, the dining scene turns more local. There are some fashionable spots here for when you want to treat yourself.

Harajuku

GOMAYA KUKI ICE CREAM ¥

Map p276 (ごまや くき; http://gomayakuki.jp; 4-6-9 Jingūmae, Shibuya-ku; 2 scoops ¥500; ⏲11am-7pm; 🚉JR Yamanote line to Harajuku, Omote-sandō exit) *Goma* (sesame) ice cream is a must-try and this speciality shop is the place to try it. There are two varieties, made from high-grade *kurogoma* (黒ごま; black sesame) or *shirogoma* (白ごま; white sesame) from Mie Prefecture. To really taste the sesame, double down and get it *chōtokunō* (super extra strong). Literally thousands of seeds go into one scoop.

SAKURA-TEI OKONOMIYAKI ¥

Map p276 (さくら亭; ☎03-3479-0039; www.sakuratei.co.jp; 3-20-1 Jingūmae, Shibuya-ku; okonomiyaki ¥1050-1500; ⏲11am-midnight; 🚭📶✍📋; 🚉JR Yamanote line to Harajuku, Takeshita exit) Grill your own *okonomiyaki* (savoury pancakes) at this funky place inside the gallery Design Festa (p1088). In addition to classic options (with pork, squid and cabbage), there are some fun fusion-style ones. There's also a great-value, two-hour, all-you-can-eat plan (¥2500 plus one drink order).

LOCAL KNOWLEDGE

AOYAMA FARMERS MARKET

Tokyo's best **farmers market** (Map p276; www.farmersmarkets.jp; 5-53-7 Jingūmae, Shibuya-ku; ⏲10am-4pm Sat & Sun; [S]Ginza line to Omote-sandō, exit B2) 🌿 – with colourful produce, pickles and preserves – sets up every weekend on the plaza in front of the United Nations University on Aoyama-dōri. There are always at least half a dozen food trucks here and the market is as much a social event as a shopping stop.

Events pop up, too, including the monthly hipster flea market Raw Tokyo (p54), the annual **Tokyo Coffee Festival** (https://tokyocoffeefestival.co/coffee) and the twice-annual **Aoyama Sake Flea** (www.facebook.com/sakeflea). Check the website for info on these and other events.

HARAJUKU GYŌZA-RŌ DUMPLINGS ¥

Map p276 (原宿餃子楼; 6-4-2 Jingūmae, Shibuya-ku; 6 gyōza ¥290; ⏲11.30am-4.30am Mon-Sat, to 10pm Sun; 🚭📋; 🚉JR Yamanote line to Harajuku, Omote-sandō exit) *Gyōza* (dumplings) are the only thing on the menu here, but you won't hear any complaints from the regulars who queue up to get their fix. Have them *sui* (boiled) or *yaki* (pan-fried), with or without *niniku* (garlic) or *nira* (chives) – they're all delicious. Expect to wait on weekends or at lunchtime, but the line moves quickly.

AGARU SAGARU NISHI-IRU HIGASHI-IRU JAPANESE ¥¥

Map p276 (上下西東; ☎03-3403-6968; basement fl, 3-25-8 Jingūmae, Shibuya-ku; small plates ¥500-900, dinner course ¥3500-5000; ⏲5.30-11.30pm Tue-Sun; 🚉JR Yamanote line to Harajuku, Takeshita exit) This chill little restaurant serves Kyoto-style food (deceptively simple, with the ingredients – always seasonal – taking centre stage) without pretense. The five-dish course (¥3500) – presented in succession and prettily plated – is perfect for when you want to indulge, but not too much. (The seven-dish course requires advance reservations.) Also, it looks like a cave.

MOMINOKI HOUSE JAPANESE ¥¥

Map p276 (もみの木ハウス; www.mominokihouse.net; 2-18-5 Jingūmae, Shibuya-ku; lunch course ¥980-1480, dinner course ¥4500; ⏲11am-3pm & 5-10pm Mon-Sat, to 9pm Sun;

1. Tokyu Plaza (p113)
Nakamura Hiroshi's castle-like mall.

2. Meiji-jingū (p107)
Tokyo's grandest Shintō shrine.

3. Takeshita-dōri (p108)
Famous fashion bazaar selling all sorts of clothing styles.

4. Yoyogi-kōen (p108)
This park attracts revellers and noisemakers of all stripes,

⊜ ✈ 📵 ; 🚇 JR Yamanote line to Harajuku, Takeshita exit) ✐ This pioneering macrobiotic restaurant has been running since 1976, long enough to see many a Harajuku trend come and go (and to see some famous visitors, like Sir Paul McCartney). Chef Yamada's menu is heavily vegan, but also includes free-range chicken and *Ezo shika* (Hokkaidō venison). Inside, the restaurant looks like a grown-up tree fort and features several cosy, semi-private booths.

★EATRIP
BISTRO ¥¥¥

Map p276 (🕿03-3409-4002; www.restauranteatrip.com; 6-31-10 Jingūmae, Shibuya-ku; course ¥5400-8640; ⊗6pm-midnight Tue-Sat, 11.30am-3pm Sat, 11.30am-5pm Sun; ⊜📵; 🚇JR Yamanote line to Harajuku, Omote-sandō exit) ✐ Eatrip is one of the big players in Tokyo's farm-to-table organic movement. Working with domestic food producers, it serves up neo-bistro-style dishes that reflect head chef Shiraishi Takayuki's global travels. Sample dish: *mahata* (grouper; from Mie Prefecture) sautéed with harissa (made in-house), squid ink and *daikon* (radish). Course menu only; reserve ahead.

When you find it (it's a little tricky; it's a house entered via a stone path), you'll be surprised that such a peaceful spot exists in Harajuku.

✖ Aoyama & Gaienmae

★MAISEN
TONKATSU ¥

Map p276 (まい泉; 🕿0120-428-485; www.maisen .com; 4-8-5 Jingūmae, Shibuya-ku; lunch/dinner from ¥990/1580; ⊗11am-10.45pm; ⊜📵🈂; 🚇Ginza line to Omote-sandō, exit A2) Maison is famous for its *tonkatsu* (breaded, deep-fried pork cutlets) and its setting (an old public bathhouse). There are different grades of pork on the menu, including prized *kurobuta* (black pig), but even the cheapest is melt-in-your-mouth divine; the very reasonable lunch set is served until 4pm.

A takeaway window (10am to 7pm) serves delicious *tonkatsu sando* (sandwich).

AOYAMA KAWAKAMI-AN
SOBA ¥

Map p276 (青山川上庵; 🕿03-5411-7171; 3-14-1 Minami-Aoyama, Minato-ku; soba ¥920-1750; ⊗11.30am-4am; ⊜📵; 🚇Ginza line to Omote-sandō, exit A5) This Aoyama outpost of famed Karuizawa soba shop serves handmade, 100% buckwheat noodles all day and (nearly) all night. Go for broke with the (truly) jumbo tempura prawns or add on sides of

Nagano specialities like *kurakake mame* (a kind of soy bean) and pickles made of *nozawana* (a kind of mustard leaf).

COMMUNE 2ND
MARKET ¥

Map p276 (www.commune2nd.com; 3-13 Minami-Aoyama, Minato-ku; meals ¥1000-1500; ⊗11am-10pm; ⊜📵; 🚇Ginza line to Omote-sandō, exit A4) Commune 2nd is a collection of vendors offering inexpensive curries, hot dogs, beer and more. Purchase what you want from any of the stalls, then grab a seat at one of the shared picnic tables; this is one of Tokyo's rare alfresco dining spots. It's very popular, on a warm Friday or Saturday night.

YANMO
SEAFOOD ¥¥¥

Map p276 (やんも; 🕿03-5466-0636; www.yanmo.co.jp/aoyama/index.html; basement fl, T Place Bldg, 5-5-25 Minami-Aoyama, Minato-ku; lunch/dinner set menu from ¥1200/7560; ⊗11.30am-2pm & 5.30-10.30pm Mon-Sat; ⊜; 🚇Ginza line to Omote-sandō, exit A5) Freshly caught seafood from the nearby Izu Peninsula is the speciality at this upscale, yet unpretentious, restaurant. The dinner courses, which include fish served as sashimi, steamed and grilled, are reasonably priced for what you get; reservations essential. The weekday grilled fish lunch set (¥1200 to ¥1500; chosen from one of several seasonal options) is a bargain; there's usually a queue.

🍷 DRINKING & NIGHTLIFE

★SAKURAI
JAPANESE TEA EXPERIENCE
TEAHOUSE

Map p276 (櫻井焙茶研究所; 🕿03-6451-1539; www.sakurai-tea.jp; 5th fl, Spiral Bldg, 5-6-23 Minami-Aoyama, Minato-ku; tea from ¥1400, course from ¥4800; ⊗11am-11pm; ⊜📵; 🚇Ginza line to Omote-sandō, exit B1) Tea master (and former bartender) Sakurai Shinya's contemporary take on the tea ceremony is a must for anyone hoping to be better acquainted with Japan's signature brew. The course includes several varieties – you might be surprised how different tea can taste – paired with small bites, including some beautiful traditional sweets. Come in the evening for tea cocktails. Reservations recommended.

AOYAMA
FLOWER MARKET TEAHOUSE
TEAHOUSE

Map p276 (🕿03-3400-0887; www.afm-teahouse. com; 5-1-2 Minami-Aoyama, Minato-ku; ⊗11am-8pm Mon-Sat, to 7pm Sun; ⊜📵; 🚇Ginza line to

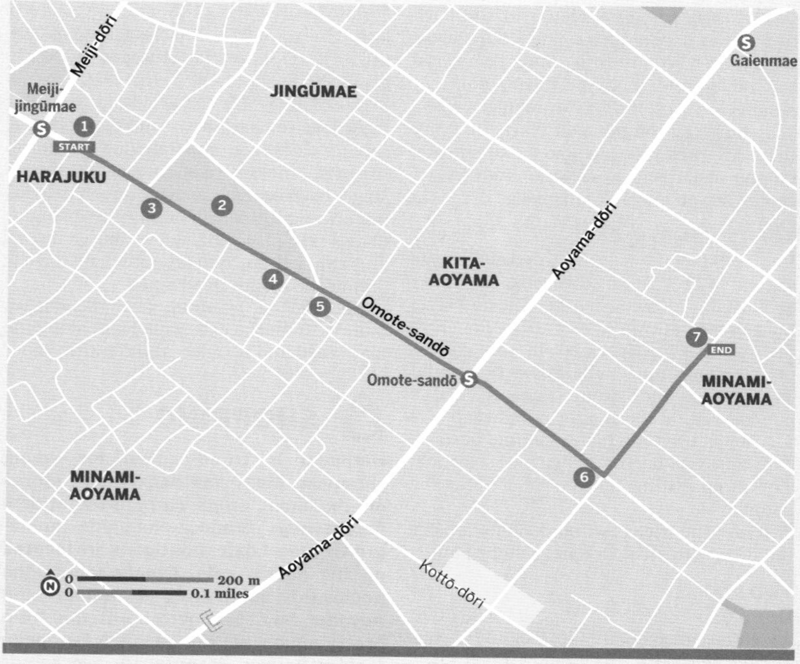

Neighbourhood Walk
Omote-sandō Architecture

START TOKYU PLAZA
END SUNNYHILLS
LENGTH 1.2KM; ONE HOUR

Start at the intersection of Omote-sandō and Meiji-dōri, at 1 **Tokyu Plaza**, a castle-like structure built in 2012 and designed by up-and-coming architect Nakamura Hiroshi. The entrance is a dizzying hall of mirrors and there's a roof garden (with a Starbucks) on top.

Continue to Tadao Ando's deceptively deep 2 **Omotesandō Hills** (2003). This high-end shopping mall spirals around a sunken central atrium. Andō's architecture uses materials such as concrete to create strong geometric shapes, often drawn from Japan's traditional architecture.

Across the street, the five-storey glass 3 **Dior building** (2003), designed by SANAA (Nishizawa Ryue and Sejima Kazuyo), has a filmy surface that seems to hang like a dress (an effect achieved with clever lighting and acrylic screens).

A couple of blocks down, Aoki Jun's 4 **Louis Vuitton building** (2002) has offset panels of tinted glass behind sheets of metal mesh that are meant to evoke a stack of trunks. There's an art gallery on the 7th floor.

Climb onto the elevated crosswalk to admire Itō Toyō's construction for 5 **Tod's** (2004). The criss-crossing strips of concrete take their inspiration from the zelkova trees below; they're also structural.

You can't miss the 6 **Prada Aoyama building** (2003) with its curvaceous exterior of convex glass bubbles. Created by Herzog & de Meuron, this is the building that escalated the design race in the neighbourhood.

Turn the corner to see Kengo Kuma's design for Taiwanese pineapple cake shop 7 **SunnyHills** (2014). Architect Kuma is known for using wood and traditional Japanese joinery techniques, and this building shows his work at its most playful. The latticework evokes a bamboo basket, but also resembles a cross-hatched pineapple.

Omote-sandō, exit A5) Secreted in the back of a flower shop is this fairy-tale teahouse with flower beds running under the glass-top tables and more overhead, plus cut blooms in vases on every available surface. Tea comes by the pot and starts at ¥750; there are pretty sweets and salad spreads on the menu too. Reservations aren't accepted so you may have to queue.

KOFFEE MAMEYA
COFFEE

Map p276 (コーヒーマメヤ; www.koffee-mameya.com; 4-15-3 Jingūmae, Shibuya-ku; coffee ¥350-1100; ⊙10am-6pm; 🚻; 🚇Ginza line to Omote-sandō, exit A2) At any given time, Koffee Mameya has 15 to 20 different beans on rotation from indie roasters around Japan (and some from overseas). Get a cup brewed on the spot or purchase beans for home use; English-speaking baristas can help you narrow down the selection. There's no seating, but you can loiter at the counter.

It's a little tricky to find; look for a beige building with an alcove and a stone path.

TWO ROOMS
BAR

Map p276 (トゥールームス; ☎03-3498-0002; www.tworooms.jp; 5th fl, AO Bldg, 3-11-7 Kita-Aoyama, Minato-ku; ⊙11.30am-2am Mon-Sat, to 10pm Sun; 🚻; 🚇Ginza line to Omote-sandō, exit B2) Expect a crowd dressed like they don't care that wine by the glass starts at ¥1600. You can eat here too, but the real scene is at night by the bar. The terrace has sweeping views towards the Shinjuku skyline. Call ahead (staff speak English) on Friday or Saturday night to reserve a spot under the stars.

☆ ENTERTAINMENT

JINGŪ BASEBALL STADIUM
BASEBALL

Map p276 (神宮球場, Jingū Kyūjō; ☎0180-993-589; www.jingu-stadium.com; 3-1 Kasumigaoka-machi, Shinjuku-ku; tickets ¥2200-5000; 🚇Ginza line to Gaienmae, exit 3) Jingū Baseball Stadium, built in 1926, is home to the Yakult Swallows, Tokyo's number-two team (but number-one when it comes to fan loyalty). Most games start at 6pm. Get tickets from the booth next to Gate 9, which is open from 11am to 5pm (or until 20 minutes after the game ends).

Same-day outfield tickets cost just ¥1800 (¥500 for children) and are usually available – unless the Swallows are playing cross-town rivals, the Yomiuri Giants.

NATIONAL NŌ THEATRE
THEATRE

Map p276 (国立能楽堂, Kokuritsu Nō-gakudō; ☎03-3423-1331; www.ntj.jac.go.jp; 4-18-1 Sendagaya, Shibuya-ku; adult ¥2700-4900, student ¥1900-2200; 🚉JR Sōbu line to Sendagaya) The traditional music, poetry and dances of nō, Japan's oldest continued mode of performing arts, unfold here on an elegant cypress stage. Each seat has a small screen displaying an English translation of the dialogue. Shows take place only a few times a month and can sell out quickly; purchase tickets online one month in advance.

The theatre is 400m from Sendagaya Station; from the exit, walk right along the main road and turn left at the traffic light.

🛍 SHOPPING

Harajuku is trend-central for young shoppers. Malls and department stores on the main drags carry international fast-fashion brands alongside home-grown ones. Edgier boutiques are located on the backstreets. Omote-sandō, the boulevard connecting Harajuku and Aoyama, has statement boutiques from pretty much all the famous European fashion houses. Many of the big names in Japanese fashion, such as Issey Miyake, Comme des Garçons and Yohji Yamamoto, have their flagship boutiques in Aoyama.

★HOUSE
@MIKIRI HASSIN
FASHION & ACCESSORIES

Map p276 (ハウス@ミキリハッシン; ☎03-3486-7673; http://house.mikirihassin.co.jp; 5-42-1 Jingūmae, Shibuya-ku; ⊙noon-9pm Thu-Tue; 🚇Ginza line to Omote-sandō, exit A1) Hidden deep in Ura-Hara (Harajuku's backstreet area), House stocks an ever-changing selection of experimental Japanese fashion brands. Contrary to what the cool merch might suggest, the sales clerks are polite and friendly – grateful, perhaps, that you made the effort to find the place. Look for 'ハウス' spelled vertically in neon.

★ARTS & SCIENCE
FASHION & ACCESSORIES

Map p276 (www.arts-science.com; 103, 105 & 109 Palace Aoyama, 6-1-6 Minami-Aoyama, Minato-ku; ⊙noon-8pm; 🚇Ginza line to Omote-sandō, exit A5) Strung along the 1st floor of a mid-century apartment (across from the Nezu Museum) is a collection of small boutiques from celebrity stylist Sonya Park. Park's signature style is a vintage-inspired minimalism in luxurious, natural fabrics. There are homewares, too.

SOU-SOU FASHION & ACCESSORIES

Map p276 (そうそう; ☎03-3407-7877; http://sou-sounetshop.jp; 5-3-10 Minami-Aoyama, Minato-ku; 🕐11am-8pm; [S]Ginza line to Omote-sandō, exit A5) Kyoto brand Sou-Sou is best known for producing the steel-toed, rubber-soled *tabi* shoes worn by Japanese construction workers in fun, playful designs – but it also has clothing and accessories that riff on traditional styles (including some really adorable stuff for kids).

PASS THE BATON VINTAGE

Map p276 (パスザバトン; ☎03-6447-0707; www.pass-the-baton.com; 4-12-10 Jingūmae, Shibuya-ku; 🕐11am-9pm Mon-Sat, to 8pm Sun; [S]Ginza line to Omote-sandō, exit A3) There are all sorts of treasures to be found at this consignment shop, from 1970s designer duds to delicate teacups, personal castaways to dead stock from long-defunct retailers. It's in the basement of Omotesandō Hills, but you'll need to enter from a separate street entrance on Omote-sandō.

MUSUBI ARTS & CRAFTS

Map p276 (むす美; ☎03-5414-5678; http://kyoto-musubi.com; 2-31-8 Jingūmae, Shibuya-ku; 🕐11am-7pm Thu-Tue; [R]JR Yamanote line to Harajuku, Takeshita exit) *Furoshiki* are versatile squares of cloth that can be folded and knotted to make shopping bags and gift wrap. This shop sells pretty ones in both traditional and contemporary patterns – sometimes in collaboration with fashion brands. There is usually an English-speaking clerk who can show you some different ways to tie them.

COMME DES GARÇONS FASHION & ACCESSORIES

Map p276 (コム・デ・ギャルソン; www.comme-des-garcons.com; 5-2-1 Minami-Aoyama, Minato-ku; 🕐11am-8pm; [S]Ginza line to Omote-sandō, exit A5) Designer Kawakubo Rei threw a wrench in the fashion machine in the early '80s with her dark, asymmetrical designs. That her work doesn't appear as shocking today as it once did speaks volumes about her far-reaching success. This eccentric, vaguely disorienting architectural creation is her brand's flagship store.

KIDDYLAND TOYS

Map p276 (キデイランド; ☎03-3409-3431; www.kiddyland.co.jp; 6-1-9 Jingūmae, Shibuya-ku; 🕐11am-9pm Mon-Fri, 10.30am-9pm Sat & Sun; [R]JR Yamanote line to Harajuku, Omote-sandō exit) This multistorey toy emporium is packed to the rafters with character goods, including all your Studio Ghibli, Sanrio and Disney faves. It's not just for kids either; you'll spot plenty of adults on a nostalgia trip down the Hello Kitty aisle.

LAFORET DEPARTMENT STORE

Map p276 (ラフォーレ; www.laforet.ne.jp; 1-11-6 Jingūmae, Shibuya-ku; 🕐11am-9pm; [R]JR Yamanote line to Harajuku, Omote-sandō exit) Laforet has been a beacon of Harajuku fashion for decades, where young brands cut their teeth and established ones hold court. Check out the avant-garde looks at ground-floor boutiques **Wall** and **Hoyajuku**.

More mainstream boutiques are on the upper floors.

SPORTS & ACTIVITIES

OHARA SCHOOL OF IKEBANA IKEBANA

Map p276 (小原流いけばな; ☎03-5774-5097; www.ohararyu.or.jp; 5-7-17 Minami-Aoyama, Minato-ku; classes ¥4000; [S]Ginza line to Omote-sandō, exit B1) This well-regarded, modern ikebana school teaches 90-minute introductory flower-arrangement classes in English every Thursday at 10am and 1pm, and at 10.30am on the first and third Sunday of the month. Sign up online by 3pm the Tuesday before (the earlier the better, as spaces are limited).

SHIMIZU-YU SENTO

Map p276 (清水湯; ☎03-3401-4404; http://shimizuyu.jp; 3-12-3 Minami-Aoyama, Minato-ku; with/without sauna ¥1000/460; 🕐noon-midnight Mon-Thu, to 11pm Sat & Sun; [R]Ginza line to Omote-sandō, exit A4) Shimizu-yu is a hip, modern *sentō* (public bath), just as likely to be filled with young shoppers – perhaps transitioning to a night out – as local grandmas. You can rent a towel (¥300) and buy soap and shampoo (¥40 to ¥50) at the counter. No tattoos.

West Tokyo

NAKANO & KŌENJI | KICHIJŌJI & MITAKA | OGIKUBO | KICHIJŌJI

Neighbourhood Top Five

1 **Ghibli Museum, Mitaka** (p118) Delighting in the creativity of Japan's legendary animator, Miyazaki Hayao, and savouring the magic and wonder of his films in the museum he designed.

2 **Inokashira-kōen** (p119) Strolling through the woodsy grounds of one of Tokyo's best parks and paying your respects to the sea goddess enshrined here.

3 **Nakano Broadway** (p119) Wandering the halls of this vintage 1960s shopping mall, a collectors' paradise and a favourite destination for *otaku* (fans of anime and manga).

4 **Kōenji** (p121) Checking out the street art, creative looks and indie music venues at this hot spot for Tokyo counterculture.

5 **Reversible Destiny Lofts** (p119) Experiencing the topsy-turvy tactile world of one of Tokyo's more eccentric contemporary buildings.

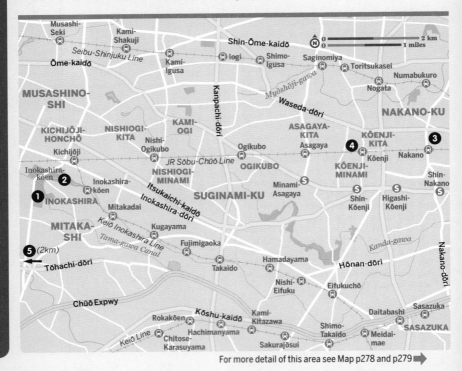

For more detail of this area see Map p278 and p279

Explore West Tokyo

What makes this part of Tokyo so fascinating is that each of the neighbourhoods along the Chūō train line has, somehow, organically developed its own particular culture. Nakano is popular with *otaku*, for example; while Kōenji, just one stop away, attracts street artists and social activists. As these are largely residential districts, there are few must-sees; rather, exploring this area west of Shinjuku is about getting a feel for Tokyoites' Tokyo.

Of course the one big attraction out here is the enchanting Ghibli Museum, Mitaka (p118). If you go, your day will be ruled by the time of your reservation. We recommend booking at 10am or 2pm so that your visit can coincide with a leisurely stroll through Inokashira-kōen (p119) and lunch in Kichijōji, either before or after. Kichijōji is a laid-back residential hub, full of fashionable boutiques and cafes, that's often voted the best place to live in Tokyo by locals.

Given that these are residential neighbourhoods it would be tempting to write them off as sleepy, but they're anything but. Each has its own *nomiyagai* (eating and drinking strips) that draw locals in the evenings. Of all the Chūō train line districts, Kōenji has the most going on after dark, with lots of shops that stay open late, restaurants, bars and live-music venues.

Local Life

➡ **Hang-outs** On weekends, performance artists and buskers gather in Kichijōji's Inokashira-kōen (p119), one of the few places the city permits them.

➡ **Eating & Drinking** Kōenji Gādo-shita (p120) and Nishi-Ogikubo's Yanagi-kōji (p120) are two popular *nomiyagai* (eating and drinking strips), for which Chūō line neighbourhoods are famous.

➡ **Music** Kōenji is the locus of Tokyo's underground scene, with several venues for punk, noise and anything goes, such as UFO Club (p122).

Getting There & Away

➡ **Train** The JR Sōbu (local) and Chūō (rapid) lines run on the same tracks (abbreviated as the Chūō-Sōbu line), heading west from Shinjuku to Nakano, Kōenji, Asagaya, Ogikubo, Nishi-Ogikubo Kichijōji and Mitaka (in that order); only Kōenji is a local-train-only stop. Beware of the 'special' rapid and 'Ome liner' trains, which go nonstop from Shinjuku to Mitaka. The Keiō Inokashira line runs from Shibuya to Kichijōji, stopping at Inokashira-kōen-mae (for the park).

➡ **Subway** The Marunouchi line runs from Shinjuku to Ogikubo, south of the Sōbu-Chūō line.

Lonely Planet's Top Tip

The JR Chūō line is only the second-most crowded line in the city, but that still means it runs at nearly 200% capacity during rush hour. Odds are you'll be going in the opposite direction, which won't be nearly as bad: heading out west in the morning when the commuters are going east towards Shinjuku, and vice versa in the evening. The local Sōbu line, which runs on the same tracks but makes more stops, is always less crowded.

 ### Best Places to Eat

➡ Tensuke (p120)
➡ Harukiya (p120)
➡ Steak House Satou (p121)

For reviews, see p119.

 ### Best Places to Drink

➡ Cocktail Shobō (p121)
➡ Sub Store (p121)
➡ Daikaijū Salon (p121)

For reviews, see p121.

Best Places to Shop

➡ Mandarake Complex (p122)
➡ Outbound (p122)
➡ Sokkyō (p122)
➡ PukuPuku (p124)

For reviews, see p122.

TOP EXPERIENCE
ENTER THE WORLD OF GHIBLI MUSEUM, MITAKA

Master animator Miyazaki Hayao and his Studio Ghibli (pronounced 'jiburi') have been responsible for some of the best-loved films in Japan – and the world. Miyazaki designed the museum himself, and it's redolent of the dreamy, vaguely steampunk atmosphere that makes his animations so enchanting.

At the Ghibli Museum, Mitaka, fans will enjoy the original sketches; kids, even if they're not familiar with the movies, will fall in love with the fairy-tale atmosphere (and the big cat bus). Don't miss the original 20-minute animated short playing on the 1st floor. This is a museum that rewards curiosity and exploration: peer through a small window, for example, and you'll see little soot sprites (as seen in *Spirited Away*; 2001); a spiral staircase leads to a purposefully overgrown rooftop terrace with a 5m-tall statue of the Robot Soldier from Laputa (*Castle in the Sky*; 1986).

Tickets must be purchased in advance, and you must choose the exact time and date you plan to visit. They can be purchased up to four months in advance from overseas travel agents or up to one month in advance through the convenience store Lawson's online ticket portal. Both options are explained in detail on the museum's website: http://www.ghibli-museum.jp/en/tickets. For July and August visits especially, we recommend buying tickets as soon as you can from an agent as they will definitely sell out early. Tickets are non-transferable; you may be asked to show an ID.

A minibus (round trip/one way ¥320/210) leaves for the museum every 20 minutes from Mitaka Station (bus stop 9). The museum is on the western edge of Inokashira-kōen and you can walk there through the park (from Kichijōji Station) in about 30 minutes.

DID YOU KNOW?

Spirited Away (2001) won the Academy Award for Best Animated Feature – the only Japanese animated film and only hand-drawn film ever to win.

PRACTICALITIES

➡ ジブリ美術館

➡ Map p279, A4

➡ www.ghibli-museum.jp

➡ 1-1-83 Shimo-Renjaku, Mitaka-shi

➡ adult ¥1000, child ¥100-700

➡ ⏰10am-6pm Wed-Mon

➡ 🚃JR Chūō-Sōbu line to Mitaka, south exit

👁 SIGHTS

👁 Nakano & Kōenji

NAKANO BROADWAY   NOTABLE BUILDING
Map p278 (中野ブロードウェイ; www.nbw.jp;
5-25-15 Nakano, Nakano-ku; ⊙varies by shop;
☎; ᴿJR Chūō-Sōbu line to Nakano, north exit)
This vintage 1960s shopping mall earned
Nakano its reputation as an underground
Akihabara: it is home to the original Mandarake Complex (p122), the famous manga
and anime goods shop, plus lots more stores
that sell collectables of all sorts (from zines
and vintage toys to antique watches and
army surplus).

At the south entrance look for the small
kiosk that has the regularly updated *Nakano Broadway Guidebook,* which lists all
the shops.

👁 Kichijōji & Mitaka

★INOKASHIRA-KŌEN   PARK
Map p279 (井の頭公園; www.kensetsu.metro.
tokyo.jp/seibuk/inokashira/index.html;   1-18-31
Gotenyama, Musashino-shi; ᴿJR Chūō-Sōbu line
to Kichijōji, Kōen exit) One of Tokyo's best parks,
Inokashira-kōen has a big pond in the middle flanked by woodsy strolling paths. You
can rent row boats (¥700 per hour) and
swan-shaped pedal boats to take out onto
the water (¥700 per 30 minutes). On weekends look for musicians, puppeteers and other assorted performance artists around the
park, as well as lots of Tokyoites of all ages.
And don't miss the ancient Inokashira Benzaiten shrine to the sea goddess Benzaiten.

HARMONICA-YOKOCHŌ   MARKET
Map p279 (ハーモニカ横丁; http://hamoyoko.
com; 1-2 Kichijōji-Honchō, Musashino-shi; ᴿJR
Chūō-Sōbu line to Kichijōji, north exit) This covered market, with its low ceilings and lots
of *aka-chōchin* (red lanterns), started life
as a black market in the post-war days.
Some of the vendors – the fishmongers, for
example – have been around for decades,
but there are several more contemporary
boutiques, restaurants and bars here, too.

REVERSIBLE DESTINY LOFTS   ARCHITECTURE
(天命反転住宅; Tenmei Hanten Jūtaku; ☎0422-
26-4966; www.rdloftsmitaka.com; 2-2-8 Ōsawa,

Mitaka-shi; adult/child ¥2700/1000; 👜; ᴿJR
Chūō-Sōbu line to Mitaka, south exit) Designed
by husband and wife Arakawa Shūsaku and
Madeleine Gins and completed in 2005,
this housing complex certainly strikes
against the mould: created 'in memory of
Helen Keller' the nine units have undulating, ridged floors, spherical dens and ceiling hooks for hammocks and swings. All
this is meant to create a sensory experience
beyond the visual (though the building is
plenty colourful). To see the inside, join one
of the monthly public tours.

The tours are in Japanese, but can be
enjoyed without understanding the explanations; tours with English-speaking trans-
lators can also be arranged. Some units are
occupied by residents, but others are available for short-term stays (p192).

From JR Mitaka Station, take bus 51 or
52 (¥220, 15 minutes, every 10 to 15 minutes) from bus stop 2 on the station's south
side and get off at Ōsawa Jūjiro (大沢十字
路); you can see the building from the bus
stop. Not all buses go this far, so show the
driver where you want to go. Bus 1 (¥220, 25
minutes, every 10 to 15 minutes) goes here
from Kichijōji Station (south exit, bus stop
3), alongside Inokashira-kōen.

INOKASHIRA BENZAITEN   SHINTO SHRINE
Map p279 (井の頭弁財天; Inokashira-kōen,
Musashino-shi; ⊙7am-4.30pm; ᴿJR Chūō-Sōbu
line to Kichijōji, Kōen exit) ᴳᴿᴱᴱ Benzaiten, one
of Japan's eight lucky gods, is actually the
octet's sole goddess; she's also the Japanese incarnation of the Hindi goddess Sar-
asvati and a patron of the arts. Her realm
is the waters, which is why you'll find this
shrine – said to have been founded in 1197
– on an island in Inokashira-kōen's central
pond.

🍴 EATING

**As these neighbourhoods don't see as
many travellers as more central ones,
fewer restaurants have English menus.
Suginami ward (which includes Kōenji,
Ogikubo and Nishi-Ogikubo) is campaigning to make its eating and drinking
scene more accessible: look for discreet
'English menu' stickers on some bars and
restaurants, which are also listed online
at http://experience-suginami.tokyo.**

WORTH A DETOUR

EDO-TOKYO OPEN AIR ARCHITECTURE MUSEUM

The fantastic yet overlooked **Edo-Tokyo Open Air Architecture Museum** (江戸東京たてもの園; www.tatemonoen.jp/english; 3-7-1 Sakura-chō, Koganei-shi; adult/child ¥400/free; ⏲9.30am-5.30pm Tue-Sun Apr-Sep, to 4.30pm Oct-Mar; 🚻; 🚉JR Chūō line to Musashi-Koganei) is a preserve for historic buildings rescued from around Tokyo during the city's decades-long construction jag. Among them are an Edo-era farmhouse, a modernist villa and a whole strip of early-20th-century shops, all of which you can enter.

The museum is inside Koganei-kōen, Tokyo's second-largest park. From the north exit of Musashi-Koganei Station (four stops past Kichijōji on the JR Chūō line), take a bus from stop 2 or 3 for Koganei-kōen Nishi-guchi, from where it's a five-minute walk to the museum through the park. There are more detailed directions on the website.

✘ Nakano & Kōenji

KŌENJI GĀDO-SHITA   STREET FOOD ¥
Map p278 (高円寺ガード下; Kōenji, Suginami-ku; ⏲5pm-late; 🚉JR Sōbu line to Kōenji, north exit) This is Kōenji's signature *nomiyagai* (eating and drinking strip), a collection of shabby (and cheap!) stalls selling *yakitori* (chicken, and other meats or vegetables, grilled on skewers), spruced-up wine bars and more seating underneath the overhead JR tracks. Since most places are super-tiny, and the rail lines provide cover, there is often seating set outside, on folding tables or overturned beer carts.

DAILY CHIKO   ICE CREAM ¥
Map p278 (デイリーチコ; basement fl, Nakano Broadway, Nakano-ku; cone from ¥280; ⏲10am-8pm; 🚉JR Chūō-Sōbu line to Nakano, north exit) A Nakano legend and one of Nakano Broadway's few original shops, this ice-cream counter features eight rotating flavours of soft-serve – and you can get them all in one towering cone (¥550). Or just two or three, if you believe in moderation.

★TENSUKE   TEMPURA ¥¥
Map p278 (天すけ; ☎03-3223-8505; 3-22-7 Kōenji-kita, Suginami-ku; lunch from ¥1000, dinner ¥1350-4600; ⏲noon-2pm & 6-10pm Tue-Sun; ☺; 🚉JR Sōbu line to Kōenji, north exit) A legitimate candidate for eighth wonder of the modern world is Tensuke's *tamago* (egg) tempura, which comes out batter-crisp on the outside and runny in the middle. It's served on rice with seafood and vegetable tempura as part of the *tamago tempura teishoku* (玉子天ぷら定食; ¥1600) or *tamago ranchi* (玉子ランチ; ¥1300; lunchtime only). There's a blue-and-orange sign out front.

Reservations not accepted; expect to queue.

✘ Ogikubo

HARUKIYA   RAMEN ¥
(春木屋; www.haruki-ya.co.jp; 1-4-6 Kami-Ogi, Suginami-ku; ramen ¥850-1350; ⏲11am-9pm Wed-Mon; ☺🚭; 🚉JR Chūō-Sōbu line to Ogikubo, north exit) Harukiya, open since 1949, is one of Tokyo's oldest existent ramen shops. It serves what has since come to be known as classic Tokyo-style ramen: with stock made of chicken and fish, seasoned with soy sauce, and with crinkly, doughy noodles.

YANAGI-KŌJI   STREET FOOD ¥¥
(柳小路; Nishi-Ogikubo, Suginami-ku; ⏲5pm-late; 🚉JR Chūō-Sōbu line to Nishi-Ogikubo, south exit) Yanagi-kōji is a classic *nomiyagai* (eating and drinking strip) and this one is particularly beloved for its nostalgic (read: crumbling) atmosphere. It's a narrow alley with tiny wooden buildings and outdoor seating under plastic tarps. Take your pick from a variety of options; expect food and drinks to cost about ¥3000 per person.

English menus are scant here, but you can always go with landmark Thai restaurant **Handsome Shokudō** (ハンサム食堂; ☎03-3335-5468; 3-11-5 Nishiogi-Minami, Suginami-ku; mains ¥600-1200; ⏲6pm-midnight Tue-Fri, from 5pm Sat & Sun, closed 1st & 3rd Tue; 🚭; 🚉JR Chūō-Sōbu line to Nishi-Ogikubo, south exit), located midway down the alley.

✘ Kichijōji

TETCHAN   YAKITORI ¥
Map p279 (てっちゃん; ☎0422-20-6811; 1-1-2 Kichijōji-Honchō, Musashino-shi; skewers & small dishes ¥130-480; ⏲3pm-midnight Mon-Sat, from noon Sat & Sun; 🚭; 🚉JR Chūō-Sōbu line to Kichijōji, north exit) Located inside labyrin-

thine market Harmonica-yokochō (p121), Tetchan has been drawing locals for years. But it's now become a bit of a tourist destination too, thanks to its interior of acrylic 'ice', designed by architect Kengo Kuma. There are chicken skewers and veggie ones, too. One-drink minimum order (from ¥330).

STEAK HOUSE SATOU
STEAK ¥¥

Map p279 (ステーキハウス　さとう; ☎0422-21-6464; www.shop-satou.com; 1-1-8 Kichijōji Honchō, Mitaka-shi; lunch set ¥1800-10,000; dinner set ¥2600-10,000; ⊙11am-2.30pm & 5-8pm Mon-Fri, 11am-2.30pm & 4.30-8.30pm Sat & Sun; ⊝▣; ▣JR Chūō-Sōbu line to Kichijōji, north exit) This is a classic Japanese-style steak house, where the meat is cooked at the counter on a *teppan* (iron hot plate), diced, then paired with rice, miso soup and pickles. The beef is high-grade *wagyū* (beef from Japanese black cattle), and priced very reasonably. We recommend ordering the chef's choice (lunch/dinner ¥4000/7000).

DRINKING & NIGHTLIFE

SUB STORE
BAR

Map p278 (☎080-3496-3883; https://substore. jimdo.com; 3-1-12 Kita-Kōenji, Suginami-ku; ⊙3pm-midnight Thu-Mon, 5pm-midnight Wed; ▣; ▣JR Sōbu line to Kōenji, north exit) Sub Store is many things: used-vinyl store, sometime art gallery, Indonesian restaurant (the original Sub Store is in Jakarta) and, most weekends, an indie live-music venue. It's always a great place to pop in for a beer (from ¥600).

DAIKAIJŪ SALON
BAR

Map p278 (大怪獣サロン; http://daikaijyu-salon. com; 1-14-16 Arai, Nakano-ku; ⊙3-11pm; ▣; ▣JR Chūō-Sōbu line to Nakano, north exit) *Daikaijū* are the 'large strange monsters' of Japanese popular cinema, including the likes of Godzilla and Mothra. Get intimately acquainted with them at this eccentric cafe where every surface is covered with monster models. Everything on the menu (drinks and dishes) is ¥800; before 6pm soft drinks cost ¥500. No cover charge, but you have to order one drink per hour.

NANTOKA BAR
BAR

Map p278 (なんとかバー; www.shirouto.org/ nantokabar; 3-4-12 Kōenji-kita, Suginami-ku; ⊙7pm-late; ▣JR Sōbu line to Kōenji, north exit) Part of the collective of spaces run by the Kōenji-based activist group Shirōto no Ran

KŌENJI COUNTERCULTURE

Tokyo has no real street-art culture (though it has lots of art museums, often with hefty admissions); the team behind BnA Hotel (p197) is working to change that. So far they've negotiated six street-facing spaces (shop fronts, apartment building walls, etc) in Kōenji for artists to do their thing. It's part of their new **Mural City Project** (http://mural-city.com); the locations are pinned on the website.

Meanwhile local activist collective Shirōto no Ran (Amateurs' Riot) – irreverent, anti-consumerist and a longtime presence in the community – runs Nantoka Bar (a good place to meet up with politically and socially minded locals), the hostel Manuke (p192) and a whole bunch of second-hand stores. Look for flyers for events at either of these spaces.

(Amateurs' Riot), Nantoka Bar is about as uncommercial as a place selling drinks can get: there's no cover charge, drinks are generous and cheap, and it's run on any given day by whoever feels like running it, which is sometimes no one at all.

BLUE SKY COFFEE
CAFE

Map p279 (ブルースカイコーヒー; 4-12 Inokashira, Mitaka-shi; coffee from ¥250; ⊙10-6pm Thu-Tue; ▣; ▣Keiō Inokashira line to Inokashira-kōen) This coffee counter looks like it could be the work of Studio Ghibli: a wooden cottage secreted in the woodsy fringes of Inokashira-kōen (p119) concealing a state-of-the-art coffee roaster and espresso machine. There are a few seats on the patio. Closed in the event of heavy rain.

COCKTAIL SHOBŌ
BAR

Map p278 (コクテイル書房; http://koenji -cocktail.info; 3-8-13 Kōenji-kita, Suginami-ku; ⊙11.30am-3pm Wed-Sun, 5-11pm daily; ▣; ▣JR Sōbu line to Kōenji, north exit) Cocktail Shobō is part used-book store, part cocktail bar, and 100% a labour of love in a vintage wooden house where the bar counter doubles as a bookshelf. Drinks start at just ¥400; the small plates of Japanese food (¥250 to ¥650) are good too, but unfortunately the menu is only in Japanese. During lunch hours, curry and coffee are served.

☆ **ENTERTAINMENT**

UFO CLUB
LIVE MUSIC

Map p278 (www.ufoclub.jp; basement fl, 1-11-6 Kōenji-Minami, Suginami-ku; S Marunouchi line to Higashi-Kōenji, exit 2) Named for the infamous 1960s London spot, Kōenji's UFO Club is committed to keeping the spirit of the era alive: the small basement space, with red-and-black swirling walls, feels like the inside of a lava lamp. Expect psychedelic music and acid rock from mostly local bands, but really anything goes so long as it's a bit weird.

It's on Ōme-kaidō, right before the big intersection with Kannana-dōri, with an English sign out front. Most gigs cost ¥2000 to ¥2500 with a one drink (¥500) minimum order.

PLAN B
PERFORMING ARTS

(☎03-3384-2051; http://i10x.com/planb; basement fl, 4-26-20 Yayoi-chō, Nakano-ku; ⬜63 to Fuji Kōko, S Marunouchi line to Nakano Fujimichō) Underground venue for avant-garde performances, often dance, including *butō* (a Japanese form of contemporary dance). Shows are irregular. Book tickets through the website's contact form or directly with the event organiser. Look for the entrance next to the Jonathan's restaurant.

Bus 63 runs between Shibuya Station and Nakano Station. More access details are on the website.

🛍 **SHOPPING**

Kichijōji is a popular shopping destination, with branches of major department stores, like Parco and Marui, and lifestyle shops like Loft and Muji, without the crowds of Shibuya or Shinjuku. Kōenji is famous for its high concentration of secondhand clothing stores. Nakano is known as underground Akihabara, with lots of shops selling anime and manga goods; many can be found in Nakano Broadway (p119).

★ MANDARAKE COMPLEX
ANIME, MANGA

Map p278 (まんだらけ; www.mandarake.co.jp; Nakano Broadway, 5-52-15 Nakano, Nakano-ku; ◷noon-8pm; ℝ JR Chūō-Sōbu line to Nakano, north exit) This is the original Mandarake, the go-to store for all things manga (Japanese comics) and anime (Japanese animation). Once a small, secondhand comic-book store, Mandarake now has some 25 shops just inside the Nakano Broadway shopping centre. Each specialises in something different, be it books, cel art or figurines.

PUKUPUKU
ANTIQUES

Map p279 (ぷくぷく; http://pukupukukichi. blogspot.jp; 2-26-2 Kichijōji-honchō, Musashino-shi; ◷11.30am-7.30pm; ℝ JR Chūō-Sōbu line to Kichijōji, north exit) The shelves of this small antiques shop are stacked with ceramics from the early Shōwa (昭和; 1926–89) period, through Taishō (大正; 1912–26) and Meiji (明治; 1868–1912) and all the way back to old Edo (江戸; 1603–1868) – stickers indicate the period. Pieces are fairly priced, with hundred-year-old saucers going for as little as a few hundred yen.

OUTBOUND
HOMEWARES

Map p279 (アウトバウンド; http://outbound. to; 2-7-4-101 Kichijōji-honchō, Musashino-shi; ◷11am-7pm Wed-Mon; ℝ JR Chūō-Sōbu line to Kichijōji, north exit) Outbound stocks beautiful homewares and objets d'art for your bohemian dream house. Works are earthy, made by contemporary artisans and displayed in gallery-like exhibitions.

SOKKYŌ
VINTAGE

Map p278 (即興; www.sokkyou.net; 102 Nakanishi Apt Bldg, 3-59-14 Kōenji-minami, Suginami-ku; ◷1-9pm, holidays irregular; ℝ JR Sōbu line to Kōenji, south exit) As far as vintage shops go, Sokkyō is more like a gallery of cool. The stock is impeccably edited down to a look that is both dreamy and modern. That said, we may have sent you on an impossible mission: the shop is in an ordinary timber-framed stucco house down an alley and marked only with a small 'open' sign.

HAYATOCHIRI
FASHION & ACCESSORIES

Map p278 (はやとちり; http://hayatochiri.the base.in; 3-4-11 Kōenji-kita, Suginami-ku; ◷3-9pm Mon-Wed & Fri, 1-9pm Sat & Sun; ℝ JR Sōbu line to Kōenji, north exit) Kōenji's Kita-Colle Building is a dilapidated shack of a structure housing a handful of seriously outré boutiques (Lady Gaga was an early fan), of which Hayatochiri is the most spectacularly out-there. Really, it's more art installation than shopping destination.

TACO CHÉ
BOOKS, MUSIC

Map p278 (タコシェ; http://tacoche.com; 3rd fl, Nakano Broadway, 5-52-15 Nakano, Nakano-ku; ◷noon-8pm; ℝ JR Chūō-Sōbu line to Nakano, north exit) Bolthole for indie comics, zines, books and music, often doubling as a gallery space.

Shinjuku & Northwest Tokyo

NISHI-SHINJUKU | SHINJUKU | MEJIRO | IKEBUKURO

Neighbourhood Top Five

❶ Golden Gai (p125) Finding your new favourite bar among the warren of rickety wooden buildings that make up this beloved, bohemian nightspot.

❷ Tokyo Metropolitan Government Building (p126) Seeing the metropolis extend all the way to the horizon from the (free!)

202m-high observatories atop Tokyo's city hall, also an architectural landmark.

❸ Shinjuku-gyoen (p126) Lazing or picnicking on the lawn at this beloved urban oasis, a former imperial garden, while gazing up at the surrounding skyscrapers.

❹ Godzilla Head (p126) Posing with this statue of Japanese film icon Godzilla, lording over Shinjuku, for the ultimate Tokyo selfie.

❺ Robot Restaurant (p132) Getting your mind blown at this love-it-or-loathe it, over-the-top, dazzling and overwhelming robot cabaret.

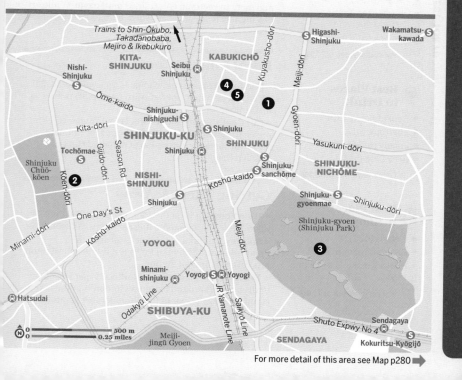

For more detail of this area see Map p280 ➡

Lonely Planet's Top Tip

Even Tokyoites get confused in Shinjuku Station. While it might seem natural to just go with the flow, your battle begins as soon as you exit the train: make sure you pick the right stairs leading to the right exit for your intended destination; otherwise you could wind up on the other side of the neighbourhood, having to circumnavigate the massive train station. The same goes for Ikebukuro, which is arguably worse: though less crowded, the signage is less consistent.

Best Places to Eat

➡ Kozue (p130)

➡ Kanae (p130)

➡ Ohitotsuzen Tanbo (p127)

➡ Donjaca (p130)

For reviews, see p127.➡

Best Places to Drink

➡ BenFiddich (p130)

➡ Zoetrope (p131)

➡ Lonely (p125)

➡ Aiiro Cafe (p131)

For reviews, see p130.➡

Best Places to Shop

➡ Isetan (p132)

➡ Beams Japan (p132)

➡ Books Kinokuniya Tokyo (p133)

For reviews, see p132.➡

Explore Shinjuku & Northwest Tokyo

Shinjuku works neatly as a day-to-night destination. Start with the skyscraper district of Nishi-Shinjuku (west of the train station), but wait until after 10am to miss the morning rush. Morning is usually the clearest time of day and thus your best chance to see Mt Fuji from the observatories atop the Tokyo Metropolitan Government Building (p126). While you're here, see the public artworks around Shinjuku I-Land (p126).

Clustered in and around Shinjuku's enormous train station are many department stores and electronics stores, which make easy work of shopping for souvenirs. On the east side of the station, grassy oasis Shinjuku-gyoen (p126) is great for a picnic (and a breather); pick up snacks in one of the department store basement food halls. There are also a few detour-worthy attractions in the neighbourhoods north of Shinjuku, including two of Tokyo's architectural highlights, St Mary's Cathedral Tokyo (p126) and Myōnichikan (p127).

Shinjuku's east side really shines at night – quite literally. Come here for dusk: as natural light gives way to arresting artificial neon, Tokyo becomes, for this magical hour, actually beautiful. There are myriad bars, *izakaya* (Japanese pub-eateries), karaoke parlours, music spots and more to keep you entertained until dawn. While Friday nights are the most crowded, Shinjuku buzzes every night of the week.

Local Life

➡ **Hang-outs** Shinjuku-nichōme is the centre of LGBT life in Tokyo; happy hour at Aiiro Cafe (p131) is an institution.

➡ **Girl Geeks** Forget Akihabara. Female *otaku* (geek) prefer Ikebukuro, home to a big branch of Animate (p133) and smaller shops along Otome Rd (literally 'Maiden Road').

Getting There & Away

➡ **Train** Shinjuku is on the JR Yamanote, Sōbu and Chūō lines. The Yamanote line also stops at Ikebukuro.

➡ **Subway** Shinjuku-sanchōme (Marunouchi, Fukutoshin and Shinjuku lines) is a useful subway stop, just east of Shinjuku Station.

➡ **Taxi** The only place you can (officially) get picked up or dropped off around Shinjuku Station is at the taxi stand on the 3rd floor of the Shinjuku Bus Terminal.

TOP EXPERIENCE
BAR-HOP THROUGH GOLDEN GAI

Golden Gai – a Shinjuku institution for over half a century – is a collection of tiny bars, often barely bigger than a closet. Each is as individual and eccentric as the 'master' or 'mama' who runs it. In a sense, Golden Gai, which has a strong visual appeal, with its low-slung wooden buildings, is their work of art. It's more than just a place to drink.

The best way to experience Golden Gai is to stroll the lanes and pick a place that suits your mood. Bars that expressly welcome tourists have English signs posted on their doors. Note that most bars have a cover charge (usually ¥500 to ¥1500), which is often posted on the door. In general, the bars here get going late, say after 9pm.

One of our favourite spots is **Lonely** (ロンリー; Map p280; 1-1-8 Kabukichō, Shinjuku-ku; ⏰6.30pm-2am Tue-Sun). 'Master' Akai-san established the bar 50 years ago because he wanted his friends to always have a place to go. Some of those friends, like the creator of classic manga *Ashita no Joe* (you'll see posters on the wall) happened to be famous. Lonely is everything you want a Golden Gai bar to be: cosy, eccentric, always fun.

Albatross G (アルバトロスG; Map p280; www.alba-s.com; 5-ban Gai, 1-1-7 Kabukichō, Shinjuku-ku; ⏰5pm-2am Sun-Thu, to 5am Fri & Sat; 🍴), which drips with chandeliers, is always a solid choice. It's also comparatively spacious, with three floors (otherwise it can be hard to squeeze into most bars with a party larger than two). Try to get the table on the 3rd floor. For a bite to eat, visit Nagi (p127).

While Golden Gai is highly photogenic, it's also private property. Do not take photos unless you have explicit permission.

DID YOU KNOW?

Golden Gai has long been a gathering spot for artists, writers and musicians. Originally, many bars here functioned more like clubhouses for various creative industries. Some bars prefer to keep their doors closed to customers who aren't regulars (foreign tourists included) to preserve that old atmosphere; others will welcome you (if there is space, of course).

PRACTICALITIES

➡ ゴールデン街

➡ Map p280, E3

➡ http://goldengai.jp

➡ 1-1 Kabukichō, Shinjuku-ku

➡ 🚉JR Yamanote line to Shinjuku, east exit

◉ SIGHTS

◉ Nishi-Shinjuku

GOLDEN GAI   AREA
See p125.

**★TOKYO METROPOLITAN
GOVERNMENT BUILDING**   OBSERVATORY
Map p280 (東京都庁, Tokyo Tochō; www.metro.
tokyo.jp/english/offices; 2-8-1 Nishi-Shinjuku,
Shinjuku-ku; ⊙observatories 9.30am-11pm;
Ⓢ Ōedo line to Tochōmae, exit A4) **FREE** Tokyo's
city hall – a landmark building designed by
Tange Kenzō – has observatories (202m)
atop both the south and north towers of
Building 1 (the views are virtually the
same). On a clear day (morning is best), you
may catch a glimpse of Mt Fuji beyond the
urban sprawl to the west; after dark, it's
illuminated buildings all the way to the
horizon. Direct-access elevators are on the
ground floor; last entry is at 10.30pm.

YAYOI KUSAMA MUSEUM   MUSEUM
(草間弥生美術館; ☑03-5273-1778; www.yayoi
kusamamuseum.jp; 07 Benten-chō, Shinjuku-ku;
adult/child ¥1000/600; ⊙11am-5.30pm Thu-
Sun; Ⓢ Tōzai line to Waseda, exit 1 or Tōei Ōedo
line to Ushigome-yanagichō, east exit) Kusama
Yayoi (b 1929) is one of Japan's most internationally famous contemporary artists,
particularly known for her obsession with
dots and pumpkins. She cut her teeth in
New York City's 1950s avant-garde scene
and remains prolific today, working from a
studio near this new museum dedicated to
her work. Kusama is in possession of most
of her works, and shows them in rotating
gallery exhibitions. Tickets for one of the
limited 90-minute viewing slots must be
purchased in advance online. They become available on the first of the month at
10am and tend to go fast.

SHINJUKU I-LAND   PUBLIC ART
Map p280 (新宿アイランド; 6-5-1 Nishi-Shinjuku,
Shinjuku-ku; Ⓢ Marunouchi line to Nishi-Shinjuku)
This otherwise ordinary office complex
is home to more than a dozen public artworks, including one of Robert Indiana's
LOVE sculptures (on the southeast corner)
and two *Tokyo Brushstroke* sculptures
by Roy Lichtenstein (at the back, towards
Ōme-kaidō). The open-air courtyard, with
stonework by Giulio Paolini and several
reasonably priced restaurants, makes an
attractive lunch or coffee stop.

◉ Shinjuku

SHINJUKU-GYOEN   PARK
Map p280 (新宿御苑; ☑03-3350-0151; www.
env.go.jp/garden/shinjukugyoen; 11 Naito-chō,
Shinjuku-ku; adult/child ¥200/50; ⊙9am-
4.30pm Tue-Sun; Ⓢ Marunouchi line to Shinjuku-
gyoenmae, exit 1) Shinjuku-gyoen was designed as an imperial retreat (completed
1906); since opening to the public in 1951,
it has become a favourite destination for
Tokyoites seeking a quick escape from the
hurly-burly of city life. The spacious manicured lawns are perfect for picnicking.
Don't miss the greenhouse; the Taiwanese-
style pavilion (Goryō-tei) that overlooks the
garden's central pond; and the cherry blossoms in spring.

GODZILLA HEAD   STATUE
Map p280 (ゴジラヘッド; Shinjuku Toho Bldg,
1-19-1 Kabukichō, Shinjuku-ku; ⊙Godzilla Terrace
6.30am-9pm; ℝJR Yamanote line to Shinjuku,
east exit) Godzilla, a portmanteau of the
Japanese words for gorilla *(gorira)* and
whale *(kujira),* is king of the *kaijū* (strange
beasts) that ruled Japanese popular cinema for decades. This giant statue of him
looking to take a bit out of a skyscraper has
become a Shinjuku landmark. Every so often he roars to life, with glowing eyes and
smoky breath.

There's an up-close view (and selfie opportunity) of the statue from the 8th-floor
'Godzilla Terrace' attached to the lobby of
the Hotel Gracery Shinjuku (p193); access
is limited to hotel guests and customers of
the hotel's cafe (though we've never been
stopped...).

HANAZONO-JINJA   SHINTO SHRINE
Map p280 (花園神社; www.hanazono-jinja.or.jp;
5-17-3 Shinjuku, Shinjuku-ku; ⊙24hr; Ⓢ Marunouchi line to Shinjuku-sanchōme, exits B10 & E2)
Merchants from nearby Kabukichō come to
this Shintō shrine to pray for the solvency
of their business ventures. Founded in the
17th century, the shrine is dedicated to the
god Inari, whose specialities include fertil-
ity and worldly success.

◉ Mejiro & Ikebukuro

ST MARY'S CATHEDRAL TOKYO   CHURCH
(東京カテドラル聖マリア大聖堂, Sekiguchi
Cathedral; http://cathedral-sekiguchi.jp; 3-16-15
Sekiguchi, Bunkyō-ku; ⊙9am-5pm; Ⓢ Yūrakuchō

line to Edogawabashi, exit 1A) **FREE** Rising nearly 40m high and glistening in the sun, this stainless-steel contemporary cathedral was completed in 1955. It's the work of Japan's foremost modern architect, Tange Kenzō, and structural and acoustic engineers from the University of Tokyo. The pipe organ was specially designed for the cathedral; free 'organ meditation' sessions are held monthly.

MYŌNICHIKAN
ARCHITECTURE

Map p280 (明日館, House of Tomorrow; ☑03-3971-7535; www.jiyu.jp; 2-31-3 Nishi-Ikebukuro, Toshima-ku; with/without coffee ¥600/400; ☑10am-4pm Tue-Sun; ☑JR Yamanote line to Ikebukuro, Metropolitan exit) Lucky are the girls who attended the Frank Lloyd Wright–designed 'School of the Free Spirit' (Jiyū Gakuen; 自由学園). Built in 1921, Myōnichikan functioned as the school's main structure until the 1970s. After restoration, it was reopened as a public space in 2001. Visitors can tour the facilities and have coffee in the light-filled hall, sitting at low tables on (mostly) original chairs.

It can be tricky to find, though there are beige and green directional signs (in Japanese) on nearby utility poles. Myōnichikan occasionally closes for private events; this info is listed on the Japanese website, but you can email in advance to check.

IKEBUKURO LIFE SAFETY LEARNING CENTER
MUSEUM

Map p280 (池袋防災館, Ikebukuro Bōsai-kan; ☑03-3590-6565; www.tfd.metro.tokyo.jp/hp-ikbskan; 2-37-8 Nishi-Ikebukuro, Tōshima-ku; ☑9am-5pm Wed-Mon, closed 3rd Wed of month; ☑JR Yamanote line to Ikebukuro, Metropolitan exit) **FREE** This public safety centre has a room that simulates a real earthquake and it's not for the faint of heart (literally): what you experience is a level seven shake, the highest on the Japanese scale and equivalent to what was felt in Sendai during the Great East Japan Earthquake.

There is a simulation session at noon (30 minutes) for foreign travellers; get there a little early and sign up at the reception desk.

✖ EATING

Shinjuku has a huge spread of eating options: it's especially good for classic izakaya. Shin-Ōkubo, Tokyo's Koreatown and one stop north on the JR Yamanote line, naturally has tonnes of Korean restaurants. For fewer crowds, head one stop south to Yoyogi.

GOCHISŌ TONJIRU
JAPANESE ¥

(ごちそうとん汁; ☑03-6883-9181; 1-33-2 Yoyogi, Shibuya-ku; meals from ¥840; ☑11.30am-midnight; ☑☑; ☑JR Yamanote line to Yoyogi, west exit) *Tonjiru*, a home-cooking classic, is a hearty miso soup packed with root veggies (such as burdock root, *daikon*/radish, potato and carrot) and chunks of pork. At this neighbourhood hang-out, styled more like a bar than a restaurant, the pork comes in the form of melting-off-the-bone barbecued spare ribs. Choose between a Kyoto-style light miso or a Tokyo-style dark miso.

OHITOTSUZEN TANBO
JAPANESE ¥

(おひつ膳田んぼ; ☑03-3320-0727; www.tanbo.co.jp; 1-41-9 Yoyogi, Shibuya-ku; meals ¥1550-2350; ☑11am-10pm; ☑☑; ☑JR Yamanote line to Yoyogi, west exit) ✐ The speciality here is the least glamorous part of the meal – the rice, which comes from an organic farm the restaurant manages in Niigata Prefecture. It's served as *ochazuke*, a classic comfort food of rice topped with meat or fish over which hot tea is poured. English instructions explain how to eat it.

BERG
CAFE ¥

Map p280 (ベルグ; www.berg.jp; basement fl, Lumine Est, 3-38-1 Shinjuku, Shinjuku-ku; morning set ¥410; ☑7am-11pm; ☑☑; ☑JR Yamanote line to Shinjuku, east exit) Wedged inside the fashion-forward Lumine Est department store (itself inside the frenetic Shinjuku Station), Berg stands still. The cramped, cult-status coffee shop still charges just ¥216 for a cup (and ¥324 for a beer). The highly recommended 'morning set' (*mōningu setto*), served until noon, includes coffee, hard-boiled egg, potato salad and toast. The front is covered in picture menus. Exiting the east exit ticket gates in JR Shinjuku Station, look for the 'Food Pocket' sign off to the left.

NAGI
RAMEN ¥

Map p280 (凪; ☑03-3205-1925; www.n-nagi.com; 2nd fl, Golden Gai G2, 1-1-10 Kabukichō, Shinjuku-ku; ramen from ¥890; ☑24hr; ☑; ☑JR Yamanote line to Shinjuku, east exit) Nagi, once an edgy upstart in the ramen world, has done well and now has branches around the city. This tiny shop, one of the originals, up a treacherous stairway in Golden Gai, is still our favourite... we're clearly not alone as there's often a line. The house speciality is *niboshi* ramen (egg

FOTOS593/SHUTTERSTOCK ©

1. Golden Gai (p125)
A collection of tiny bars, many
barely bigger than a closet.

2. Shinjuku-gyoen (p126)
Spacious manicured lawns and
cherry blossoms.

**3. Tokyo Metropolitan
Government Building
(p126)**
Tokyo's city hall, by Tange Kenzō,
has observatories on both towers.

**4. Robot Restaurant
(p132)**
A true 'wacky Japan' spectacle.

3

DEPARTMENT STORE FOOD COURTS

Should you want to grab a quick bite to eat – without having to brave the crowded streets – head to one of the food courts on the top floors of the shopping centres in and around Shinjuku Station. **Takashimaya Restaurant Park** (レストランズパーク; Map p280; www.restaurants-park.jp; 12-14 fl, Takashimaya Times Sq; ⏱11am-11pm; 🚇🚻; 🚆JR Yamanote line to Shinjuku, new south exit) has the nicest one, though it is also the priciest, with meals starting around ¥2000 per person. **Lumine** (ルミネ; Map p280; www.lumine.ne.jp/shinjuku; ⏱11am-10.30pm; 🚇🚻; 🚆JR Yamanote line to Shinjuku, south exit) and **Mylord** (ミロード; Map p280; www.shinjuku-mylord.com; ⏱11am-11pm; 🚇🚻; 🚆JR Yamanote line to Shinjuku, south exit) are cheaper, catering to young shoppers.

Within Shinjuku Station, before you reach the new south exit ticket gates, there are a number of good takeaway vendors – perfect when you're catching the Narita Express or a long-distance bus; you can also sit and eat on the terrace outside the ticket gates, adjacent to the NEWoMan (p133) mall.

From Shinjuku-sanchōme subway station you can directly access Isetan (p132), which has a fantastic basement food hall, with *bentō* (boxed meals), fresh bread and more. The department store also has a little-known free rooftop garden, where you can sit and eat.

noodles in a broth flavoured with dried sardines. Look for the sign with a red circle.

OMOIDE-YOKOCHŌ YAKITORI ¥
Map p280 (思い出横丁; Nishi-Shinjuku 1-chōme, Shinjuku-ku; skewers from ¥150; ⏱varies by shop; 🚻; 🚆JR Yamanote line to Shinjuku, west exit) Literally 'Memory Lane' (and less politely known as Shonben-yokochō, or 'Piss Alley'), Omoide-yokochō started as a postwar black market and managed to stick around. Today, it's one of Tokyo's most recognisable sights. Dozens of small restaurants serving *yakitori* (chicken, and other meats or vegetables, grilled on skewers) are packed into the alley here; several have English menus.

★KANAE IZAKAYA ¥¥
Map p280 (鼎; ☎050-3467-1376; basement fl, 3-12-12 Shinjuku, Shinjuku-ku; cover charge ¥540; dishes ¥660-1980; ⏱5pm-midnight Mon-Sat, 4.30-11pm Sun; 🚻; 🚆JR Yamanote line to Shinjuku, east exit) Kanae is a perfect example of one of Shinjuku-sanchōme's excellent and all but undiscoverable *izakaya*: delicious sashimi, seasonal dishes and simple staples (the potato salad is famous) in the basement of an unremarkable building (there's a white sign with a sake barrel out front). Seating is at the counter or at a handful of tables; reservations recommended.

DONJACA IZAKAYA ¥¥
Map p280 (呑者家; ☎03-3341-2497; 3-9-10 Shinjuku, Shinjuku-ku; cover charge ¥300, dishes ¥350-900; ⏱5pm-7am; 🚻; 🚇Marunouchi line to Shinjuku-sanchōme, exit C6) Donjaca, in busi-

ness since 1979, has many telltale signs of a classic Shōwa-era (1926–89) *izakaya*: red vinyl stools, lantern lighting and handwritten menus covering the wall. The food is equal parts classic (grilled fish and fried chicken) and inventive: a house speciality is *nattō gyōza* (dumplings stuffed with fermented soybeans). Excellent sake, too.

Warning: Donjaca can get smoky. If the main shop is full, staff will likely direct you around the corner to the larger annex.

★KOZUE JAPANESE ¥¥¥
Map p280 (梢; ☎03-5323-3460; www.hyatt.com; 40th fl, Park Hyatt Tokyo, 3-7-1-2 Nishi-Shinjuku, Shinjuku-ku; lunch set menu ¥2480-10,800, dinner set menu ¥14,040-24,850; ⏱11.30am-2.30pm & 5.30-9.30pm; 🚇🚻; 🚇Ōedo line to Tochōmae, exit A4) It's hard to beat Kozue's combination of exquisite seasonal Japanese cuisine, artisan crockery and distractingly good views over Shinjuku. As the kimono-clad staff speak English and the restaurant caters well to dietary restrictions and personal preferences, this is a good splurge spot for diners who don't want to give up complete control. Reservations essential for dinner and recommended for lunch; 15% service charge.

DRINKING & NIGHTLIFE

★BENFIDDICH COCKTAIL BAR
Map p280 (ベンフィディッチ; ☎03-6279-4223; 9th fl, 1-13-7 Nishi-Shinjuku, Shinjuku-ku; ⏱6pm-3am Mon-Sat; 🚆JR Yamanote line to Shinjuku,

west exit) BenFiddich is dark and tiny, with vials of infusions on the shelves and herbs hung to dry from the ceiling. The English-speaking barman, Kayama Hiroyasu, in a white suit, moves like a magician. There's no menu, so just tell him what you like and he'll concoct something delicious for you (we like the gimlet with herbs). Expect to pay around ¥2000 per drink.

There's no sign on the street, but it's the building in between the karaoke parlour and the curry shop. You'll see the wooden door when you exit the elevator.

★ZOETROPE BAR

Map p280 (ゾートロープ; ☎03-3363-0162; 3rd fl, 7-10-14 Nishi-Shinjuku, Shinjuku-ku; ⏲5pm-midnight Mon-Sat; 📶; 🚂JR Yamanote line to Shinjuku, west exit) A must-visit for whisky fans, Zoetrope has some 300 varieties of Japanese whisky behind its small counter – including hard-to-find bottles from small batch distilleries. It's a one-person show and the owner speaks English well. Cover charge ¥600; whisky by the glass from ¥400 to ¥19,000, though most are reasonably priced (around ¥800 to ¥1200), and there are some good-value tasting flights, too.

NEW YORK BAR BAR

Map p280 (ニューヨークバー; ☎03-5323-3458; http://restaurants.tokyo.park.hyatt.co.jp/en/nyb.html; 52nd fl, Park Hyatt Tokyo, 3-7-1-2 Nishi-Shinjuku, Shinjuku-ku; ⏲5pm-midnight Sun-Wed, to 1am Thu-Sat; 📶; 🚂Ōedo line to Tochōmae, exit A4) Head to the Park Hyatt's 52nd floor to swoon over the sweeping nightscape from the floor-to-ceiling windows at this bar of *Lost in Translation* fame. There's a cover charge of ¥2500 if you visit or stay past 8pm (7pm Sunday); go earlier and watch the sky fade to black. Cocktails start at ¥2160. Note: dress code enforced and 15% service charge levied. Unfortunately, he bar doesn't take bookings, but you probably will want to go early anyway to score a table by the windows.

AIIRO CAFE GAY & LESBIAN

Map p280 (アイイロ　カフェ; ☎03-6273-0740; www.aliving.net; 2-18-1 Shinjuku, Shinjuku-ku; ⏲6pm-2am Mon-Thu, to 5am Fri & Sat, to midnight Sun; 📶; [S]Marunouchi line to Shinjuku-sanchōme, exit C8) Aiiro is the best place to start any night out in Shinjuku-nichōme, thanks to the all-you-can-drink beer for ¥1000 happy-hour special from 6pm to 9pm daily. The bar itself is teeny-tiny; the action happens on the street corner outside, which swells to block-party proportions when the weather is nice. There's a red *torii* out front; you can't miss it.

Aiiro is welcoming to all and staff speak excellent English. This is a great place to find out about other events and happenings in Ni-chōme.

EAGLE GAY

Map p280 (www.eagletokyo.com; 2-12-3 Shinjuku, Shinjuku-ku; ⏲6pm-1am Sun-Thu, to 4am Fri & Sat; 📶; 🚂JR Yamanote line to Shinjuku, east exit) There's much to love about new Shinjuku-nichōme bar Eagle: the friendly staff, the happy-hour prices (¥500 drinks from 5pm to 8pm; otherwise they're ¥700), but especially the instantly iconic mural from proudly out manga artist Inuyoshi. Pick up a free copy of the artist's bilingual manga *Nippondanji* here.

SAMURAI BAR

Map p280 (サムライ; http://jazz-samurai.seesaa.net; 5th fl, 3-35-5 Shinjuku, Shinjuku-ku; ⏲6pm-1am; 📶; 🚂JR Yamanote line to Shinjuku, southeast exit) Never mind the impressive record collection, this eccentric jazz *kissa* (cafe where jazz records are played) is worth a visit just for the owner's overwhelming collection of 2500 *maneki-neko* (beckoning cats). It's on the alleyway alongside the highway, with a small sign on the front of the building. There's a ¥300 cover charge (¥500 after 9pm); drinks from ¥650.

BAR GOLDFINGER GAY & LESBIAN

Map p280 (☎03-6383-4649; www.goldfingerparty.com; 2-12-11 Shinjuku, Shinjuku-ku; ⏲6pm-2am Sun-Thu, to 5am Fri & Sat; [S]Marunouchi line to Shinjuku-sanchōme, exit C8) Goldfinger is a long-running ladies' spot in Shinjuku-nichōme (but open to all, save for Saturdays). The bar has a lowbrow-chic decor designed to look like a '70s motel, a friendly vibe and fun events, like Friday-night karaoke. Drinks from ¥700; no cover unless there's an event.

ROOF TOP BAR & TERRACE G BAR

Map p280 (☎03-5155-2412; www.granbellhotel.jp/shinjuku/restaurant/bar/; 13th fl, Shinjuku Granbell Hotel, 2-14-5 Kabukichō, Shinjuku-ku; ⏲5pm-2am Mon-Sat, to 11pm Sun; [S]Ōedo line to Higashi-Shinjuku, exit A1) The drinks and decor here are totally uninteresting, but we're a sucker for an open-air rooftop bar – not as common as you'd think in Tokyo, where the night views are always divine (even if, in this case, it's partly of the gentrifying red-light district). Beer is ¥500 during happy hour (5pm to 7pm); otherwise drinks start at ¥800. There's a ¥500 cover charge.

The bar is inside Shinjuku Granbell Hotel and the cover charge is waived for hotel guests.

REN
BAR

Map p280 (蓮; ☑03-6723-9736; www.ren-shinjuku.com; 3rd fl, Shinjuku Robot Bldg, 1-7-1 Kabukichō, Shinjuku-ku; ◷10pm-5am; Ⓓ; Ⓡ JR Yamanote line to Shinjuku, east exit) This over-the-top lounge bar is from the same people behind the equally over-the-top Robot Restaurant, and is in the same building; enter around the back. It's open to Robot Restaurant ticket holders only until 10pm, after which anyone can enter to marvel at the gilded plastic, game-show-set aesthetic. Minimum purchase of one drink and one food item (from ¥500 each).

⭐ ENTERTAINMENT

★ SHINJUKU PIT INN
JAZZ

Map p280 (新宿ピットイン; ☑03-3354-2024; www.pit-inn.com; basement, 2-12-4 Shinjuku, Shinjuku-ku; from ¥3000; ◷matinee 2.30pm, evening show 7.30pm; Ⓢ Marunouchi line to Shinjuku-sanchōme, exit C5) This is Tokyo's best jazz spot: intimate, unpretentious and with an always solid line-up of influential, avant-garde, crossover and up-and-coming musicians from Japan and abroad. If you're already a fan of jazz, you'll want to make it a point to visit; and if you're not, Pit Inn is the kind of place that just might win you over.

TOKYO OPERA
CITY CONCERT HALL
CLASSICAL MUSIC

(東京オペラシティコンサートホール; ☑03-5353-9999; www.operacity.jp; 3rd fl, Tokyo Opera City, 3-20-2 Nishi-Shinjuku, Shinjuku-ku; Ⓡ Keiō New line to Hatsudai, east exit) This beautiful, oak-panelled, A-frame concert hall, with legendary acoustics, hosts the Tokyo Philharmonic Orchestra among other well-regarded ensembles; *bugaku* (dance pieces played by court orchestras in ancient Japan) is also sometimes performed here. Free lunchtime organ performances take place monthly, usually on Fridays. Get information and tickets from the box office

next to the entrance to the Tokyo Opera City Art Gallery.

ROBOT RESTAURANT
CABARET

Map p280 (ロボットレストラン; ☑03-3200-5500; www.shinjuku-robot.com; 1-7-1 Kabukichō, Shinjuku-ku; tickets ¥8000; ◷shows at 5.55pm, 7.50pm & 9.45pm, additional show at 4pm Fri-Sun; Ⓡ JR Yamanote line to Shinjuku, east exit) This Kabukichō spectacle has hit it big with its vision of 'wacky Japan': bikini-clad women ride around on giant robots against a backdrop of animated screens and enough LED lights to illuminate all of Shinjuku. You can book ahead online (at full price) or save up to ¥2000 per person by purchasing at the venue with a discount flyer (available at Tourist Information Centers and hotels).

The show receives mixed reviews: some love it (you'll get great photos), while others recoil at the price and tourist-trappiness of it. You can have a small, free taste just by basking in the glow of the exterior, where two robo-glamazons are parked outside (also great for photos). For the full experience, head to sister bar Ren.

🛍 SHOPPING

Shinjuku and Ikebukuro are major shopping hubs, with department and electronics stores clustered around both train stations.

★ BEAMS JAPAN
FASHION & ACCESSORIES

Map p280 (ビームス・ジャパン; www.beams.co.jp; 3-32-6 Shinjuku, Shinjuku-ku; ◷11am-8pm; Ⓡ JR Yamanote line to Shinjuku, east exit) Beams, a national chain of trendsetting boutiques, is a Japanese cultural institution and this multistorey Shinjuku branch has a particular audience in mind: you, the traveller. It's full of the latest Japanese streetwear labels, traditional fashions with cool modern twists, artisan crafts, pop art and more – all contenders for that perfect only-in-Tokyo souvenir. Set your budget before you enter.

★ ISETAN
DEPARTMENT STORE

Map p280 (伊勢丹; ☑03-3352-1111; www.isetan.co.jp; 3-14-1 Shinjuku, Shinjuku-ku; ◷10.30am-8pm; Ⓢ Marunouchi line to Shinjuku-sanchōme, exit B3, B4 or B5) Isetan is our favourite Tokyo department store for several reasons: the up-and-coming Japanese fashion designers (check the 2nd-floor Tokyo

Closet and 3rd-floor Re-Style boutiques in the main building, and the 2nd floor of the men's building); the homewares from contemporary artisans (5th floor); and the quite literally mouth-watering *depachika* (basement food floor).

DISK UNION SHINJUKU
MUSIC

Map p280 (ディスクユニオン新宿; http://diskunion.net; 3-31-4 Shinjuku, Shinjuku-ku; ⊗11am-9pm Mon-Sat, to 8pm Sun; ℝJR Yamanote line to Shinjuku, east exit) Keeping the dream alive for fans of physical music, Disk Union has eight storeys of used CDs and records, including whole floors for genres like '70s prog and '80s new wave. There are a few more branches nearby with even more specific (and obscure) foci; see the map out front.

It's mostly CDs but there's enough vinyl here to entertain crate diggers. For more records, head to the chain's new **Union Record Shinjuku** (ユニオンレコード新宿; Map p280; 3-34-1 Shinjuku, Shinjuku-ku; ⊗11am-9pm Mon-Sat, to 8pm Sun) around the corner.

BOOKS KINOKUNIYA TOKYO
BOOKS

Map p280 (紀伊國屋書店; ☎03-5361-3316; www.kinokuniya.co.jp/c/store/Books-Kinokuniya-Tokyo; 6th fl, Takashimaya Times Sq Minami-kan, 5-24-2 Sendagaya, Shibuya-ku; ⊗10am-8.30pm; ℝJR Yamanote line to Shinjuku, south exit) A long-time lifeline for Tokyo expats, Kinokuniya stocks a broad selection of foreign-language books and magazines. Particularly of note is its fantastic collection of books on Japan in English and Japanese literature in translation; we love the notes handwritten by the staff with their recommendations.

ANIMATE IKEBUKURO
MANGA & ANIME

Map p280 (アニメイト池袋本店; ☎03-3988-1351; www.animate.co.jp; 1-20-7 Higashi-Ikebukuro, Toshima-ku; ⊗10am-9pm; ℝJR Yamanote line to Ikebukuro, east exit) Akihabara might get more attention, but Ikebukuro is a major player in the anime-manga-gamer universe. Case in point: Animate's Ikebukuro store is the largest of its kind in Japan. It also gets extra kudos from girl geeks (who are known to prefer Ikebukuro to Akiba), thanks to several floors devoted to their favourite series.

NEWOMAN
MALL

Map p280 (www.newoman.jp; 4-1-6 Shinjuku, Shinjuku-ku; ⊗11am-9.30pm, food hall 8am-10pm; ℝJR Yamanote line to Shinjuku, new south exit) Awkward name and unlikely location (within the Shinjuku Bus Terminal complex) aside, this newish mall is one of Tokyo's swankiest places to shop. There's an outpost of excellent food and kitchenware shop Akomeya (p77) in the basement and a line-up of posh takeaway vendors on the 2nd-floor terrace (where you can sit and eat).

🏃 SPORTS & ACTIVITIES

SKY CIRCUS
AMUSEMENT PARK

Map p280 (スカイサーカス; ☎03-3989-3457; www.skycircus.jp; Sunshine 60, 3-1-1 Higashi-Ikebukuro, Toshima-ku; observatory ticket adult/child ¥1200/600, attractions extra; ⊗10am-10pm; ℝJR Yamanote line to Ikebukuro, east exit) One of Tokyo's better virtual-reality parks, Sky Circus has an aerial roller-coaster that snakes between Ikebukuro's skyscrapers (Swing Coaster; ¥400) and a cannon attraction that sends you bouncing around a futuristic version of Tokyo's more famous attractions (Tokyo Bullet Flight; ¥600). Basic instructions are given in English. If you are prone to motion sickness you will feel it, possibly acutely.

You have to first buy a ticket to the 60th-floor observatory – which is nice in its own right – from the ticket counter in the basement of Sunshine 60 (part of Sunshine City). You can get your hand stamped for in-and-out entry all day. Attraction tickets can be bought on the 60th floor. Last ticket sales are at 8.50pm. To ride the attractions, children must be over seven years of age and taller than 130cm; grown-ups no bigger than 2m and 100kg.

THERMAE-YU
ONSEN

Map p280 (テルマー湯; ☎03-5285-1726; www.thermae-yu.jp; 1-1-2 Kabukichō, Shinjuku-ku; weekdays/weekends & holidays ¥2365/2690; ⊗11am-9am; ℝJR Yamanote line to Shinjuku, east exit) The best (and most literal) example to date that red-light district Kabukichō is cleaning up its act: this sparkling-clean onsen (hot springs) complex. The tubs, which include several indoor and outdoor ones (sex-segregated), are filled with honest-to-goodness natural hot-spring water. There are several saunas, including a hot-stone sauna (*ganbanyoku*; ¥810 extra). Towels included. No tattoos allowed.

Kōrakuen & Akihabara

KŌRAKUEN | KUDANSHITA | KANDA | AKIHABARA | KAGURAZAKA

Neighbourhood Top Five

❶ Koishikawa Kōrakuen (p136) Slipping into the beautiful verdant world of this classic traditional garden with its central pond, charming bridges and seasonal flowerings.

❷ Kanda Myōjin (p136) Saying a prayer at this venerable Shintō shrine in Akiba.

❸ 3331 Arts Chiyoda (p136) Encountering dinosaurs made from old plastic toys among the contemporary art galleries in this former school turned arts-and-culture centre.

❹ Akagi-jinja (p137) Threading your way through the narrow, stone-flagged streets of Kagurazaka to

find this thoroughly modern shrine.

❺ TeNQ (p136) Gazing down in wonder at the videos of the solar system projected across an 11m-diameter screen and taking part in fun, educational activities focussing on space science.

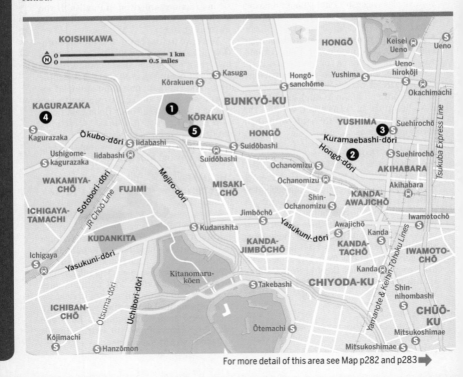

For more detail of this area see Map p282 and p283 ➡

Explore Kōrakuen & Akihabara

These relatively overlooked neighbourhoods north and northwest of the Imperial Palace have some fascinating sights. Start with a stroll through the serene traditional garden Koishikawa Kōrakuen (p136). Next door is the entertainment complex Tokyo Dome (p139), which includes a baseball stadium, an amusement park, a giant spa complex and the excellent TeNQ (p138) space museum.

South of Kōrakuen, in Kudanshita, is the controversial shrine Yasukuni-jinja (p138). Nearby Kagurazaka, with its narrow cobblestone lanes, presents a charming alternative picture of Tokyo – that of a hundred years ago.

Whizz back to 21st-century Tokyo in Akihabara, the electronics district that has become synonymous with *otaku* (geeks) and their love of anime (Japanese animation), manga (Japanese comics) and J-pop culture. Even if you haven't the faintest idea of who or what AKB48 or Gundam is, Akiba, as it's popularly known, is still worth visiting for its buzzing, quirky atmosphere, and the contemporary arts of 3331 Arts Chiyoda (p136). West of Akihabara, in the vicinity of Ochanomizu, is the area's major shrine, Kanda Myōjin (p136).

Local Life

⇢ **Go-karting** Experience the wacky *otaku* culture of Akiba while taking a go-kart for a spin dressed in a *cosplay* (costume play) outfit with MariCAR (p141).

⇢ **Eating** Kagurazaka is known to harbour many great restaurants, such as Kado (p137).

⇢ **Books & Coffee** Neighbourhood Jimbōchō is famous for its secondhand bookstores, such as Ohya Shobō (p140) and Komiyama Shoten (p140), and its coffee shops, like Sabōru (p138) – for reading in, of course.

Getting There & Away

⇢ **Train** The JR Yamanote, Sōbu and Keihin-Tōhoku lines stop at Akihabara and Kanda. Sōbu line stops Iidabashi (for Kagurazaka), Suidōbashi (for Kōrakuen) and Ochanomizu are also convenient. Rapid-service JR Chūō line trains stop at Ochanomizu and Kanda.

⇢ **Subway** The Hibiya line stops near Akihabara, while the Ginza line stops at Suehirochō and Kanda. Other useful stations include Iidabashi (Nanboku, Yūrakuchō, Tōzai and Ōedo lines), Kōrakuen (Nanboku and Marunouchi lines), Kagurazaka (Tōzai line) and Kudanshita (Hanzōmon, Tōzai and Shinjuku lines).

Lonely Planet's Top Tip

Check electronics prices in your home country online before buying big-ticket items in Akihabara; they may or may not be a good deal. If you do buy, have your passport handy since travellers spending more than ¥5000 in a single day at selected shops can get a refund of the consumption tax. For a list of duty-free shops offering this service, see http://akiba.or.jp.

 ### Best Places to Eat

➡ Isegen (p138)

➡ Kado (p137)

➡ Kagawa Ippuku (p137)

➡ Mensho Tokyo (p138)

For reviews, see p137.⇥

 ### Best Places to Drink

➡ Imasa (p138)

➡ Beer-Ma Kanda (p138)

➡ Sabōru (p138)

➡ Cocktail Works (p138)

➡ Craft Beer Server Land (p138)

For reviews, see p138.⇥

 ### Best Places to Shop

➡ 2k540 Aki-Oka Artisan (p139)

➡ Chabara (p140)

➡ Mandarake Complex (p140)

➡ Y. & Sons (p139)

For reviews, see p139.⇥

KŌRAKUEN & AKIHABARA

◉ SIGHTS

◉ Kōrakuen & Kudanshita

★ KOISHIKAWA KŌRAKUEN   GARDENS

Map p282 (小石川後楽園; ☎03-3811-3015; www.tokyo-park.or.jp/teien; 1-6-6 Kōraku, Bunkyō-ku; adult/child ¥300/free; ⊙9am-5pm; ▣Ōedo line to Iidabashi, exit C3) Established in the mid-17th century as the property of the Tokugawa clan, this formal strolling garden incorporates elements of Chinese and Japanese landscaping. It's among Tokyo's most attractive gardens, although nowadays the *shakkei* (borrowed scenery) also includes the contemporary skyline of Tokyo Dome (p139).

Don't miss the **Engetsu-kyō** (Full-Moon Bridge), which dates from the early Edo period (the name will make sense when you see it), and the beautiful vermilion wooden bridge **Tsuten-kyō**. The garden is particularly well known for its plum blossoms in February, irises in June and autumn leaves.

TENQ   MUSEUM

Map p282 (テンキュー; ☎03-3814-0109; www.tokyo-dome.co.jp; 6F Tokyo Dome City, Yellow Bldg, 1-3-61 Kōraku, Bunkyō-ku; adult/child ¥1800/1200; ⊙11am-9pm Mon-Fri, from 10am Sat & Sun; ♿; ▣JR Sobu line to Suidōbashi, west exit) This nifty, interactive museum is devoted to outer-space exploration and science. Timed entry tickets start you off with one of three impressive high-resolution videos projected across an 11m-diameter screen that you stand around. Good English captions throughout make it a fine educational experience. Set aside a couple of hours to do the museum justice.

Other fun things to do here include taking part in a Mars research project being run by Tokyo University (which has a lab on-site) and playing an astro-ball robot control game.

YASUKUNI-JINJA   SHINTO SHRINE

Map p282 (靖国神社; ☎03-3261-8326; www.yasukuni.or.jp; 3-1-1 Kudan-kita, Chiyoda-ku; ⊙6am-5pm; ▣Hanzōmon line to Kudanshita, exit 1) Literally 'For the Peace of the Country Shrine', Yasukuni is the memorial shrine to Japan's war dead, around 2.5 million souls. First built in 1869, it is a peaceful and green place but also incredibly controversial: in 1979, 14 class-A war criminals, including WWII general Hideki Tōjō, were enshrined here.

The main approach is fronted by a 25m-tall steel-and-bronze *torii* (entrance gate); seek out the serene grove of mossy trees and ornamental pond behind the main shrine.

For politicians, a visit to Yasukuni, particularly on 15 August, the anniversary of Japan's defeat in WWII, is considered a political statement. It's a move that pleases hawkish constituents but also one that draws a strong rebuke from Japan's Asian neighbours, who suffered greatly in Japan's wars of expansion during the 20th century.

TOKAS HONGO   GALLERY

Map p283 (☎03-5689-5331; www.tokyoartsandspace.jp; 2-4-16 Hongō, Bunkyō-ku; ⊙11am-7pm Tue-Sun; ▣Mita line to Suidōbashi, exit A1) FREE Operated by the Tokyo Metropolitan Government, TOKAS (short for Tokyo Arts and Space) comprises three floors of galleries with the aim of promoting new and emerging artists. There is a regularly changing program of exhibitions, competitions and lectures in media ranging from painting to video art. Check the website before setting out as opening hours can change.

◉ Kanda & Akihabara

KANDA MYŌJIN   SHINTO SHRINE

Map p283 (神田明神, Kanda Shrine; ☎03-3254-0753; www.kandamyoujin.or.jp; 2-16-2 Soto-kanda, Chiyoda-ku; ▣JR Chūō or Sōbu lines to Ochanomizu, Hijiri-bashi exit) FREE Tracing back to AD 730, this splendid Shintō shrine boasts vermilion-lacquered halls with a stately courtyard. Its present location dates from 1616 and the *kami* (gods) enshrined here are said to bring luck in business and in finding a spouse. There are also plenty of anime characters, since this is Akiba's local shrine.

3331 ARTS CHIYODA   GALLERY

Map p283 (☎03-6803-2441; www.3331.jp; 6-11-14 Soto-Kanda, Chiyoda-ku; ⊙ground fl 10am-9pm, exhibition space noon-7pm Wed-Mon; 📷♿; ▣Ginza line to Suehirochō, exit 4) FREE A major exhibition space, smaller art galleries and creative studios now occupy this former high school, which has evolved into a forward-thinking arts hub for Akiba. It's a fascinating place to explore. On the ground floor, there's a good cafe and a shop selling cute design items, as well as a play area for kids stocked with recycled toys and colourful giant dinosaurs made of old plastic toys.

ORIGAMI KAIKAN   GALLERY

Map p283 (おりがみ会館; ☎03-3811-4025; www.origamikaikan.co.jp; 1-7-14 Yushima, Bunkyō-ku; ⊙shop 9.30am-6pm, gallery 10am-5.30pm Mon-Sat; ♿; ▣JR Chūō or Sōbu lines to Ochanomizu,

WORTH A DETOUR

KAGURAZAKA

At the start of the 20th century, Kagurazaka was a fashionable *hanamachi* – a pleasure quarter where geisha entertained. Though there are far fewer geisha today (they're seldom seen by tourists), the neighbourhood retains its glamour and charm. It's a popular destination for Tokyoites, who enjoy wandering the cobblestone lanes or whiling away time in one of the area's many cafes.

A highlight is **Akagi-jinja** (赤城神社; Map p282; ☎9am-5pm 03-3260-5071; www.akagi-jinja.jp; 1-10 Akagi-Motomachi, Shinjuku-ku; [S]Tōzai line to Kagurazaka, exit 1), Kagurazaka's signature shrine. In 2010 the shrine, which dates back centuries, was remodelled by Kengo Kuma, one of Japan's most prominent architects. The result is a sleek glass box.

Kagurazaka has many *ryōtei*, exclusive, traditional Japanese restaurants, but there are some attractive, affordable options, too. Set in an old wooden house with a white lantern out the front, **Kado** (カド; Map p282; ☎03-3268-2410; http://kagurazaka-kado.com; 1-32 Akagi-Motomachi, Shinjuku-ku; set menus ¥3000-5000; ⏲restaurant 5-11pm Tue-Fri, bar from 4pm Tue-Fri & 2pm Sat & Sun; 🚭📖; 🚆Tōzai line to Kagurazaka, exit 1) specialises in *katei-ryōri* (home-cooking). Dinner is a set course of seasonal dishes (such as grilled quail or fresh tofu). Bookings are required for the full selection of courses, but you can try turning up on the night and if there's space, you'll be able to eat. In the entrance is a *tachinomi-ya* (standing bar), where you can order small dishes (around ¥300) à la carte, paired with sake and other drinks.

Hijiri-bashi exit) [FREE] This exhibition centre and workshop is dedicated to the quintessential Japanese art of origami, which you can learn to do yourself in classes here. There's a shop-gallery on the 1st floor, a gallery on the 2nd, and a workshop on the 4th where you can watch the process of making, dyeing and decorating origami paper.

🍴 EATING

Kanda is home to some of Tokyo's most traditional restaurants in lovely old buildings, as well as come-as-you-are noodle bars and *izakaya* (Japanese pub-eateries) packed with carousing salarymen. Akihabara and Jimbōchō are known for their Japanese curry cafes and other cheap places to eat.

🍴 Kanda & Akihabara

★KAGAWA IPPUKU
UDON ¥

Map p283 (香川　一福　神田店; ☎03-557-3644; www.udon-ippuku-kanda.com; 1st fl, Tokyo Royal Plaza,1-18-11 Uchikanda, Chiyoda-ku; udon ¥430-820; ⏲11am-8pm Mon-Sat, also closed 1st Mon of month; 📖; 🚆Yamanote line to Kanda, west exit) Proof you don't need to shell out a small fortune to eat well in Tokyo is this humble restaurant specialising in *Sanuki-udon,* wheat noodles from Kagawa in Shikoku. Pay at the vending machine; you'll be handed an English menu to help with the options, which include the amount of noodles you wish and the toppings. The curry noodles are excellent.

KANDA YABU SOBA
SOBA ¥

Map p283 (神田やぶそば; ☎03-3251-0287; www.yabusoba.net; 2-10 Kanda-Awajichō, Chiyoda-ku; noodles ¥670-1910; ⏲11.30am-8.30pm Thu-Tue; 🚭📖; [S]Marunouchi line to Awajichō, exit A3) Totally rebuilt following a fire in 2013, this is one of Tokyo's most venerable buckwheat noodle shops, in business since 1880. Come here for classic handmade noodles and accompaniments such as shrimp tempura *(ten-seiro soba)* or slices of duck *(kamo-nanban soba).*

KIKANBŌ
RAMEN ¥

Map p283 (鬼金棒; ☎03-6206-0239; http://karashibi.com; 2-10-8 Kaji-chō, Chiyoda-ku; ramen from ¥800; ⏲11am-9.30pm Mon-Sat, to 4pm Sun; 🚭; 🚆JR Yamanote line to Kanda, north exit) The *karashibi* (カラシビ) spicy *miso-rāmen* here has a cult following. Choose your level of *kara* (spice) and *shibi* (a strange mouth-numbing sensation created by Japanese *sanshō* pepper). We recommend *futsu-futsu* (regular for both) for first-timers; *oni* (devil) level costs an extra ¥100. Look for the black door curtains. The sister shop next door, with red curtains, specialises in *tsukemen* (noodles with condensed soup on the side for dipping).

AMANOYA
DESSERTS ¥

Map p283 (天野屋; ☏03-3251-7911; www.
amanoya.jp; 2-8-15 Soto-Kanda, Chiyoda-ku;
desserts from ¥500; ⊙10am-6pm Mon-Sat;
⊜🅿; 🚆JR Chūō or Sōbu lines to Ochanomizu,
Hijiri-bashi exit) The owner of this charming
dessert cafe is a bit of a collector, as you'll
discover from the eclectic bits and bobs
on display ranging from model trains to
carved masks. Motherly women dole out
sweet treats, such as *mochi* rice cakes, as
well *amazake,* a mildly alcoholic milky sake
beverage that's long been a house speciality.

★ISEGEN
JAPANESE ¥¥

Map p283 (いせ源; ☏03-3251-1229; www.isegen.
com; 1-11-1 Kanda-Sudachō, Chiyoda-ku; lunch/
dinner from ¥1000/3500; ⊙11.30am-2pm &
5-9pm, closed Sat & Sun Apr-Oct; 🅿; 🚇Marunouchi
line to Awajichō, exit A3) This illustrious fish
restaurant, in business since the 1830s, operates out of a handsome 1930 wooden building. The speciality is *ankō-nabe* (monkfish
stew; ¥3500 per person, minimum order for
two only in the evening), served in a splendid
communal tatami room. Get a side of *kimo-
zashi* (monkfish liver; ¥1500) – a prized deli-
cacy – served pâté-style. Lunchtime options
include *yanagawa-nabe* (loach in rich egg
and dashi stock; ¥1800).

🍴 Kōrakuen & Kudanshita

MENSHO TOKYO
RAMEN ¥

Map p282 (☏03-3830-0842; http://menya-sho
no.com/tokyo; 1-15-9 Kasuga, Bunkyō-ku; noodles from ¥750; ⊙11am-3pm & 5-11pm Wed-Mon;
🚇Nambuku line to Kōrakuen, exits 5 & 6) The
speciality at this branch of the innovative
ramen chain is noodles prepared with lamb
– the lamb and pork stock is topped with
lamb *chāshū* (sliced roast meat). For a real
treat, opt for the lamb soba (¥900) – dry
noodles that you mix in the bowl with spicy
minced lamb and other condiments.

DRINKING & NIGHTLIFE

★IMASA
CAFE

Map p283 (井政; ☏03-3255-3565; www.kanda-
imasa.co.jp; 2-16 Soto-Kanda, Chiyoda-ku; drinks
¥600; ⊙11am-4pm Mon-Fri; ⊜; 🚆JR Chūō or
Sōbu lines to Ochanomizu, Hijiri-bashi exit) It's
not every day you get to sip your coffee or
tea in a cultural property. Imasa is the real
deal, an old timber merchant's shophouse
dating from 1927 but with Edo-era design
and detail, and a few pieces of contemporary furniture.

Very few houses like this exist in Tokyo
or are open to the public.

★BEER-MA KANDA
CRAFT BEER

Map p283 (びあマ神田; ☏03-3527-1900; www.fa
cebook.com/kanda.wbm; 1-6-4 Kajichō, Chiyoda-
ku; ⊙4-11pm Mon-Sat, 3-9pm Sun; 🚆JR lines to
Kanda, south exit) Down an alley of sketchy-
looking drinking dens is this nirvana for
craft-beer lovers. It's principally a bottle
shop stocking hundreds of different beer
brands all of which you can buy and drink
on the premises (corkage ¥200). There's
also eight taps of barrel beer available with
servings in a range of sizes.

CRAFT BEER SERVER LAND
CRAFT BEER

Map p282 (☏03-6228-1891; Okawa Bldg B1F, 2-9
Kagurazaka, Shinjuku-ku; service charge ¥380;
⊙5pm-midnight Mon-Fri, from noon Sat & Sun;
📶; 🚆JR Sōbu line to Iidabashi, west exit) With
some 14 Japanese craft beers on tap, going
for a reasonable ¥500/840 a glass/pint, plus
good food (the deep-fried eel in batter and
chips is excellent), this brightly lit basement
bar with wooden furniture and a slight
Scandi feel is a winner.

SABŌRU
CAFE

Map p283 (さぼうる; ☏03-3291-8404; 1-11
Kanda-Jimbōchō, Chiyoda-ku; coffee from ¥450;
⊙9.30am-11pm Mon-Sat; 🚇Hanzōmon line to
Jimbōchō, exit A7) Sabōru checks the boxes of
a classic mid-20th-century *kissaten* (coffee
shop): dim lighting, low tables, lots of dark
wood and strong *burendo kōhī* ('blend' coffee). And then it adds a few of its own plus-
es: totem poles, a Robinson Crusoe–vibe
and copious potted plants.

Come before 11am for the good-value
morning set (coffee, hard-boiled egg and
two rolls for ¥500).

COCKTAIL WORKS
COCKTAIL BAR

Map p283 (カクテルワークス; ☏03-6886-2138;
3-7-13 Ogawamachi, Chiyoda-ku; ⊙6pm-3am
Mon-Sat; 🚇Mita line to Jimbōchō, exit 9) Award-
winning mixologist Eiji Miyazawa brings
sophisticated style to studenty Jimbōchō
with this spacious bar selling cocktails from
¥1400. Gin lovers will be in heaven with
some 160-plus versions to choose from including several local artisan brands.

HITACHINO BREWING LAB
CRAFT BEER

Map p283 (☑03-3254 3434; http://hitachino. cc; 1-25-4 Kanda-Sudachō, Chiyoda-ku; ☉11am-11pm Mon-Sat, until 9pm Sun; ⊠Chūō or Sōbu lines to Akihabara, Electric Town exit) Sake brewery Kiuchi has been brewing its excellent range of Hitachino Nest craft beers since 1996. At this dedicated outlet you can have a very merry time working your way from the white beer to the sweet stout while gazing across the Kanda-gawa from the terrace seating alongside mAAch Ecute (p140).

@HOME CAFE
CAFE

Map p283 (@ほぉ～むカフェ; ☑03-3255-2808; www.cafe-athome.com; 4th-7th fl, 1-11-4 Soto-Kanda, Chiyoda-ku; ☉11am-10pm Mon-Fri, from 10am Sat & Sun; 🗋; ⊠JR Yamanote line to Akihabara, Electric Town exit) 'Maid cafes' with *kawaii* (cute) waitresses, dressed as saucy French or prim Victorian maids, are a stock-in-trade of Akiba, and @Home is one that's suitable if you have kids in tow.

You'll be welcomed as *go-shujinsama* (master) or *o-jōsama* (miss) the minute you come through the door. Admission is ¥700 for one hour plus one drink order (from ¥570).

⭐ ENTERTAINMENT

⭐TOKYO DOME
BASEBALL

Map p282 (東京ドーム; www.tokyo-dome.co.jp; 1-3 Kōraku, Bunkyō-ku; tickets ¥1700-6200; ⊠JR Chūō line to Suidōbashi, west exit) Tokyo Dome (aka 'Big Egg') is home to the Yomiuri Giants. Love 'em or hate 'em, they're the most consistently successful team in Japanese baseball. If you're looking to see the Giants in action, the baseball season runs from the end of March to the end of October. Tickets usually sell out in advance; get them early at www.giants.jp.

Any tickets left on the day of the game are sold from the ticket office in front of the Dome's Gate 22 from 10am.

If you'd rather root for the underdog (whoever is playing the Giants), you can drown your sorrows in the beer served by the *uriko*, young women with kegs strapped to their backs, who work the aisles with tireless cheer.

Tokyo Dome is also used for pop concerts by major Japanese and visiting singers and groups.

ℹ️ AKIBA INFO

If you're hunting for specific anime or manga merchandise or anything else in Akihabara, try the helpful English-speaking information desk **Akiba Info** (Map p283; ☑080-3413-4800; www. akiba-information.jp; 2nd fl, Akihabara UDX Bldg, 4-14-1 Soto-Kanda, Chiyoda-ku; ☉11am-5.30pm Tue-Sun; 📶; ⊠JR Yamanote line to Akihabara, Electric Town exit). There's also a shop that sells a variety of character goods.

CLUB GOODMAN
LIVE MUSIC

Map p283 (クラブグッドマン; ☑03-3862-9010; www.clubgoodman.com; basement, AS Bldg, 55 Kanda-Sakumagashi, Chiyoda-ku; cover charge ¥100-5500; ⊠JR Yamanote line to Akihabara, Shōwa-dōri exit) In the basement of a building with a guitar shop and recording studios, it's no surprise that this live house is a favourite with Tokyo's indie-scene bands and their fans. Entry charges depend on the bands playing.

🔒 SHOPPING

⭐2K540 AKI-OKA ARTISAN
ARTS & CRAFTS

Map p283 (アキオカアルチザン; ☑03-6806 0254; www.jrtk.jp/2k540; 5-9-23 Ueno, Taitō-ku; ☉11am-7pm Thu-Tue; ⊠Ginza line to Suehirochō, exit 2) This ace arcade under the JR tracks (its name refers to the distance from Tokyo Station) offers an eclectic range of stores selling Japanese-made goods – everything from pottery and leatherwork to cute aliens, a nod to Akihabara from a mall that is more akin to Kyoto than Electric Town. The best for colourful crafts is **Nippon Hyakkuten** (日本百貨店; http://nippon-dept.jp).

⭐Y. & SONS
FASHION & ACCESSORIES

Map p283 (☑03-5294-7521; www.yandsons.com; 2-17-2 Soto-Kanda, Chiyoda-ku; ☉11am-8pm Thu-Tue; ⊠JR Chūō line to Ochanomizu, Ochanomizu-bashi exit) Every once in a while in Tokyo, you'll spot a gentleman in a silk-wool kimono and a fedora, looking as if he's stepped out of the 1900s. Bespoke tailor Y. & Sons would like to see this more often. Custom kimonos with obi (sash) start at around ¥65,000 and take two weeks to complete; international shipping is available.

CHABARA
FOOD

Map p283 (ちゃばら; www.jrtk.jp/chabara; 8-2 Kanda Neribei-chō, Chiyoda-ku; ⏱11am-8pm; 🚆JR Yamanote line to Akihabara, Electric Town exit) This under-the-train-tracks shopping mall focuses on artisan food and drinks from across Japan, including premium sake, soy sauce, sweets, teas and crackers – all great souvenirs and presents.

MANDARAKE COMPLEX
MANGA, ANIME

Map p283 (まんだらけコンプレックス; ☎03-3252-7007; www.mandarake.co.jp; 3-11-12 Soto-Kanda, Chiyoda-ku; ⏱noon-8pm; 🚆JR Yamanote line to Akihabara, Electric Town exit) When *otaku* (geeks) dream of heaven, it probably looks a lot like this giant go-to store for manga and anime. Eight storeys are piled high with comic books, action figures, *cosplay* accessories and cel art just for starters. The 1st floor has cases of some (very expensive) vintage toys.

OKUNA KARUTA-TEN
TOYS

Map p283 (奥野かるた店; ☎03-3264-8031; www.okunokaruta.com; 2-26 Kanda-Jimbōchō, Chiyoda-ku; ⏱11am-6pm, closed 2nd & 3rd Sun; 🚇Shinjuku line to Jimbōchō, exit A4) This shop, established in 1921, is the go-to place for traditional Japanese card games such as *hyakunin isshu* and *hanafuda,* which make for unusual lightweight souvenirs, For some games they have English translations and explanation books. Also available are mah-jong and chess sets and various puzzle games.

YODOBASHI-AKIBA
ELECTRONICS

Map p283 (ヨドバシカメラAkiba; ☎03-5209 1010; www.yodobashi-akiba.com; 1-1 Kanda Hanaoka-chō, Chiyoda-ku; ⏱9.30am-10pm; 🚆JR Yamanote line to Akihabara, Shōwa-tōriguchi exit) This is the monster branch of Yodobashi Camera where many locals shop. It has eight floors not only of electronics, state-of-the-art camera and audio equipment, and household appliances but also toys, cosmetics and even food at competitive prices. Ask about export models and VAT-free purchases.

OHYA SHOBŌ
BOOKS

Map p283 (大屋書房; ☎03-3291-0062; www.ohya-shobo.com; 1-1 Kanda-Jimbōchō, Chiyoda-ku; ⏱10am-6pm Mon-Sat; 🚇Hanzōmon line to Jimbōchō, exit A7) This splendid, musty old bookshop specialises in *ukiyo-e* (woodblock prints), both old and newly printed (from ¥2000). There are antique books and maps, too. The staff are friendly and can help you with whatever you're looking for. All purchases are tagged with a small origami crane.

KOMIYAMA SHOTEN
BOOKS

Map p283 (小宮山書店; ☎03-3291-0495; www.book-komiyama.co.jp; 1-7 Kanda-Jimbōchō, Chiyoda-ku; ⏱11am-6.30pm Mon-Sat, to 5.30pm Sun; 🚇Hanzōmon line to Jimbōchō, exit A7) In business since 1939, this shop stocks an incredible selection of art and photography books, posters and prints with some very famous Japanese and international artists represented. Every spare inch of wall is given over to gallery space.

AKIHABARA RADIO KAIKAN
MANGA, ANIME

Map p283 (秋葉原ラジオ会館; http://akihabara-radiokaikan.co.jp; 1-15-6 Soto-kanda, Chiyoda-ku; ⏱11am-8pm; 🚆JR Yamanote line to Akihabara, Electric Town exit) Despite its name, Radio Kaikan has nothing to do with radios and everything to do with Japanese pop culture. It was completely rebuilt in 2014 to include nine floors of shops selling manga, anime, collectables such as models and figurines, fanzines, costumes and gear.

MAACH ECUTE
MALL

Map p283 (☎03-3257-8910; www.ecute.jp/maach; 1-25-4 Kanda-Sudachō, Chiyoda-ku; ⏱11am-9pm Mon-Sat, to 8pm Sun; 🚆Chūō or Sōbu lines to Akihabara, Electric Town exit) Mansei-bashi Station was Tokyo's original eastern terminus, completed two years before Tokyo Station (p64) in 1912. It closed in 1943 and was reborn at long last some 70 years later as this stylish shopping and dining centre. Crafts, homewares, fashions and food from across Japan are sold here, under the red-brick railway arches.

🏃 SPORTS & ACTIVITIES

⭐TOYOKUNI ATELIER GALLERY
ARTS & CRAFTS

Map p282 (豊國アトリエ; ☎090-4069-8410; www.nekomachi.com; 3-1-13 Kanda-Jimbōchō, Chiyoda-ku; 1hr class ¥2000; ⏱gallery noon-5pm Tue-Thu & Sat & Sun, classes 1pm, 3pm or 5pm; 🚇Shinjuku line to Jimbōchō, exit A1) Get a taster of *sumie*, the delicate art of ink painting on *washi* (Japanese handmade paper), at this gallery displaying the artworks of master ink painter Honda Toyokuni. The one-hour

GO-KARTING AROUND TOKYO

If you've seen the many online videos and photos, go-karting around Tokyo dressed in a *cosplay* onesie is sure to be top of your to-do list. Despite appearances to the contrary, the activity has nothing to do with Nintendo's *Super Mario Brothers* – the main operator, **MariCAR** (マリカー; Map p283; ☎080-8899-8899; https://maricar.com; 4-12-9 Soto-Kanda, Chiyoda-ku; 1/2/3hr tours ¥5000/7500/10,000; 🕙10am-8pm; [S]Ginza line to Suehirochō, exit 1), is engaged in an ongoing legal tussle with Nintendo for claimed infringement of the game company's intellectual property and brand.

Don't let this put you off what can be one of the most fun things to do in Tokyo. However, before donning your character outfit and getting behind the wheel, there's a few important things you should note:

➡ Advance reservations are pretty much essential and you *must* have a valid International Driving Permit (or a Japanese driver's licence).

➡ Safe, lawful driving is key – it may feel like it, but this is *not* a video game. Also the low-lying go-karts can easily become involved in accidents, so pay full attention to the safety briefing and make sure you have insurance cover for any accidents.

➡ There's a wide variety of courses lasting between one and three hours, held either during the day or night, and covering different areas of the city depending on which branch you book with. Think about what you want to see and how long you feel comfortable driving – you will be breathing in a lot of exhaust fumes!

➡ Discounts are available by booking online via Voyagin (www.govoyagin.com).

class is taught by his English-speaking, affable son Yuta, and highly recommended for budding artists of all ages. Reservations are essential. Classes with 73-year-old Toyokuni cost ¥15,000 and last two hours.

★SPA LAQUA — ONSEN

Map p282 (スパ　ラクーア; ☎03-5800-9999; www.laqua.jp; 5th-9th fl, Tokyo Dome City, 1-1-1 Kasuga, Bunkyō-ku; weekday/weekend ¥2850/3174; 🕙11am-9am; [S]Marunouchi line to Kōrakuen, exit 2) One of Tokyo's few true onsen, this chic spa complex, renovated in 2017, relies on natural hot-spring water from 1700m below ground. There are indoor and outdoor baths, saunas and a bunch of add-on options, such as *akasuri* (Korean-style whole-body exfoliation). It's a fascinating introduction to Japanese health and beauty rituals.

An extra ¥865 gives you access to the Healing Baden area, with even more varieties of saunas and a lounge area styled like a Balinese resort; here men and women can hang out together (everyone gets a pair of rental pyjamas). There are lounging areas too, with reclining chairs. For an extra ¥1950 you can overnight here.

TOKYO DOME CITY ATTRACTIONS — AMUSEMENT PARK

Map p282 (東京ドームシティアトラクションズ; ☎03-5800-9999; www.tokyo-dome.co.jp; 1-3-61 Kōraku, Bunkyō-ku; day pass adult/child/teenager ¥3900/2500/3400; 🕙10am-9pm; 👪; 🚆JR Chūō line to Suidōbashi, west exit) The top attraction at this amusement park next to Tokyo Dome (p139) is the 'Thunder Dolphin' (¥1030), a roller coaster that cuts a heart-in-your-throat course in and around the tightly packed buildings of downtown. There are plenty of low-key, child-friendly rides as well. You can buy individual-ride tickets, day passes, night passes (valid from 5pm) and a five-ride pass (¥2600).

Ueno & Yanesen

UENO | YANESEN

Neighbourhood Top Five

❶ Tokyo National Museum (p145) Getting schooled in Japanese art history at the finest collection of Japanese art and cultural artefacts in the world.

❷ Rikugi-en (p144) Admiring the poetically inspired views across one of Tokyo's most beautiful formal gardens with its central pond,

teahouses, stone bridges and manicured foliage.

❸ Ueno-kōen (p148) Strolling through this expansive park chock-a-block with museums, temples and even a zoo.

❹ Nezu-jinja (p149) Paying your respects at this picturesque shrine with its corridor of mini red *torii*

(entrance gates) and azalea bushes, then continuing to explore the wider Yanesen area.

❺ Ameya-yokochō (p151) Absorbing the sights, sounds and smells of this old-fashioned partially outdoor market that's also a great spot for street food.

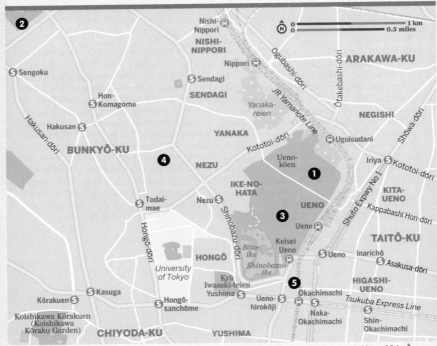

For more detail of this area see Map p284 ➡

Explore Ueno & Yanesen

Ueno is one of Tokyo's top destinations and you could easily spend a whole day just exploring the sights in and around Ueno-kōen (p148). Start in the morning at the Tokyo National Museum (p145) and wend your way southward, hitting a few other museums, the zoo (p148) and the centuries-old shrines and temples that dot the park. Wrap up the day with a stroll through the retro street market Ameya-yokochō (p151).

Within walking distance of Ueno are a trio of neighbourhoods that time seemingly forgot. Much of Yanaka, Nezu and Sendagi, collectively known as Yanesen, miraculously survived the Great Kantō Earthquake and the allied fire-bombing of WWII (not to mention the slash-and-burn modernising of the postwar years). Yanaka in particular has a high concentration of vintage wooden structures. But that's not all that makes Yanesen unique: it has more than a hundred temples and shrines, some relocated from around Tokyo during an Edo-era episode of urban restructuring. Others, such as beautiful Nezu-jinja (p149), have been here for much longer. This area is is popular with Tokyoites, too, so can get crowded on weekends.

A worthy detour is Rikugi-en (p144), one of Tokyo's most spectacular traditional gardens, accessed from Komagome station.

With the exception of the area immediately around Ueno Station, these districts get pretty quiet at night, though Yanaka has a few hip hang-outs.

Local Life

→ **Park Life** On weekends, look for buskers, acrobats and food vendors in Ueno-kōen (p148).

→ **Night Market** In and around Ameya-yokochō (p151) are several casual restaurants that open onto the street. It's a fun place to dine in the evening.

Getting There & Away

→ **Train** The JR Yamanote line stops at Ueno and Nippori (for Yanaka). Keisei line trains from Narita Airport stop at Keisei Ueno Station (just south of JR Ueno Station).

→ **Subway** The Ginza and Hibiya lines stop at Ueno. The Chiyoda line runs along the west side of Ueno-kōen (p148), stopping at Yushima, Nezu and Sendagi; the latter two stops are convenient for Yanaka.

→ **Bus** The *tōzai* (東西; east–west) route of the **Megurin** (めぐりん; www.city.taito.lg.jp/index/kurashi/kotsu/megurin; single ride/day pass ¥100/300; ⊙7am-7pm, every 15min) community bus does a helpful loop around the area. Stops are announced on the bus.

Lonely Planet's Top Tip

Ueno-kōen and Yanesen are lovely locations to stroll; they're also great places to cycle.

 Best Places to Eat

→ Hantei (p151)
→ Innsyoutei (p149)
→ Kamachiku (p150)
→ Ueno-Sakuragi Nanohana (p150)
→ Tayori (p150)

For reviews, see p149.

Best Places to Drink

→ Yanaka Beer Hall (p151)
→ Kayaba Coffee (p151)
→ Torindō (p151)

For reviews, see p151.

Best Places to Shop

→ Ameya-yokochō (p151)
→ Geidai Art Plaza (p153)
→ Yanaka Matsunoya (p153)
→ Isetatsu (p153)

For reviews, see p151.

UENO & YANESEN

TOP EXPERIENCE
TAKE A STROLL THROUGH RIKUGI-EN

Considered by many to be Tokyo's most elegant garden, Rikugi-en was originally completed in 1702, at the behest of a feudal lord. It is designed to evoke scenes from classical literature and mythology, complete with wooded walkways, stone bridges, a central pond, trickling streams and wooden teahouses.

Rikugi-en is a classic example of an Edo-era strolling garden. Such gardens are designed as a series of sensory encounters (often visual, but they can be auditory too – eg rushing water) that unfold along a meandering path.

Rikugi-en has 88 viewpoints that evoke scenes from poetry and legend or recreate (in miniature) famous vistas found in Japan and China. One example is the bridge, **Togetsukyō**, created from two huge stone slabs, that references a poem about a crane flying over a moonlit field. Another is the craggy rock in the pond, called **Hōrai-jima**, which represents the Taoist 'Isle of Immortals'.

Stone markers make note of some other scenic viewpoints (even the most erudite Japanese visitor wouldn't get them all); some are signposted with English explanations as well.

Rikugi-en has two vintage teahouses: **Tsutsuji-chaya** dates to the Meiji period and is perfectly primed for viewing the maples in autumn. **Takimi-chaya** is perched on the edge of the stream where you can enjoy the view of a mini water-fall over rocks and giant *koi* (carp) swimming in the water.

Something is almost always in bloom at Rikugi-en. It is most famous for its maple leaves, which turn bright red usually around late November and early December. During this time, the park stays open until 9pm and the trees are illuminated after sunset. In early spring you can catch plum blossoms, followed by the flowering of the magnificent weeping cherry tree near the entrance.

DON'T MISS

➡ Teahouses
➡ Togetsukyō
➡ Maples in late autumn

PRACTICALITIES

➡ 六義園
➡ ☏03-3941-2222
➡ http://teien.tokyo-park.or.jp/en/rikugien
➡ 6-16-3 Hon-Komagome, Bunkyō-ku
➡ adult/child/senior ¥300/free/150
➡ ⏱9am-5pm
➡ Ⓢ Namboku line to Komagome, exit 2; Ⓡ JR Yamanote line to Komagome.

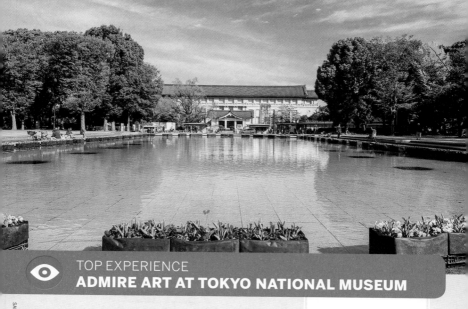

TOP EXPERIENCE
ADMIRE ART AT TOKYO NATIONAL MUSEUM

If you visit only one museum in Tokyo, make it this one. Established in 1872, this unprecedented collection of Japanese art covers ancient pottery, Buddhist sculpture, samurai swords, colourful *ukiyo-e* (woodblock prints), gorgeous kimonos and much, much more.

The museum is divided into several buildings, the most important of which is the **Honkan** (Japanese Gallery), which houses the main collection. If you only have an hour or two, this is where you should spend it. The building itself is in the Imperial Style of the 1930s, with art-deco flourishes throughout inside.

Next visit the enchanting **Gallery of Hōryū-ji Treasures** (法隆寺宝物館; Map p284), which displays masks, scrolls and gilt Buddhas from Hōryū-ji (in Nara Prefecture, dating from 607) in an elegant, box-shaped contemporary building (1999) by Taniguchi Yoshio. Nearby, to the west of the main gate, is the **Kuro-mon** (黒門; Black Gate; Map p284), transported from the Edo-era mansion of a feudal lord. On weekends it opens for visitors to pass through.

Visitors with more time can explore the three-storied **Tōyōkan** (Gallery of Asian Art; Map p284), with Asian artworks, including delicate Chinese ceramics, and a theatre screening short documentaries on historical art subjects.

The **Heiseikan** (平成館; Map p284), which can be accessed via a passage on the 1st floor of the Honkan, houses the Japanese Archaeological Gallery as well temporary exhibitions (which cost extra); these can be fantastic, but sometimes lack the English signage found throughout the rest of the museum.

Also only used for special exhibitions and events is the 1909-vintage **Hyokeikan** (表慶館; Map p284). For more on Tokyo National Museum, see p146.

DON'T MISS

➜ Honkan
➜ Gallery of Hōryū-ji Treasures
➜ Kuro-mon
➜ Tōyōkan

PRACTICALITIES

➜ 東京国立博物館, Tokyo Kokuritsu Hakubutsukan
➜ Map p284, D4
➜ 03-3822-1111
➜ www.tnm.jp
➜ 13-9 Ueno-kōen, Taitō-ku
➜ adult/child ¥620/free
➜ 9.30am-5pm Tue-Thu, to 9pm Fri & Sat, to 6pm Sun
➜ JR lines to Ueno, Ueno-kōen exit

Tokyo National Museum

HISTORIC HIGHLIGHTS

The Honkan (Japanese Gallery) is designed to give visitors a crash course in Japanese art history from the Jōmon era (13,000–300 BC) to the Edo era (AD 1603–1868). The works on display here are rotated regularly, to protect fragile ones and to create seasonal exhibitions, so you're always guaranteed to see something new.

Buy your ticket from outside the main gate then head straight to the Honkan with its sloping tile roof. Stow your coat in a locker and take the central staircase up to the 2nd floor, where the exhibitions are arranged chronologically. Allow two hours for this tour of the highlights.

The first room on your right starts from the beginning with **ancient Japanese art ❶**. Pick up a free copy of the brochure *Highlights of Japanese Art* at the entrance to the first room on your right. The exhibition starts here with the **Dawn of Japanese Art**.

Continue to the **National Treasure Gallery ❷**. 'National Treasure' is the highest distinction awarded to a work of art in Japan. Keep an eye out for more National Treasures, labelled in red, on display in other rooms throughout the museum.

Moving on into the Heian era (794–1185), considered the first flourishing of what we think of as Japanese culture, stop to admire the **courtly art ❸**. Next is the medieval art: ink brush scrolls, tea ceremony pottery and **samurai armour and swords ❹**; and then the *ukiyo-e* and **kimono ❺** of the 17th and 18th centuries.

Head to the ground floor, where rooms are arranged by theme (such as lacquerware). Particularly noteworthy is the collection of **Buddhist sculptures ❻** and the **Ainu and Ryūkyū cultural artefacts ❼**.

Finish your visit with a look inside the enchanting **Gallery of Hōryū-ji Treasures ❽**.

Ukiyo-e & Kimono (Room 10)
Chic silken kimono and lushly coloured *ukiyo-e* (woodblock prints) are two icons of the Edo-era (AD 1603–1868) *ukiyo* – the 'floating world', or world of fleeting beauty and pleasure.

Japanese Sculpture (Room 11)
Many of Japan's most famous sculptures, religious in nature, are locked away in temple reliquaries. This is a rare chance to see them up close.

MUSEUM GARDEN
Don't miss the garden if you visit in spring and autumn during the few weeks it's open to the public.

Heiseikan & Japanese Archaeology Gallery

Research & Information Centre

Hyōkeikan

Kuro-mon

Main Gate

Gallery of Hōryū-ji Treasures
Surround yourself with miniature gilt Buddhas from Hōryū-ji, one of Japan's oldest Buddhist temples, founded in 607. Don't miss the graceful Pitcher with Dragon Head, a National Treasure.

Samurai Armour & Swords (Rooms 5 & 6)
Glistening swords, finely stitched armour and imposing helmets bring to life the samurai, those iconic warriors of Japan's medieval age.

Courtly Art (Room 3-2)
Literature works, calligraphy and narrative picture scrolls are displayed alongside decorative art objects, which allude to the life of elegance led by courtesans a thousand years ago.

Honkan (Japanese Gallery) 2nd Floor

Honkan (Japanese Gallery) 1st Floor

National Treasure Gallery (Room 2)
A single, superlative work from the museum's collection of 88 National Treasures (perhaps a painted screen, or a gilded, hand-drawn sutra) is displayed in a serene, contemplative setting.

Museum Garden & Teahouses

Honkan (Japanese Gallery)

Tōyōkan (Gallery of Asian Art)

GIFT SHOP
The museum gift shop, on the 1st floor of the Honkan, has an excellent collection of Japanese art books in English.

Dawn of Japanese Art (Room 1)
The rise of the imperial court and the introduction of Buddhism changed the Japanese aesthetic forever. These clay works from previous eras show what came before.

Ainu and Ryūkyū Collection (Room 16)
Japanese culture is often considered a monolith, but before Japan colonized Hokkaidō (home of the indigenous Ainu people) and the Ryūkyū Empire, each had its own rich culture.

👁 SIGHTS

RIKUGI-EN   GARDENS
See p144.

👁 Ueno

TOKYO NATIONAL MUSEUM   MUSEUM
See p145.

UENO-KŌEN   PARK
Map p284 (上野公園; www.ueno-bunka.jp; Taitō-ku; 🚉JR lines to Ueno, Ueno-kōen or Shinobazu exit) One of Tokyo's top spots for springtime cherry-blossoms, sprawling Ueno-kōen is also home to many of Ueno's sights, including the Tokyo National Museum, Ueno Zoo, the National Museum of Nature & Science, Kiyōmizu Kannon-dō and Ueno Tōshō-gū. Navigating the park's wooded paths and large plazas is easy, thanks to large maps in English.

KURODA MEMORIAL HALL   GALLERY
Map p284 (黒田記念室; ☎03-5777-8600; www.tobunken.go.jp/kuroda/index_e.html; 13-9 Ueno-kōen, Taitō-ku; ⊙9.30am-5pm Tue-Sun; 🚉JR lines to Ueno, Ueno-kōen exit) **FREE** Kuroda Seiki (1866–1924) is considered the father of modern Western-style painting in Japan. This 1928-vintage hall, an annex to the national museum (p145), displays key works from different points in his career (which took him to France, first to study law and then painting). The most famous works in the collection, including *Reading* (1891) and *Lakeside* (1897), are in a room that only opens a few times a year; check the website for a schedule.

SHINOBAZU-IKE   LAKE
Map p284 (不忍池; Ueno-kōen, Taitō-ku; 🚉JR lines to Ueno, Shinobazu exit) A key feature of Ueno-kōen is this large, natural pond, divided into three sections (one of which lies within the boundaries of Ueno Zoo). The largest section is dominated by giant lotuses, which completely cover its surface in summer. Go bird- and botany-spotting on the boardwalk at the pond's southern end and around the temple **Benten-dō** (Map p284; 弁天堂; ☎03-3821-4638; ⊙9am-5pm) **FREE**.

UENO ZOO   ZOO
Map p284 (上野動物園, Ueno Dōbutsu-en; ☎03-3828-5171; www.tokyo-zoo.net; 9-83 Ueno-kōen, Taitō-ku; adult/child ¥600/free; ⊙9.30am-5pm Tue-Sun; 🚉JR lines to Ueno, Ueno-kōen exit) Japan's oldest zoo, established in 1882, is home to animals from around the globe, but the biggest attractions are the giant pandas that arrived from China in 2011 – Rī Rī and Shin Shin who welcomed a cub, Xiang Xiang, in 2017. There's also a whole area devoted to lemurs, which makes sense given Tokyoites' love of all things cute.

UENO TŌSHŌ-GŪ   SHINTO SHRINE
Map p284 (上野東照宮; ☎03-3822-3455; www.uenotoshogu.com; 9-88 Ueno-kōen, Taitō-ku; adult/child ¥500/200; ⊙9am-5.30pm Mar-Sep, to 4.30pm Oct-Feb; 🚉JR lines to Ueno, Shinobazu exit) This shrine inside Ueno-kōen was built in honour of Tokugawa Ieyasu, the warlord who unified Japan. Resplendent in gold leaf and ornate details, it dates to 1651 (though it has had recent touch-ups). You can get a pretty good look from outside the gate, if you want to skip the admission fee.

KIYŌMIZU KANNON-DŌ   BUDDHIST TEMPLE
Map p284 (清水観音堂; ☎03-3821-4749; http://kiyomizu.kaneiji.jp; 1-29 Ueno-kōen, Taitō-ku; ⊙9am-5pm; 🚉JR lines to Ueno, Shinobazu exit) Ueno-kōen's Kiyōmizu Kannon-dō is one of Tokyo's oldest structures: established in 1631 and in its present position since 1698, it has survived every disaster that has come its way. It's a miniature of the famous Kiyomizu-dera in Kyoto and is a pilgrimage site for women hoping to conceive as it enshrines Kosodate Kannon, the protector of childbearing and child-raising.

**NATIONAL MUSEUM
OF NATURE & SCIENCE**   MUSEUM
Map p284 (国立科学博物館; ☎03-5777-8600; www.kahaku.go.jp/english; 7-20 Ueno-kōen, Taitō-ku; adult/child ¥600/free; ⊙9am-5pm Tue-Thu, Sat & Sun, to 8pm Fri; 🚉JR lines to Ueno, Ueno-kōen exit) The Japan Gallery here showcases the rich and varied wildlife of the Japanese archipelago, from the bears of Hokkaidō to the giant beetles of Okinawa. Elsewhere in this fascinating museum: a rocket launcher, an Edo-era mummy and a digital seismograph that charts earthquakes in real time. There's English signage throughout, plus an English-language audio guide (¥300).

**INTERNATIONAL LIBRARY
OF CHILDREN'S LITERATURE**   LIBRARY
Map p284 (☎03-3827-2053; www.kodomo.go.jp; 12-49 Ueno-kōen, Taitō-ku; ⊙9.30am-5pm Tue-Sun & 3rd Wed of month; 📷♿; 🚉JR lines to Ueno, Ueno-kōen exit) **FREE** This branch of the National Diet Library stores hundreds of thousands of volumes including picture and kids' story

books from around the world. Exhibitions are held here and there is a cafe with an inexpensive menu that aims to please children.

KYŪ IWASAKI-TEIEN HISTORIC BUILDING

Map p284 (旧岩崎邸庭園; ☎03-3823-8340; http://teien.tokyo-park.or.jp/en/kyu-iwasaki/index.html; 1-3-45 Ike-no-hata, Taitō-ku; adult/child ¥400/free; ⏰9am-5pm; [S]Chiyoda line to Yushima, exit 1) This grand residence has a Western-style mansion designed by Josiah Conder in 1896, connected to a Japanese house built by Ōkawa Kijuro at the same time, and gardens. It was the home of Hisaya Iwasaki, son of the founder of Mitsubishi, and is a fascinating example of how the cultural elite of the early Meiji period synthesised east and west.

Yanesen

★ASAKURA MUSEUM OF SCULPTURE, TAITŌ MUSEUM

Map p284 (朝倉彫塑館; ☎03-3821-4549; www.taitocity.net/taito/asakura; 7-16-10 Yanaka, Taitō-ku; adult/child ¥500/250; ⏰9.30am-4.30pm Tue, Wed & Fri-Sun; 🚉JR Yamanote line to Nippori, north exit) Sculptor Asakura Fumio (artist name Chōso; 1883–1964) designed this atmospheric house himself. It combined his original Japanese home and garden with a large studio that incorporated vaulted ceilings, a 'sunrise room' and a rooftop garden with wonderful neighbourhood views. It's now a reverential museum with many of the artist's signature realist works, mostly of people and cats, on display.

NEZU-JINJA SHINTO SHRINE

Map p284 (根津神社; ☎03-3822-0753; www.nedujinja.or.jp; 1-28-9 Nezu, Bunkyō-ku; ⏰6am-5pm; [S]Chiyoda line to Nezu, exit 1) Not only is this one of Japan's oldest shrines, it is also easily the most beautiful in a district packed with attractive religious buildings. The vermilion-and-gold structure dates from the early 18th century and is one of the city's miraculous survivors. The long corridor of small red *torii* makes for great photos.

YANAKA GINZA AREA

Map p284 (谷中銀座; www.yanakaginza.com; 🚉JR Yamanote line to Nippori, north exit) Yanaka Ginza is pure, vintage mid-20th-century Tokyo, a pedestrian street lined with butcher shops, vegetable vendors and the like. Most Tokyo neighbourhoods once had stretches like these (until supermarkets took over). It's popular with Tokyoites from all over the city, who come to soak up the nostalgic atmosphere, plus the locals who shop here.

YANAKA-REIEN CEMETERY

Map p284 (谷中霊園; ☎03-3821-4456; www.tokyo-park.or.jp/reien; 7-5-24 Yanaka, Taitō-ku; 🚉JR Yamanote line to Nippori, west exit) One of Tokyo's largest graveyards, Yanaka-reien is the final resting place of more than 7000 souls, many of whom were quite well known in their day. It's also where you'll find the tomb of Yoshinobu Tokugawa (徳川慶喜の墓), the last shogun. Come spring it is also a popular cherry-blossom-viewing spot.

SCAI THE BATHHOUSE GALLERY

Map p284 (スカイザバスハウス; ☎03-3821-1144; www.scaithebathhouse.com; 6-1-23 Yanaka, Taitō-ku; ⏰noon-6pm Tue-Sat; [S]Chiyoda line to Nezu, exit 1) [FREE] This 200-year-old bathhouse has for several decades been an avant-garde gallery space, showcasing Japanese and international artists in its austere vaulted space. Closed between exhibitions.

SUDO-KŌEN PARK

Map p284 (須藤公園; 3-4 Sendagi, Bunkyō-ku; [S]Chiyoda line to Sendagi, exit 2) [FREE] Looking like something straight from a woodblock print, this gorgeous pocket park is worth the stroll from the Sendagi end of Yanaka to view its brilliant vermilion bridge over an ornamental pond to the small shrine for the deity Benzaiten. In the background a waterfall splashes over rocks down the hill.

SHITAMACHI MUSEUM MUSEUM

Map p284 (下町風俗資料館; ☎03-3823-7451; www.taitocity.net/zaidan/shitamachi; 2-1 Ueno-kōen, Taitō-ku; adult/child ¥300/100; ⏰9.30am-4.30pm Tue-Sun; 🚉JR lines to Ueno, Shinobazu exit) This small museum recreates life in the plebeian quarters of Tokyo during the Meiji and Taishō periods (1868–1926), before the city was twice destroyed by the Great Kantō Earthquake and WWII. There are old tenement houses and shops that you can enter.

🍴 EATING

🍴 Ueno

★INNSYOUTEI JAPANESE ¥

Map p284 (韻松亭; ☎03-3821-8126; www.innsyoutei.jp; 4-59 Ueno-kōen, Taitō-ku; lunch/dinner from ¥1680/5500; ⏰restaurant 11am-3pm &

5-9.30pm, tearoom 3-5pm; [🖥]; [🚆]JR lines to Ueno, Ueno-kōen exit) In a gorgeous wooden building dating to 1875, Innsyoutei (pronounced 'inshotei' and meaning 'rhyme of the pine cottage') has long been a favourite spot for fancy *kaiseki*-style meals while visiting Ueno-kōen (p148). Without a booking (essential for dinner) you'll have a long wait but it's worth it. Lunchtime *bentō* (boxed meals) offer beautifully presented morsels and are great value.

Between lunch and dinner the attached rustic teahouse serves *matcha* (powdered green tea) and traditional desserts from ¥600.

YANGXIANG AJIBO   CHINESE ¥

Map p284 (羊香味坊; [☎]03-6803-0168; 3-12-6 Ueno, Taitō-ku; mains ¥500-2000; [🕑]11.30am-11pm Mon-Sat, 1-10pm Sun; [🚆]JR lines to Okachimachi, north exit) Lamb isn't a common meat on Tokyo's menus, but at this casual eatery specialising in the cuisine of northeastern China, it's the *raison d'etre*. Sample it served as grilled chops, on skewers, in luscious dumplings and as a base for the peppery broth used for ramen.

UENO-SAKURAGI NANOHANA   JAPANESE ¥¥

Map p284 (上野桜木　菜の花; [☎]03-3827-3511; 1-10-26 Ueno-Sakuragi, Taitō-ku; lunch/dinner ¥1580/5400; [🕑]11am-2pm & 5.30-9.30pm Tue-Sat, 11am-4pm Sun; [🚇]Chiyoda line to Nezu, exit 1) The family that runs this charming restaurant sources many of the organic ingredients (including the rice, pickles and vegetables for side dishes) from the chef's mother, who lives on Sado-ga-shima. The house speciality is *ochazuke* – rice mixed with cuts of raw fish, other toppings and a clear broth.

SASA-NO-YUKI   TOFU ¥¥

Map p284 (笹乃雪; [☎]03-3873-1145; www. sasanoyuki.com; 2-15-10 Negishi, Taitō-ku; dishes ¥400-700, lunch/dinner course from ¥2400/5600; [🕑]11.30am-8.30pm Tue-Sun, [🖥]; [🚆]JR Yamanote line to Uguisudani, north exit) [✐] Sasa-no-Yuki opened its doors in the Edo period and continues to serve its signature dishes with tofu made fresh every morning using water from the shop's own well. Some treats to expect: *ankake-dofu* (tofu in a thick, sweet sauce) and *goma-dofu* (sesame tofu). Vegetarians should not assume everything is purely veggie – ask before ordering. There is bamboo out the front.

The best-value lunch set (¥2400) is served from 11.30am to 2pm Tuesday to Friday.

SHINSUKE   IZAKAYA ¥¥

Map p284 (シンスケ; [☎]03-3832-0469; 3-31-5 Yushima, Bunkyō-ku; dishes ¥500-2500, cover charge ¥300; [🕑]5-9.30pm Mon-Fri, to 9pm Sat; [🖥]; [🚇]Chiyoda line to Yushima, exit 3) In business since 1925, Shinsuke has honed the concept of an ideal *izakaya* (Japanese pub-eatery) to perfection: long cedar counter, 'master' in *happi* (traditional short coat) and *hachimaki* (traditional headband), and smooth-as-silk *daiginjō* (premium-grade sake). The menu, updated monthly, includes house specialities (such as *kitsune raclette* – deep-fried tofu stuffed with raclette cheese) and seasonal dishes; note portions are small. Reservations recommended.

Also, unlike other storied *izakaya* that can be intimidating to foreigners, the staff here are friendly and go out of their way to explain the menu in English.

✖ Yanesen

★ KAMACHIKU   UDON ¥

Map p284 (釜竹; [☎]03-5815-4675; www.kamachiku.com; 2-14-18 Nezu, Bunkyō-ku; noodles from ¥850, small dishes ¥350-950; [🕑]11.30am-2pm Tue-Sun, 5.30-9pm Tue-Sat; [🖥]; [🚇]Chiyoda line to Nezu, exit 1) Freshly made udon are the speciality at this popular restaurant, in a beautifully restored brick warehouse from 1910 that's incorporated into a building designed by Kuma Kengo. In addition to noodles, the menu includes a good selection of sake and lots of small dishes (such as grilled fish, veggies and a delicious Japanese-style omelette).

TAYORI   JAPANESE ¥

Map p284 ([☎]03-5834-7026; www.tayori-osozai.jp; 3-12-4 Yanaka, Taitō-ku; set meals ¥1000; [🕑]11.30am-8pm Wed-Mon; [📶][🖥]; [🚆]Yamanote line to Nippori, Yanaka exit) Tucked down an alley off Yanaka Ginza (p149) is this design-savvy deli and cafe that subscribes to the farm-to-table ethos by telling customers all about its ingredients' provenance. The set meals are excellent value and the cool, artisan atmosphere makes it a prime spot to revive while you explore the area.

HAGI CAFE   CAFE ¥

Map p284 (ハギカフェ; [☎]03-5832-9808; www.hagiso.jp; 3-10-25 Yanaka, Taitō-ku; mains ¥850-1445; [🕑]8-10.30am & noon-9pm; [🖥]; [🚇]Chiyoda line to Sendagi, exit 2) Part of the gallery and event space Hagiso, run by students from Tokyo University of the Arts (Geidai), this is a good all-rounder for meals, drinks and sweets in the heart of Yanaka. Its Japanese-style breakfast is a great deal at ¥325; later in the day there's curry, pasta, cakes and sundaes. Expect to wait on weekends as it's popular.

★HANTEI JAPANESE ¥¥

Map p284 (はん亭; ☎03-3287-9000; www.hantei.co.jp; 2-12-15 Nezu, Bunkyō-ku; lunch/dinner from ¥3200/3000; ⏰noon-3pm & 5-10pm Tue-Sun; 📖; [S]Chiyoda line to Nezu, exit 2) Housed in a beautifully maintained, century-old traditional wooden building, Hantei is a local landmark. Delectable skewers of seasonal *kushiage* (fried meat, fish and vegetables) are served with small, refreshing side dishes. Lunch includes eight or 12 sticks; dinner starts with six, after which you can order additional rounds (three/six skewers ¥800/1600).

DRINKING & NIGHTLIFE

Ueno

TORINDŌ TEAHOUSE

Map p284 (桃林堂; ☎03-3828-9826; 1-5-7 Ueno-Sakuragi, Taitō-ku; ⏰9.30am-5pm Tue-Sun; [S]Chiyoda line to Nezu, exit 1) Sample a cup of paint-thick *matcha* (¥450) at this tiny teahouse on the edge of Ueno-kōen (p148). Tradition dictates that the bitter tea be paired with something sweet, so choose from the artful desserts (¥280 to ¥435) in the glass counter, then pull up a stool at the communal table. It's a white building on a corner.

Yanesen

YANAKA BEER HALL CRAFT BEER

Map p284 (谷中ビアホール; ☎03-5834-2381; www.facebook.com/yanakabeerhall; 2-15-6 Ueno-sakuragi, Taitō-ku; ⏰noon-8.30pm Tue-Fri, from 11am Sat & Sun; 🚭📖; [S]Chiyoda line to Nezu, exit 1) Exploring Yanesen can be thirsty work so thank heavens for this craft-beer bar, a cosy place with some outdoor seating. It's part of a charming complex of old wooden buildings that also houses a bakery-cafe, a bistro and an events space. It has several brews on tap, including a Yanaka lager (¥970) that's only available here.

KAYABA COFFEE CAFE

Map p284 (カヤバ珈琲; ☎03-3823-3545; http://kayaba-coffee.com; 6-1-29 Yanaka, Taitō-ku; coffee ¥450; ⏰8am-9pm Mon-Sat, to 6pm Sun; 📖; [S]Chiyoda line to Nezu, exit 1) This vintage 1930s coffee shop (the building is actually from the '20s) in Yanaka is a hang-out for local students and artists. Come early for the 'morning set' (coffee and a sandwich for ¥800; served 8am to 11am). In the evenings, Kayaba morphs into a bar.

ENTERTAINMENT

TOKYO BUNKA KAIKAN CLASSICAL MUSIC

Map p284 (東京文化会館; ☎03-3828-2111; www.t-bunka.jp; 5-45 Ueno-kōen, Taitō-ku; ⏰library 1-8pm Tue-Sat, to 5pm Sun, closed irregularly; 🚉JR lines to Ueno, Ueno-kōen exit) The Tokyo Metropolitan Symphony Orchestra and the Tokyo Ballet make regular appearances at this concrete bunker of a building designed by Maekawa Kunio, an apprentice of Le Corbusier. Prices vary wildly; look out for monthly morning classical-music performances that cost only ¥500. The gorgeously decorated auditorium, with cloud-shaped acoustic panels on the wall, has superb acoustics.

TOKYO UNIVERSITY OF THE ARTS PERFORMING ARTS CENTER CLASSICAL MUSIC

Map p284 (東京藝術大学奏楽堂; ☎050-5525-2465; www.pac.geidai.ac.jp; 12-8 Ueno-kōen, Taitō-ku; tickets ¥1000-5000) With its stage dominated by a French Garnier Organ and a ceiling that can be moved to create optimum acoustics, the university's intimate hall is a superb spot to take in a classical concert. Check online for the schedule and enquire about the occasional morning concerts usually starting at 11am and costing ¥1000.

SHOPPING

Ueno

★AMEYA-YOKOCHŌ MARKET

Map p284 (アメヤ横町; www.ameyoko.net; 4 Ueno, Taitō-ku; ⏰10am-7pm, some shops close Wed; 🚉JR lines to Okachimachi, north exit) Step into this partially open-air market paralleling and beneath the JR line tracks, and ritzy, glitzy Tokyo feels like a distant

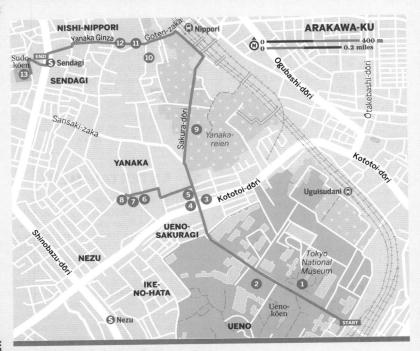

Neighbourhood Walk
Strolling Yanaka

START TOKYO NATIONAL MUSEUM
END SENDAGI STATION
LENGTH 3KM; TWO HOURS

If you have time, visit the ❶ **Tokyo National Museum** (p145) before you start exploring Yanaka, with its temples, galleries and old wooden buildings. If not, simply follow the road northwest out of ❷ **Ueno-kōen** until you hit Kototoi-dōri. At the corner is the ❸ **Shitamachi Museum Annex** (2-10-6 Ueno-sakuragi), actually a preserved, century-old liquor store. Across the street is ❹ **Kayaba Coffee** (p151), if you need a pick-me-up.

❺ **SCAI the Bathhouse** (p149) is a public bathhouse turned contemporary art gallery. Continue down to the studio of painter ❻ **Allan West** (p153). Beside it, on the corner, is an ancient, thick-trunked ❼ **Himalayan cedar tree**. Around here, you'll pass many temples, including ❽ **Enju-ji** (1-7-36 Yanaka), where Nichika-sama, the 'god of strong legs', is enshrined; it's popular with runners. You can stop in any of the temples; just be respectful and keep your voice low.

Double back towards the entrance of ❾ **Yanaka-reien** (p149), one of Tokyo's most atmospheric and prestigious cemeteries (also a favourite sunning spot of the neighborhood's many stray cats). When you exit the cemetery, continue with the train tracks on your right, climbing until you reach the bridge, which overlooks the tracks (a favourite destination for trainspotters).

Head left and look for the sign pointing towards the ❿ **Asakura Museum of Sculpture, Taitō** (p149), the home studio of an early-20th century sculptor and now an attractive museum. Back on the main drag, continue down the ⓫ **Yūyake Dandan** – literally the 'Sunset Stairs' – to the classic mid-20th-century shopping street ⓬ **Yanaka Ginza** (p149). Pick up some snacks from the vendors here, then hunker down on a milk crate on the side of the road with the locals and wash it all down with a beer. Walk west and you can pick up the subway at Sendagi Station, after taking a peek at the gorgeous pocket park ⓭ **Sudo-kōen** (p149).

memory. It got its start as a black market, post-WWII, when American goods (which included *ameya* – candy and chocolates) were sold here. Today you can pick up everything from fresh seafood to vintage jeans and bargain sneakers.

★ GEIDAI ART PLAZA   ARTS & CRAFTS
Map p284 (☎050-5525-2102; www.artplaza. geidai.ac.jp; Tokyo University of the Arts, 12-8 Ueno-kōen, Taitō-ku; ☺10am-6pm Tue-Sun; ℝJR lines to Ueno, Ueno-kōen exit) On the campus of Tokyo's top arts university this shop, opened in 2018, showcases creative pieces in a range of media by the institute's staff, students and graduates. It's well worth a browse and if you can't afford an original work, there are plenty of affordable things too including books, comics and specially designed biscuits.

🏠 Yanesen

YANAKA MATSUNOYA   HOMEWARES
Map p284 (谷中松野屋; ☎03-3823-7441; www. yanakamatsunoya.jp; 3-14-14 Nishi-Nippori, Arakawa-ku; ☺11am-7pm Mon & Wed-Fri, from 10am Sat & Sun) At the top of Yanaka Ginza (p149), Matsunoya sets out its stall with an attractive range of mainly household goods – baskets, brooms and canvas totes, for example – simple in beauty and form, and handmade by local artisans.

ART SANCTUARY ALLAN WEST   ART
Map p284 (繪処アラン・ウエスト; ☎03-3827-1907; www.allanwest.jp; 1-6-17 Yanaka, Taitō-ku; ☺1.30-4.30pm Mon-Wed, Fri & Sat, from 3pm Sun; ⓢChiyoda line to Nezu, exit 1) **FREE** In this masterfully converted garage, long-time Yanaka resident Allan West paints gorgeous screens and scrolls in the traditional Japanese style, making his paints from

scratch just as local artists have done for centuries. Smaller votive-shaped paintings start at ¥5000; the screens clock in at a cool ¥6 million.

ISETATSU   ARTS & CRAFTS
Map p284 (いせ辰; ☎03-3823-1453; www.ise tatsu.com; 2-18-9 Yanaka, Taitō-ku; ☺10am-6pm; ⓢChiyoda line to Sendagi, exit 1) Dating back to 1864, this venerable stationery shop specialises in *chiyogami* – gorgeous, colourful paper made using woodblocks – as well as papier-mâché figures and masks.

 # SPORTS & ACTIVITIES

KITCHEN KUJO TOKYO   COOKING
Map p284 (☎03-5832-9452; www.kujo.tokyo; 1-2-10 Yanaka, Taitō-ku; classes ¥6000-12,000; ☺classes 10.30am or 1.30pm, bar 6-10.30pm Mon-Sat; ⓢChiyoda line to Nezu, exit 2) The Kobayashi family and their translator/ramen chef Jun offer an interesting variety of cooking and culture classes at this studio devoted to cooking with organic products. Learn how to make tofu, miso, vegan ramen and curry rice with guest instructor Curryman (who dresses in a wacky costume). Also available are calligraphy, tea-ceremony and yoga classes.

BUDDHA BELLIES   COOKING
Map p284 (☎080-5001-9395; www.buddha belliestokyo.jimdo.com; classes ¥5500-10,000; ⓢChiyoda line to Yushima, exit 3) English-speaking professional sushi chef and sake sommelier Ayuko and her husband lead small hands-on classes in sushi, *bentō* (boxed lunch), udon and *wagashi* (Japanese sweets) making. Classes are held at Ayuko's home close to Yushima Station (she'll meet you at exit 3) and run usually from 11am, lasting 2½ hours. Book early. Vegetarian, vegan and halal menus are also available.

Asakusa & Sumida River

ASAKUSA | OSHIAGE | RYŌGOKU | KIYOSUMI-SHIRAKAWA | FUKAGAWA

Neighbourhood Top Five

1 **Sensō-ji** (p156) Soaking up the atmosphere (and the incense) at Asakusa's centuries-old temple complex and browsing the craft stalls of Nakamise-dōri.

2 **Ryōgoku Kokugikan** (p158) Catching the salt-slinging, belly-slapping ritual of sumo at one of the city's four annual tournaments.

3 **Edo-Tokyo Museum** (p157) Learning about life in old Edo at this excellent history museum with full-scale reconstructions of famous buildings.

4 **Tokyo Sky Tree** (p157) Scaling the world's tallest communication tower, seeing the capital stretch to the horizon, then browsing the Solamachi mall at the base afterwards.

5 **Fukagawa Fudō-dō** (p163) Being blown away by the theatre of the fire ritual at this Shingon sect temple.

For more detail of this area see Map p286 and p287 ➡

Explore Asakusa & Sumida River

Welcome to Tokyo's east side, the area long known as Shitamachi (the 'Low City'), where the city's merchants and artisans lived during the Edo period (1603–1868). Asakusa (ah-*saku*-sah), centred around the bustling temple complex Sensō-ji (p156), is one of Tokyo's principal tourist destinations. Step off the main drags to find far fewer tourists, and the craft shops and small restaurants that have long defined these quarters. Looming over them all is Tokyo Sky Tree (p157), just across the river from Asakusa in Oshiage. Make it your last stop of the day to see the city all lit up at night.

Of the other neighbourhoods east of Sumida-gawa prioritise Ryōgoku. where you'll find the sumo stadium (p158), the Edo-Tokyo Museum (p157) and the Sumida Hokusai Museum (p157). All these can be covered in a day or less. If you have more time, it's rewarding to explore off-the-radar Kiyosumi-shirakawa and Fukagawa, where highlights include Kiyosumi-teien (p162), the Museum of Contemporary Art, Tokyo (MOT) (p162) and the temple Fukagawa Fudō-dō (p163). Walking around these peaceful east-side neighbourhoods can give you a feel for the old city culture (there are also pockets of hipster cool).

Asakusa has some of the city's longest running and most traditional restaurants. There are some bars here too, but generally this is a quieter part of Tokyo after dark.

Local Life

→ **Street Food** Asakusa brims with street-food vendors, especially along Sensō-ji's Nakamise-dōri.

→ **Market** A good flea market is held at Tomioka Hachiman-gū (p163) on the first and second Sunday of every month.

→ **Riverside Park** Pleasant Sumida-kōen runs along both sides of the river around Asakusa.

Getting There & Away

→ **Train** The Tsukuba Express stops at Tsukuba Express Asakusa Station, west of Sensō-ji. The Tōbu Sky Tree line leaves from Tōbu Asakusa Station for Tokyo Sky Tree Station. The JR Sōbu line goes to Ryōgoku.

→ **Subway** The Ginza line stops at Asakusa. The Asakusa line stops at a separate Asakusa Station and at Oshiage. The Ōedo line stops at Ryōgoku and Kiyosumi-shirakawa stations.

→ **Water Bus** Tokyo Cruise (p232) and Tokyo Mizube Cruising Line (p232) ferries stop at separate piers in Asakusa; Tokyo Mizube Cruising Line might stop again in Ryōgoku in time for the Olympics.

Lonely Planet's Top Tip

The roof terrace of the Asakusa Culture Tourist Information Center (p243) has fantastic views of Tokyo Sky Tree (p157) and the Nakamise-dōri approach to Sensō-ji (p156). Free events are sometimes held here, including geisha dances and craft-making demonstrations – check with the centre for the schedule.

 ASAKUSA & SUMIDA RIVER

Best Places to Eat

→ Asakusa Imahan (p159)

→ Kappō Yoshiba (p159)

→ Otafuku (p159)

→ Misojyu (p158)

For reviews, see p158.

Best Places to Drink

→ Popeye (p160)

→ Dandelion Chocolate (p160)

→ Café Otonova (p160)

→ Fuglen (p160)

For reviews, see p160.

Best Places to Shop

→ Marugoto Nippon (p161)

→ Babaghuri (p162)

→ Bengara (p161)

→ Kama-asa (p161)

→ Yoshitoku Dolls (p161)

For reviews, see p161.

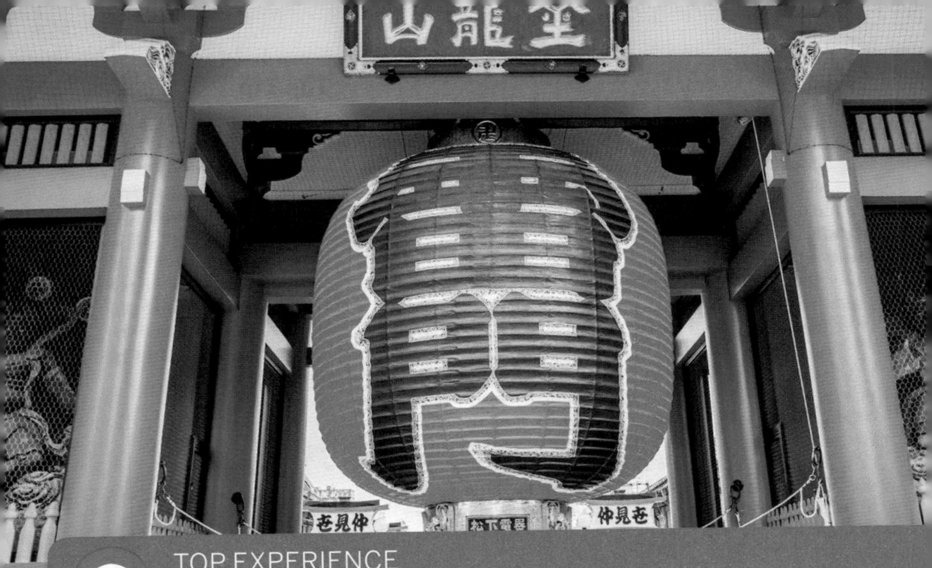

PAKPOOM PHUMMEE/SHUTTERSTOCK ©

TOP EXPERIENCE

SOAK UP THE ATMOSPHERE AT SENSŌ-JI

Sensō-ji is the capital's oldest temple, far older than Tokyo itself. According to legend, in AD 628, two fishermen brothers pulled out a golden image of Kannon (the Bodhisattva of compassion) from the nearby Sumida-gawa. Sensō-ji was built to enshrine it. Today the temple stands out for its atmosphere of an older Japan, rarely visible in Tokyo today.

The main entrance to the temple complex is via the fantastic, red **Kaminari-mon** (雷門; Thunder Gate; Map p286). An enormous *chōchin* (lantern), which weighs 670kg, hangs from the centre. On either side are a pair of ferocious protective deities: Fūjin, the god of wind, on the right; and Raijin, the god of thunder, on the left. Beyond the gate is the shopping street **Nakamise-dōri** with stalls selling everything from tourist trinkets to genuine Edo-style crafts.

In front of the grand **Hondō** (Main Hall), with its dramatic sloping roof, is a large cauldron with smoking incense. The smoke is said to bestow health and you'll see people wafting it over their bodies. The current Hondō was constructed in 1958, replacing the one destroyed in WWII air raids. The Main Hall and its gates are illuminated every day from sunset until 11pm. The **Kannon image** (a tiny 6cm) is cloistered away from view deep inside the Main Hall (and admittedly may not exist at all).

DON'T MISS

- Kaminari-mon
- Nakamise-dōri stalls
- Incense cauldron at the Main Hall
- Temple lights at sunset

PRACTICALITIES

- 浅草寺
- Map p286, C2
- ☎03-3842-0181
- www.senso-ji.jp
- 2-3-1 Asakusa, Taitō-ku
- admission free
- 🕒24hr
- [S]Ginza line to Asakusa, exit 1

Off the courtyard stands a 53m-high **Five-Storey Pagoda** (五重塔; Map p286), a 1973 reconstruction of a pagoda built by Tokugawa Iemitsu; it was renovated in 2017. It's the second-tallest pagoda in Japan.

Consider the crowds part of the experience, as there doesn't seem to be a time of day when Sensō-ji isn't packed.

👁 SIGHTS

👁 Asakusa

ASAKUSA-JINJA SHINTO SHRINE

Map p286 (浅草神社; ☎03-3844-1575; www.asakusajinja.jp; 2-3-1 Asakusa, Taitō-ku; ⏱9am-4.30pm; ⓢGinza line to Asakusa, exit 1) Asakusa-jinja was built in honour of the brothers who discovered the Kannon statue that inspired the construction of Sensō-ji (p160). The current building, painted a deep shade of red, dates to 1649 and is a rare example of early Edo architecture.

ASAHI SUPER DRY HALL ARCHITECTURE

Map p286 (フラムドール; Flamme d'Or; 1-23-1 Azuma-bashi, Sumida-ku; ⓢGinza line to Asakusa, exit 4) Also known as Asahi Beer Hall, the headquarters of the brewery – designed by Philippe Starck and completed in 1989 – remains one of Tokyo's most distinctive buildings.

The tower, with its golden glass facade and white top floors, is supposed to evoke a giant mug of beer, while the golden blob atop the lower jet-black building is the flame (locals, however, refer to it as the 'golden turd').

ASAKUSA GALLERY

Map p286 (浅草; ☎050-5532-3237; www.asakusa-o.com; 1-6-16 Nishi-Asakusa, Taitō-ku; ⏱noon-7pm Sat-Mon; ⓢGinza line to Tawaramachi, exit 3) FREE Worth searching out is this quirky 40-sq-metre exhibition space in an unmarked old house, hiding down a narrow alley. It's run by contemporary art curator Ōsaka Koichiro and features an eclectic range of shows and events by local and international artists. Look for it beside the shop with the sign コーザイ.

👁 Ryōgoku

⭐EDO-TOKYO MUSEUM MUSEUM

Map p287 (江戸東京博物館; ☎03-3626-9974; www.edo-tokyo-museum.or.jp; 1-4-1 Yokoami, Sumida-ku; adult/child ¥600/free; ⏱9.30am-5.30pm, to 7.30pm Sat, closed Mon; ®JR Sōbu line to Ryōgoku, west exit) Tokyo's history museum documents the city's transformation from tidal flatlands to feudal capital to modern metropolis via detailed scale re-creations of townscapes, villas and tenement homes,

plus artefacts such as *ukiyo-e* and old maps. Reopened in 2018 after a renovation, the museum also has interactive displays, multilingual touch-screen panels and audio guides. Still, the best way to tour the museum is with one of the gracious English-speaking volunteer guides, who can really bring the history to life.

JAPANESE SWORD MUSEUM MUSEUM

Map p287 (刀剣博物館; ☎03-6284-1000; www.touken.or.jp; 1-12-9 Yokoami, Sumida-ku; adult/child ¥1000/free; ⏱9.30am-5pm Tue-Sun; ®JR Sōbu line to Ryōgoku, west exit) For visitors with a keen interest in Japanese sword-making – an art that continues to this day – this museum, which relocated to a new building in 2018, features exhibitions from contemporary craftspeople. There's good English information on the different styles and components (and more English-language references for sale in the small gift shop).

SUMIDA HOKUSAI MUSEUM MUSEUM

Map p287 (すみだ北斎美術館; ☎03-5777-8600; http://hokusai-museum.jp; 2-7-2 Kamezawa, Sumida-ku; adult/child/student & senior ¥400/free/300; ⏱9.30am-5.30pm Tue-Sun; ⓢOedo line to Ryōgoku, exit A4) The woodblock artist Hokusai Katsushika (1760–1849) was born and died close to the location of this museum, which opened in 2016 in a striking aluminium-clad building designed by Pritzker Prize–winning architect Sejima Kazuyo.

The small permanent exhibition gives an overview of his life and work, mostly through replicas.

👁 Oshiage

TOKYO SKY TREE TOWER

Map p286 (東京スカイツリー; ☎0570-55-0102; www.tokyo-skytree.jp; 1-1-2 Oshiage, Sumida-ku; 350m/450m observation decks ¥2060/3090; ⏱8am-10pm; ⓢHanzōmon line to Oshiage, Tokyo Sky Tree exit) Tokyo Sky Tree opened in May 2012 as the world's tallest 'free-standing tower' at 634m. Its silvery exterior of steel mesh morphs from a triangle at the base to a circle at 300m. There are two observation decks, at 350m and 450m. You can see more of the city during daylight hours – at peak visibility you can see up to 100km away, all the way to Mt Fuji – but it is at night that Tokyo appears truly beautiful.

✖ EATING

✖ Asakusa

★MISOJYU
JAPANESE ✖

Map p286 (☎03-5830-3101; www.misojyu.jp; 1-7-5 Asakusa, Taitō-ku; miso soup ¥780, set menu from ¥1280; ⊙8.30am-7pm Tue-Sun; ⓇTsukuba Express to Asakusa, exit 4) The Japanese meal staples of rice and miso soup, are given a stylish update at Misojyu. All ingredients are organic and recipes range from traditional to contemporary, such as miso soup with beef and tomato and brown rice *onigiri* covered in tea leaves. A limited breakfast menu is served until 11am.

ONIGIRI YADOROKU
JAPANESE ✖

Map p286 (おにぎり　浅草　宿六; ☎03-3874-1615; www.onigiriyadoroku.com; 3-9-10 Asakusa, Taitō-ku; set lunch 2/3 onigiri from ¥690/930, onigiri ¥280-690; ⊙11.30am-5pm Mon-Sat, 6pm-2am Thu-Tue; ⊜🎫; ⓇTsukuba Express to Asakusa, exit 1) *Onigiri,* wrapped in crispy sheets of *nori* (seaweed), are a great Japanese culinary invention. Try them freshly made at Tokyo's oldest *onigiri* shop, which feels more like a classy sushi counter. The set lunches are a great deal; at night there's a large range of flavours to choose from, along with alcohol.

HOPPY-DŌRI
IZAKAYA ✖

Map p286 (ホッピー通り; 2-5 Asakusa, Taitō-ku; dishes ¥500-700; ⊙noon until late, varies by shop; ⓇTsukuba Express to Asakusa, exit 4) Along either side of the street popularly known as Hoppy-dōri – 'hoppy' is a cheap malt beverage – are rows of *izakaya* (Japanese pub-eateries) with outdoor seating on rickety stools and plastic tarps for awnings. Don't let that put you off – this is one of Asakusa's most atmospheric eating and drinking strips.

Many shops have picture menus. Try the *gyū-suji nikomi* (stewed beef tendons), a speciality of the street.

SUZUKIEN
ICE CREAM ✖

Map p286 (壽々喜園; ☎03-3873-0311; http://to cha.co.jp; 3-4-3 Asakusa, Taitō-ku; ice cream from ¥370; ⊙10am-5pm, closed 3rd Wed of the month; 🎫; ⓇTsukuba Express to Asakusa, exit 1) Suzukien boasts of having the most *matcha*-ful *matcha* ice cream around, and the deep moss-green Premium No 7 does not disappoint. In addition to the seven levels of

---

◉ TOP EXPERIENCE
SEE SUMO AT RYŌGOKU KOKUGIKAN

If you're in town when a tournament is on, don't miss the chance to catch the big boys of Japanese wrestling in action at the country's largest sumo stadium. The key spectacle is around 3.45pm when the *makuuchi* (top division) wrestlers in elaborately decorated aprons parade into the ring. Tickets can be bought online one month before the start of the tournament.

Tournaments run for 15 days each January, May and September. Doors open at 8am, but the action doesn't heat up until the senior wrestlers hit the ring around 2pm.

For the opening and closing days and the days in between that fall on the weekend you can expect advance purchase seats to sell out. Around 200 general-admission tickets (¥2100) are sold on the day of the match from the box office in front of the stadium. You'll have to line up very early (at the latest from 6am) to buy one.

If you arrive in the morning when the stadium is still fairly empty, you can usually sneak down to the box seats for a closer view. Rent a radio (¥100 fee, plus ¥2000 deposit) to listen to commentary in English.

DID YOU KNOW?

Chanko-nabe is the protein-rich stew eaten by the wrestlers to put on weight. You can sample it for just ¥300 a bowl in the stadium's basement banquet hall.

PRACTICALITIES

➡ 両国国技館, Ryōgoku Sumo Stadium

➡ Map p287, B2

➡ ☎03-3623-5111

➡ www.sumo.or.jp

➡ 1-3-28 Yokoami, Sumida-ku

➡ tickets ¥3800-11,700

➡ ⓇJR Sōbu line to Ryōgoku, west exit

matcha, you can try ice cream in *hōjicha* (roasted green tea), *genmaicha* (brown rice tea) and *kōcha* (black tea) flavours.

DAIKOKUYA   TEMPURA ¥

Map p286 (大黒家; ☎03-3844-1111; www.tempura.co.jp; 1-38-10 Asakusa, Taitō-ku; meals ¥1550-2100; ⏰11am-8.30pm Sun-Fri, to 9pm Sat; 🔞; ⓢGinza line to Asakusa, exit 1) This is the place to get old-fashioned tempura fried in pure sesame oil, an Asakusa speciality. It's in a white building with a tile roof. If there's a queue (and there often is), you can try your luck at the annex one block over – it also serves set-course meals.

SOMETARŌ   OKONOMIYAKI ¥

Map p286 (染太郎; ☎03-3844-9502; 2-2-2 Nishi-Asakusa, Taitō-ku; mains from ¥700; ⏰noon-10pm; 🔞; ⓢGinza line to Tawaramachi, exit 3) Sometarō is a fun and funky place to try *okonomiyaki* (savoury Japanese-style pancakes filled with meat, seafood and vegetables that you cook yourself). This historic, vine-covered house is a friendly spot where the menu includes a how-to guide for novice cooks. Tatami seating; cash only.

OTAFUKU   JAPANESE ¥¥

Map p286 (大多福; ☎03-3871-2521; www.otafuku.ne.jp; 3rd fl, 1-2-6 Hanakawado, Taitō-ku; oden ¥100-500; ⏰11.30am-2pm & 5-11pm Tue-Fri, 4-11pm Sat, until 9pm Sun; 🔞; ⓡGinza line to Asakusa, exit 5) In business for over a century, Otafuku specialises in *oden*, a classic Japanese hotpot dish of vegetables and seafood simmered in a soy sauce and *dashi* (fish stock) broth. You can dine cheaply on radishes and kelp, or splash out on scallops and tuna or a full-course menu for ¥5400. It's above the Daily Yamazaki shop.

Its original location, undergoing renovation, is set to reopen late in 2019 so check online for the current address.

★ASAKUSA IMAHAN   JAPANESE ¥¥¥

Map p286 (浅草今半; ☎03-3841-1114; www.asakusaimahan.co.jp; 3-1-12 Nishi-Asakusa, Taitō-ku; lunch/dinner from ¥2000/8000; ⏰11.30am-9.30pm; 🍴🔞; ⓡTsukuba Express to Asakusa, exit 4) For a meal to remember, swing by this famous beef restaurant, in business since 1895. Choose between courses of sukiyaki and *shabu-shabu*; prices rise according to the grade of meat. For diners on a budget, Imahan sells 20 servings of a *gyudon* (rice topped with beef; ¥1500) per day.

✕ Ryōgoku

★KAPPŌ YOSHIBA   JAPANESE ¥¥

Map p287 (割烹吉葉; ☎03-3623-4480; www.kapou-yoshiba.jp; 2-14-5 Yokoami, Sumida-ku; dishes ¥650-7800; ⏰11.30am-2pm & 5-10pm Mon-Sat; 🔞; ⓢŌedo line to Ryōgoku, exit 1) The former Miyagino sumo stable is the location for this one-of-a-kind restaurant that has preserved the *dōyō* (practice ring) as its centrepiece. Playing up to its sumo roots, you can order the protein-packed stew *chanko-nabe* (for two people from ¥5200), but Yoshiba's real strength is its sushi, which is freshly prepared in jumbo portions.

The lunch *nigiri* set menu (¥1000) is a bargain, but you'll probably want to come in the evening when the *dōyō* becomes a stage for traditional live-music performances.

At 7.30pm on Monday, Wednesday, Friday and Saturday, former wrestlers sing *sumo jinku* (a type of folk song) for 15 minutes, while at 7pm on Tuesday and Thursday the female duo Kitamura Shimai plays a short concert on *shamisen* (three-stringed instruments resembling a lute or banjo). This is followed at 8pm by a pianist tinkling the ivories on the grand piano by the sushi counter (and stained-glass window of a sumo wrestler!).

EDO NOREN   FOOD HALL ¥¥

Map p287 (江戸NOREN; ☎03-6658-8033; www.jrtk.jp/edonoren; 1-3-20 Yokoami, Sumida-ku; meals from ¥1000-4000; ⏰most restaurants 11am-11pm; 🍴; ⓡJR Sōbu line to Ryōgoku, west exit) The old Ryōgoku Station has been transformed into this touristy, sumo-themed food hall with souvenir shops and 11 different restaurants on two floors. In the middle is a full-scale sumo ring.

TOMOEGATA   HOTPOT ¥¥

Map p287 (巴潟; ☎03-3632-5600; www.tomoegata.com; 2-17-6 Ryōgoku, Sumida-ku; lunch/dinner from ¥860/3130; ⏰11.30am-2pm & 5-10pm; 🔞; ⓡJR Sōbu line to Ryōgoku, east exit) If you're keen to try *chanko-nabe*, Tomoegata is a great place to do it. The daily lunch special includes a reasonably sized individual serving of *chanko-nabe*. In the evening, groups can splash out on huge steaming pots filled with beef, scallops, mushrooms and tofu.

🍷 DRINKING & NIGHTLIFE

★ DANDELION CHOCOLATE
CAFE

Map p287 (📞03-5833-7270; http://dandelion chocolate.jp; 4-14-6 Kuramae, Taitō-ku; ⏰10am-8pm; 🚭🛜; 🚇Asakusa line to Kuramae, exit A3) Perhaps the most compelling reason to have Kuramae on your to-visit list is this superior cafe specialising in bean-to-bar small batch chocolate, made on the premises. The stylish, barnlike setting and delicious drink and food offerings are impossible to resist. There's also a pleasant community park opposite should you prefer to take away.

★ POPEYE
PUB

Map p287 (ポパイ; 📞03-3633-2120; www.lares. dti.ne.jp/~ppy; 2-18-7 Ryōgoku, Sumida-ku; sampler set of 3/10 beers ¥630/1750; ⏰5-11.30pm Mon-Fri, from 3pm Sat; 🚭🛜; 🚃JR Sōbu line to Ryōgoku, west exit) Popeye boasts an astounding 100 beers on tap, including a huge selection of Japanese beers – from Echigo Weizen to Hitachino Nest Espresso Stout. The happy-hour deal (5pm to 8pm, from 3pm on Saturday) offers select brews with free plates of pizza, sausages and other munchables. It's extremely popular and fills up fast; get here early to grab a seat. From the station's west exit, take a left on the main road and pass under the tracks; take the second left and look for Popeye on the right.

FUGLEN
COFFEE

Map p286 (📞03-5811-1756; www.fuglen.com; 2-6-15 Asakusa, Taitō-ku; ⏰7am-10pm, until 1am Wed & Thu, until 2am Fri & Sat; 🛜🛜; 🚇Ginza line to Tawaramachi, exit 3) This Norwegian coffee and cocktail bar brings its oh-so-cool vintage Scandi stylings to Asakusa at this outlet opened in 2018. The coffee is very good but it's also a sophisticated place to chill in the evening over delicious concoctions, such as a rum and maple marmalade cocktail.

CAFÉ OTONOVA
CAFE

Map p286 (カフェ・オトノヴァ; 📞03-5830-7663; www.cafeotonova.net/#3eme; 3-10-4 Nishi-Asakusa, Taitō-ku; ⏰noon-11pm, to 9pm Sun; 🚇) This charming cafe occupies an old house on an alley running parallel to Kappabashi-dōri. Exposed beams are whitewashed and an atrium has been created, with tables upstairs and a big communal table downstairs in front of the DJ booth. It's a stylish cafe by day and a romantic bolthole for drinks at night, with no table charge.

KAMIYA BAR
BAR

Map p286 (神谷バー; 📞03-3841-5400; www.kamiya-bar.com; 1-1-1 Asakusa, Taitō-ku; ⏰11.30am-10pm Wed-Mon; 🚭🛜; 🚇Ginza line to Asakusa, exit 3) One of Tokyo's oldest Western-style bars, Kamiya opened in 1880 and is still hugely popular. The house drink for over a century has been Denki Bran, a secret mix of brandy, gin, wine, curaçao and medicinal herbs. Order either 'blanc' (30 proof) or the 40 proof 'old' at the counter, then give your tickets to the server.

The bar is also famous for its enormous, cheap draught Asahi beer (¥1050 per litre).

ASAHI SKY ROOM
BAR

Map p286 (アサヒスカイルーム; 📞03-5608-5277; www.asahibeer.co.jp/area/search/shop.psp. html/90218704.htm; 22nd fl, Asahi Super Dry Bldg, 1-23-1 Azuma-bashi, Sumida-ku; ⏰10am-10pm; 🛜; 🚇Ginza line to Asakusa, exit 4) Spend the day at the religious sites and end at the Asahi altar, on the 22nd floor of the golden-tinged Asahi Super Dry Building. The venue itself isn't noteworthy, but the views over Sumida-gawa are spectacular, especially at sunset.

'CUZN HOMEGROUND
BAR

Map p286 (カズンホームグラウンド; 📞03-5246-4380; www.homeground.jpn.com; 2-17-9 Asakusa, Taitō-ku; beer ¥900; ⏰noon-5am; 🛜🛜; 🚇Ginza line to Tawaramachi, exit 3) Run by a wild gang of local hippies, 'Cuzn is the kind of bar where anything can happen: a barbecue, a jam session or all-night karaoke, for example.

☆ ENTERTAINMENT

RYŌGOKU KOKUGIKAN
SPECTATOR SPORT

See p158.

OIWAKE
TRADITIONAL MUSIC

Map p286 (追分; 📞03-3844-6283; www.oiwake. info; 3-28-11 Nishi-Asakusa, Taitō-ku; ¥2000 plus 1 food item & 1 drink; ⏰5.30pm-midnight Tue-Sun; 🚃Tsukuba Express to Asakusa, exit 1) Oiwake is one of Tokyo's few *minyō izakaya*, pubs where traditional folk music is performed. It's a homely place, where the waitstaff and the musicians – who play *shamisen* (a banjo-like instrument), hand drums and bamboo flute – are one and the same. Sets start at 7pm and 9pm; children are welcome for the early show. Seating is on tatami.

LOCAL KNOWLEDGE

KAPPABASHI KITCHENWARE TOWN

Kappabashi-dōri (合羽橋通り; Map p286; www.kappabashi.or.jp; 🕒most shops 10am-5pm Mon-Sat; [S]Ginza line to Tawaramachi, exit 3) is the country's largest wholesale restaurant-supply and kitchenware district. Gourmet accessories include bamboo steamer baskets, lacquer trays, neon signs and *chōchin* (paper lanterns). It's also where restaurants get their freakishly realistic plastic food models.

Ganso Shokuhin Sample-ya (元祖食品サンプル屋; Map p286; www.ganso-sample.com; 3-7-6 Nishi-Asakusa, Taitō-ku; 🕒10am-5.30pm; [S]Ginza line to Tawaramachi, exit 3) has a showroom of tongue-in-cheek food models, plus key chains and kits to make your own. Staff at **Kama-asa** (Map p286; ☎03-3841-9355; www.kama-asa.co.jp; 2-24-1 Matsugaya, Taitō-ku; 🕒10am-5.30pm; [S]Ginza line to Tawaramachi, exit 3) 🍃 can advise you in English and French on the best locally made knife from their excellent selection – if you're in town for a week or more, you can have them engrave your name or choice of words onto a knife for free. Also drop by **Soi** (Map p286; ☎03-6802-7732; www.soi-2.jp; 3-25-11 Nishi-Asakusa, Taitō-ku; 🕒11am-6pm Tue-Sun; 🚆Tsukuba Express to Asakusa, exit 2) for a well-edited selection of ceramics and glassware, new and vintage, plus some really cute *tenugui* to wrap them in.

SHOPPING

Asakusa is one of the best places in Tokyo for souvenir shopping as it is packed with shops, many specialising in traditional crafts. To the south is Kuramae, dotted with boutiques selling more-contemporary crafts.

★MARUGOTO NIPPON — FOOD & DRINKS

Map p286 (まるごとにっぽん; ☎03-3845-0510; www.marugotonippon.com; 2-6-7 Asakusa, Taitō-ku; 🕒10am-8pm; [S]Ginza line to Tawaramachi, exit 3) Think of this as a minimall, showcasing the best of Japan's speciality food and drink (ground floor) and arts and crafts (2nd floor). The 3rd floor showcases the products and attractions of different Japanese regions on a regularly changing basis.

BENGARA — ARTS & CRAFTS

Map p286 (べんがら; ☎03-3841-6613; www.bengara.com; 1-35-6 Asakusa, Taitō-ku; 🕒10am-6pm Mon-Fri, to 7pm Sat & Sun, closed 3rd Thu of the month; [S]Ginza line to Asakusa, exit 1) *Noren* are the curtains that hang in front of shop doors. This store sells beautiful ones, made of linen and coloured with natural dyes (such as indigo or persimmon) or decorated with ink-brush paintings. There are smaller items too, such as pouches and book covers, made of traditional textiles.

YOSHITOKU DOLLS — ARTS & CRAFTS

Map p287 (吉徳人形; ☎03-3863-4419; www.yoshitoku.co.jp; 1-9-14 Asakusabashi, Taitō-ku; 🕒9am-5.45pm Mon-Fri; 🚆JR Sobu line to Asakusabashi, east exit) Founded in 1711, this traditional Japanese doll manufacturer is the place to come to see the exquisite craftsmanship of these ornamental figurines, ranging from geisha in beautiful kimono and samurai in full armour to the elaborate sets of dolls displayed during Hina Matsuri in March.

The shop stocks many other craft products, too.

INK STAND — STATIONERY

Map p287 (☎050-1744-8547; http://inkstand.jp; 4-20-12 Kuramae, Taitō-ku; 🕒11am-7pm Tue-Sun; [S]Asakusa line to Kuramae, exit A3) If the basic black or blue ink of pens is too common for you, let Ink Stand help you create your own personalised colour. For ¥2700 for a 33ml bottle, you can blend your unique shade from 17 basic colours. It's best to make an advance reservation (details are online). The whole process takes around 1½ hours.

MAITO — FASHION & ACCESSORIES

Map p287 (マイト; ☎03-3863-1128; http://maitokomuro.com; 4-14-2 Kuramae, Taitō-ku; 🕒11.30am-6.30pm Tue-Sun; [S]Asakusa line to Kuramae, exit A3) Everything is natural about Maito's clothing and accessories, including the fabrics used (mainly cotton and wool) and the plant-based dyes. Choose from a rainbow-coloured selection of scarves, *tabi* socks, canvas bags, shirts and knits dyed using traditional techniques.

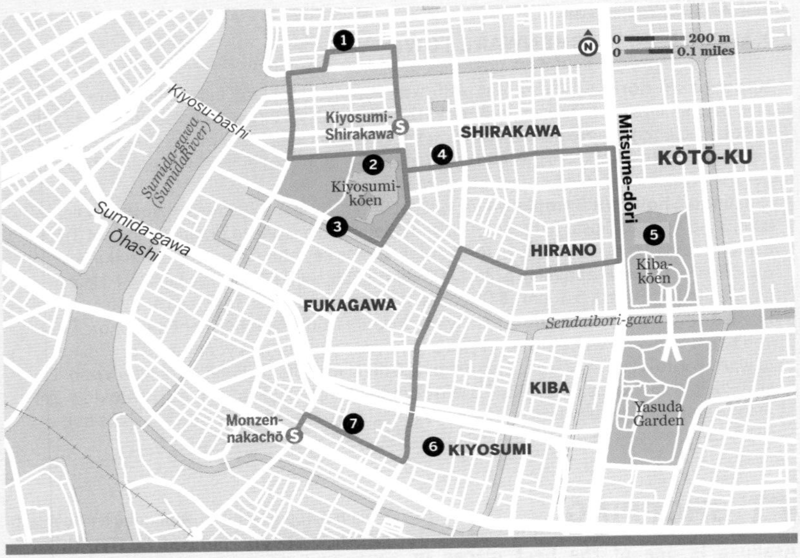

Local Life
Kiyosumi-shirakawa & Fukagawa

These peaceful residential areas east of Sumida-gawa have become a base for small galleries, cool cafes and artisan businesses to set up shop. Spend a pleasant day away from the bustle of central Tokyo as you sip lattes, stroll around a traditional garden, ponder contemporary art and witness a spectacular fire ritual at a Buddhist temple.

1 Iki Espresso

Start the day at this perfectly formed Aussie-style **cafe** (www.ikiespresso.com; 2-2-12 Tokiwa, Kōtō-ku; mains ¥1200-1350; ⏰8am-7pm; 🚭📶📋; [S] Ōedo line to Kiyosumi-shirakawa, exit A1) with a great breakfast of freshly cooked eggs, avocado on toast or a muffin, all washed down with a hand-poured coffee or a fresh juice.

2 Kiyosumi-teien

This picturesque **garden** (清澄庭園; 3-3-9 Kiyosumi, Kōtō-ku; adult/child ¥150/free; ⏰9am-5pm; [S] Ōedo line to Kiyosumi-shirakawa, exit A3) dates back to 1721. In the early 20th century Iwasaki Yatarō, founder of the Mitsubishi Corporation, purchased the property. He added prize stones from across Japan, which are set around a pond ringed with beautiful trees and flowers.

3 Babaghuri

Renewable, natural or recycled materials are used for the rustically beautiful clothes, pottery, tableware and linens sold in this **boutique** (www.babaghuri.jp; 3-1-7 Kiyosumi, Koto-ku; ⏰11am-7pm irregular holidays; [S] Ōedo line to Kiyosumi-shirakawa, exit A3). The chic fashion brand was created by German-born, Japan-based designer Jurgen Lehl, who passed away in 2014.

4 Fukagawa Edo Museum

See what this area once looked liked during the Edo period (1603–1868) at this small **museum** (深川江戸資料館; www.kcf.or.jp/fukagawa; 1-3-28 Shirakawa, Kōtō-ku; adult/child ¥400/50; ⏰9.30am-5pm, closed 2nd & 4th Mon of month; [S] Ōedo line to Kiyosumi-shirakawa, exit A3) on an attractive shopping street. Inside is a full-scale recreation of an Edo-era streetscape complete with a fire-lookout tower, buildings you can enter and furnished rooms.

5 Museum of Contemporary Art, Tokyo (MOT)

Reopened in 2019 following major renovations, this is Tokyo's premier contemporary arts **museum** (東京都現代美術館; www.

Kiyosumi-teien

mot-art-museum.jp; 4-1-1 Miyoshi, Kōtō-ku; adult/child ¥500/free; ⏰10am-6pm Tue-Sun; ⒮Ōedo line to Kiyosumi-shirakawa, exit B2). The exhibitions cover all the major movements of post-WWII Japanese art, and include temporary shows on fashion, architecture and design.

❻ Tomioka Hachiman-gū

Founded in 1627, this attractive **shrine** (富岡八幡宮; 1-20-3 Tomioka, Kōtō-ku; ⒮Ōedo line to Monzen-nakachō, exit 1) is famous as the birthplace of the sumo tournament. Around the back of the main building is the *yokozuna* (sumo grand champions) stone, carved with the names of each of these champion wrestlers.

❼ Fukagawa Fudō-dō

Attend the 5pm *goma* (fire ritual) at **Fukagawa Fudō-dō** (深川不動尊; www.fukagawafudou.gr.jp; 1-17-13 Tomioka, Kōtō-ku; ⏰8am-6pm, to 8pm on festival days; ⒮Ōedo line to Monzen-nakachō, exit 1). Sutras are chanted, drums are pounded and flames are raised on the main altar as an offering to the deity. There's a trippy prayer corridor with 9500 miniature Fudōmyō (a fierce-looking representation of Buddha's determination) crystal statues.

KURODAYA
STATIONERY

Map p286 (黒田屋; ☎03-3844-7511; 1-2-5 Asakusa, Taitō-ku; ⏰10am-7pm Tue-Sun; ⒮Ginza line to Asakusa, exit 3) Since 1856, Kurodaya has been specialising in *washi* (traditional Japanese paper) and products made from paper, such as cards, kites and papiermâché folk-art figures. It sells its own designs and many others from across Japan.

TOKYO HOTARUDO
VINTAGE

Map p286 (東京蛍堂; ☎03-3845-7563; http://tokyohotarudo.com; 1-41-8 Asakusa, Taitō-ku; ⏰11am-8pm Wed-Sun; ⒭Tsukuba Express to Asakusa, exit 5) This curio shop is run by an eccentric young man who prefers to dress as if the 20th century hasn't come and gone already. If you think that sounds marvellous, you'll want to check out his collection of vintage dresses and bags, antique lamps, watches and decorative *objets*. The entrance is tricky: look for a vertical black sign with a pointing finger.

FUJIYA
ARTS & CRAFTS

Map p286 (ふじ屋; ☎03-3841-2283; 2-2-15 Asakusa, Taitō-ku; ⏰10am-6pm Thu-Tue; ⒮Ginza line to Asakusa, exit 1) Fujiya specialises in *tenugui*: dyed cloths of thin cotton that can be used as tea towels, handkerchiefs, gift wrapping (the list goes on – they're surprisingly versatile). Here they come in traditional designs and humorous modern ones.

SOLAMACHI
MALL

Map p286 (ソラマチ; www.tokyo-solamachi.jp; 1-1-2 Oshiage, Sumida-ku; ⏰10am-9pm; ☎; ⒮Hanzōmon line to Oshiage, exit B3) It's not all cheesy Sky Tree (p157) swag at this mall under the tower (though you can get 634m-long rolls of Sky Tree toilet paper). Shops on the 4th floor offer a better-than-usual selection of Japanesey souvenirs, including pretty trinkets made from kimono fabric and quirky fashion items.

🏃 SPORTS & ACTIVITIES

★ WANARIYA
TRADITIONAL CRAFT

Map p286 (和なり屋; ☎03-5603-9169; www.wanariya.jp; 1-8-10 Senzoku, Taitō-ku; indigo dyeing/weaving from ¥1920/1980; ⏰10am-7pm irregular holidays; ⒮Hibiya line to Iriya, exit 1) A team of young and friendly Japanese operates this indigo-dyeing and traditional *hataori*

RICKSHAW RIDES

Around the Kaminari-mon (p156) entrance to Sensō-ji (as well as elsewhere in Asakusa) you may well get approached by a scantily clad, strapping young man offering you...a ride in his *jinrikisha* (rickshaw). Rides start at ¥4000 per 10 minutes for two people (¥3000 for one person).

(hand-loom-weaving) workshop. In under an hour you can learn to dye a T-shirt or a tote bag or weave a pair of coasters.

It's a fantastic opportunity to make your own souvenirs. Book at least three days in advance.

★ **MOKUHANKAN**   TRADITIONAL CRAFT

Map p286 (木版館; ☑070-5011-1418; www.moku hankan.com; 1-41-8 Asakusa, Taitō-ku; per person ¥2000; ☺10am-5.30pm Wed-Mon; ⒭Tsukuba Express to Asakusa, exit 5) Try your hand at making *ukiyo-e* (woodblock prints) at this studio run by expat David Bull. Hour-long 'print parties' are great fun and take place daily; sign up online. There's a shop here too, where you can buy vintage prints as well as Bull's and Jed Henry's humorous *Ukiyo-e Heroes* series – contemporary prints featuring video-game characters in traditional settings.

ZAC   KAYAKING

(☑03-6671-0201; www.zacsports.com; adult/ child ¥5500/4500; ⒮Shinjuku line to Higashi-ōshima, Komatsugawa exit) Choose either day or night to go on these 1½-hour kayaking

tours of Kyunaka-gawa (actually a canal) way out east of Ryūgoku. It's a wonderful way to get an alternative view of the city, plus some light exercise. If there is just one person on the tour, add ¥1000 to the pricing.

The website has instructions on how to dress and where to meet for the tours. Guides speak basic English.

EDOYŪ   SPA

Map p287 (江戸湯; ☑03-3621-2611; www.edoyu. com/ryougoku; 1-5-8 Kamezawa, Sumida-ku; ¥2380; ☺11am-9am; ⒮Ōedo line to Ryōgoku, exit A3 or A4) The images of Hokusai, local artist made good, provide the inspiration for some of the decorative touches at this elegant modern spa. Over five floors there are nine types of bath in which to soak away your aches and pains, as well as various spa treatments and massages. Free green tea and sweets are served at 4pm and 8pm.

Bathe between 6am and 8am and entry is reduced to only ¥1100; from 1am to 6am there's a ¥320 surcharge per hour.

TOKYO KITCHEN   COOKING

Map p286 (☑090-9104-4329; www.asakusa-to kyokitchen.com; 502 Ayumi Bldg, 1-11-1 Hana-kawado, Taitō-ku; per person from ¥7560; ⒮Ginza line to Asakusa, exit 4A) English-speaking Yoshimi is an Asakusa-based cook who teaches small groups of visitors how to make a range of Japanese dishes. Her menu list is broad and includes mosaic sushi rolls, tempura, ramen and *gyōza*. Vegetarians and those with gluten intolerance are catered for too. Yoshimi will meet you at the subway exit and guide you to her kitchen.

Odaiba & Tokyo Bay

Neighbourhood Top Five

❶ teamLab Borderless (p167) Immersing yourself in the fluid, animated world of this interactive digital art museum – one of Tokyo hottest new attractions.

❷ Toyosu Market (p168) Getting a peek inside the city's busy wholesale market and then treating yourself to

sushi breakfast at a market restaurant.

❸ Unicorn Gundam (p168) Looking up at Odaiba's unofficial mascot, this towering statue from the iconic anime series Gundam, illuminated against the skyline.

❹ National Museum of Emerging Science &

Innovation (p168) Meeting the robots of the future at this museum of cutting-edge technology.

❺ Ōedo Onsen Monogatari (p170) Soaking in some honest-to-goodness natural hot springs (and experiencing an onsen theme park) right here on the bay.

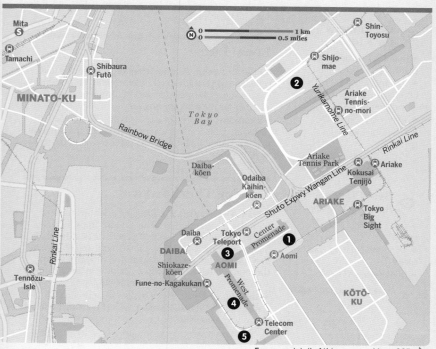

For more detail of this area see Map p265 ➡

Lonely Planet's Top Tip

The automated (driver-less) Yurikamome line runs above-ground from Shimbashi to Toyosu via the islands that make up Odaiba. While principally a means of getting around, the ride itself is a treat: the train wends between skyscrapers downtown before doing a loop to reach Rainbow Bridge. Fares are from ¥190 to ¥360; a one-day pass – a good deal if you plan to see many sights here – costs ¥820/¥410 per adult/child.

Best Places to Eat

➡ Sushi Dai (p169)

➡ Daiwa Sushi (p169)

➡ Mosuke Dango (p169)

For reviews, see p169.

⊙ Best Places for Kids

➡ teamLab Borderless (p166)

➡ National Museum of Emerging Science & Innovation (p168)

➡ Tokyo Joypolis (p170)

➡ Tokyo Disney Resort (p170)

For reviews, see p168. ➡

⊙ Best Places for Bay Views

➡ Odaiba Kaihin-kōen (p168)

➡ Jicoo the Floating Bar (p169)

➡ Dai-kanransha (p170)

For reviews, see p168.

Explore Odaiba & Tokyo Bay

If you have any interest in Tokyo's food culture, you'll want to start the day with a visit to the city's new wholesale market (p168) in Toyosu – from where many of the city's top restaurants source their seafood. If you get here early (by 6am!) you can watch the tuna auction in action, and then head over to Sushi Dai (p169) for the most decadent of breakfasts.

Odaiba is a collective of man-made islands on Tokyo Bay, where the atmosphere is notably different from older parts of the city – big box structures and wide streets. Here, it's what's inside that counts: the immersive digital art centre teamLab Borderless (p167) is fantastic. To do it justice, budget a few hours; it's great for kids, too.

One of Odaiba's biggest selling points is its family-friendly factor. Other fun spots include the interactive National Museum of Emerging Science & Innovation (p168) and the virtual reality arcade Tokyo Joypolis (p170). All of these are indoors (teamLab Borderless included) – perfect for rainy days. On the other hand, there's little to do here at night. Stick around until evening to see Unicorn Gundam (p168) lit up against the night sky, or head to hot-spring complex Ōedo Onsen Monogatari (p170) – admission is discounted after 6pm! – for a good soak.

Further afield, along the bay, are some other family attractions, such as Tokyo Disney Resort (p174) and Tokyo Sea Life Park (p172).

Local Life

➡ **Boat Cruises** A floating banquet with friends and colleagues on a traditional *yakatabune* (flat-bottomed boat) is a popular pastime, especially during the summer for the cool bay breezes.

➡ **Viewpoint** Waterfront park Odaiba Kaihin-kōen (p168), and especially the terrace between the Aqua City mall and Odaiba Hilton, is the place to watch the sun go down over Tokyo Bay.

Getting There & Away

➡ **Train** The elevated Yurikamome line runs from Shimbashi through Odaiba to Toyosu; stops include Odaiba Kaihin-kōen, Daiba, Telecom Center, Tokyo Big Sight (formerly Kokusai-tenjijō-seimon) and Shijō-mae (for Toyosu Market). The Rinkai line runs from Ōsaki through Odaiba to Shin-Kiba, stopping at Tennōzu Isle, Tokyo Teleport and Kokusai-tenjijō stations.

➡ **Boat** Tokyo Cruise water buses run between Odaiba Kaihin-kōen (Odaiba Marine Park), Hinode Pier and all the way to Asakusa.

◉ TOP EXPERIENCE
GET ARTY AT TEAMLAB BORDERLESS

Digital art collective teamLab created 60 installations for this museum, opened in 2018, that blurs the boundary between art and the viewer: many works are interactive. Not sure how? That's the point – approach the installations, move and touch them (or just stand still) and see how they react. There is no suggested route; teamLab Borderless is all about exploration.

Many of the artworks here are optimised for photography, none more so than the magical **Forest of Lamps**. Approach one of the Venetian glass lamps and watch it bloom into colour, setting off a chain reaction. Only a limited number of people are allowed in for a few minutes at a time. As this is among the most popular installations, you'll likely have to queue for it.

Many installations are designed with kids in mind and there are no minimum age requirements; however, keep in mind the museum is dark and often crowded. **Athletics Forest**, a collection of installations on the 2nd floor, is the best for little ones. Here they (and you!) can add colour to a drawing of an animal or insect and watch as it is born into an animated creature – then follow it on its course along the crags and divots of this playful indoor landscape.

Make sure to stop for a cup of tea (¥500) at digitally enhanced **En Teahouse** and see flowers come to life in your teacup; the petals blow away in the breeze when you've finished. And while you're here, don't miss the digital calligraphy installation of an *ensō*, a circle drawn in one stroke and a classic symbol of Zen Buddhism.

Buy tickets in advance online, as they often sell out. Note that some of the installations have mirrored floors; for this reason we recommend wearing trousers. Trainers are a good idea too.

DON'T MISS

➡ Forest of Lamps
➡ Athletics Forest
➡ En Teahouse

PRACTICALITIES

➡ Map p265, C3
➡ ☎ 03-6406-3949
➡ https://borderless.teamlab.art
➡ 1-3-8 Aomi, Kōtō-ku
➡ adult/child ¥3200/1000
➡ ⏲ 10am-7pm Mon-Thu & Sun, to 9pm Fri & Sat, closed 2nd & 4th Tue
➡ ♿
➡ 🚉 Yurikamome line to Aomi

👁 SIGHTS

TEAMLAB BORDERLESS · MUSEUM
See p167.

★ NATIONAL MUSEUM OF EMERGING SCIENCE & INNOVATION (MIRAIKAN) · MUSEUM

Map p265 (未来館; www.miraikan.jst.go.jp; 2-3-6 Aomi, Kōtō-ku; adult/child ¥620/210; ⏰10am-5pm Wed-Mon; 📱; 🚉Yurikamome line to Telecom Center, north exit) *Miraikan* means 'hall of the future', and the hands-on exhibits here present the science and technology that will possibly shape the years to come. Don't miss the demonstrations of humanoid robot ASIMO (11am, 1pm, 2pm and 4pm) and the lifelike android Otonaroid (demonstration 11.30am; interactive experience 3pm to 5pm). The Gaia dome theatre/planetarium (adult/child ¥300/100) has an English audio option and is popular; book online one week in advance. A multilingual smartphone app makes a game out of visiting.

TOYOSU MARKET · MARKET

Map p265 (豊洲市場, Toyosu Shijō; www.shijou.metro.tokyo.jp; 6-chōme Toyosu, Kōtō-ku; ⏰5am-5pm Mon-Sat, closed some Wed; 🚉Yurikamome line to Shijō-mae) In 2018, Tokyo's central wholesale market moved from its iconic Tsukiji location to this new facility in Toyosu. It's a structure dreamed up by bureaucrats; access is limited, but smoother than it was at Tsukiji. The early-morning tuna auction and other parts of the market are visible from glass-walled viewing platforms; visitors aren't allowed on the market floor. The upper floors have some shops and restaurants, including sushi counters originally at Tsukiji. Get here early to make the most of your visit.

The market is divided into three blocks (5, 6 and 7), all connected via promenades that also run directly to the train station, and is well signposted in English.

The highlight for many visitors is the tuna auction, where the *naka-oroshi* (intermediate wholesalers) gamble on bluefin tuna brought in from all over the world. The auction starts around 5am and finishes by 6.30am. A limited number of visitors can observe the auction up close from a mezzanine-level viewing platform that is only partially shielded by glass; for details see the market website. Otherwise anyone can watch it from the glassed-in corridors on the 2nd floor of block 7. On your way here from the train station, you'll pass a row of restaurants; traditional sweets shop Mosuke Dango (p169) is here.

In block 6 is the produce market; auctions take place here at 6.30am and are also visible from the corridors above. Daiwa Sushi (p169) is in this building, on the ground floor (enter from outside).

The intermediate wholesaler market – where sushi chefs and fishmongers come to buy from the *naka-oroshi* – is in building 5. You can peer down into it from windows on the 3rd floor but the view isn't great. Also on the 3rd floor is another collection of restaurants, including Sushi Dai (p169); the 4th floor has shops selling tea, knives, *katsuo-bushi* (dried bonito flakes), miso and more. Above is a grassy rooftop garden.

The metropolitan government decided to move the city's wholesale market from Tsukiji to Toyosu in 2012, citing outdated facilities (Tsukiji Market was built in 1935). But the move, finally completed in October 2018, was a controversial one, fought by many vendors and citizens. While the new site is significantly larger than the old and far more contemporary, the Toyosu building's position on the former site of a gas refinery was concerning for some, particularly as the ground water has tested high for toxic chemicals in the past.

UNICORN GUNDAM · STATUE

Map p265 (ユニコーンガンダム; 1-1-10 Aomi, Kōtō-ku; 🚉Yurikamome line to Daiba, south exit) This is truly an only-in-Tokyo sight: a 19.7m-tall model of an RX-0 Unicorn Gundam from the iconic Mobile Suit Gundam anime franchise. It undergoes a transformation four times a day (at 11am, 1pm, 3pm and 5pm) into 'destroy mode'; light shows take place on the half-hour between 7pm and 9.30pm. The statue is in front of the Diver City mall.

TOKYO SEA LIFE PARK · AQUARIUM

(葛西臨海水族園, Kasai Rinkai Suizokuken; www.tokyo-zoo.net; 6-2-3 Rinkai-chō, Edogawa-ku; adult/child ¥700/free; ⏰9.30am-5pm Thu-Tue; 🚉JR Keiyō line to Kasai Rinkai-kōen) Tokyo Sea Life Park is the city's best aquarium. Particularly interesting is the exhibit that recreates Tokyo Bay's ecosystem – in case you were wondering what lived in these waters. There is also a doughnut-shaped tank filled with sleek, silvery bluefin tuna.

ODAIBA KAIHIN-KŌEN · PARK

Map p265 (お台場海浜公園, Odaiba Marine Park; www.tptc.co.jp; 1-4-1 Daiba, Minato-ku; ⏰24hr;

Yurikamome line to Odaiba Kaihin-kōen) There are good views of Tokyo from this park's promenades and elevated walkways – especially at night when old-fashioned *yakatabune*, decorated with lanterns, traverse the bay. Note that swimming here is not permitted.

 EATING

The best place to eat around Tokyo Bay is at the new Toyosu Market (p168). Odaiba's malls are packed with mostly uninspiring but family-friendly food courts and chain restaurants.

MOSUKE DANGO SWEETS ¥

Map p265 (茂助だんご; ☑03-6633-0873; 2nd fl, Bldg 7, Toyosu Market, 6-6-1 Toyosu, Kōtō-ku; per piece from ¥170; ☺5.30am-1pm, closed Sun & market holidays; ☑☑; ☒Yurikamome line to Shijō-mae) The original Mosuke, a street vendor, began making *dango* (soft rice-flour balls) in 1898, back when the fish market was in Nihombashi. Now on its third market, Mosuke Dango still serves its famous *shōyu dango* (with soy-sauce glaze) and *tsubuan dango* (made from chunky *azuki*-bean paste), but with the addition of a cafe eat-in space (*matcha* ¥500).

★**SUSHI DAI** SUSHI ¥¥

Map p265 (寿司大; ☑03-6633-0042; 3rd fl, Bldg 6, Toyosu Market, 6-5-1 Toyosu, Kōtō-ku; course meal ¥4500; ☺5.30am-1pm, closed Sun & market holidays; ☺☑☑; ☒Yurikamome line to Shijō-mae) There is no better-value sushi in Tokyo than the *omakase* (chef's choice) course here. The menu changes daily (and sometimes hourly), but you're guaranteed to get 10 pieces of *nigiri* (hand-pressed) sushi made from seafood picked up from the fish market downstairs, prepared one at a time, pre-seasoned to perfection (and with zero boring fillers). Expect to queue.

You can order à la carte, but considering each piece costs ¥500 to ¥800 (based on market rates), the course is the way to go; you also get to choose your last piece. The shop also offers a course for customers who can't eat raw fish (¥4500) and a smaller children's course (¥3000). Staff speak some English and you'll be dining with plenty of fellow travellers, but don't write this off as a tourist spot – locals love it, too.

Cash-only Sushi Dai is one of the shops that made the move from Tsukiji to Toyosu; there's a big photo of the old shop on the wall. It's in the same building as the intermediate wholesalers market. Sushi Dai closes the same days as the market so check the market schedule online.

★**DAIWA SUSHI** SUSHI ¥¥

Map p265 (大和寿司; ☑03-6633-0220; 1st fl, Bldg 5, Toyosu Market, 6-3-1 Toyosu, Kōtō-ku; course meal from ¥4320; ☺5.30am-1pm, closed Sun & market holidays; ☺; ☒Yurikamome line to Shijō-mae) One of Tsukiji's most famous sushi restaurants has made the move to the new Toyosu Market. The course meal includes seven pieces of *nigiri* (hand-pressed) sushi and one roll – all made with premium seafood. If you're still hungry you can order more sushi à la carte (¥300 to ¥800 per piece). Go early (before 9am), or there might be a queue.

BILLS INTERNATIONAL ¥¥

Map p265 (ビルズ; www.bills-jp.net; 3rd fl, Seaside Mall, DECKS Tokyo Beach, 1-6-1 Daiba, Minato-ku; breakfast & lunch mains ¥1425-2375, dinner mains ¥1650-2700; ☺9am-10pm Mon-Fri, 8am-10pm Sat & Sun; ☺☞☑☑; ☒Yurikamome line to Odaiba Kaihin-kōen) Australian chef Bill Granger has had a big hit with his restaurant chain in Japan – unsurprising given how inviting and spacious a place this is. The menu includes his breakfast classics, like creamy scrambled eggs and ricotta hotcakes, and lunch and dinner mains like *wagyū* burgers and prawn and chilli linguine. The terrace has great bay views.

🍷 **DRINKING & NIGHTLIFE**

JICOO THE FLOATING BAR COCKTAIL BAR

Map p265 (ジークザフローティングバー; ☑11am-8pm 0120-049-490; www.jicoofloatingbar.com; cover from ¥2600; ☺8-10.30pm Thu-Sat; ☑; ☒Yurikamome line to Hinode or Odaiba Kaihin-kōen, north exit) For a few nights a week, the futuristic cruise-boat *Himiko*, designed by manga and anime artist Leiji Matsumoto, morphs into this floating bar. Board on the hour at Hinode pier and the half-hour at Odaiba Kaihin-kōen (p168). The evening-long 'floating pass' usually includes some sort of live music; check the schedule online as sometimes events drive up the price.

Note that this won't run in the event of a typhoon or similarly inclement weather.

AGEHA
CLUB

(アゲハ; www.ageha.com; 2-2-10 Shin-Kiba, Kōtō-ku; ⏰11pm-5am Fri & Sat; S Yūrakuchō line to Shin-Kiba, main exit) This gigantic waterside club is Tokyo's largest, complete with a pool and food trucks. Best to come in a group and definitely check the schedule in advance (there's not always something happening and events vary). Free buses run between the club and a bus stop on the east side of Shibuya Station (on Roppongi-dōri) all night. Cover around ¥3000; bring photo ID.

SPORTS & ACTIVITIES

ŌEDO ONSEN MONOGATARI
ONSEN

Map p265 (大江戸温泉物語; ☎03-5500-1126; www.ooedoonsen.jp; 2-6-3 Aomi, Kōtō-ku; adult/child ¥2720/1058, surcharge Sat & Sun ¥220; ⏰11am-9am, last entry 7am; ☎Yurikamome line to Telecom Center, south exit or Rinkai line to Tokyo Teleport, exit B with free shuttle bus) Come experience the truly Japanese phenomenon that is an amusement park centred on bathing. There are multiple tubs to choose from, filled with real hot-spring water (pumped from 1400m below Tokyo Bay), and a lantern-lit re-creation of an old Tokyo downtown area. Come after 6pm for a ¥540 discount. Visitors with tattoos will be denied admission.

Upon entering, you'll get to choose a colourful *yukata* (light cotton kimono) to wear around the complex. The main bathing areas are gender-segregated but the town area is communal, so unlike most city day spas there's space for mixed-groups and families to hang out.

There's a huge variety of baths here, including jet baths, pools of natural rock and, on the ladies' side, personal bucket-shaped baths made of cedar. The town area has food stalls and carnival games. There's also an outdoor foot bath, set in a garden, which is also communal.

TOKYO DISNEY RESORT
AMUSEMENT PARK

(東京ディズニーリゾート; ☎domestic calls 0570-00-8632, from overseas +81-45-330-5211; www.tokyodisneyresort.jp; 1-1 Maihama, Urayasu-shi, Chiba-ken; 1-day ticket for 1 park adult/child ¥7400/4800, after 6pm ¥4200; ⏰varies by sea-son; ☎JR Keiyō line to Maihama, south exit) Tokyo Disney Resort includes Tokyo Disneyland, modelled after the one in California, and Tokyo DisneySea, an original theme park with seven 'ports' evoking locales real and imagined (the Mediterranean and 'Mermaid Lagoon', for example). DisneySea targets a more grown-up crowd, but still has many attractions for kids. Both resorts get extremely crowded, especially on weekends and during summer holidays; you'll have to be strategic with your FastPasses. Book admission tickets online to save time.

TOKYO JOYPOLIS
AMUSEMENT PARK

Map p265 (東京ジョイポリス; http://tokyo-joypolis.com; 3rd-5th fl, DECKS Tokyo Beach, 1-6-1 Daiba, Minato-ku; adult/child ¥800/500, all-rides passport ¥4300/3300, passport after 5pm ¥3300/2300; ⏰10am-10pm; ☎Yurikamome line to Odaiba Kaihin-kōen, north exit) This indoor amusement park is stacked with virtual-reality attractions and thrill rides, such as the video-enhanced Halfpipe Tokyo; there are rides for little ones, too. Separate admission and individual ride tickets (¥500 to ¥800) are available, but if you plan to ride more than a few, the unlimited 'passport' makes sense.

Bring your passport for a slight discount on admission.

FUNASEI
CRUISE

(船清; ☎for bookings 03-5770-5131; www.funasei.com; 1-16-8 Kita-Shinagawa, Shinagawa-ku; per person ¥10,800; ☎Keikyū line to Kita-Shinagawa) Take an evening cruise on a classic wooden *yakatabune;* packages include sashimi and tempura dinners and all-you-can-drink beer, wine and sake. Bookings (essential) are possible for a minimum of two people. HIS travel agency handles reservations; see the website for details.

The 2¾-hour cruises depart at 5.45pm or 6.30pm from Kita-Shinagawa, from where you'll sail on Tokyo Bay and up the Sumidagawa to Asakusa (for views of Tokyo Sky Tree) and back.

DAI-KANRANSHA
FERRIS WHEEL

Map p265 (大観覧車; www.daikanransha.com; 1-3-10 Aomi, Kōtō-ku; adult/child ¥1000/500; ⏰10am-10pm Sun-Thu, to 11pm Fri & Sat; ☎Yurikamome line to Aomi) The world's tallest Ferris wheel when it opened in 1999 (a title it lost the following year), this Odaiba landmark offers unobstructed views over the city and the bay. It's also great eye-candy when illuminated at night in a rainbow of colours.

Day Trips from Tokyo

Climbn Marvellous Mt Fuji p172

Follow the pilgrim trail up Japan's most famous peak for a sunrise to beat all others.

Nikkō p174

Ancient moss clinging to a stone wall, rows of perfectly aligned stone lanterns, vermilion gates and towering cedars – this is a scene from Nikkō, famous for its 17th-century shrines and temples.

Hakone p177

A hot-spring resort in the mist-shrouded hills southwest of Tokyo, Hakone offers Mt Fuji views, scenery straight out of a woodblock painting, a volcano and plenty of onsen.

Kamakura p181

An ancient feudal capital and centre of Zen Buddhism, seaside Kamakura is packed with temples, plus the Daibutsu (Big Buddha) statue, but it also has a laid-back, earthy vibe and great restaurants.

TOP EXPERIENCE
CLIMB MARVELLOUS MT FUJI

Catching a glimpse of Mt Fuji (富士山; 3776m), Japan's highest and most famous peak, will take your breath away. Climbing it and watching the sunrise from the summit is one of Japan's superlative experiences (though it's often cloudy). The official climbing season runs from 1 July to 31 August, though in recent years this has often been extended to 10 September.

Climbing Mt Fuji

The Japanese proverb 'He who climbs Mt Fuji once is a wise man, he who climbs it twice is a fool' remains as valid as ever. While reaching the top brings a great sense of achievement, it's a gruelling climb not known for its beautiful scenery or for being at one with nature.

The mountain is divided into 10 'stations' from base (First Station) to summit (Tenth). These days most climbers start from the halfway point at one of the four Fifth Stations. The **Yoshida Trail** is by far the most popular route. It's accessed from Fuji Subaru Line Fifth Station (2305m; aka Kawaguchi-ko Fifth Station), has the most modern facilities and is easiest to reach from Tokyo. Allow five to six hours to reach the top (though some climb it in half the time) and about three hours to descend, plus 1½ hours for circling the crater at the top.

The other trails are: **Subashiri** (1980m), **Fujinomiya** (2380m) and **Gotemba** (1440m); the latter is considered the toughest.

Know Before You Go

Mt Fuji is a serious mountain, high enough for altitude sickness, and on the summit it can go from sunny and warm to wet, windy and cold remarkably quickly. Even if conditions are fine, you can count on it being close to freezing in the morning, even in summer. Also be aware that visibility can rapidly disappear with a blanket of mist rolling in suddenly.

At a minimum, bring clothing appropriate for cold and wet weather, including a hat and gloves. Also bring at least two litres of water (you can buy more on the mountain during the climbing season), as well as a map, snacks and cash for other necessities, such as toilets (¥200). If you're climbing at night, bring a torch (flashlight) or headlamp, and spare batteries.

When to Go

To time your arrival for dawn you can either start up in the afternoon, stay overnight in a mountain hut and continue early in the morning, or climb the whole way at night. You do not want to arrive on the top too long before dawn, as it will be very cold and windy, even at the height of summer.

The Yoshida Trail is very busy during the climbing season. To avoid the worst of the crush head up on a weekday or start earlier during the day. Or consider taking a tour that makes use of one of the other trails not easily reached by public transport.

Authorities strongly caution against climbing outside the regular season, when the weather is highly unpredictable and first-aid stations on the mountain are closed. Outside of the climbing season, check weather conditions carefully before setting out, bring appropriate equipment, do not climb alone, and be prepared to retreat at any time. A guide will be invaluable. Once snow or ice is on the mountain, Fuji becomes a very

GETTING THERE

During the climbing season, **Keiō Dentetsu Bus** (☏03-5376-2222; www.highwaybus.com) runs direct buses (¥2700, 2½ hours; reservations necessary) to Fuji Subaru Line Fifth Station (aka Kawaguchi-ko Fifth Station) from Shinjuku Bus Terminal (p233). Outside the official season, take a bus or train from Shinjuku to Kawaguchi-ko, and then a bus or taxi to the mountain.

serious and dangerous undertaking and should only be attempted by those with winter mountaineering equipment and plenty of experience.

Off-season climbers should register with the local police department; fill out the necessary form at the **Kawaguchi-ko Tourist Information Center** (☎0555-72-6700; ⏰8.30am-5.30pm).

Mountain Huts

Mountain huts offer spartan sleeping conditions and hot meals. Reservations are recommended and are essential on weekends. These two, at the Eighth Station of the Yoshida Trail, usually have English-speaking staff. Both accept reservations from 1 April.

At **Taishikan** (太子館; ☎0555-22-1947; www.mfi.or.jp/w3/home0/taisikan; per person incl 2 meals from ¥8500), warm sleeping bags are provided, and vegetarian or halal meals are available if requested in advance. Cash only.

Fujisan Hotel (富士山ホテル; ☎late Jun–mid-Sep 0555-24-6512, reservations 0555-22-0237; www.fujisanhotel.com; per person with/without 2 meals from ¥8350/5950; ☯) is one of the largest and most popular rest huts. Credit cards accepted.

Tours

Fuji Mountain Guides (☎042-445-0798; www.fujimountainguides.com; 2-day Mt Fuji tours per person ¥48,600) runs both in and out of season by highly experienced and very professional bilingual American guides. Transport to and from Tokyo, mountain guide, two meals and one night in a mountain hut is included; gear rental is available for extra. Tours use the Subashiri Trail. Fuji Mountain Guides can also assist independent travellers in making reservations at mountain huts for a fee of ¥1000 per booking.

Discover Japan Tours (www.discover-japan-tours.com; tours per person from ¥10,000) has self-guided overnight treks to/from Shinjuku, timed for sunrise arrival, on summer Saturdays, with a stop at a public hot spring on the way back. Groups of up to eight can arrange a private tour (¥60,000) any day of the week, including outside the climbing season.

Around Mt Fuji

On the north side of Mt Fuji is the resort area of **Fuji Five Lakes** (富士五湖), which offers year-round hiking and hot springs. The most developed lake is Kawaguchi-ko, also a transport hub for the region. An excellent place to stay here – and to meet fellow travellers/climbers – is **K's House Mt Fuji** (☎0555-83-5556; www.kshouse.jp; 6713-108 Funatsu; dm from ¥2500; d with/without bathroom from ¥8800/7200; ☯@☎).

DAY TRIPS FROM TOKYO TOP EXPERIENCE

GEAR RENTAL

Want to climb Mt Fuji, but don't want to invest in (or schlep) all the requisite gear? **Yamadōgu Rental** (やまどうぐレンタル屋; Map p280; ☎050-5865-1615; www.yamarent.com; 6th fl, 1-13-7 Nishi-Shinjuku, Shinjuku-ku; ⏰noon-7pm Mon-Sat Sep-May, noon-7pm Wed-Mon Jun, 6.30am-7pm every day Jul & Aug; ☒JR Yamanote line to Shinjuku, west exit) can set you up with individual items (shoes, poles, rain jacket etc) or a full kit including a backpack from ¥10,500 for two days. Most of the gear is from Japanese outdoor brand Montbell. You can rent directly from the shop (same-day rental is possible, pending availability) or place an order online and have the gear shipped to your accommodation. During the Fuji climbing season, they have a shop at Fuji Subaru Line Fifth Station where you can return your gear after coming down the mountain.

Two useful resources for climbing Mt Fuji are the official website (www.fujisan-climb.jp) and www.snow-forecast.com/resorts/Mount-Fuji/6day/top, where you can check summit weather conditions before a climb – a must outside the official season.

Nikkō

Explore

Nikkō (日光) is one of Japan's major attractions, conveniently accessible from Tokyo and compact. You can accomplish a lot in a day; the problem is crowds, most common in high season (summer and autumn) and at weekends. Spending the night here allows for an early start on the day trippers. (Otherwise we recommend a very early morning train from Tokyo). There are some wonderful places for lunch, but it's a sleepy town after the sights close.

The Best...

⇒ **Sight** Tōshō-gū

⇒ **Place to Eat** Gyōshintei (p181)

⇒ **Place to Drink** Nikkō Coffee (p181)

Top Tip

On days when Nikkō is crowded, it's a good idea to buy your return ticket to Tokyo early in the day, as popular late afternoon and early evening express trains can sell out.

Getting There & Around

Nikkō is best reached from Tokyo via the Tōbu Nikkō line from Asakusa Station. You can usually get last-minute seats on the hourly reserved *tokkyū* (limited-express) trains (¥2800, 1¾ hours). *Kaisoku* (rapid) trains (¥1360, 2½ hours, hourly from 6.20am to 5.30pm) require no reservation, but you may have to change at Shimoimaichi. Be sure to ride in the last two cars to reach Nikkō (some cars may separate at an intermediate stop).

The main sights are a 20-minute walk uphill along the main road from Tōbu Nikkō Station. You can also take a bus from the station to the Shin-kyō bus stop (¥200), at the top of the main road.

Need to Know

⇒ **Area Code** ☑0288

⇒ **Population** 84,197

⇒ **Location** 120km north of Tokyo

⇒ **Tourist Office** (☑0288-54-0864; Tōbu Nikkō Station; ☺8.30am-5pm)

◉ SIGHTS

★ TŌSHŌ-GŪ   SHINTO SHRINE

(東照宮; www.toshogu.jp; 2301 Sannai; adult/child ¥1300/450; ☺8am-4.30pm Apr-Oct, to 3.30pm Nov-Mar) A Unesco World Heritage Site in an idyllic natural setting, Tōshō-gū is a lavishly ornate Shintō complex within which Tokugawa Ieyasu (1543–1616), the first shogun and founder of the Tokugawa Bakufu (Japan's last feudal military government) is enshrined. Among its standout structures are the dazzling **Yōmei-mon** (陽明門; Sunset Gate), **Gōjūnotō** (五重塔; Five Storey Pagoda; ¥300) and the grand **Honji-dō** (本地堂) with its famous 'crying dragon'. Most of what you see was commissioned by Ieyasu's grandson in 1636.

Sections of the shrine may be closed for repairs until 2020.

The stone steps of **Omotesandō** lead past the towering stone *torii* (entrance gate) **Ishi-dorii** and the Gōjūnotō, an 1819 reconstruction of the original mid-17th-century pagoda, to **Omote-mon** (表門), Tōshō-gū's main gateway, protected on either side by deva kings.

In Tōshō-gū's initial courtyard are the **Sanjinko** (三神庫; Three Sacred Storehouses); on the upper storey of the **Kami-jinko** (upper storehouse) are relief carvings of 'imaginary elephants' by an artist who had never seen the real thing. Nearby is the **Shinkyūsha** (神厩舎; Sacred Stable), adorned with relief carvings of monkeys. The allegorical 'hear no evil, see no evil, speak no evil' simians demonstrate three principles of Tendai Buddhism.

Further into Tōshō-gū's precincts, to the left of the drum tower, is Honji-dō, a hall known for the painting on its ceiling of the Nakiryū (Crying Dragon). Monks demonstrate the hall's acoustic properties by clapping two sticks together. The dragon 'roars' (a bit of a stretch) when the sticks are clapped beneath its mouth, but not elsewhere.

Restored in 2017, the Yōmei-mon dazzles with its gold leaf and delicate carvings of flowers, dancing girls, mythical beasts and Chinese sages. Worrying that the gate's perfection might arouse envy in the gods, those responsible for its construction had the final supporting pillar placed upside down as a deliberate error.

Gōhonsha (御本社), the main inner courtyard, includes the **Honden** (本殿; Main Hall) and **Haiden** (拝殿; Hall of Wor-

Nikkō

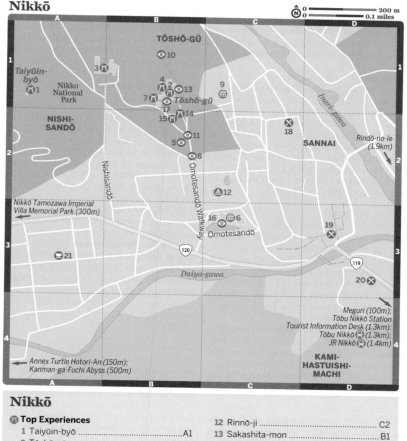

Nikkō

ship). Inside these halls are paintings of the 36 immortal poets of Kyoto, and a ceiling-painting pattern from the Momoyama period; note the 100 dragons, each different. *Fusuma* (sliding door) paintings depict a *kirin* (a mythical beast that's part giraffe and part dragon).

To the right of Gōhonsha is **Sakashita-mon** (坂下門), into which is carved a tiny wooden sculpture of the **Nemuri-neko**

(眠り猫) that's famous for its lifelike appearance (though admittedly the attraction is lost on some visitors). From here it's an uphill path through towering cedars to the appropriately solemn **Okumiya** (奥宮), Ieyasu's tomb.

Bypassed by nearly everyone at Tōshō-gū is the marvellous **Nikkō Tōshō-gū Museum of Art** (日光東照宮美術館; ☎0288-54-0560; www.toshogu.jp/shisetsu/bijutsu.html; 2301 Yamanouchi; adult/child ¥800/400; ☉9am-5pm Apr-Oct, to 4pm Nov-Mar) in the old shrine offices, showcasing fine paintings on its doors, sliding screens, frames and decorative scrolls, some by masters including Yokoyama Taikan and Nakamura Gakuryo. Follow the path to the right of Omote-mon to find it.

⭐**TAIYŪIN-BYŌ**　　　　SHINTO SHRINE
(大猷院廟; adult/child ¥550/250; ☉8am-4.30pm Apr-Oct, to 3.30pm Nov-Mar) Ieyasu's grandson Iemitsu (1604–51) is buried here, and although the shrine houses many of the same elements as Tōshō-gū (drum tower, Chinese-style gates etc), the more intimate scale, lighter tourist footfall and gorgeous setting in a cryptomeria forest make it hugely appealing.

Look for dozens of lanterns donated by *daimyō* (domain lords), and the gate **Niō-mon**, whose guardian deities have a hand up (to welcome those with pure hearts) and a hand down (to suppress those with impure hearts).

FUTARASAN-JINJA　　　SHINTO SHRINE
(二荒山神社; www.futarasan.jp; 2307 Sannai; adult/child ¥200/100) Set among cypress trees, this atmospheric shrine was founded by Shōdō Shōnin; the current building dates from 1619, making it Nikkō's oldest. It's the protector shrine of Nikkō itself, dedicated to Nantai-san (2484m), the mountain's consort, Nyotai-san, and their mountainous progeny, Tarō.

There are other branches of the shrine on Nantai-san and by Chūzenji-ko. At the time of research, parts of the shrine were closed for restoration.

NIKKŌ TAMOZAWA IMPERIAL VILLA MEMORIAL PARK　　HISTORIC SITE
(日光田母沢御用邸記念公園; ☎0288-53-6767; www.park-tochigi.com/tamozawa; 8-27 Hon-chō; adult/child ¥510/250; ☉9am-4.30pm Wed-Mon) About 1km west of Shin-kyō bridge, this splendidly restored imperial palace (c 1899)

of more than 100 rooms showcases superb artisanship, with parts of the complex dating from the Edo, Meiji and Taishō eras. Apart from the construction skills involved there are brilliantly detailed screen paintings and serene garden views framed from nearly every window. Visit in autumn to see the gardens at their most spectacular.

RINNŌ-JI　　　　BUDDHIST TEMPLE
(輪王寺; ☎0288-54-0531; www.rinnoji.or.jp; 2300 Yamanouchi; adult/child ¥400/200; ☉8am-5pm Apr-Oct, to 4pm Nov-Mar) This Tendai-sect temple was founded 1200 years ago by Shōdō Shōnin. The main hall (Sanbutsu-dō) houses a trio of 8m gilded wooden Buddha statues: Amida Nyorai (a primal deity in the Mahayana Buddhist canon) flanked by Senjū (deity of mercy and compassion) and Batō (a horse-headed Kannon). Its exterior may still be under wraps for restoration.

Rinnō-ji's **Hōmotsu-den** (宝物殿, Treasure Hall; ¥300) houses some 6000 treasures associated with the temple; the separate admission ticket includes entrance to the **Shōyō-en** (逍遥園) strolling garden.

You can buy a combination ticket that covers entry to Rinnō-ji and Taiyūin-byō for ¥900.

KANMAN-GA-FUCHI ABYSS　　　PARK
(憾満ガ淵) Escape the crowds along this riverside path lined with a collection of Jizō statues, the small stone effigies of the Buddhist protector of travellers and children. It's said that if you try to count the statues there and again on the way back, you'll end up with a different number, hence the nickname 'Bake-jizō' (ghost Jizō). To find it, follow Daiya-gawa west for about 1km from the Shin-kyō bridge, crossing another bridge near Jyoko-ji temple en route.

EATING & DRINKING

A local speciality is *yuba* (the skin that forms when making tofu) cut into strips; it's a staple of *shōjin-ryōri* (Buddhist vegetarian cuisine).

HONGŪ CAFE　　　CAFE ¥
(本宮カフェ; ☎0288-54-1669; www.hongu cafe.com; 2384 Sannai; espresso ¥400, dessert sets from ¥650; ☉10am-5pm, closed Thu; 🖼) Refresh with a cup of espresso or a traditional Japanese dessert set of *matcha*

and *yomogi-mochi* (mugwort dumplings topped with sweet *azuki*-bean paste) – it tastes better than it sounds. Set in a refurbished historic house near the entrance of the national park, this cafe is a great place to take a breather après-shrine.

NIKKŌ COFFEE   CAFE ¥

(日光珈琲; www.nikko-coffee.com; 3-13 Honchō; coffee from ¥550; ☺10am-6pm Tue-Sun, closed 1st & 3rd Tue of every month) A century-old rice shop has been reinvented as this retro-chic cafe with a garden, where house-roasted coffee is served alongside pastries and snacks like savoury *galettes* (buckwheat pancakes) and pork curry with rice (meals from ¥1650). Expect queues.

NAGOMI-CHAYA   JAPANESE ¥¥

(和み茶屋; ☎0288-54-3770; 1016 Kamihatsuishi; set meals from ¥1620; ☺11.30am-4pm, closed Wed) The beautifully prepared *kaiseki*-style lunches are a great deal at this sophisticated arts-and-crafts-style cafe near the top of Nikkō's main drag, but be prepared to wait in line. Last order for lunch is 2.30pm.

MEGURI   VEGAN ¥¥

(自然茶寮 廻; ☎0288-25-3122; 909 Nakahatsuishi-machi; lunch ¥1400; ☺11.30am-6pm, closed Thu; 🖉🍴) Enjoy lovingly prepared Japanese vegan meals in this antique former art shop that also boasts a grand, faded ceiling fresco. Arrive as soon as it opens if you want to eat lunch – it's a popular place and once it's run out of food, it's sweets and drinks only. Look for the retro sign that says 'Oriental Fine Art & Curios'.

★ GYŌSHINTEI   KAISEKI ¥¥¥

(尭心亭; ☎0288-53-3751; www.meiji-yakata.com/gyoushin; 2339-1 Sannai; sets ¥3800-5500; ☺11am-7pm, closed Thu; 🖉🍴) Splash out on deluxe spreads of vegetarian *shōjin-ryōri*, featuring local bean curd and vegetables served in delectable ways, or the *kaiseki* courses that include fish. The elegant tatami dining room overlooks a bonsai-filled garden, which is part of the Meji-no-Yakata compound of chic restaurants close to the World Heritage Site.

🛏 SLEEPING

RINDŌ-NO-IE   MINSHUKU ¥

(りんどうの家; ☎53-0131; 1462 Tokorono; r per person without bathroom from ¥3500;

😊❀@🛜) Run by a lovely older couple, this small but well-maintained *minshuku* (guesthouse) offers spacious tatami rooms, generous meals and a pick-up service. Breakfast/dinner is ¥700. It's across the river, a 15-minute walk northwest of the train station.

ANNEX TURTLE HOTORI-AN   INN ¥¥

(アネックス―ほとり庵; ☎0288-53-3663; www.turtle-nikko.com; 8-28 Takumi-chō; s/tw from ¥6700/13,800; 😊❀@🛜) Only steps away from the trailhead to Kanman-ga-Fuchi Abyss, this tidy, comfortable inn offers Japanese- and Western-style rooms, plus river views from the house onsen. It's a lovely spot in a quiet neighbourhood that gives way to open space.

Hakone

Explore

Hakone (箱根) is made up of seven distinct hot-spring villages, the most developed of which are Hakone-Yumoto and Gōra. Hakone-Yumoto is the nearest to Tokyo and has some excellent day spas. Beyond onsen, there is a lot to do in Hakone: the classic route includes a stop at the volcano, Ōwakudani (p180), and a cruise on the lake, Ashino-ko (芦ノ湖), famous for its Mt Fuji views and the floating *torii* of Hakone-jinja (p180).

Naturally, this is all quite attractive, so it can feel crammed, particularly at weekends and holidays. It's easiest to go with the flow, from train to cable car to ferry, though this can feel highly packaged. Working out your own itinerary will give you a more personalised experience.

Overnighting here means more time to relax in the springs (and lots of places to stay have them). Hakone is also a great place to experience a ryokan (traditional Japanese inn).

The Best...

➡ **Sight** Hakone Open-Air Museum (p179)
➡ **Place to Eat** Itoh Dining by Nobu (p180)
➡ **Place to Drink** Amazake-chaya (p180)

Hakone

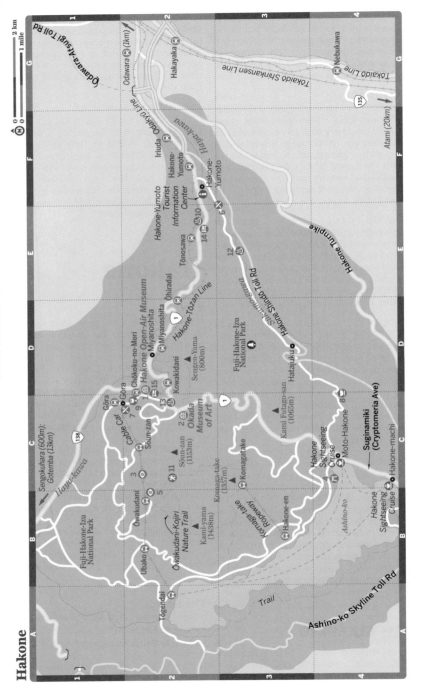

Hakone

Top Tip

Odakyū's **Hakone Freepass** (two-day pass, adult/child ¥5140/1500) covers the return fare between Shinjuku and Hakone and unlimited use of most modes of transport within the region, plus discounts at museums and facilities in the area. Freepass-holders need to pay an additional limited-express surcharge (¥890 each way) to ride the Romance Car. Purchase it at Odakyū Shinjuku Station.

Getting There & Around

The Odakyū line (www.odakyu.jp) from Shinjuku Station goes directly into Hakone-Yumoto, the region's transit hub. Use either the convenient Romance Car (¥2280, 1½ hours) or *kyūkō* (regular-express) service (¥1190, two hours); the latter usually requires a transfer at Odawara.

In Hakone-Yumoto, the narrow-gauge, switchback Hakone-Tōzan line runs to Gōra (¥400, 40 minutes). From Gōra, a funicular (¥420, 10 minutes) heads up to near the 1153m-high summit of **Sōun-zan**, from where you can catch the **Hakone Ropeway** (箱根ロープウェイ; www.hakoneropeway.co.jp; one way/return ¥1450/2550; ⏰9am-5pm Mar-Nov, to 4.15pm Dec-Feb) to **Ōwakudani** and **Tōgendai**.

☐ From Tōgendai, sightseeing boats crisscross Ashino-ko to **Hakone-machi** and **Moto-Hakone** between 9.30am and 5pm (one way/return ¥1000/1840, 30 minutes).

Of course you can do the whole circuit in reverse. For more details, see www.odakyu.jp/english/course/hakone.

The Hakone-Tōzan and Izu Hakone bus companies also service the Hakone area, linking most of the sights.

Need to Know

➡ **Area Code** ☎0460

➡ **Population** 11,389

➡ **Location** 92km southwest of Tokyo

➡ **Tourist Office** (☎0460-85-8911; www.hakone.or.jp; 706-35 Yumoto; ⏰9am-5.45pm)

👁 SIGHTS

⭐ **HAKONE OPEN-AIR MUSEUM**　MUSEUM

(彫刻の森美術館; ☎0460-82-1161; www.hakone-oam.or.jp; 1121 Ninotaira; adult/child ¥1600/800; ⏰9am-5pm) Occupying a verdant swath of Hakone hillside is this unmissable art safari, leading visitors past a rich array of 19th- and 20th-century sculptures and installations by leading Japanese artists as well as the likes of Henry Moore, Rodin and Miró, harmoniously plonked into the landscape. If it's raining, take shelter in the humongous Picasso Pavilion with more than 300 of his works inside, ranging from paintings and glass art to tapestry.

⭐ **OKADA MUSEUM OF ART**　MUSEUM

(岡田美術館; ☎0460-87-3931; www.okada-museum.com; 483-1 Kowakidani; adult/student ¥2800/1800; ⏰9am-5pm) This mammoth museum showcases the dazzling Japanese, Chinese and Korean art treasures of industrialist Okada Kazuo. You could easily spend hours marvelling at the beauty of many pieces, including detailed screen paintings and exquisite pottery. Interactive, multilingual interpretive displays enhance the experience. The museum is opposite the Kowakien bus stop. As well as admiring the treasures on display, you can explore the lush hillside garden and woodland, soak in the outdoor footbath or relax in the cafe-restaurant housed in a traditional wooden villa.

ŌWAKUDANI
VOLCANO

(大桶谷; www.kanagawa-park.or.jp/owakudani) FREE The 'Great Boiling Valley' was created 3000 years ago when Kami-yama erupted and collapsed, also forming Ashino-ko. Hydrogen sulphide steams from the yellow ground (the yellow is crystallised sulphur) and the hot water is used to boil onsen *tamago*, eggs blackened in the sulphurous waters, which you can buy from the tourist shops beside the ropeway station. Occasionally Ōwakudani is closed due to volcanic activity.

HAKONE-JINJA
SHINTO SHRINE

(箱根神社; ◎9am-4pm) A pleasant stroll around Ashino-ko follows a cedar-lined path to this shrine set in a wooded grove, in Moto-Hakone. Its signature red *torii* rises from the lake; get your camera ready for that picture-postcard shot.

EATING & DRINKING

Most overnight guests eat at their inns so many restaurants close early in the day. Gōra and Hakone-Yumoto and have the best options.

COCO-HAKONE
CHICKEN ¥

(☏70-4006-5212; 475-8 Yumoto; meals around ¥1000; ◎11am-4.30pm Wed-Sun; 🌐) The 'Hakone lava' chicken over rice looks burnt to a crisp at this casual joint, but actually it's a juicy, tasty treat and simply a bit of gastronomic trickery. You can drink Hakone craft beer here, too, and nerds will appreciate the glass cabinet stuffed with vintage Star Wars toys (sorry, it's locked).

SUKUMO
SOBA ¥¥

(自然薯自然薯すくも; ☏0460-86-4126; 208 Yumoto-chaya; soba from ¥1100; ◎11.30am-4.30pm Fri-Wed) This serene riverside soba restaurant is perfect for a bite after visiting the neighbouring Tenzan Tōji-kyō onsen complex. Find it through an arched gate just beside the bridge. The chef speaks English.

ITOH DINING BY NOBU
JAPANESE ¥¥¥

(伊藤ダイニング　バイノブ; ☏0460-83-8209; www.itoh-dining.co.jp; 1300-64 Gōra; lunch/dinner from ¥3000/7000; ◎11.30am-3pm & 5-9.30pm; 🚠🌐) Savour premium Japanese beef, cooked *teppanyaki*-style in front of you by the chef, at this elegant restaurant, an outpost of the celeb chef Nobu's dining empire. It's just uphill from Koenshimo Station on the funicular, one stop from Gōra.

★ GORA BREWERY & GRILL
CRAFT BEER

(☏0460-83-8107; www.itoh-dining.co.jp; 1300-72 Gōra; ◎1-4pm & 5-9.30pm; 🌐🌐) Sup on a Gora IPA or a Black Belt stout, among other ales from this stylish brewery venue, run by the folk behind Itoh Dining by Nobu. Grill treats include house-made sausages, Peruvian-style lamb and Nobu's signature black cod with miso. It's a three-minute walk from Koenshimo Station on the funicular, or a 10-minute uphill slog from Gora.

★ AMAZAKE-CHAYA
TEAHOUSE

(甘酒茶屋; ☏0460-83-6418; www.amasake-chaya.jp; 395-1 Futoko-yama; amazake ¥400, snacks from ¥250; ◎7am-5.30pm) This historic thatched-roofed teahouse, the last of several that once lined the Old Hakone Highway, has been relieving road-weary travellers with *amazake* (a sweet drink made from rice used to make sake) and seasoned *mochi* (sticky rice cakes) for more than 360 years. If you visit in the chillier months, you can warm yourself around the *irori*.

Amazake-chaya is about 550m along the cobbled Old Hakone Highway from Moto-Hakone, or take a Hakone-Yumoto–bound bus from Moto-Hakone and get off at the Amazake-chaya stop. The staff will give you some warning when the last bus back to Hakone-Yumoto is approaching (just after 5pm).

SPORTS & ACTIVITIES

★ TENZAN TŌJI-KYŌ
ONSEN

(天山湯治郷; ☏0460-86-4126; www.tenzan.jp; 208 Yumoto-chaya; adult/child ¥1300/650; ◎9am-10pm) Soak in tranquil *rotemburo* (outdoor baths) of varying temperatures and designs (one, for women only, is constructed to resemble a natural cave) at this stylish complex by gushing Haya-kawa. To get here, take the 'B' course shuttle bus from the bridge outside Hakone-Yumoto Station (¥100, five minutes). Tattoos are allowed.

HAKONE YURYŌ
ONSEN

(箱根湯寮; ☎0460-85-8411; www.hakone yuryo.jp; 4 Tōnosawa; adult/child ¥1400/700, private bath ¥4000-6000; ◷10am-9pm Mon-Fri, to 10pm Sat & Sun) Relax in spacious *rotemburo* under the trees at this idyllic complex ensconced in the forest, or book yourself a private bath in advance. A free shuttle bus (9am to 8pm, every 10 to 15 minutes) will whisk you here from Hakone-Yumoto Station, or it's a five-minute walk along a narrow path from Tōnosawa Station on the Hakone-Tōzan line. No tattoos allowed.

YUNESSUN
ONSEN

(箱根小涌園ユネッサン; www.yunessun.com; 1297 Ninotaira; Yunessun adult/child ¥2900/1600, Mori-no-Yu ¥1900/1200, both ¥4100/2100; ◷9am-7pm Mar-Oct, to 6pm Nov-Feb) This modern, family-oriented complex is more like an onsen amusement park, with outdoor water slides and a variety of baths (including some filled with coffee, green tea and even sake!) as well as indoor swimming pools with a retro leisure centre vibe. Mixed bathing so you'll need a swimsuit. The connected Mori-no-Yu complex (11am to 8pm) is traditional single-sex bathing.

Take a bus from Hakone-machi, Gōra or Hakone-Yumoto to the Kowakien bus stop. There's also a variety of accommodation here.

SŌUN-ZAN
HIKING

(早雲山) There are various hiking trails on this mountain including one to Kamiyama, Hakone's highest peak (1¾ hours) and another up to Ōwakudani (1¼ hours). The latter is sometimes closed due to the mountain's toxic gases. Check at the tourist information office.

🛏 SLEEPING

At Hakone-Yumoto Station, deposit your luggage with **Hakone Baggage Delivery Service** (箱根キャリーサービス; ☎0460-86-4140; 2nd fl, Hakone-Yumoto Station; S/M/L suitcase ¥800/1000/1500; ◷8.30am-7pm) by 12.30pm, and it will be delivered to your inn within Hakone from 3pm. Alternatively, you can check your bag at your inn by 10am and pick it up after 1pm at Hakone-Yumoto Station. Hakone Freepass holders get a discount of ¥100 per bag.

★ GUESTHOUSE TENMAKU
HOSTEL ¥

(囲炉裏ゲストハウス天幕; ☎0460-83-9348; 1121 Ninotaira; dm/tw/f from ¥3500/9000/18000, deluxe dorm 1/2 people ¥5500/8500; ❄✳@🛜🅿) The centrepiece of this impeccably designed hostel is the *irori* (sunken hearth) in the bar-lounge, around which communal feasts of grilled fish, rice and miso soup are shared between guests (¥1000). The 'deluxe dorm' is worth considering – private timber cabins/capsules furnished with double beds. There's a good selection of rooms for families, too, and kids of all ages are welcome.

★ FUKUZUMIRŌ
RYOKAN ¥¥¥

(福住楼; ☎0460-85-5301; www.fukuzumi-ro.com; 74 Tōnosawa; s/d incl 2 meals from ¥25,000/44,000; ✳🛜) Established in 1890, this antique inn boasts a trio of onsen and fine woodwork throughout its tatami guestrooms, some with terraces overlooking Haya-kawa. One of the rooms was a favourite of Nobel Prize–winning author Kawabata Yasunori. Buses heading up the hill from Hakone-Yumoto stop just outside, or it's a 10-minute walk from Tōnosawa Station (on the Hakone-Tōzan railway).

Kamakura

Explore

Kamakura (鎌倉) has two clusters of sights: the temples around Kita-Kamakura Station and those in and around town, where Kamakura Station is located. A popular itinerary starts in Kita-Kamakura, with a visit to Engaku-ji (p183) and Kenchō-ji (p183), and then follows a hiking trail (p184) through the hills to the Daibutsu (p182).

Temples aside, Kamakura is an attractive city, with its own food scene (with lots of organic and vegetarian restaurants) and some bars. It's a very popular day trip for Tokyoites and tends to get packed on weekends and holidays, so plan accordingly (evenings are quieter and more local). In summer, head to Kamakura's beach, Yuigahama, where seasonal shacks set up on the sand selling food and drink.

Kamakura

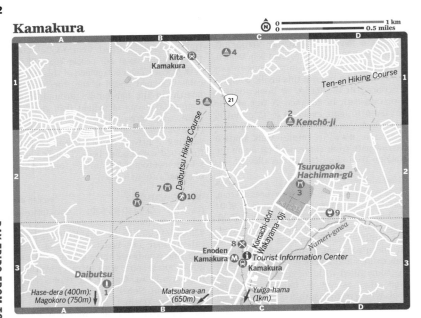

The Best...

→ **Sight** Daibutsu

→ **Place to Eat** Matsubara-an (p184)

→ **Place to Drink** Magnetico (p184)

Top Tip

Bicycles are great for touring Kamakura's shrines and temples; **Kamakura Rent-a-Cycle** (レンタサイクル; ☎0467-24-3944; www.jrbustech.co.jp/kamakura; 1-1 Komachi; per hr/day ¥800/1800; ☺8.30am-5pm) is outside the east exit of Kamakura Station, and right up the incline.

Getting There & Around

JR Yokosuka-line trains run to Kamakura from Tokyo (¥920, 54 minutes) and Shinagawa (¥720, 46 minutes), via Yokohama (¥340, 25 minutes). Alternatively, the Shōnan Shinjuku line runs from the west side of Tokyo (Shibuya, Shinjuku and Ikebukuro, all ¥920) in about one hour, though some trains require a transfer at Ōfuna. The last train from Kamakura back to Tokyo Station is at 11.19pm and Shinjuku at 9.48pm.

You can walk to most temples and shrines from Kamakura or Kita-Kamakura stations. Sites in the west, like the Daibutsu, can be reached via the Enoden Enoshima line from Kamakura Station to Hase (¥190) or by bus from Kamakura Station stops 1 and 6.

Need to Know

→ **Area Code** ☎0467

→ **Population** 172,306

→ **Location** 65km southwest of Tokyo

→ **Tourist Office** (鎌倉市観光総合案内所; ☎0467-22-3350; www.kamakura-info.jp; 1-1-1 Komachi; ☺9am-5pm)

◉ SIGHTS

★ DAIBUTSU   MONUMENT

(大仏; ☎0467-22-0703; www.kotoku-in.jp; Kōtoku-in, 4-2-28 Hase; adult/child ¥200/150; ☺8am-5.30pm Apr-Sep, to 5pm Oct-Nov) Kamakura's most iconic sight, an 11.4m bronze statue of Amida Buddha (*amitābha* in Sanskrit), is in Kōtoku-in, a Jōdo sect temple. Completed in 1252, it's said to have been inspired by Yoritomo's visit to Nara (where Japan's biggest Daibutsu holds court) after the Minamoto clan's victory over the Taira clan. Once housed in a huge hall, today the

Kamakura

statue sits in the open, the hall having been washed away by a tsunami in 1498.

For an extra ¥20, you can duck inside to see how the sculptors pieced the 850-tonne statue together.

Buses from stops 1 and 6 at the east exit of Kamakura Station run to the Daibutsu-mae stop (¥200). Alternatively, take the Enoden Enoshima line to Hase Station and walk north for about eight minutes. Better yet, take the Daibutsu Hiking Course (p184).

★**KENCHŌ-JI**   BUDDHIST TEMPLE
(建長寺; www.kenchoji.com; 8 Yamanouchi; adult/child ¥300/100; ⊗8.30am-4.30pm) Established in 1253, Japan's oldest Zen monastery is still active today. The central Butsuden (Buddha Hall) was brought piece by piece from Tokyo in 1647. Its Jizō Bosatsu statue, unusual for a Zen temple, reflects the valley's ancient function as an execution ground – Jizō consoles lost souls. Other highlights include a bell cast in 1253 and a juniper grove, believed to have sprouted from seeds brought from China by Kenchō-ji's founder some seven centuries ago.

The temple once comprised seven buildings and 49 subtemples, most of which were destroyed in fires during the 14th and 15th centuries. However, the 17th and 18th centuries saw its restoration, and you can still get a sense of its original splendour.

Kenchō-ji offers beginner-friendly, public *zazen* sessions from 5pm to 6pm on Fridays and Saturdays (enter before 4.30pm). Instruction is in Japanese, but you can easily manage by watching everyone else; arrive at least 15 minutes early. *Zazen* sessions in English (¥1000) are scheduled for specific dates every couple of months, for which you must apply in advance; see website for details.

★**TSURUGAOKA HACHIMAN-GŪ**   SHINTO SHRINE
(鶴岡八幡宮; ☏0467-22-0315; www.tsuruga oka-hachimangu.jp; 2-1-31 Yukinoshita; ⊗5am-8.30pm Apr-Sep, from 6am Oct-Mar) FREE Kamakura's most important shrine is, naturally, dedicated to Hachiman, the god of war. Minamoto no Yoritomo himself ordered its construction in 1191 and designed the pine-flanked central promenade that leads from the shrine to the coast. The sprawling grounds are ripe with historical symbolism: the Gempei Pond, bisected by bridges, is said to depict the rift between the Minamoto (Genji) and Taira (Heike) clans.

HASE-DERA   BUDDHIST TEMPLE
(長谷寺; Hase Kannon; ☏0467-22-6300; www. hasedera.jp; 3-11-2 Hase; adult/child ¥300/100; ⊗8am-5pm Mar-Sep, to 4.30pm Oct-Feb) The focal point of this Jōdo sect temple, one of the most popular in the Kantō region, is a 9m-high carved wooden *jūichimen* (11-faced) Kannon statue. Kannon (*avalokiteshvara* in Sanskrit) is the Bodhisattva of infinite compassion and, along with Jizō, is one of Japan's most popular Buddhist deities. The temple is about 10 minutes' walk from the Daibutsu and dates back to AD 736, when the statue is said to have washed up on the shore near Kamakura.

ENGAKU-JI   BUDDHIST TEMPLE
(円覚寺; ☏0467-22-0478; www.engakuji.or.jp; 409 Yamanouchi; adult/child ¥300/100; ⊗8am-4.30pm Mar-Nov, to 4pm Dec-Feb) One of Kamakura's five major Rinzai Zen temples, Engaku-ji was founded in 1282 as a place where Zen monks might pray for soldiers who lost their lives defending Japan against Kublai Khan. All of the temple structures have been rebuilt over the centuries; the Shariden, a Song-style reliquary, is the oldest,

DAIBUTSU HIKING COURSE

This 3km wooded trail connects Kita-Kamakura with the Daibutsu (p182) in Hase (allow about 1½ hours) and passes several small, quiet temples and shrines. The path begins at the steps just up the lane from pretty **Jōchi-ji** (浄智寺; 1402 Yamanouchi; adult/child ¥200/100; ⏱9am-4.30pm), down the road from Kita-Kamakura Station.

Along the way, you'll pass the shrine **Zeniarai-benten** (銭洗弁天; 2-25-16 Sasuke; ⏱8am-4.30pm) **FREE**. A cavelike entrance here leads to a clearing where visitors come to bathe their money in natural springs, with the hope of bringing financial success.

Then continue down the paved road, turning right at the first intersection, walking along a path lined with cryptomeria and ascending through a succession of *torii* to **Sasuke-inari-jinja** (佐助稲荷神社; 2-22-10 Sasuke; ⏱24hr) **FREE**, a hilltop enclave strewn with *kitsune*, or fox totems, before meeting up with the Daibutsu path once again. To hike in the opposite direction, follow the road beyond Daibutsu and the trail entrance is on the right, just before a tunnel.

last rebuilt in the 16th century. At the top of the long flight of stairs is the Engaku-ji bell, the largest bell in Kamakura, cast in 1301.

✖ EATING & DRINKING

SÔNG BÉ CAFE   ASIAN ¥

(ソンベカフェ; www.song-be-cafe.com; 13-32 Onarimachi; dishes from ¥800; ⏱11.30am-8pm Thu-Sun; 🖉🖫) This mellow day-to-evening joint serves up dishes such as *pad thai* (stir-fried rice noodles) and green curry, with veggies sourced from the local farmers market, and Southeast Asian beers to match. The friendly owner also serves a good selection of teas and desserts like yuzu honey cheesecake and banana cake with coconut milk.

★ MATSUBARA-AN   SOBA ¥¥

(松原庵; 🖉0467-61-3838; www.matsubara-an. com/shops/kamakura.php; 4-10-3 Yuiga-hama; mains ¥960-1850, set meals from ¥3200; ⏱11am-10pm; 🖫) Dinner reservations are recommended for this upscale soba restaurant in a lovely old house. Try the *goma seiro soba* (al dente noodles served cold with sesame

dipping sauce). Dine alfresco or indoors where you can watch noodles being handmade. From Yuiga-hama Station (Enoden Enoshima line) head towards the beach and then take the first right. Look for the blue sign.

MAGOKORO   FUSION ¥¥

(麻心; 🖉0467-38-7355; www.magokoroworld.jp; 2nd fl, 2-8-11 Hase; meals ¥800-1400; ⏱11.30am-8pm Tue-Sun; 🛜🖉🖫) 🖉 Boho beachfront spot mixing ocean views with an organic hemp-based menu, including vegetarian hemp taco rice, several vegan options, macrobiotic cakes and hemp beer (no, it doesn't get you high). From Hase Station, walk to the beach then turn left on the coastal road.

MAGNETICO   BAR

(🖉467-33-5952; 4-1-19 Yukinoshita; ⏱11.30am-3pm & 5.30-10pm Mon, Tue, Thu & Fri, 11.30am-11pm Sat & Sun; 🛜🖫) Run by a couple of relaxed reggae dudes, this louche hang-out has Japanese craft beers on tap, island rhythms on the stereo and a menu of tacos, fried chicken and other comfort food. It's a five-minute walk east from the main entrance of Tsurugaoka Hachiman-gū, Kamakura's main shrine.

 # Sleeping

As in any major city, accommodation will take up a big chunk of your Tokyo budget. But there's good news: there are plenty of attractive budget and midrange options, and levels of cleanliness and service are generally high. You can play it safe with a standard hotel or change it up with a more local option, like a ryokan (traditional inn with Japanese-style bedding) or a capsule hotel.

Apartment Hotels

Tokyo has a few hotels that offer rooms with the amenities of a small studio apartment, including kitchenettes and in-room laundry facilities. These can sometimes sleep more than two, which makes them a good option for families. **Tokyu Stay** (www.tokyustay. co.jp/e) is a reliable chain that has apartment-style rooms.

Boutique & Design Hotels

Tokyo has some very cool boutique and design hotels. While stylish, some are milking the design factor a little too much: be wary of ones with rooms that are really no bigger than those of a business hotel and, alternatively, ones that out-price even the luxury hotel franchises, but often don't have the same level of practised concierges that the established-name hotels have. A double room for ¥20,000 to ¥25,000 is around the sweet spot.

Business Hotels

Functional and economical, 'business hotels' have compact rooms, usually with semi-double beds (140cm across; roomy for one, a bit of a squeeze for two) and tiny en-suite bathrooms. If cost performance is your chief deciding factor – and you don't plan to spend much time in your room – then a business hotel is your best bet.

They're famous for being deeply unfashionable, though many chains have updated their look in recent years. Expect to pay from ¥10,000 to ¥15,000 (or ¥15,000 to ¥20,000 for double occupancy). In major hubs, front desk staff should speak some English.

Reliable chains include cheap and ubiquitous **Toyoko Inn** (www.toyoko-inn.com/ eng) and **Dormy Inn** (www.hotespa.net/dor myinn/english), which has some extra amenities like large communal baths, as well as in-room showers.

Capsule & Cabin Hotels

Capsule hotels offer a space the size of a single bed, with just enough headroom for you to sit up – like a bunk bed with more privacy: there's usually a curtain to seal off the entrance in addition to walls on three sides. Older capsule hotels have large communal baths (in which case visitors with visible tattoos are not allowed to stay); newer ones, geared more towards international travellers, often just have showers. Prices range from ¥3500 to ¥5000.

They're a neat experience as an alternative to a hostel, but bear in mind that capsule hotels are not ideally set up for multiple-night stays. Most will allow you to stay consecutive days if you book and pay upfront, without having to check out and back in. They do, however, want you and your stuff to be out of the capsule for a few hours, usually around noon, when cleaning staff roll through. You can put your stuff in one of the lockers (typically big enough for a backpack); larger suitcases can usually be held at the front desk.

Some places will let you opt-out of cleaning services, in which case you won't have to move out. Though as capsules lack security, you might want to put your stuff in the locker anyway.

Cabin hotels are a new concept, falling somewhere in between capsule hotels and business hotels: they're not bunked so you have room to stand, but the 'door' is only a sliding curtain; facilities are shared. Price-wise, they also fall in between (¥5500 to ¥8000). The same caveats about cleaning time and security apply here.

In both capsule and cabin hotels, floors and facilities are sex-segregated and front-desk service is typically limited.

Hotels

Bigger space and better front-desk service than a business hotel, but without the perks of a luxury hotel, an ordinary hotel is the obvious compromise, in the ¥20,000 to ¥35,000 range for a double room. They're often well located for public transport and some have rooms with good city views. Note that these are unlikely to have fitness centres; for that you'll need a luxury hotel.

Hostels

Tokyo excels at hostels: they're clean and well managed, with a mixture of dorms and private rooms. Staff typically speak good English and are often very helpful, offering more personalised service than you'd get at a business hotel. Some hostels put on cultural activities and social events for guests.

Laundry facilities are common; some but not all hostels have cooking facilities. Expect to pay about ¥3000 for a dorm and ¥8000 for a private room (double occupancy) and possibly extra for amenities like towels; check ahead to avoid surprises. Tokyo also has some new boutique guest-houses for the flashpacker crowd, with stylish interiors, hip bars and DJ nights; the average price of a dorm is ¥5000, while a double is around ¥12,000.

Love Hotels

'Love hotels', (in Japanese *rabu hoteru,* or *rabuho* for short) are designed for hook ups and can be found clustered around entertainment districts, such as Kabukichō in Shinjuku and Dōgenzaka in Shibuya. (Also good in a pinch if you've stayed out past last train but can't keep going until the first one

starts). They are cheaper than even business hotels: an overnight 'stay' costs around ¥7000; you can also stop for a short afternoon 'rest' (around ¥3000).

Reservations wouldn't be expected, though some love hotels have started listing themselves on booking sites – if you see a hotel listed as 'adults only', you're probably about to book a love hotel. Love hotels are famous for having decor designed to evoke exotic getaways; pictures of the rooms are usually displayed out front.

Luxury Hotels

Name-brand luxury hotels have big rooms full of mod-cons and luxe amenities, but the biggest perk of all is the English-language concierge service. A good concierge can do a lot, not the least of which is help you score hard-to-come-by restaurant reservations.

Many luxury hotels are atop high-rise buildings and offer fantastic city views; they also have direct airport access (via the Limousine Bus) and taxis on call. One downside is that some are in rather inconvenient locations that all but require you to rely on taxis. Prices vary wildly – and you can sometimes find amazing online deals – but average around ¥50,000 for a double room.

Ryokan

Ryokan (Japanese-style inns) offer a traditional experience, with tatami (woven-mat floor) rooms and futons (traditional quilt-like mattresses) instead of beds. Most have family rooms that can sleep four or five – an economical choice if you're travelling as a group or with kids. Some offer rooms with private baths, in addition to the communal (sex-segregated) ones designed for long soaks. Most inns provide cotton robes called *yukata*, which you can wear to and from the baths.

Some ryokan are in gorgeous old wooden buildings; some are in ostensibly ordinary, modern ones, but have traditional Japanese interiors. Prices vary wildly: a budget ryokan can cost as little as ¥8000 for two, a nice one goes for around ¥20,000, and a luxury one can top ¥100,000. Many ryokan have half-board packages.

Lonely Planet's Top Choices

BnA STUDIO Akihabara
(p194) Spacious studio apartments with cool interiors created by local artists.

Hanare (p195) Hip guesthouse in an old Yanaka house, renovated by Tokyo University of the Arts students.

Mustard Hotel (p191) New designer hot spot convenient for Shibuya, Ebisu and Daikanyama.

Sawanoya Ryokan (p195) Long-running traveller favourite with wonderfully kind service, in Yanaka.

Best by Budget

¥

Citan (p189) Flashpacker style without the price upgrade.

Mustard Hotel (p191) This design hostel in Shibuya also has budget-traveller friendly dorms.

Bay Hotel Ginza (p189) Great value at this capsule hotel in a typically pricey neighbourhood.

¥¥

Apartment Hotel Mimaru Akasaka (p190) Studio apartments priced nearly as low as a business hotel room.

Wired Hotel Asakusa (p196) Good-value design hotel, near the sights in Asakusa.

Hotel Niwa Tokyo (p194) Traditional design flourishes at this better-than-ordinary hotel in centrally located Suidōbashi.

¥¥¥

Park Hyatt Tokyo (p194) Palatial high-rise atop a Shinjuku skyscraper.

Hilltop Hotel (p195) Art-deco style and literary cred (and not really all that expensive).

Aman Tokyo (p193) Go big or go home: this is the ultimate Tokyo splurge.

Best Ryokan

Hoshinoya Tokyo (p189) The ultimate luxury ryokan experience.

Kimi Ryokan (p193) The gracious hospitality of a high-end ryokan, without the price tag.

Best Hostels

Citan (p189) Hipster hostel with DJ events in up-and-coming Bakurachō.

Kaisu (p190) Bed down in a former traditional Japanese restaurant, where geisha once performed.

Book and Bed Shinjuku (p193) Bunks built into well-stocked bookshelves – need we say more?

Best for Families

Apartment Hotel Mimaru Akasaka (p190) Great-value apartment-style rooms that sleep up to five.

Kimi Ryokan (p197) The largest rooms at this traditional inn sleep up to five on futons.

Sakura Hotel Ikebukuro (p193) Hostel with family rooms featuring a double bed and two bunks.

Best for Art & Design

BnA STUDIO Akihabara
(p194) Each room is the work of a single artist or studio, who shares in the hotels' profits.

Park Hotel Tokyo (p194) Original paintings adorn the walls of every room on the 31st floor.

SLEEPING

Where to Stay

Neighbourhood	For	Against
Marunouchi & Nihombashi	Convenient for sightseeing and travel in all directions.	This is largely a business district: expensive and quiet on weekends.
Ginza & Tsukiji	Central, with Ginza's shops and restaurants at your doorstep.	A pricier part of town.
Roppongi & Around	Fairly central with both daytime sights and nighttime attractions nearby.	Roppongi can be noisy at night; if you're not here for nightlife give it a pass.
Ebisu, Meguro & Around	Near major hubs but with fewer crowds; great bars and restaurants.	Few sleeping options and no major sights here.
Shibuya & Shimo-Kitazawa	Good transit links; lots going on after dark and a buzzing vibe.	The crowds and constant activity in Shibuya can get exhausting.
Harajuku & Aoyama	Sights, restaurants and shops galore.	Very limited sleeping options and crowded by day.
West Tokyo	Slightly cheaper rates than central Tokyo; local vibe.	Far from most sights, requiring a commute on the crowded Chūō line.
Shinjuku & Northwest Tokyo	Shinjuku is a convenient hub, with lots of sleeping options and plenty of restaurants and bars; Ikebukuro is a good budget choice.	Shinjuku Station can feel overwhelming; many cheap options in Shinjuku are in the red-light district.
Kōrakuen & Akihabara	Central, reasonable prices and with good transport links.	Though central, this part of town can feel strangely quiet at night.
Ueno & Yanaka	Ryokans abound; lots of greenery and museums; easy airport access.	Some options are in residential pockets, a bit of a walk from amenities.
Asakusa & Sumida River	Atmospheric old city feel; convenient for east Tokyo sights; great budget options and backpacker vibe.	Asakusa is quiet at night, and a good 20-minute subway ride to more central areas.
Odaiba & Tokyo Bay	Proximity to family-friendly attractions.	Over-priced and awkward for travel to the rest of the city.

USEFUL WEBSITES

Often it is cheapest to book online directly with the accommodation.

Jalan (www.jalan.net) Popular local discount accommodation site.

Japanese Inn Group (www.japaneseinngroup.com) Bookings for ryokan and other small, family-run inns.

Lonely Planet (lonelyplanet.com/Japan/Tokyo/hotels) Reviews, recommendations and bookings.

🛏 Marunouchi & Nihombashi

★CITAN HOSTEL ¥

Map p266 (☎03-6661-7559; https://backpackersjapan.co.jp/citan; 15-2 Nihombashi-Odenmachō, Chūō-ku; dm/tw/d from ¥3000/8400/8500; ❄📶; [S]Shinjuku line to Bakuro-Yokoyama, exit A1) The Bakurochō area has exploded with flashpacker hostels in the last few years – this is one of the biggest and the best. The trendy young staff are very helpful, and both dorms and private rooms (all share bathrooms) sport a pared-back contemporary look.

Also here is a spacious and buzzy basement cafe-bar (open 8am to 10.30pm), which serves craft beer and decent food and hosts occasional events and DJ nights.

KIKKA HOSTEL ¥

Map p266 (☎03-5825-4826; https://seven-garden.com/ja/hotel/KIKKA; 1-3-3 Higashi-Kanda, Chiyoda-ku; dm/r from ¥2900/9800; [S]Shinjuku line to Bakuro-Yokoyama, exit A2) Kikka offers decent, wooden-box-style dorm bunks but it's the good private rooms with their own bathrooms that are the draw here. In what is now a tried-and-true format for this area, Kikka also combines cool contemporary styling with a convivial ground-floor cafe-bar where you can enjoy healthy food.

★AMAN TOKYO DESIGN HOTEL ¥¥¥

Map p266 (☎03-5224-3333; www.aman.com; 1-5-6 Ōtemachi, Chiyoda-ku; r from ¥120,000; 🚭❄[@]📶🏊; [S]Marunouchi line to Ōtemachi, exit A5) Overlooking the Imperial Palace (p60) from atop Ōtemachi Tower, this outstanding hotel incorporates natural materials – including dark stone walls, blonde wood and white *washi* (Japanese handmade paper) – into its elegant, minimalist design. Enormous rooms all have baths with stunning city views – something you also get from the giant stone bath filled with onsen water in the spa.

★HOSHINOYA TOKYO RYOKAN ¥¥¥

Map p266 (星のや東京; ☎050-3786-1144; www.hoshinoyatokyo.com; 1-9-1 Ōtemachi, Chiyoda-ku; r incl breakfast from ¥166,000; [S]Marunouchi line to Ōtemachi, exit A1) In creating this contemporary ryokan in the heart of Tokyo, Hoshinoya has barely put a foot wrong, overcoming a location boxed in by office towers. Staying here is all about insulating yourself from the city in a building that incorporates timeless artisanship and the best of traditional Japanese design and service.

PENINSULA TOKYO HOTEL ¥¥¥

Map p266 (ザ・ペニンシュラ東京; ☎03-6270-2288; www.peninsula.com/tokyo; 1-8-1 Yūrakuchō, Chiyoda-ku; r from ¥54,000; 🚭❄[@]📶🏊; 🚉JR lines to Yūrakuchō, Hibiya exit) One almost gets a feeling of guilty extravagance when sprawling out in the Peninsula's vast rooms (starting at 51 sq metres). Latticed caramel woodwork, sumptuous marble bathrooms and a dark central atrium unite in a delicious symphony of design.

🛏 Ginza & Tsukiji

★PRIME POD GINZA TOKYO CAPSULE HOTEL ¥

Map p268 (☎03-5550-0147; http://theprimepod.jp; 13th fl, Duplex Tower, 5/13 Bldg, 5-13-19 Ginza, Chūō-ku; capsules from ¥4000; [S]Hibiya line to Higashi-Ginza, exit 3) One of the cheapest places to sleep in Ginza is this capsule hotel, which is suitably contemporary in its stylings. For a bit more headroom than in your average capsule, request a corner pod when you book. Rates are cheaper online.

BAY HOTEL GINZA CAPSULE HOTEL ¥

Map p268 (☎03-6226-1078; www.bay-hotel.jp/ginza; 7-13-15 Ginza, Chūō-ku; capsule ¥3500; 🚭❄📶; [S]Asakusa or Hibiya line to Higashi-Ginza, exit A3) You're unlikely to find anywhere cheaper to stay in central Ginza than this branch of a capsule hotel chain. The footbath to soak weary feet at the ground-floor entrance is a nice touch and it has a women-only floor, too. Cooking facilities are fairly basic, limited to a kettle and a microwave.

★PARK HOTEL TOKYO DESIGN HOTEL ¥¥¥

Map p268 (☎03-6252-1111; www.parkhoteltokyo.com; Shiodome Media Tower, 1-7-1 Higashi-Shimbashi, Minato-ku; s/d from ¥17,000/20,000, art rooms from ¥20,000/22,400; 🚭❄[@]📶; [S]Ōedo line to Shimbashi, exit 7) Kudos to the Park Hotel for commissioning 31 artists to decorate 31 of its 31st-floor rooms. The results are very impressive with all-Japanese themes ranging from sumo and Zen to *yokai* (monsters) and geisha. See the various themes online and book well in advance for popular rooms such as the cherry-blossom one.

APARTMENT RENTALS

Apartment rentals are strictly regulated in Tokyo (and Japan in general). Very few places are currently able to meet the requirements to qualify. Those that appear on AirBnB have completed the proper registration process. **Housing Japan** (https://housingjapan.com) can also arrange legal short-term stays. Options may increase in the near future, as more and more operators are able to get their paperwork through the approval process.

MILLENNIUM MITSUI GARDEN HOTEL TOKYO
HOTEL ¥¥¥

Map p268 (ミレニアム 三井ガーデンホテル 東京; ☑03-3549-3331; www.gardenhotels.co.jp/eng/millennium-tokyo; 5-11-1 Ginza, Chūō-ku; r from ¥27,000; ➋✴@🛜; ⓢHibiya line to Higashi-Ginza, exit A1) Mitsui Garden's upmarket business hotel has a super-convenient Ginza location, and with online deals the rates can be affordable. It's all quite contemporary with deep-purple design accents in the rooms and striking digital art in the lobby.

IMPERIAL HOTEL
HOTEL ¥¥¥

Map p268 (帝国ホテル; ☑03-3504-1111; www.imperialhotel.co.jp; 1-1-1 Uchisaiwai-chō, Chiyoda-ku; s/d from ¥45,360/48,600; ➋✴@🛜♒; ⓢHibiya line to Hibiya, exit A13) This hotel's present building is the successor to Frank Lloyd Wright's 1923 masterpiece, and small tributes to the architect's style can be found in the lobby and elsewhere. The rooms, split across the main building and a connected tower, may not be Tokyo's most stylish, but they are large, comfortable and generally have impressive views. Service is excellent.

🛏 Roppongi & Around

★KAISU
HOSTEL ¥

Map p270 (☑03-5797-7711; www.kaisu.jp; 6-13-5 Akasaka, Minato-ku; dm/r without bathroom from ¥3900/10,500; ➋✴🛜; ⓢChiyoda line to Akasaka, exit 7) Occupying a former *ryōtei* (geisha house), Kaisu is a flashpacker hostel with mid-century-modern and surfer-chic stylings. Dorms offer wooden bunks with the gorgeous old building's exposed beams on show. English-speaking staff are very

friendly and there's a great cafe-bar (10am to 11pm) where you can mingle with locals.

★APARTMENT HOTEL MIMARU AKASAKA
APARTMENT ¥¥

Map p270 (☑03-6807-4344; www.mimaruhotels.com; 7-9-6 Akasaka, Minato-ku; apt from ¥18,000; ✴🛜; ⓢChiyoda line to Akasaka, exit 7) Opened in 2018, Mimaru has beautifully designed rooms with fully equipped kitchens and proper bathrooms (no pokey unit baths!). Its apartment studios, some with Japanese tatami areas, sleep up to four people. Online deals via its Facebook page can make it a great accommodation option, particularly for families or groups.

★HOTEL S
BOUTIQUE HOTEL ¥¥

Map p270 (ホテル S; ☑03-5771-2469; www.hr-roppongi.jp; 1-11-6 Nishi-Azabu, Minato-ku; r from ¥16,000, apt per month from ¥216,000; ➋✴@🛜; ⓢHibiya line to Roppongi, exit 2) The various styles of room at this boutique property capture the arty design spirit of Roppongi. Some of the more expensive duplex-type rooms have Japanese design elements such as tatami (in charcoal) and circular *hinoki* (wooden baths). The entry-level rooms are also a cut above the usual.

CANDEO HOTELS TOKYO ROPPONGI
HOTEL ¥¥

Map p270 (カンデオホテルズ東京六本木; ☑03-5413-6950; www.candeohotels.com/roppongi; 6-7-11 Roppongi, Minato-ku; s from ¥20,000, d & tw from ¥25,000; ➋✴🛜; ⓢHibiya line to Roppongi, exit 3) Designed in burnished metallic tones, the Candeo rises up from the heart of Roppongi, its high-level rooms all offering good views towards either Roppongi Hills or Tokyo Tower. There's comfy seating by the windows for taking it all in or you can relax in the rooftop communal bath (from 3pm to 11am), also with a view.

★HOTEL ŌKURA
HOTEL ¥¥¥

Map p270 (ホテルオークラ東京; ☑03-3582-0111; www.okura.com; 2-10-4 Toranomon, Minato-ku; s/d from ¥35,840/36,040; ➋✴@🛜♒; ⓢHibiya line to Kamiyachō, exit 4B) While the beloved original 1962 hotel has been demolished to make way for a new building (set to open in September 2019), the Ōkura's elegant South Wing remains intact – and long may it do so! Rooms are bright, and large, with tasteful Japanese design touches. The public areas ooze retro glamour and service is courteous to a fault.

🛏 Ebisu, Meguro & Around

DORMY INN EXPRESS
MEGURO AOBADAI   BUSINESS HOTEL ¥¥
Map p274 (ドーミーインエクスプレス目黒青葉台; ☎03-6894-5489; www.hotespa.net/hotels/meguro; 3-21-8 Aobadai, Meguro-ku; s/d from ¥14,000/20,600; ☺❄🤖; Ⓢ Hibiya line to Naka-Meguro) If you prefer to base yourself somewhere less hectic – but no less fun – try this business hotel along the canal in Naka-Meguro.

This chain sets itself apart with its evening cup noodle service and free bicycles (up to two hours; afterwards it's ¥200 per hour up to five hours). Rooms are small (naturally), but sufficiently up-to-date.

🛏 Shibuya & Shimo-Kitazawa

★ MUSTARD HOTEL   DESIGN HOTEL, HOSTEL ¥¥
Map p272 (マスタードホテル; ☎03-6459-2842; www.mustardhotel.com; 1-29 Higashi, Shibuya-ku; dm/s/d with shared bathroom from ¥4000/10,000/15,000, s/d with bathroom from ¥20,000/25,000; ☺❄🤖; Ⓡ JR Yamanote line to Shibuya, new south exit) Mustard is the most exciting of Shibuya's new crop of hotels. The glossy white interior is the work of design firm Tripstar, and there are a variety of sleeping spaces to accommodate different budgets.

The hotel is within walking distance of Shibuya, Daikanyama and Ebisu (though 10 minutes from the nearest station, Shibuya). The English-speaking front desk staff have tips for local hang-outs.

TURNTABLE   HOSTEL ¥¥
Map p272 (ターンテーブル; ☎03-3461-7722; www.turntable.jp; 10-3 Shinsen-chō, Shibuya-ku; d/s/tw from ¥6750/12,000/20,000; ☺❄🤖; Ⓡ Keio Inokashira line to Shinsen, south exit) This stylish, upscale hostel is pricier than average but has more amenities and services, like fresh towels every day and sheets changed every other day. The dorms are comfy and well designed, and the breakfast is a buffet of home-style Japanese cooking served in the ground-floor cafe. Shinsen is the closest station, but you can walk to Shibuya Station in 10 minutes.

MILLENNIALS   CAPSULE HOTEL ¥¥
Map p272 (☎03-6824-9410; www.themillennials.jp/shibuya; 1-20-13 Jinnan, Shibuya-ku; capsule incl breakfast from ¥8000; ☺❄🤖; Ⓡ JR Yamanote line to Shibuya, Hachikō exit) This new Shibuya capsule hotel has cabin-style rooms: single-decker, divided on the sides by walls, but with curtains for doors; they're literally the size of a single bed (put your luggage underneath). It's located in the heart of Shibuya, and among the neighbourhood's cheapest options. Complimentary breakfast (continental style), happy-hour beer and all-day coffee sweeten the deal.

Unlike other capsule and cabin-style hotels, the Millennials doesn't require you to pack up daily for cleaning purposes. Actually if you want your bed redone with fresh sheets, you have to specifically request it (¥1000).

HOTEL KOÉ TOKYO   DESIGN HOTEL ¥¥¥
Map p272 (ホテル コエ トーキョー; ☎03-6712-7251; 3-7 Udagawachō, Shibuya-ku; s/d from ¥20,000/25,000; ☺❄🤖; Ⓡ JR Yamanote line to Shibuya, Hachikō exit) The 10 rooms here, with walls the colour of the ocean at night and slate, glass-enclosed bathrooms (the work of Suppose Design Office), are beautiful, but you do pay dearly for them: the entry-level rooms are small and the suites are devastatingly expensive. The location, though, is suburb: dead-central Shibuya but with zero street noise.

All rooms have access to a private lounge where a welcome drink of *matcha* and complementary breakfast from the bakery downstairs are served.

SHIBUYA STREAM
EXCEL HOTEL TOKYU   HOTEL ¥¥¥
Map p272 (渋谷ストリームエクセルホテル東急; ☎03-3406-1090; www.tokyuhotelsjapan.com/global/stream-e; 3-21-3 Shibuya, Shibuya-ku; s/d from ¥24,200/34,400; ☺❄🤖; Ⓢ Ginza, Hanzōmon & Fukutoshin lines to Shibuya, exit 16b, Ⓡ JR Yamanote line to Shibuya, new south exit) Tokyu's new property in the Shibuya Stream complex (p99) is going for a boutique vibe with a decor of earthy textiles and mid-century furnishings, but honestly it could be dressed in potato sacks and we'd still take it: it's got direct access to Shibuya Station (via the subway) plus all the easy dining options at Shibuya Stream.

HOTEL METS SHIBUYA BUSINESS HOTEL ¥¥¥

Map p272 (ホテルメッツ渋谷; ☎03-3409-0011; www.hotelmets.jp/shibuya; 3-29-17 Shibuya, Shibuya-ku; s/d incl breakfast from ¥20,700/25,200; ❄❈🛜; ☒JR Yamanote line to Shibuya, new south exit) Hotel Mets is part of Shibuya Station's quiet south side, with direct access to the JR lines; the location can be confusing at first, but once you get the hang of it, it's convenient. Rooms are modern and comfortable, with the double beds clocking in at a roomy 160cm. JR Pass holders get a 10% discount. The free breakfast is good.

The hotel is especially convenient for the Narita Express airport train, as the platform is very near the south exit.

EXCEL HOTEL TOKYU HOTEL ¥¥¥

Map p272 (エクセルホテル東急; ☎03-5457-0109; www.tokyuhotelsjapan.com; 1-12-2 Dōgenzaka, Shibuya-ku; s/d from ¥29,900/38,400; ❄❈🛜; ☒JR Yamanote line to Shibuya, Mark City exit) This hotel is part of Shibuya Station's 'Mark City' complex with direct access to Shibuya train station, a not negligible convenience factor. Rooms are spacious, comfortable and modern, though nothing special. Prices rise along with the floor numbers, but you can get a pretty good view with a simple upgrade for ¥2000 per night to a 'city view' room.

CERULEAN TOWER TŌKYŪ HOTEL LUXURY HOTEL ¥¥¥

Map p272 (セルリアンタワー東急ホテル; ☎03-3476-3000; www.ceruleantower-hotel.com/en; 26-1 Sakuragaoka-chō, Shibuya-ku; d from ¥47,000; ❄❈🛜; ☒JR Yamanote line to Shibuya, south exit) The Cerulean is Shibuya's only luxury hotel, just slightly removed from the train station area and up a small hill. It has big rooms with big beds; stylish, modern decor; and huge picture windows with views across Shibuya to the Shinjuku skyline and beyond or towards Tokyo Bay – your pick.

🛏 Harajuku & Aoyama

DORMY INN PREMIUM SHIBUYA JINGŪMAE BUSINESS HOTEL ¥¥

Map p276 (ドーミーインプレミアム渋谷神宮前; ☎03-5774-5489; www.hotespa.net/hotels/shibuya; 6-24-4 Jingūmae, Shibuya-ku; s/d from ¥13,790/18,590; ❄❈🛜; ☒JR Yamanote line to Harajuku, Omote-sandō exit) Dormy is a popular chain of business hotels that offers some perks that others don't, like a traditional-style communal bath and sauna (in addition to in-room showers) and bicycle rentals (pending availability).

Rooms are pretty ordinary: typically small with double beds (140cm). There's a free morning shuttle service to Shibuya Station.

🛏 West Tokyo

MANUKE HOSTEL ¥

Map p278 (マヌケ; ☎after 8pm 080-3576-2939, noon-8pm 080-4899-5799; http://manuke.asia; 4th fl, 3-8-12 Kōenji-kita, Suginami-ku; dm/s/d ¥2500/4500/6000, per week dm ¥14,000; ❄❈🛜; ☒JR Sōbu line to Kōenji, north exit) There's no pretence of style at this barebones hostel run by local activist group Shiroto no Ran (Amateurs' Riot) – just two dorms (one mixed and one female, with bunk beds), two private tatami rooms with futons and a small lounge. It's fairly clean, though, and you'll likely mix with some interesting characters.

REVERSIBLE DESTINY LOFTS APARTMENT ¥¥

(天命反転住宅, Tenmei Hanten Jūtaku; ☎0422-26-4966; www.rdloftsmitaka.com/english; 2-2-8 Ōsawa, Mitaka-shi; per stay ¥26,000 plus per night s/d/tr/q ¥10,800/13,800/17,800/20,800; ❄❈🛜🚲; ☒JR Chūō-Sōbu line to Mitaka, south exit) This is a rare opportunity to sleep within one of Tokyo's most eccentric architectural landmarks. The two apartments – one has one bedroom sleeping two, the other has two bedrooms, sleeping four – were designed for maximum wonderment, with contrasting colours and textures and oddly shaped rooms. Both have washing machines, kitchens and hammocks. You need to book a minimum of four nights.

BNA HOTEL DESIGN HOTEL ¥¥

Map p278 (www.bna-hotel.com; 2-4-7 Kōenji-kita, Suginami-ku; tw from ¥20,000; ❄❈🛜; ☒JR Sōbu line to Kōenji, north exit) There's a lot to love about Kōenji hotel BnA: it's in a fun neighbourhood, just a minute's walk from the train station; the rooms are decorated by local artists, who get a percentage of the hotel's profit; and the lobby doubles as a bar. There's just not a lot of space: only two small rooms – so book well in advance.

AIRPORT ACCOMMODATION

For late-night arrivals and early-morning departures, sleeping at the airport is an economical option.

9 Hours (☏0476-33-5109; http://ninehours.co.jp/en/narita; Narita International Airport Terminal 2; capsule ¥4900; ☺❄☎) Capsule hotel inside Narita Airport. It's also possible to stay for only a few hours (between 9am and 6pm; ¥1500 for the first hour, plus ¥500 per additional hour) or just use the shower room (24 hours; ¥1000).

Royal Park Hotel the Haneda (ロイヤルパークホテル ザ 羽田; ☏03-6830-1111; www.the-royalpark.jp/the/tokyohaneda; Haneda Airport International Terminal; s/d from ¥18,500/24,4100; ☺❄☎) Attached to Haneda Airport's international terminal.

🛏 Shinjuku & Northwest Tokyo

BOOK AND BED SHINJUKU HOSTEL ¥

Map p280 (☏03-6233-9511; www.bookandbedtokyo.com; 8th fl, AMP Kabukichō Bldg, 1-27-5 Kabukichō, Shinjuku-ku; dm from ¥5300, r with shared bathroom ¥12,000; ☺❄☎; ⓇJR Yamanote line to Shinjuku, east exit) If bookstores are your happy place you'll feel right at home at this hostel where the beds are fitted into bookshelves. The capsule-style bunks have privacy curtains and there are even ones with double beds (from ¥10,000). One downside: nonguests can pay to access the lounge during the day (from 1pm to 6pm), which can get crowded. Payment by credit card only.

9 HOURS SHINJUKU-NORTH CAPSULE HOTEL ¥

(☏03-5291-7337; https://ninehours.co.jp/en/shinjuku-north; 1-4-15 Hyakunin-chō, Shinjuku-ku; capsule from ¥4900; ☺❄☎; ⓇJR Yamanote line to Shin-Ōkubo) 9 Hours calls its capsules 'pods' which fits with the space-station sleek design, hushed vibe and views of the Shinjuku skyline (just one train stop away). As this is a capsule hotel, floors and facilities are gender segregated. You can stay for consecutive days but you must be out (with your stuff in one of the lockers) between 10am and 1pm.

SAKURA HOTEL IKEBUKURO HOSTEL ¥

Map p280 (サクラホテル池袋; ☏03-3971-2237; www.sakura-hotel.co.jp; 2-40-7 Ikebukuro, Toshima-ku; dm/s/d ¥3300/7000/9300; ☺❄@☎⌂; ⓇJR Yamanote line to Ikebukuro) This old standby lacks the designer charm of Tokyo's newer hostels but makes up for it with its multilingual, four-star-hotel-level front-desk service. There's a diverse spread of spartan room arrangements, including rare-in-Japan family rooms with a double bed and bunks. Other perks include discounted rates for stays of a week or more and cultural activities.

KIMI RYOKAN RYOKAN ¥

Map p280 (貴美旅館; ☏03-3971-3766; www.kimi-ryokan.jp; 2-36-8 Ikebukuro, Toshima-ku; s/d from ¥5400/8100; ☺❄@☎⌂; ⓇJR Yamanote line to Ikebukuro, west exit) Kimi Ryokan has been a traveller favourite for decades and it's easy to see why: the tatami rooms and shared bathrooms (including a Japanese cypress bath that can be used privately) are clean and well kept; the service (in multiple languages) is gracious and helpful; and there's a lounge and a rooftop terrace. Oh, and the eminently reasonable price. Book well in advance.

HOTEL SUNROUTE PLAZA SHINJUKU HOTEL ¥¥

Map p280 (ホテルサンルートプラザ新宿; ☏03-3375-3211; http://en.sunrouteplazashinjuku.jp/en/; 2-3-1 Yoyogi, Shibuya-ku; d from ¥16,000; ☺❄☎; ⓇJR Yamanote line to Shinjuku, south exit) This large outpost of the rather generic Japanese hotel chain Sunroute offers a winning combination of price and location. The comfortably modern rooms are a tad larger than those of a typical business hotel, front-desk staff speak English and Shinjuku Station is just a couple of minutes walk away. Book early.

Upgrade for around ¥2000 per night for a double room with a bigger bed (160cm).

HOTEL GRACERY SHINJUKU HOTEL ¥¥

Map p280 (ホテルグレイスリー新宿; ☏03-6833-2489; http://shinjuku.gracery.com; 1-19-1 Kabukichō, Shinjuku-ku; s/d from ¥16,200/22,200; ☺❄☎; ⓇJR Yamanote line to Shinjuku, east exit) The big draw of this huge

(970 rooms!) hotel is the enormous Godzilla statue (p126) atop it (which means you, and taxi drivers, will have no trouble finding it). It's fairly new and still feels fresh, and the size means you can usually score good rates (but also note that the lobby is routinely crowded). Note that it's in Kabukichō, the red-light district.

SEKITEI RYOKAN ¥¥

(石亭; ☏03-3365-5931; https://la-hotelgroup. com/sekitei; 2-15-10 Hyakunin-chō, Shinjuku-ku; d from ¥10,800; ❄✳☎; ☒JR Yamanote line to Shin-Ōkubo) A 15-minute walk north of Shinjuku Station (five minutes from Shin-Ōkubo Station), Sekitei is a traditional inn with clean and comfortable tatami rooms. Try to book the one with the rock garden running through the centre. Staff speak English, and there are coin laundry machines. There are only 11 rooms, so book well in advance.

NISHITETSU INN SHINJUKU BUSINESS HOTEL ¥¥

Map p280 (西鉄イン新宿; ☏03-3367-5454; www.n-inn.jp/english/hotels/shinjuku; 7-23-2 Nishi-Shinjuku, Shinjuku-ku; s/tw from ¥15,000/ 18,500; ❄✳☎; ☒Marunouchi line to Nishi-Shinjuku, exit 1) This is really an ordinary business hotel masquerading as a boutique one, but the stylish lobby, local info and helpful English-speaking front-desk staff really are convincing.

Nishitetsu is right next door to the Nishi-Shinjuku subway station (on the useful Marunouchi line) and is a 10-minute walk west of Shinjuku Station. Rooms are simple, clean and predictably small.

★PARK HYATT TOKYO LUXURY HOTEL ¥¥¥

Map p280 (パークハイアット東京; ☏03-5322-1234; http://tokyo.park.hyatt.com; 3-7-1-2 Nishi-Shinjuku, Shinjuku-ku; d from ¥60,000; ❄@✳☎♿; ☒Ōedo line to Tochōmae, exit A4) This eyrie atop a Tange Kenzō–designed skyscraper in west Shinjuku looks no less tasteful and elegant than when it opened more than 20 years ago, and it remains a popular spot for visiting celebrities. The rooms are on the 42nd to 51st floors, meaning even the entry-level rooms have fantastic views; west-facing rooms look out towards Mt Fuji.

Perks include fitness classes in the naturally lit studio on the 47th floor and access to a private library full of art books.

HOTEL CENTURY SOUTHERN TOWER HOTEL ¥¥¥

Map p280 (ホテルセンチュリーサザンタワー; ☏03-5354-0111; www.southerntower.co.jp; 2-2-1 Yoyogi, Shibuya-ku; s/d from ¥16,400/20,520; ❄✳☎; ☒JR Yamanote line to Shinjuku, south exit) This is the only upmarket accommodation in Shinjuku that seems to assume its guests will actually be getting around by public transport – it's just steps from Shinjuku Station's south exit. The hotel occupies the 20th to 35th floors, so the rooms (spacious with big beds) have views over Shinjuku. If you can lock in a good rate, this is a great deal.

🛏 Kōrakuen & Akihabara

★UNPLAN KAGURAZAKA HOSTEL ¥

Map p282 (☏03-6457-5171; www.unplan.jp; 23-1 Tenjinchō, Shinjuku-ku; dm/r ¥3800/16,700; ✳☎; ☒Tōzai line to Kagurazaka, exit 2) A standout among Tokyo's new breed of flash-packer digs, Unplan offers comfy dorms in Scandinavian wood tones. The private rooms are very pleasant, and a superbly handy addition are the free smartphones for guests to use. There's a common room with cooking facilities as well as a pleasant cafe on the ground floor.

HOTEL NIWA TOKYO HOTEL ¥¥

Map p283 (庭のホテル; ☏03-3293-0028; www. hotelniwatokyo.com; 1-1-6 Misaki-chō, Chiyoda-ku; s/d/tw from ¥14,600/17,200/20,600; ✳@☎; ☒JR Sōbu line to Suidōbashi, east exit) A traditional Japanese design with a contemporary spin in the public areas and the reasonably spacious hotel rooms put Niwa well ahead of the usual bland midrangers. We like the rock garden and bamboo grove out the front and the *shōji* (traditional paper screens) across the windows in the rooms.

The central location is also great – close to the JR station but also on a quiet backstreet.

★BNA STUDIO AKIHABARA APARTMENT ¥¥¥

Map p283 (☏03-5846-8876; www.bna-aki habara.com; 6-3-3 Soto-Kanda, Chiyoda-ku; apt from ¥26,000; ✳☎; ☒Ginza line to Suehirochō, exit 4) Five different artists and artist groups have brought their creative visions to the studio apartments here. Designs are influenced by colourful street art and local culture – we love the minimalist Zen Garden from which you can gaze on a *kare-*

sansui (dry landscape) on the balcony. All the rooms all spacious, with enormous bathrooms, fully equipped kitchens and washing machines.

HILLTOP HOTEL
HISTORIC HOTEL ¥¥¥

Map p283 (山の上ホテル; ☑03-3293-2311; www.yamanoue-hotel.co.jp; 1-1 Kanda-Surugadai, Chiyoda-ku; s/d from ¥22,575/33,265; ❋@☎; ℝJR Chūō or Sōbu lines to Ochanomizu, Ochanomizu exit) This art deco gem from the 1930s exudes personality and charm, with antique wooden furniture and a wood-panelled lounge. Mishima Yukio wrote his last few novels here. The older rooms in the main building come with antique writing desks and leather chairs.

🛏 Ueno & Yanesen

TOCO
HOSTEL ¥

(トコ; ☑03-6458-1686; http://backpackersjapan.co.jp; 2-13-21 Shitaya, Taitō-ku; dm from ¥3000; ❋@☎; ⓢHibiya line to Iriya, exit 4) This is your chance to stay in a beautiful wooden building (which dates to 1920) that has been turned into one of Tokyo's most attractive hostels. Dorms with wooden bunks open onto a deck with a view of a traditional garden. The hostel is behind a trendy bar-lounge (open 7pm to 11.30pm) in a modern building at the front.

★NOHGA HOTEL
DESIGN HOTEL ¥¥

Map p284 (☑03-5816-0213; www.nohgahotel.com; 2-21-10 Higashi-Ueno, Taitō-ku; r from ¥20,000; ℝJR lines to Ueno, Asakusa exit) Opened in November 2018, this super-stylish hotel ups the ante on midrange digs around Ueno. Fronted by attractive greenery and with a very pleasant restaurant-lounge area, Nohga's developers have incorporated products from local artisans and contemporary brands (such as Tokyobike for its rental cyles) into the overall design. Rooms are comfortable and tastefully decorated in soft grey.

★HANARE
GUESTHOUSE ¥¥

Map p284 (☑03-5834-7301; http://hanare.hagiso.jp; 3-10-25 Yanaka, Taitō-ku; s/d incl breakfast from ¥11,505/18,200; ⓢChiyoda line to Sendagi, exit 2) A project of Tokyo University of the Arts, Hanare offers five immaculate tatami rooms in an old dormitory house, which has been tastefully upgraded to retain original features such as wooden beams. There is a shared bathroom, but you'll be given tickets to the local *sentō* (public bath), as the concept is to use Yanaka as an extension of the guesthouse. Reception is in the nearby Hagiso building, the same location as Hagi Cafe (p150) where you'll be served a traditional breakfast.

★SAWANOYA RYOKAN
RYOKAN ¥¥

Map p284 (旅館澤の屋; ☑03-3822-2251; www.sawanoya.com; 2-3-11 Yanaka, Taitō-ku; s/d from ¥5615/10,585; ➹❋@☎📵; ⓢChiyoda line to Nezu, exit 1) Sawanoya is a gem in quiet Yanaka, run by a very friendly family and with all the traditional hospitality you would expect of a ryokan. The shared cypress and earthenware baths are the perfect balm after a long day (a couple of slightly more expensive rooms have their own bath, too). The lobby overflows with information about travel options in Japan.

ANNEX KATSUTARŌ RYOKAN
RYOKAN ¥¥

Map p284 (アネックス勝太郎旅館; ☑03-3828-2500; www.katsutaro.com; 3-8-4 Yanaka, Taitō-ku; s/d from ¥6600/13,200; ➹❋@☎; ⓢChiyoda line to Sendagi, exit 2) More like a modern hotel than a traditional ryokan, the family-run Annex Katsutarō has spotless, thoughtfully arranged tatami rooms. It's ideal for exploring the old Yanaka district. Breakfast (from ¥430) and bicycles (a bargain ¥300 a day) are also available.

🛏 Asakusa & Sumida River

★ANDON RYOKAN
RYOKAN ¥

(行燈旅館; ☑03-3873-8611; www.andon.co.jp; 2-34-10 Nihonzutsumi, Taitō-ku; s/d from ¥6500/7560; ➹❋@☎; ⓢHibiya line to Minowa, exit 3) About 2km north of Asakusa, the contemporary Andon Ryokan is fabulously designed in form and function. It has 20 tiny but immaculate tatami rooms, bathrooms decorated with specially commissioned manga art, and a spectacular upper-floor spa with a manga-style mural, which can be used privately. Toshiko, the friendly owner, collects antiques, which are displayed around the ryokan.

BUNKA HOSTEL TOKYO
HOSTEL ¥

Map p286 (☑03-5806-3444; www.bunkahostel.jp; 1-13-5 Asakusa, Taitō-ku; dm/f from ¥3000/16,800; ℝTsukuba Express to Asakusa, exit 4) This is one of the most stylish of the several

Tokyo hostels that combine a cafe or a bar open to the public in the foyer with a hostel above. Bunka offers capsule-style bunks; roomier versions where you can stand up go for ¥5000 a bed. The family room sleeping up to four offers great views across the area.

NUI HOSTEL ¥

Map p287 (ヌイ; ☎03-6240-9854; https://backpackersjapan.co.jp/nui; 2-14-13 Kuramae, Taitō-ku; dm/tw/d from ¥2800/8000/8500; 🚭❄@📶; [S]Ōedo line to Kuramae, exit A7) In a former warehouse, this stylish hostel has rooms with high ceilings, translating to bunks you can comfortably sit up in. There's also an enormous shared kitchen and work space. Best of all is the ground-floor cafe-bar and lounge (open 8am to 1am), with furniture made from salvaged timber; it's a popular local hang-out.

LYURO THE SHARE HOTELS HOSTEL ¥

Map p287 (☎03-6458-5540; www.thesharehotels.com; 1-1-7 Kiyosumi, Kōtō-ku; dm/d from ¥3000/10,000; 🚭❄📶; [S]Hanzomon or Ōedo line to Kiyosumi-shirakawa, exit A3 or B1) The riverside location, nicely designed dorms and rooms in cool blues with a Nordic feel and an on-site craft brewery and restaurant are all appealing factors at this flashpackers. There may be some noise from the neighbouring newspaper printing factory, though.

KHAOSAN WORLD HOSTEL ¥

Map p286 (☎03-3843-0153; http://khaosan-tokyo.com/en/world; 3-15-1 Nishi-Asakusa, Taitō-ku; dm/d from ¥2100/8000; 🚭❄@📶👪; 🚆Tsukuba Express to Asakusa, exit A2) One of Tokyo's most oddball hostels, Khaosan World occupies an ageing love hotel with many of the original design elements intact – things like mirrored ceilings and glittering brocade wallpaper (don't worry: it's clean). There's a wide variety of rooms to choose from, including ones with tatami floors and capsule-style bunks. There are cooking and laundry facilities, too.

TOKYO RYOKAN RYOKAN ¥

Map p286 (東京旅館; ☎090-8879-3599; www.tokyoryokan.com; 2-4-8 Nishi-Asakusa, Taitō-ku; s/d from ¥6000/7000; 🚭❄📶; [S]Ginza line to Tawaramachi, exit 3) This tidy little inn has only three small tatami rooms and no en-suite bathrooms but tons of charm. There are touches of calligraphy, attractive woodwork and sliding screens.

Kenichi, the owner, is an avid traveller, speaks fluent English and Chinese, and is super-knowledgeable about Asakusa and the surrounding area.

WIRED HOTEL ASAKUSA DESIGN HOTEL ¥¥

Map p286 (☎03-5830-7931; www.wiredhotel.com; 2-16-2 Asakusa, Taitō-ku; tw/d from ¥13,000/14,000; 🚭❄📶; [S]Ginza line to Asakusa, exit 1) This boutique-style hotel is an appealing mix of retro and contemporary design.

Each room is has subtly different decor, but all have decent-sized bathrooms and beds graced by a gorgeous indigo-dye throw. Events are sometimes held in the ground-floor cafe-bar.

Understand Tokyo

History

Tokyo is one of the world's great cities. While its history might be comparatively short – a mere four centuries – the city has already played many roles: samurai stronghold, imperial capital and modern metropolis. Its latest identity, city of the future – as it is often portrayed in manga, anime and think pieces – is just another example of Tokyo's protean nature.

Early History

Japan as we know it began to coalesce around CE 300 in what is now known as the Kansai region, an area to the west of Tokyo encompassing the present day cities of Kyoto, Osaka and Nara. Though the Japanese archipelago had been inhabited for at least 30,000 years, waves of immigration from the continent began to shake things up at this time, with the introduction of new technologies, such as wet rice farming.

The period from the 6th to the 8th centuries was one of great exchange between the Yamato court (the proto-Japanese empire), the Korean kingdom of Baekji and Tang-dynasty China. From its continental neighbours, Japan imported Buddhism, a written language (in the form of Chinese characters) and sophisticated ideas of statecraft. These, combined with existing customs – Japan's Shintō religion predates Buddhism – formed the foundation of Japan's political and social ideologies.

At the start of the Heian era (794–1185), the Yamato court established a capital at Kyoto, which would go on to be the nation's capital for the better part of a millennium. About a hundred or so years after the foundation of Kyoto, the court stopped its practice of sending emissaries to China; Japanese culture set off on its own track, with less influence from the outside. This pattern of looking outward and then inward would repeat itself several times over the centuries and is one of the defining characteristics of Japanese history from the early days to the present.

During the Heian era, Kyoto enjoyed a golden age of cultural refinement, captured famously in the novel *The Tale of Genji*, written by the

The Imperial House traces its lineage back 125 generations to the 6th century BCE; historians are sceptical about the early emperors, but are reasonably certain that number 29, Emperor Kinmei (reign CE 539–71), really existed. Either way, the Yamato dynasty is the longest unbroken monarchy in the world.

TIMELINE	794	early 1000s	1192
	The imperial capital moves to Heian-kyō, renamed Kyoto in the 11th century, laid out in a grid in accordance with Chinese geomancy principles.	Lady of the court, Murasaki Shikibu, writes *The Tale of Genji*. Considered to be the world's first novel, it documents courtly life in the Heian era.	Newly minted shogun Minamoto no Yoritomo establishes Japan's first *bakufu* (feudal government) in Kamakura.

court-lady Murasaki Shikibu. By her accounts, courtiers indulged in diversions such as moonlit excursions for the purpose of composing *waka* (31-syllable poems). Hers was a world that encouraged aesthetic sensibilities, such as the appreciation of *mono no aware* – the inherent sorrow of nature's transient beauty, a concept rooted in Buddhism and one that still resonates today in the celebration of the cherry blossoms.

The Age of Warriors

Early Japanese culture was one of refinement, but also one of conquest as the Yamato court sought to spread its influence beyond the Kansai region. Warrior clans were dispatched from the capital to subjugate the tribes (particularly in eastern and northern Japan) that had thus far resisted Yamato hegemony. These clans were often established and led by minor nobles barred from succession claims; their warriors would evolve into Japan's fearsome fighters, the samurai.

The nobility, who had been manipulating court politics from the get-go, also relied on warrior clans as muscle for advancing their interests. In the 12th century, two rival clans – the Minamoto (also known as Genji) and the Taira (also known as Heike) – backing different claimants to the imperial throne, entered an all-out feud, sparking a civil war that would upend the political order of Japan.

After decades of fighting, the general of the victors, Minamoto no Yoritomo (1147–99), demanded the emperor grant him the title *Sei-i Taishōgun* (Commander-in-chief of barbarian subjugation) – or shogun, for short. The emperor would still be the emperor, but from this point onward it would be the warrior clans, not the nobility, behind the machinations of the court, wielding the real power. The feudal era had begun.

The Minamoto set up their seat of power in Kamakura, 65km south of present-day Tokyo. They, and the Hōjō clan who succeeded them, would only hold onto it for 150 years before it was sacked by the Ashikaga clan in 1333, who brought the institution of shogun to Kyoto, where they ruled until the mid-16th century.

But the ascendancy of the warrior class wasn't just about political change: the Kamakura shogunate reopened trade and communication with what was now Song-dynasty China; among the many new ideas and technologies gained was Zen Buddhism. Zen's emphasis on austerity and self-discipline appealed to the warriors and as the loci of culture shifted from the court to the palaces of the shoguns and the monasteries, new ideals such as *wabi* (a kind of restrained, austere beauty) and *sabi* (a rustic or timeworn patina) entered the Japanese idiom.

Samurai were the warriors retained by *daimyō* (feudal lords) to defend (or advance) positions, to enforce rules and to keep the peace. Instantly recognisable with their plated armour knit with silken cords, terrifying face guards and helmets sprouting crests or horns, they are one of the most enduring images of Japan.

12th century	1274 & 1281	1457	1543
Monks returning from study in China introduce Zen Buddhism and tea drinking to Japan, which would have profound effects on the culture.	Under Kublai Khan, the Mongols twice attempt to invade Japan, but fail due to poor planning, spirited Japanese resistance and, especially, the destruction of their fleets by typhoons.	Ōta Dōkan orders construction of the first Edo Castle, putting Edo (present-day Tokyo) on the map.	Portuguese sailors arrive in Japan (by accident), the first Westerners known to land on the islands; the Portuguese later introduce firearms and Christianity.

Warring States & Reunification

The Ashikaga shoguns had Kyoto but they had trouble holding down the rest of the country; by the 15th century, provincial warlords (called *daimyō*) had succeeded in carving it up into a patchwork of fiefdoms. This is when Tokyo, then called Edo (meaning 'mouth of the river'), first enters the picture: a castle was erected in what was then an obscure fishing village by a warrior poet named Ōta Dōkan (1432–86).

Starting with the Ōnin War (1467–77), which all but destroyed Kyoto, for the next hundred years the country was in a near constant state of civil war. By now, Portuguese traders had introduced firearms, which upped the ante significantly. A succession of powerful *daimyō* made bloody stabs at unifying the country (under their own iron fists): first Oda Nobunaga (1534–82), then Toyotomi Hideyoshi (1537–98) and finally Tokugawa Ieyasu (1543–1616).

Tokugawa was the son of a minor lord allied to Oda. A brief contest for power with Toyotomi ended in truce, with Toyotomi granting Tokugawa control over eight provinces in eastern Japan (including present day Tokyo). On his deathbed, Toyotomi entrusted Tokugawa, who had proven to be one of his ablest generals, with safeguarding the country and the succession of his young son Hideyori (1593–1615). Tokugawa, however, soon went to war against those loyal to Hideyori, and after winning the decisive Battle of Sekigahara in 1600, moved into a position of supreme power.

In 1603 the emperor named Tokugawa shogun; breaking centuries of tradition, Tokugawa decided to locate his government not in Kyoto, but within his own stronghold in eastern Japan, choosing Edo for his capital.

Besides loyal samurai, Tokugawa Ieyasu stocked his capital with ninja. Their commander was Hattori Hanzō, renowned for his cunning and deadly tactics that helped Ieyasu at key moments in his career. The ninja master's legacy was enshrined in Hanzōmon, a gate that still exists today at the Imperial Palace.

Tokugawa Rule

The Tokugawa shoguns would rule from Edo for two and half centuries, a period of relative peace known as the Edo era (1603–1868). Tokugawa Ieyasu was both an ambitious ruler and an ambitious city planner. He built the world's largest fortress, Edo-jō (Edo Castle); around the castle, a spiral of moats were dug (by samurai attached to the clans who had opposed Tokugawa), as well as a canal system to bring water to the population that had quickly swelled to 500,000 by 1650. By the early 1700s, Edo's population topped one million, dwarfing much older London and Paris.

Much of Edo's stability and swift rise can be attributed to a canny move by the Tokugawa regime that ensured its hegemony: a system called *sankin kōtai* that demanded that all *daimyō* in Japan spend alternate years in Edo. Their wives and children remained in Edo (hos-

1600	1657	1689	1707
Tokugawa Ieyasu, victor in the Battle of Sekigahara, establishes his capital in Edo, beginning 250 years of Tokugawa rule, known as the Edo period.	Great Meireki Fire devastates Edo, killing over 100,000 people and destroying two-thirds of the city.	Matsuo Bashō, the greatest name in haiku poetry, departs Edo for northern Japan, a journey that would be documented in his most famous collection of poems, *The Narrow Road to the Deep North*.	Mt Fuji erupts, spewing ash over the streets of Edo 100km to the northeast. The stratovolcano is still active today but with a low risk of eruption.

LIFE IN EDO

Society in Edo was rigidly hierarchical, comprising (in descending order of importance) the nobility, who had nominal power; the *daimyō* and their samurai; the farmers; and finally the artisans and merchants, collectively known as *chōnin* (townspeople). Class dress, living quarters and even manner of speech were all strictly codified, and inter-class movement was prohibited.

Though they sat at the bottom of the hierarchy, in reality many merchants grew fabulously wealthy. Shut out from established status symbols by law – they were not allowed, for example, to wear embroidered silk – the *chōnin* created their own culture, one that revolved around the Kabuki theatre, sumo tournaments and the pleasure quarters of the Yoshiwara, often enjoying a *joie de vivre* that the dour lords of Edo Castle frowned upon. The height of fashion was *iki*, a kind of rakish dandyism. Today, the best glimpses we have of this time are in the form of *ukiyo-e*, woodblock prints.

The uncompromising boundaries of Edo society also applied to the city itself. The *daimyō* and their samurai lived in sprawling villas in the Yamanote (literally 'hand of the mountains'), the highland area to the west of the palace (including present day neighbourhoods like Yotsuya, Koishikawa, Hongō, Akasaka and Aoyama). The *chōnin*, meanwhile, occupied Shitamachi (the 'low city'), the low-lying land along the Sumida-gawa delta (encompassing Kanda, Ueno, Yanaka, Asakusa, Ryōgoku and Fukagawa).

The average Shitamachi resident lived in a cramped wooden tenement house with an earthen floor and communal facilities, like a well, in the alleys behind. Fires, known as *Edo-no-hana* ('flowers of Edo'), were frequent, a reminder that even in peacetime life was precarious.

Tokyo has several museums that look at life in the Edo period, including the Edo-Tokyo Museum (p157), the Shitamachi Museum (p149) and the Fukagawa Edo Museum (p162).

tages, essentially) while the *daimyō* returned to administer their home provinces. This dislocating policy made it hard for ambitious *daimyō* to usurp the Tokugawas and the high costs of travelling back and forth (with sufficiently large retinues) eroded their finances. Meanwhile the services and goods required to maintain the lords' lifestyles in Edo channelled money to the city's merchants and artisans.

Another defining policy of the Edo period was *sakoku* (closure to the outside world). The Tokugawa regime was fearful of the potentially destabilising effect of Christianity (which had entered the country in the 16th century along with firearms) and expelled all Westerners except the Protestant Dutch, who were confined to an island off the coast of Naga-saki, in 1638. Overseas travel for Japanese was banned (as well as the re-turn of those already overseas). The country did not remain completely

1721	1853	1868	1889
Edo's population grows to 1.1 million as people move in from rural areas, making it the world's largest city. Meanwhile, London's population is roughly 650,000.	The US Navy succeeds in forcing Japan open to foreign trade; an international port is established in Yokohama in 1859.	Meiji Restoration; Tokugawa shogunate loyalists are defeated in civil war. The imperial residence moves to Edo, which is renamed Tokyo.	Constitution of the Empire of Japan declared. Based on a Prussian model of constitutional monarchy, the emperor shares power with an elected parliament.

cut off: trade with Asia and the West continued through the Dutch and Chinese settlements in Nagasaki and also through the Ryūkyū Empire (now Okinawa) – it was just tightly controlled and, along with the exchange of ideas, funnelled exclusively to the shogunate.

The Meiji Restoration

In 1853 and again the following year, US Commodore Matthew Perry steamed into Edo-wan (now Tokyo Bay) with a show of gunships and demanded Japan open up to trade and provisioning. The shogunate, which by then was stultifying, had no match for Perry's firepower and acquiesced. Soon an American consul arrived, and other Western powers followed suit. Japan was obliged to sign what came to be called the 'unequal treaties', opening ports and giving Western nations control over tariffs.

In 1867–68, civil war broke out between Tokugawa loyalists and a band of *daimyō* from southern Kyūshū. The latter were victorious; faced with widespread antigovernment feeling and accusations that the shogunate had failed to prepare Japan for the threat of the West, the last Tokugawa shogun resigned. Power reverted to Emperor Meiji in what became known as the Meiji Restoration (and those southern lords became the new political strategists). In 1868, the seat of imperial power was moved from Kyoto to Edo – Edo-jō became the Imperial Palace – and the city was renamed Tokyo (Eastern Capital).

Above all, the new leaders of Japan – keen observers of what was happening throughout Asia – feared colonisation by Western powers. They moved quickly to modernise (as defined by the West), to prove they could stand on an equal footing with those Western colonisers. The government embarked on a grand project of industrialisation and militarisation. A great exchange began between Japan and the West: Japanese scholars were dispatched to Europe to study everything from literature and engineering to nation building and modern warfare. Western scholars were invited to teach in Japan's nascent universities.

On a darker note, the Japanese also proved able imperialists themselves: following military victories over China (1894–95) and Russia (1904–05) the country annexed Taiwan (1895), then Korea (1910) and Micronesia (1914).

World War II

The early decades of the 20th century were a time of optimism, when democratic ideals seemed to be overtaking feudal-era loyalties. But there was a dark undercurrent of dissatisfaction, both among certain political and military factions (who felt they were still not held in equal

In 1904, the kimono shop Echigoya, founded in 1673, decided to reinvent itself as Japan's first Western-style department store, Mitsukoshi. The shop in Nihombashi (opened in 1914) was called the grandest building east of the Suez Canal. The retailer remains one of the most prestigious shops in Tokyo.

1923	1923	1926	1944–45
Great Kantō Earthquake kills more than 140,000. An estimated 300,000 houses are destroyed.	Yamanote train line completed. One of Japan's busiest lines, today the 34.5km loop around the heart of Tokyo has 29 stations. It takes trains about an hour to circle the city.	Hirohito ascends the throne to become the Shōwa emperor. Presiding over Japan's military expansion across East Asia and atrocities, he is spared trial by Allied forces after WWII.	Allied air raids during WWII destroy large swaths of the city, including the Imperial Palace; casualties of more than 100,000 are reported.

TOKYO: THE MODERN CAPITAL

The Meiji Restoration introduced far-reaching social changes. The four-tier class system was scrapped; after centuries of having everything prescribed for them, citizens were now free to choose their occupations and places of residence. Many moved to the cities to join the growing workforce in the new manufacturing and white-collar sectors. In 1898, Tokyo's population was just shy of 1.5 million; by 1909 it had surpassed two million.

Tokyo became a showcase city for the new, modern Japan, with electric lighting and Western-style brick buildings first introduced in Ginza, establishing the neighbourhood as a fashion centre. By the 1920s, Western fashions and ideas, initially the domain of only the most elite, began to trickle down to the middle class. More and more Tokyoites began adopting Western dress (which they most likely traded for kimonos as soon as they got home). Cafes and dance halls flourished.

Women began to work outside the home, in offices, department stores and factories, enjoying a new freedom and disposable income. Like women around the world in the 1920s, they cut their hair short and wore pants – and became symbols for both the optimism and the dread that the new modern era inspired.

esteem by Western powers) and by the poor (rural and urban alike, as the Great Depression hit Japan), appalled by what they saw as an elite under the sway of Western decadence.

By the 1930s, outright nationalism and militaristic fervour began to take hold. The armed forces began acting of their own accord, manufacturing a conflict with China (the Manchurian Incident of 1931) that escalated into Japan taking control of Manchuria – an act that was widely condemned by the international community (and especially the US) and led to Japan leaving the League of Nations.

Japan signed a pact with Germany and Italy in 1940 and, after diplomatic attempts to gain US neutrality failed, drew the US into WWII with a surprise attack on its Pacific Fleet in Hawaii's Pearl Harbor on 7 December 1941. Initially, Japan's war efforts were successful, as its armies and navies fanned out, claiming territory throughout nearly all of Southeast Asia; but in the end the war proved disastrous for Japan. Tokyo was all but destroyed by incendiary bombing, the most devastating of which took place over the nights of 9 and 10 March 1945, when some two-fifths of the city went up in smoke and tens of thousands of lives were lost.

In August the declaration of war by the Soviet Union and the atomic bombs dropped by the USA on Hiroshima and Nagasaki were the final straws: the emperor formally surrendered on 15 August 1945 and

When NHK, Japan's national broadcaster, played a message prerecorded by Emperor Hirohito declaring Japan's surrender to the Allies in WWII, it was the first time the people of Japan had heard their emperor speak.

1947	1948	1951	1954
New constitution adopted, including Article 9, in which Japan renounces war and the possession of armed forces.	Tokyo War Crimes Tribunal concludes, resulting in the execution of six wartime Japanese leaders. In 1978, they are secretly enshrined at Yasukuni-jinja.	Japan signs San Francisco Peace Treaty, officially ending WWII, renouncing Japan's claims to overseas colonies and outlining compensation to Allied territories.	Godzilla makes his first appearance in an enponymous film directed by Honda Ishirō, with the premise that Godzilla was a monster created by the atomic bombings of WWII.

THE GREAT KANTŌ EARTHQUAKE

At noon on 1 September 1923, a magnitude 7.9 earthquake struck Japan just south of Tokyo in Sagami Bay. More damaging were the fires that spread through the city as a result, lasting some 40 hours and killing an estimated 142,000 people.

Until the earthquake, Tokyo retained much of old Edo's layout, with Sumida-gawa as its central artery and the population concentrated in the old merchants' quarters in the river delta – and it was these areas that went up in flames.

Tokyo started rebuilding immediately, but its landscape would be altered permanently: many Shitamachi residents whose homes and businesses had been destroyed chose to resettle in what was then the westernmost fringe of Tokyo, in districts like Shibuya and Shinjuku that were provincial by comparison.

From this point onward, the city's centre – both literally and figuratively – would be pulled increasingly to the west.

American forces, under the command of General Douglas MacArthur, occupied the country. Japan was obligated to give up its territorial claims in Korea and China and adopt a new constitution that dismantled the political power of the emperor, denounced war and banned a Japanese military.

Reconstruction & the Boom Years

In the early postwar years, conditions in Tokyo remained dire: food was scarce and unemployment was high; many relied on black markets and prostitution to survive. By 1951, however, with a boom in Japanese profits arising from the Korean War, Tokyo began to rapidly rebuild. And Tokyoites threw themselves into the project, putting in the long hours that a reinvigorated corporate Japan demanded of them.

The 1964 Tokyo Summer Olympics are seen by many as a turning point in the nation's history – the moment when Japan finally recovered from the devastation of WWII to emerge as a fully fledged member of the modern world economy. In preparation, the city embarked on a frenzy of construction unequalled in its history – much of the city's current infrastructure, such as the city highway system, dates to this period.

Starting in the 1970s Nishi-Shinjuku was developed as a *fukutoshin* (urban sub-centre) as part of an effort to decentralise the city, taking the strain off overcrowded central business districts Marunouchi and Yurakuchō (and continuing the westward shift of the city that began in

During the US occupation, American pop culture poured into the country and along with it a yearning for the comfortable and affluent lifestyles portrayed on the big and small screens. The most coveted items were televisions, refrigerators and washing machines; by 1964, 90% of Japanese households had them.

1955	1960s	1964	1989
Liberal Democratic Party (LDP) founded; it has a virtually uninterrupted hold on power into the 21st century, despite recurring corruption scandals and deep-seated factionalism.	Protests against the signing of the 'Treaty of Mutual Cooperation and Security between the United States and Japan' (known as ANPO) erupt in 1960, ushering in a decade of social agitation.	Tokyo Olympic Games held, marking Japan's postwar reintegration into the international community and the first time the Games are hosted by a non-Western country.	Death of Emperor Hirohito; Heisei era begins as Hirohito's son, Akihito, ascends the throne; stock market decline begins, initiating a decade-long economic slump in Japan.

the aftermath of the Great Kantō Earthquake). Dozens of skyscrapers – including the new city hall – went up, organised around a geometric grid, like Manhattan.

In the 1980s, inflated real-estate prices and stock speculation created what is now known as the 'bubble economy'. Back then it seemed like the city and the economy would never stop growing – these were heady times when it looked like all the relentless work of the postwar years had paid off and Japan might even overtake the US; Tokyoites (well the lucky ones, anyway) spent wildly and freely.

Heisei Doldrums

In 1991, just two years after the Heisei emperor ascended the throne, the bubble burst and Japan's economy went into a tailspin. The 1990s were christened the 'Lost Decade', but that has since turned into two, and then three, as the economy continues to slump along, despite government intervention. By now, a whole generation has come of age in a Japan where lifelong employment – the backbone of the middle class – is no longer a guarantee.

There have also been other disturbing troubles, which have transformed the optimism of the boom years into a stubborn, increasing pessimism: the 1995 attack on the crowded Tokyo subways by the Aum Shinrikyō doomsday cult; a series of corporate scandals that left indelible stains on the once proud brand of Japan Inc; and the 2011 earthquake, tsunami and nuclear meltdown in northeastern Japan.

When Emperor Akihito abdicated and his son, Crown Prince Naruhito ascended the chrysanthemum throne in 2019, the Heisei era ended and a new one, the Reiwa era, began. Of course, the starts and ends of Japan's historic periods – in modern times determined by the passing of emperors – depend on nature, yet they really do seem to effectively bracket the culture's shifting moods. The Heisei era had become symbolic of stagnation and uncertainty; perhaps Reiwa would be better?

Japan was looking with optimism to the 2020 Tokyo Summer Olympics, hoping that, like the 1964 games, it would reassert the country's position on the global stage and Tokyo's place in the pantheon of the world's great cities. Then the COVID-19 pandemic hit: borders closed, the Olympics were postponed to 2021 and life in Tokyo was curtailed by a series of states of emergencies.

Based on the price paid for the most expensive real estate in the late 1980s, the land value of Tokyo exceeded that of the entire USA.

1995	2011	2016	2019
Doomsday cult Aum Shinrikyō releases sarin gas on the Tokyo subway, killing 12 and injuring more than 5000. Guru Shōkō Asahara is sentenced to death in 2004 and executed in 2018.	Magnitude 9.0 earthquake strikes off Sendai in Tōhoku, unleashing tsunami waves, killing nearly 20,000, and crippling the Fukushima Dai-ichi nuclear plant.	Tokyo elects its first female governor, Koike Yuriko; an independent, Koike ran on a platform of reining in backroom dealing and improving transparency.	Emperor Akihito (b 1933), the first Japanese emperor of the modern age to abdicate, steps down on 30 April, ushering in a new era.

Tokyo Pop!

A Studio Ghibli movie, a manga by Tezuka Osamu, day-glo accessories from cutesy pioneer 6% Dokidok, the latest Sony PlayStation: Tokyo is a master at crafting pop-cultural products that catch the attention of the world. Here more people read manga (Japanese comics) than newspapers, street fashion is dynamic and constantly evolving, robots are the stars of anime (Japanese animation) as well as real-life marvels of technology, and everyone, including the police, has a *kawaii* (cute) cartoon mascot.

Manga

Above: Games arcade in Akihabara (p134)

Walk into any Tokyo convenience store and you can pick up several phone-directory-sized weekly manga anthologies. Inside you'll find about 25 comic narratives spanning everything from gangster sagas and teen romance to bicycle racing to *shōgi* (Japanese chess), often with generous helpings of sex and violence. The more successful series are collected in volumes *(tankōbon),* which occupy major sections of bookshops.

As Japan's publishing industry faces a severe decline in sales across the board, manga is the one bright hope. In particular, the market is booming for *keitai* manga – comics read on smartphones; sales of digital manga racked up around ¥171.1 billion in 2017. Top seller *One Piece* shifted nearly 11.5 million units alone in 2017. Major publishers, including Kodansha and Kadokawa, are based in Tokyo and this is where many *mangaka* (manga artists) get their start in the industry.

Comiket (コミケット; www.comiket.co.jp) is a massive twice-yearly convention for fan-produced amateur manga known as *dōjinshi.* To the untrained eye, *dōjinshi* looks like 'official' manga, but most are parodies (sometimes of a sexual nature) of famous manga titles.

Top Manga

Astro Boy

Barefoot Gen

Black Jack

Doraemon

Lone Wolf
and Cub

Nausicaä of the
Valley of the Wind

Rose of Versailles

Anime

Many manga have inspired anime for TV and cinema. For example, *Nausicaä of the Valley of the Wind,* a 1982 manga by Miyazaki Hayao, Japan's most revered living animator, was made into a movie in 1984. Beloved TV anime *Astro Boy* and *Kimba the White Lion* were the first successful manga for Tezuka Osamu (1928–89), an artist frequently referred to as *manga no kamisama* – the 'god of manga'.

Studio Ghibli (www.ghibli.jp) is Japan's most critically acclaimed and commercially successful producer of animated movies. Its films include classics such as the Oscar-winning *Spirited Away,* directed by Miyazaki Hayao. In 2017 Miyazaki announced he was coming out of retirement to work on *How Do You Live?,* an adaptation of a children's story by Yoshino Genzaburo – it is unlikely to be released before 2021.

Sadly, in 2018, Takahata Isao, Miyazaki's creative partner at Studio Ghibli, passed away. Takahata directed anime classics including *Grave of the Fireflies* (1988), *Only Yesterday* (1991) and the Oscar-nominated *The Tale of Princess Kaguya* (2013).

Studio Ghibli's premium product is far superior to the vast majority of low-budget anime, which tends to feature saucer-eyed schoolgirls, cute fluorescent monsters and mechatronic superheroes in recycled and tweaked plots. Nevertheless, the international success of series such as *Mobile Suit Gundam* and *Pokémon* continues to tempt many fans to anime's creative source in Tokyo.

Leading the pack of current talented anime directors is Shinkai Makoto, hailed the 'new Miyazaki' for beautifully realised movies, including the 2015 smash-hit *Kimi no Na wa* (Your Name), the highest grossing anime movie ever. Hiromasa Yonebayashi, who also directed Ghibli's *When Marnie Was There* (2014) and *The Secret World of Arrietty* (2010), had a critical hit in 2017 with *Mary and the Witch's Flower.* Also look out for movies by Hosoda Mamoru, including *The Girl Who Leapt Through Time* (2009) and *Boy and the Beast* (2015).

Top Anime

Akira (1988)

My Neighbor
Totoro (1988)

Ghost in the Shell
(1995)

Tokyo Godfathers
(2003)

The Tale of
Princess Kaguya
(2013)

Your Name (2016)

Hyperfashion

Visitors are often in awe of Tokyo's incredible sense of style and its broad range of subcultures. Fashion trends come and go in the blink of a heavily made-up eye in Tokyo. The streets of Harajuku and Shibuya remain the best places to view the latest looks.

It's not uncommon to see Japanese wearing kimonos for special occasions, and *yukata* (light summer kimonos) for fireworks shows and festivals in summer. Everyday wear ranges from the standard-issue salaryman suit (overwhelmingly dark blue or black) to the split-toed shoes and baggy trousers of construction workers.

Shop in Takeshita-dōri (p108)

Tokyo's fashion designers who have become international superstars include Issey Miyake, Yohji Yamamoto and, more recently, Rei Kawakubo of Comme des Garçons. Other designers include Fujiwara Hiroshi, a renowned streetwear fashion arbiter, who has a huge impact on what Japanese youth wear.

J-Pop

Top pop-culture books include Hector Garcia's *A Geek in Japan* (2011), Peter Carey's *Wrong about Japan* (2006) and *Cruising the Anime City: An Otaku Guide to Neo Tokyo* (Patrick Macias and Machiyama Tomohiro; 2004).

Japanese pop music, commonly shortened to J-pop, is a major driver of the country's fashion industry. An icon of the scene is Kyary Pamyu Pamyu (http://kyary.asobisystem.com). A runaway success since her musical debut in 2011 with PonPonPon, Kyary (whose real name is Takemura Kiriko) has been compared to Lady Gaga for her outrageous fashions and self-promotion, which includes being the Harajuku ambassador of *kawaii* (cuteness).

Avex is one of Japan's biggest recording labels and one of its brightest stars is Hamasaki Ayumi (http://avex.jp/ayu). Noted for her chameleon style and high-concept videos, Ayu – as she is known to her adoring fans – has shifted more than 50 million records since her debut in 1998.

Digital Delights

The creative intersection of Japanese technology and pop culture has resulted in several digitally driven attractions across Tokyo, which if nothing else makes for dazzling eye candy. At the forefront is teamLab (www.teamlab.art), having a smash hit with its teamLab Borderless (p167) and *Planets* interactive exhibitions in Odaiba. Also see its digital waterfall cascading down a wall of Ginza Six (p77).

Neon signs in Akihabara (p134)

Working in a similar visual digital arena is creative team Naked, whose past projects have included Tokyo Art City (http://tokyoartcity. tokyo) and who also have collaborated on the theme restaurant Trees by Naked (http://treebynaked.jp).

Virtual reality (VR) video games and experiences are showcased at Odaiba's Tokyo Joypolis (p170) and Ikebukuro's Sky Circus (p133).

Pop Culture Districts

Akihabara is ground central on any pop-culture Tokyo tour. With its multitude of stores selling anime- and manga-related goods, not to mention maid cafes and all the electronic gizmos imaginable, Akiba (as it's known to locals) is peak geek territory.

Die-hard anime fans will also want to schedule time in Nakano, in west Tokyo, to cruise the aisles of pop-culture emporium Mandarake Complex (p122).

Ikebukuro, in northwest Tokyo, is home to a cluster of anime- and manga-related shops aimed at geek gals.

The artificial island Odaiba with its outlandish architecture and zippy monorail feels like an anime version of Tokyo. For robots, don't miss Odaiba's National Museum of Emerging Science & Innovation (Miraikan; p168). Anime fans will be in raptures over the Unicorn Gundam (p168), a 19.7m-tall model of an RX-0 Unicorn Gundam from the iconic *Mobile Suit Gundam* anime franchise.

Pop Culture Events

Tokyo Game Show (http://expo.nik keibp.co.jp/tgs) September

Comiket (www. comiket.co.jp) August and December

AnimeJapan (www.anime -japan.jp) March

Design Festa (http://design festa.com) May and November

The Arts & Architecture Scene

Tokyo has an arts scene that is broad, dynamic and scattered – much like the city itself. It offers a beguiling blend of traditional and modern, and is rivalled only by Kyoto for position as Japan's centre of arts and culture. Highlights include the city's contemporary art museums and those devoted to Tokyo's signature visual art form, *ukiyo*-e (woodblock prints), its old-world kabuki stage and the fascinating creations of Japan's 20th-century architects, which line many a downtown street.

Classical Arts

Above: Black lacquer tea caddy

Japan has a long artistic tradition of painting, calligraphy, lacquerware, ceramics, metalwork and textiles. Lacquerware, in particular, is very old: it's believed to go back 5000 years. Since the early days of the court and during periods of openness, Japan imported styles, techniques and themes from its nearest Asian neighbours, China and Korea. During times of retreat, Japan's artists refined these techniques, filtered styles through local sensibilities and tweaked themes to correspond with the times and materials at hand.

These are all still very much living arts: you'll see historic works in museums but also the works of contemporary artists in galleries and department stores and in high-end restaurants and teahouses.

Traditionally paintings were done in black ink or mineral pigments on *washi* (Japanese handmade paper; itself an art form), scrolls (that either unfurled horizontally or were designed to hang vertically), folding screens or sliding doors. There is no one style: over the centuries painting modes have included colourful, highly stylised scenes of courtly life (called *yamato-e*); monochromatic suggestions of craggy mountains executed with a few lively brushstrokes (called *sumi-e*); and flattened compositions of seasonal motifs, boldly outlined against a backdrop of solid gold leaf (associated with works of the Kano school).

Metalwork includes bronze statues of Buddhist deities and ritual elements, as well as tea kettles for the tea ceremony and intricately designed hand guards for swords. Lacquerware – sometimes black, sometimes red and sometimes inlaid with mother-of-pearl or sprinkled with gold leaf – appears on boxes for storing sutras or writing implements and serving trays. Japan's skilled weavers, dyers and embroiderers come together to create lavish kimonos, historically worn by the nobility and today seen on actors on the *nō* and kabuki stages. Pottery covers the whole spectrum from rough earthenware to delicate enamelled porcelain.

Early on, Buddhist imagery was prominent in the arts, less so as time went by. More consistently running through all of this is the use of symbolic motifs. These might evoke a particular season (say a pine tree for winter or a cherry blossom for spring) or a kind of good fortune (such as a crane for longevity or a gourd for prosperity). Museum exhibitions in Tokyo are often seasonal, so if you visit in autumn, you'll likely see many works with autumn motifs – a good reason to visit again at a different time of the year.

The Arts of the Tea Ceremony

Chanoyu (literally 'water for tea') is usually translated as 'tea ceremony', but it's more like performance art, with each element – from the gestures of the host to the feel of the tea bowl in your hand – carefully designed to articulate an aesthetic experience. It's had a profound and lasting influence in Japan, one that has percolated through all the divergent arts wrapped up in it: architecture, landscape design, ikebana (flower arranging), ceramics and calligraphy.

The culture of drinking *matcha* (powdered green tea) entered Japan along with Zen Buddhism in the 12th century. Like everything else in monastic life – the sweeping of the temple grounds and the tending of the garden, for example – the preparation of tea was approached as a kind of working meditation. The practice was later taken up by the ruling class, and the famous tea master Sen no Rikkyū (1522–91) is credited with laying down the foundations of *wabi-sabi* and raising tea to an art form.

Wabi roughly means 'rustic' and connotes the loneliness of the wilderness, while *sabi* can be interpreted as 'weathered', 'waning' or 'altered with age'. Together the two words signify an object's natural imperfections, arising in its inception, and the acquired beauty that comes with the patina of time. Ceramics selected for tea ceremonies

Arts Courses

Mokuhankan (p164; Asakusa)

Ohara School of Ikebana (p115; Harajuku & Aoyama)

Toyokuni Atelier Gallery (p140; Kōrakuen & Akihabara)

Wanariya (p163; (Asakusa)

THE ARTS & ARCHITECTURE SCENE THE ARTS OF THE TEA CEREMONY

Arts Info

Contemporary Japanese Literature (https:// japaneselit.net) New in translation.

Real Tokyo (www. realtokyo.co.jp) Cultural reviews.

Tokyo Art Beat (www.tokyoart beat.com) Exhibition listings.

Traditional tea ceremony

were often dented, misshapen or rough in texture, with drips of glaze running down the edges – and all the more prized for it. Tea didn't stop and end with *wabi-sabi* – it evolved too, and new styles like *kirei-sabi* (a kind of simple elegance) later emerged – but it remained a driver of the arts well into the modern period.

Traditionally tea ceremonies are performed in teahouses built especially for the purpose and located in the gardens of a villa. Like Japan's classical art tradition, the tea ceremony is highly attuned to the seasons, which dictate what hanging scroll and sprig of flowers or leaves are placed in the teahouse alcove; perhaps even more so, because of its emphasis on naturalness. Some historic teahouses still exist. These relatively humble structures were easy to dismantle and move, in order to keep them safe, and the Tokyo National Museum (p145) has five in its garden, open for a few weeks each spring and autumn.

While it's not the same as experiencing the whole ritual, Tokyo has some lovely spots to enjoy *matcha* prepared in the formal way, including **Nakajima no Ochaya** (中島の御茶屋; 1-1 Hama-rikyū Onshi-teien, Chūō-ku; tea ¥510 or ¥720; ⊙9am-4.30pm; 🍵🚻; 🚇Ōedo line to Shiodome, exit A1), in the garden Hama-rikyū Onshi-teien (p73) and Chashitsu Kaboku (p68), the Tokyo outpost of famed 300-year-old Kyoto tea purveyor Ippodō.

Ukiyo-e

Ukiyo was a play on words: spelt with one set of Chinese characters, it meant the 'fleeting world', our tenuous, temporary abode on earth and a pivotal concept in Japanese Buddhism for centuries. Change the first character, however, and you got the homophone the 'floating world', which was used to describe the urban pleasure quarters of the Edo period. In this topsy-turvy world, the social hierarchies dictated by

Matsuo Bashō (1644–94) is Japan's most famous haiku poet. Before he left for the wilds of northern Honshū to pen his opus, *Oku no Hosomichi* (The Narrow Road to the Deep North; 1702) he lived in a little hut with a banana tree in Tokyo's Fukagawa district.

Landscape by Utagawa Hiroshige

the Tokugawa shogunate were inverted: money meant more than rank, kabuki actors were the arbiters of style and courtesans were the most accomplished of artists.

Ukiyo-e were literally pictures of the floating world, capturing famed beauties, pleasure boats and outings under the cherry blossoms. They were also postcards from the world beyond; at a time when rigid laws prevented much of the populace from travelling, woodblock prints presented compelling scenes from around Japan. The famous *ukiyo-e* artists Katsushika Hokusai (1760–1849) and Utagawa Hiroshige (1797–1858) are best known, respectively, for their series *Fifty Three Stations of the Tōkaidō* and *One Hundred Famous Views of Edo*.

The vivid colours, novel composition and flowing lines of *ukiyo-e* caused great excitement when they finally arrived in the West; the French came to dub it 'Japonisme'. *Ukiyo-e* was a key influence on Impressionists and post-Impressionists (including Toulouse-Lautrec, Manet and Degas). Yet among the Japanese, the prints were hardly given more than passing consideration – millions were produced annually in Edo, often thrown away or used as wrapping paper for pottery.

20th-Century Modernism

When Japan opened up to the world in the late 19th century, new forms and ideas came spilling in – oil painting, figurative sculpture, the novel – which was exciting, but also fraught. A painting tradition with a 1000-year history was flattened into the catch-all term *nihonga* (Japanese-style painting) as a foil to the new *yōga* (Western-style painting). Making art now meant either a rejection or an embrace of Western influence, a choice that was hard to divorce from politics.

Public Art

LOVE (p126) by
Robert Indiana
(Shinjuku)

Maman (p81) by
Louise Bourgeois
(Roppongi)

Myth of Tomorrow
(p99) by Okamoto
Tarō (Shibuya)

White Deer by
Nawa Kōhei
(Akasaka)

This shift raised a number of questions: should the old styles stay just that? And, if not, how could they possibly evolve organically without addressing the elephant (Western influence) in the room? Could works in Western mediums ever transcend mere imitation? And who would be the new patrons of the arts, now that the old power structure had been dismantled? Some critics argue that these same questions haunt the arts to this day.

Literature and film, with their narrative qualities, were perhaps the best mediums in which to parse the profound disorientation that had settled upon Japan by the early 20th century. Novels such as Sōseki Natsume's *Kokoro* (1914) and Kawabata Yasunari's *Yukiguni* (Snow Country; 1935–37) address the conflict between Japan's nostalgia for the past and its rush towards the future, between its rural heartland and its burgeoning metropolises. These are themes still explored today: just watch recent anime hit *Your Name*.

Film, meanwhile, was as new to Japan as the rest of the world – which conferred upon the medium an enviable freedom. Ozu Yasujirō (1903–63), Japan's first great auteur, created family dramas of grace and depth, looking at the rapid change that left different generations all but isolated from each other. His *Tokyo Story* will break your heart. And it was with film that Japanese artists first achieved major international recognition in the 20th century, most notably Kurosawa Akira (1910–98), who won the Golden Lion at the Venice International Film Festival for the haunting *Rashōmon* (1950) and later an honorary Oscar. Kurosawa is an oft-cited influence for film-makers around the world.

Tokyo Pop & Beyond

The '90s was a big decade for Japanese contemporary art: love him or hate him, Murakami Takashi (b 1962) brought Japan back into an international spotlight it hadn't enjoyed since 19th-century collectors went wild for *ukiyo-e* (woodblock prints). His work makes fantastic use of the flat planes, clear lines and decorative techniques associated with *nihonga* (Japanese-style painting), while lifting motifs from the lowbrow subculture of manga (Japanese comics).

As much an artist as a clever theorist, Murakami proclaimed in his 'Superflat' manifesto that his work picked up where Japanese artists left off after the Meiji Restoration – and might just be the future of painting, given that most of us now view the world through the portals of two-dimensional screens. Murakami inspired a whole generation of artists who worked in his 'factory', Kaikai Kiki, and presented their works at his Geisai art fairs.

Murakami might have made the biggest splash, but he was just one of many artists from the '90s (and beyond) working to deconstruct Japanese art history and untangle it from the stubborn legacy of West-centric art criticism. For example, there's also Aida Makoto (b 1965), who revels in resurrecting the rather ribald tradition of *ukiyo-e* (many were rather racy or grotesque), creating sometimes shocking works; he also riffs on pop culture, including Japan's infatuation with cute mascots.

And there are also artists who have nothing to do with the old styles. The collective known as ChimPom (http://chimpom.jp), formed by a group of 20-somethings in the mid-aughts, is one of the more daring presences in Tokyo's art scene: their conceptual installations directly address (sometimes confrontationally and often cheekily) contemporary issues in Japanese, and global, society.

Tokyo is serious about street performers and buskers (perhaps too serious): they have to audition for approval and can only perform in certain areas. Ueno-kōen is the best spot, with almost daily performances; on weekends look for them at Inokashira-kōen and Yoyogi-kōen.

Above: Life-size geisha doll at Edo-Tokyo Museum (157)
Right: Busker, Inokashira-kōen (p119)

Kabuki performer

Performing Arts

Tokyo, when it was Edo (1603–1868), had a rich theatre culture. Above all, there was kabuki – Japan's most famous form of performing arts, known for its exaggerated poses and fearsome expressions, dramatic stage makeup and boldly coloured costumes. It is this intensely visual nature and heightened sense of drama that makes kabuki so appealing to foreign audiences – you don't really have to know the story to enjoy the spectacle.

Other forms of traditional theatre that can be seen on Tokyo stages include *nō* (an even older form of stylised dance-drama), bunraku (classic puppet theatre using huge puppets to portray dramas similar to kabuki) and *bugaku* (dance pieces played by court orchestras in ancient Japan). The Japan Arts Council (www.ntj.jac.go.jp), which runs Tokyo's national theatres, does a good job of making these old art forms accessible with English subtitles or synopses; the same goes for contemporary Japanese audiences, who – with the exception of devout connoisseurs – would be equally lost without the same crutches in their own language.

Unfortunately, the same isn't true for Tokyo's contemporary theatre offerings. There is a small but active and interesting fringe scene, but it is near impossible to access without some Japanese-language ability. Meanwhile, mainstream theatre is made up of mostly Western works in translation, especially musicals, or unchallenging performances starring celebrities from film and TV. One contemporary movement that fortunately requires no language comprehension is *butō*, a style of dance that is raw, electrifying and often unsettling.

Contemporary theatre is at its most accessible during the month-long theatre festival, Festival/Tokyo (http://festival-tokyo.jp/en; Octo-

Kabukiza theatre (p74)

ber to November), which features both domestic and international productions; some of these have English subtitles or synopses, while others require no language ability to appreciate.

Kabuki

Kabuki actually got its start in Kyoto: around the year 1600, a charismatic shrine priestess and her entourage began publicly performing a new (and a bit bawdy) style of dance. People dubbed it 'kabuki', a slang expression that meant 'cool' or 'in vogue' at the time. It was also a gateway to prostitution, which eventually led the shogunate to ban the female performers. Adolescent men took their place, though that didn't solve the problem. Finally, in 1653, the authorities mandated that only adult men with shorn forelocks could perform kabuki, which gave rise to one of kabuki's most fascinating elements, the *onnagata* (actors who specialise in portraying women).

But it was in the urbane circles of Edo that kabuki evolved into what we think of today. Those exaggerated moves? They're not-so-subtle references to the off-duty samurai or the dandyish merchant swaggering around the pleasure quarters – both characters lifted from everyday life. Kabuki deals in archetypes; the make-up signals whether a character is good or evil, noble or ruled by passion. But it is not simplistic: though it gets lost in translation (even for modern Japanese) many of the plays, and especially the confrontations, are meant to be funny.

More than by plot, however, kabuki is driven by its actors, who train for the profession from childhood. In its heyday, kabuki actors outshone even those swaggering samurai and merchants; they were the ultimate influencers. Sons (biological or adopted) follow their fathers into a *yago* (kabuki acting house); the leading families of modern kabuki (such as

Bandō and Ichikawa) go back many generations. At pivotal moments in a performance, like when the actors pause in dramatic poses (called *mie*), enthusiastic fans shout out the actor's *yago* – an act called *kakegoe*.

Ginza's Kabukiza (p74), in business since 1889, is the last of Tokyo's dedicated kabuki theatres.

Nō

Nō, which emerged in 14th-century Kyoto, is the oldest existent Japanese performing art (older than Tokyo). Its roots are likely older still: *nō* is believed to be a pastiche of earlier traditions, including Shintō rites, popular entertainments like pantomime and acrobatics, and *gagaku* (the traditional music and dance of the imperial court).

Rather than a drama in the usual sense of a story in motion, *nō* seeks to express a poetic moment by symbolic and almost abstract means: glorious movements, sonorous chorus and music, and subtle expression. Its principal aesthetic, *yūgen* – a kind of gentle and mysterious, yet profound, grace – was laid down by the dramatist Zeami Motokiyo (1363–1443), who wrote many of the plays still performed today. Characters speak in the language of the medieval court.

The *nō* stage is furnished with only a single pine tree. There are two principal characters: the *shite*, who is sometimes a living person but more often a ghost whose soul cannot rest or a demon, and the *waki*, who leads the main character towards the play's climactic moment.

Haunting masks, carved from wood, are used to depict female or nonhuman characters. Often they are designed to appear different when tilted at varying angles – an effect heightened by the lighting of the stage (traditionally torch-lit). Many still in use are hundreds of years old (the oil and sweat from the actors' faces keeps the wood supple). Adult male characters are played without masks.

Some viewers find this all captivating; others (including most Japanese today) find its subtlety all too subtle. As if anticipating this, comic vignettes known as *kyōgen* are part of the programs of *nō* plays, taking the spectator from the sublime realm to the ridiculous world of the everyday. Using the colloquial language of the time and a cast of stock characters, *kyōgen* poke fun at such subjects as cowardly samurai, depraved priests and faithless women.

Tokyo has its own public theatre dedicated to *nō*, the National Nō Theatre (p114), near Harajuku. Masks and costumes are on display at the Tokyo National Museum (p145). *Nō* is also performed occasionally, usually in October, as it was intended to be: outdoors and torch-lit (this is called *takigi-nō*). It makes for a fascinating visual spectacle, though you won't get the same language help that the national theatre offers.

Butō

Butō is Japan's unique and fascinating contribution to contemporary dance. It was born out of a rejection of the excessive formalisation that characterises traditional forms of Japanese dance and of an intention to return to more ancient roots. Hijikata Tatsumi (1928–86), born in the remote northern province of Akita, is credited with giving the first *butō* performance in 1959; Ōno Kazuo (1906–2010) was also a key figure.

During a performance, dancers use their naked or seminaked bodies to express the most elemental and intense human emotions. Nothing is forbidden in *butō* and performances often deal with taboo topics such as sexuality and death. For this reason, critics often describe *butō* as scandalous, and *butō* dancers delight in pushing the boundaries of what can be considered beautiful in artistic performance. It's also entirely visual, meaning Japanese and non-Japanese spectators are on level footing.

Dairakudakan dance troupe

Though performers have toured internationally, in Japan *butō* has remained a largely underground scene. It is sometimes performed at the Setagaya Public Theatre; Dairakudakan (www.dairakudakan.com), which operates out of a small performance space in Kichijōji, is one of the more active troupes today.

Architecture & Gardens

Japan's traditional design aesthetic of clean lines, natural materials, heightened spatial awareness and subtle enhancement has inspired artists and designers around the world. Meanwhile, the country's contemporary architects, riffing on old and contemplating the new, are among the most internationally acclaimed and influential. Since ancient times landscape design has been inseparable from architecture, and Tokyo has several fantastic gardens, though the structures attached to them may be long gone.

Traditional Architecture

Japan's abundant forests were an easy source of wood, which has historically been the building material of choice. Stone appears in foundations, bridges or castle ramparts; however, the frequency of earthquakes in Japan made it an unsuitable material for walls. Other natural materials also come into play: mulberry bark is fashioned into *washi*, which is employed in varying degrees of thickness on *shoji* (sliding wooden doors covered with translucent *washi*) and *fusama* (sliding screens covered with opaque *washi*, used to partition rooms and closets); dried reeds are woven into floor mats (tatami) and window shades.

Traditionally, Japanese constructions use a post and lintel system, which, when combined with the gridlike composition of latticed

Traditional Japanese room, with *shoji* doors

screens and tatami-mat floors, give buildings an overwhelmingly recti-linear appearance. Another defining feature of traditional buildings is that they are designed for a life largely lived on the floor. Tatami mats cushion the floor where people sit on *zabuton* (floor pillows) around low tables and sleep on futons (floor mattresses). Space is also modu-lar: *fusama* can be employed according to need; *shoji* can be removed, eliminating the barrier between inside and outside.

Up until a century ago, Tokyo's buildings – save for a few Western-style showpieces created in the late 19th and early 20th centuries – were almost entirely constructed of wood and paper, with clay tile roofs. Early photos of the city show a remarkable visual harmony in the old skyline. Unfortunately, such structures were also highly flammable and few survived the twin conflagrations of the first half of the 20th century: the fires that followed the Great Kantō Earthquake and the fire-bombings of WWII.

The fires at least were to be expected, and only monumental build-ings were designed with some degree of permanency in mind. Tradi-tional wooden buildings require a great deal of maintenance to live beyond their natural shelf life, and of those that survived the first half of the 20th century, many were replaced with buildings made of reinforced concrete (which was deemed safer and easier to maintain) in later years.

The neighbourhood of Yanaka (p152) is famous for having a high concentration of wooden structures from the early 20th century. There is also a fantastic collection of classic wooden shops, dissembled and reassembled at the Edo-Tokyo Open Air Architecture Museum (p120). And while many buildings may appear modern on the outside, they often make use of traditional Japanese design elements on the inside.

Edo-Era Buildings

Kiyōmizu Kannon-dō (1631; p148)

Asakusa-jinja (1649; p157)

Tōshō-gū (1651; p148)

Nezu-jinja (1706; p149)

TEMPLE OR SHRINE?

Buddhist temples and Shintō shrines were historically intertwined, until they were forcibly separated by government decree in 1868. But centuries of coexistence means the two resemble each other architecturally; you'll also often find small temples within shrines and vice versa. The easiest way to tell the two apart though is to check the gate. The main entrance of a shrine is a *torii* (gate), usually composed of two upright pillars, joined at the top by two horizontal crossbars, the upper of which is normally slightly curved. *Torii* are often painted a bright vermilion. In contrast, the *mon* (main entrance gate) of a temple is often a much more substantial affair, constructed of several pillars or casements, joined at the top by a multitiered roof. Temple gates often contain guardian figures, usually *Niō* (deva kings).

Foreign Influences

When Japan opened its doors to Western influence following the Meiji Restoration (1868), the city's urban planners sought to remake downtown Tokyo in the image of a European city. A century-long push and pull ensued, between enthusiasts and detractors, architects who embraced the new styles and materials, and those who rejected them. Tokyo Station (p64), with its brick facade and domes looking very much like a European terminus, went up in 1914. Meanwhile, the Tokyo National Museum (p145), from 1938, was done in what was called the Imperial Style, a sturdy, modern rendering of traditional design.

There was also some meeting in the middle: around the turn of the 20th century it became fashionable among the elite to build houses with both Japanese and Western-style wings; the Kyū Iwasaki-teien (p149) is one example. Built up gradually over the decades of the early 20th century, the home studio of sculptor Asakura Fumio, now the Asakura Museum of Sculpture, Taitō (p235), is another interesting, more organic example of a hybrid structure.

A few decades later the International Style – characterised by sleek lines, cubic forms and materials such as glass, steel and brick – arrived in Japan, settling the debate and putting an end (mostly) to the idea that modern-style (ie Western) buildings need to incorporate neoclassical flourishes. It was also a style that squared more neatly with Japan's own architectural tradition. Many structures in this style were put up in the central business districts of Marunouchi and Nihombashi; though many have since been rebuilt to add more floors, the street-floor facades of some buildings pay homage to the original structures.

Meiji-era Buildings

Former Ministry of Justice (1895)

....

Bank of Japan (1896)

....

Kyū Iwasaki-teien (p149) (1896)

....

Tokyo National Museum's Hyokeikan (p145) (1908)

....

Akasaka Palace (p83) (1909)

Modernism & Postmodernism

Modern Japanese architecture really came into its own in the 1960s. The best known of Japan's 20th-century builders was Tange Kenzō (1913–2005), who was influenced by traditional Japanese forms, as well as the aggressively sculptural works of French architect Le Corbusier. Some of Tange's noteworthy works include St Mary's Cathedral (p126) (1964), the National Gymnasium (1964), the Tokyo Metropolitan Government Building (p126) (1991) and the Fuji Television Japan Broadcast Centre (1996).

Concurrent with Tange were the postmodern 'Metabolists', Shinohara Kazuo, Kurokawa Kishō, Maki Fumihiko and Kikutake Kiyonori. The Metabolism movement promoted flexible spaces and functions at the expense of fixed forms in building. Kurokawa's Nakagin Capsule Tower (p73) (1972) is a seminal work, designed using pods that could be removed whole from a central core and replaced elsewhere. Kikutake went on to design the Edo-Tokyo Museum (p157) (1992). This enormous

Above: Asakusa Culture Tourist Information Center (p243); architect Kengo Kuma
Left: St Mary's Cathedral Tokyo (p126); architect Tange Kenzō

Edo-Tokyo Museum (p157)

structure encompasses almost 50,000 sq metres of built space and reaches 62.2m (the height of Edo Castle) at its peak.

Contemporary Architects

Since the 1980s a new generation of Japanese architects has emerged who continue to explore both modernism and postmodernism, while mining Japan's architectural heritage. Among the more influential ones are Andō Tadao (b 1941) and Itō Toyō (b 1941). Andō's works tend to be grounded and monumental, yet unobtrusive, with no unnecessary flourishes; he works in modern materials such as concrete and steel. 21_21 Design Sight (p82) is a great example.

Itō's designs are lighter and more conceptual, meditating on the ideas of borders between inside and outside, public and private. Two of his protégés, Sejima Kazuyo and Nishizawa Ryūe, went on to form the firm SANAA. Their own luminous form-follows-function creations have also been influential. Both Itō and SANAA have designed boutiques on Omote-sandō in Harajuku.

The architect whose work you're most likely to encounter in Tokyo is Kengo Kuma (b 1954), who has been the go-to architect for high-profile commissions over the last decade. In terms of his impact on the texture of the city, he is Tange's successor, but their works are entirely different: Kengo is famous for his use of wood, employing cutting-edge computer drafting technology to that age-old staple of Japanese construction. He's behind the new National Stadium for the latest Tokyo Summer Olympics and also the redesigns for the Nezu Museum (p108), Akagi-jinja (p137) and the Asakusa Culture Tourist Information Center (p243), among many others. Walking around Tokyo you'll soon be able to identify his works and signature style.

Standing 634m tall, Tokyo Sky Tree (2012) is the world's tallest free-standing tower. It employs an ancient construction technique used in pagodas: a *shimbashira* column (made of contemporary reinforced concrete), structurally separate from the exterior truss. It acts as a counterweight when the tower sways, cutting vibrations by 50%.

Kiyosumi-teien (p162)

Landscape Gardens

In the Edo period (1603–1868) no *daimyō* (feudal lord) would dare have a villa in the capital without a landscaped strolling garden, which would serve as both a retreat and a place to entertain guests. In the Meiji period (1868–1912), when the class system was dismantled, wealthy merchants picked up the tradition and, in some cases, the properties themselves. Though many of these villas have long since disappeared, there remain some beautifully preserved gardens in Tokyo.

Flowering plants are only one component of the Japanese garden, which may be composed of any combination of vegetation (including trees, shrubs and moss), stones of varying sizes and water. Some gardens are not limited to that which falls within their walls, but take into account the scenery beyond (a technique called *shakkei* or 'borrowed scenery'). Often they are meant to evoke a landscape in miniature, with rocks standing in for famous mountains of myth or Chinese literature; raked gravel may represent flowing water. Garden elements are arranged asymmetrically and shapes, such as the outline of a pond, are often irregular. The idea is that the garden should appear natural, or more like nature in its ideal state; in reality most gardens are meticulously maintained – and entirely by hand.

Strolling gardens are meant to be entered and viewed from multiple vantage points along a path that wends around a central pond. Such gardens have several interesting architectural elements, such as bridges, which may be a graceful sloping arch or a simple slab of stone; pavilions, which were created as places for rest or for moon-viewing; and stone pagodas, often much older than the garden (or even Tokyo!) itself.

The ideal garden is designed to be attractive in all seasons, though most are associated with a particular time of year, be it the blooming of the azaleas in April or the turning of the maples in November.

The Japanese Art of Bathing

Don't be shy! Many Japanese would argue that you couldn't possibly understand their culture without taking a dip in an onsen (natural hot-spring bath). The blissful relaxation that follows can turn a sceptic into a convert. Don't let Tokyo's slick surface and countless diversions fool you; underneath the city it's pure, bubbling primordial pleasure. In the city, onsen can be found in elaborate day spas or humble public bathhouses (called *sentō*).

Bathing Basics

First of all, relax: really. All you need to know to avoid causing alarm is to wash yourself before getting into the bath. But yes, you do need to get naked. Baths and changing rooms are gender segregated, though

Above: Onsen, Hakone (p177)

Mori-no-Yu hot springs, Yunessun onsen, Hakone (p181)

Day spas typically refuse entry to customers with tattoos because of the association of tattoos with the *yakuza*; some *sentō* allow visitors with tattoos (Jakotsu-yu is an example). In either case, the policy (with obvious signage) will likely be posted at the entrance.

some day spas have communal areas where guests wear bathing suits or pyjamas (for saunas).

Upon entering a spa or bathhouse, the first thing you'll encounter is a row of lockers for your shoes. At the front desk you'll either pay your admission up front (always the case at *sentō*) or be given a wristband (often the case at spas). The wristband can be used to open and close your locker in the changing room and also to charge any food, drinks or additional services to your tab, which you'll settle upon checking out. Some places may keep your shoe locker key at the front desk as a deposit.

Next, head to the correct changing room. Take everything off here, storing your clothes and belongings in the lockers or baskets provided. If there are no lockers, you can ask to leave valuables at the front desk.

Enter the bathing room with only a small towel. Park yourself on a stool in front of one of the taps and give yourself a thorough wash. Make sure you rinse off all the suds. When you're done, it's polite to rinse off the stool for the next person.

That little towel performs a variety of functions: you can use it to wash (but make sure you give it a good rinse afterwards) or to cover yourself as you walk around. It is not supposed to touch the water though, so leave it on the side of the bath or – as the locals do – folded on top of your head.

In the baths, keep splashing to a minimum and your head above the water (and your heart above water if you're prone to dizziness). Before heading back to the changing room, wipe yourself down with the towel to avoid dripping on the floor.

Ōedo Onsen Monogatari (p170)

Day Spas

Day spas offer a huge variety of baths and saunas, often including *rotemburo* (outdoor baths) and *ganbanyoku* (heated stone saunas). They also usually offer massages, facials and body scrubs. It's entirely possible to spend the better part of a day in one. Or night: they're usually open 24 hours and, for an extra fee, you can overnight here, sleeping on a reclining chair in the lounge. (Yes, this is a real thing people do.)

Those in central Tokyo are used to foreign visitors and usually have dos and don'ts posted in multiple languages. Towels and robes or pyjamas are provided and the washing and changing rooms have toiletries, disposable razors and combs, hair dryers and anything else you might need.

Spa LaQua (p141), in Kōrakuen, and Ōedo Onsen Monogatari (p170), in Odaiba, are Tokyo's two biggest day spas; the latter bills itself as an onsen 'theme park' and includes a recreation of an old Edo downtown. In Shinjuku, newcomer Thermae-yu (p133) is popular. All use natural hot-spring waters in their baths.

Sentō

As little as 50 years ago, many private homes in Japan did not have baths, so in the evenings people headed off to the local neighbourhood *sentō* (public bath). More than just a place to wash oneself, the *sentō* served as a kind of community meeting hall, where news and gossip were traded and social ties strengthened. In 1968, at the peak of their popularity, Tokyo had 2687 *sentō;* now there are around 1000.

Tokyo Sentō (www.1010.or.jp/index.php), run by the Tokyo Sentō Association, has information on *sentō* culture and bathing etiquette, and a select list of public bathhouses in the city.

Most *sentō*-goers are neighbourhood regulars. This can be a little intimidating for first-timers, but don't let that put you off; just give your fellow bathers a brief nod and go about your business.

Bathhouses can be identified by their distinctive *noren* (half-length curtains over the doorway), which usually bear the hiragana (ゆ; yu) for hot water (occasionally, it may be written in kanji: 湯). Most open from around 3pm to midnight. Admission is ¥460; sometimes more if you add on admission to the sauna. You're expected to bring your own towel and toiletries; however, you can show up empty-handed and rent a towel and purchase soap, shampoo etc for a small price.

Some, though not most, *sentō* are fed by onsen water. In Tokyo, a public bathhouse with hot-spring water is **Jakotsu-yu** (蛇骨湯; ☑03-3841-8645; www.jakotsuyu.co.jp; 1-11-11 Asakusa, Taitō-ku; adult/child ¥460/180; ◉1pm-midnight Wed-Mon; ⓢGinza line to Tawaramachi, exit 3) in Asakusa. While it just uses ordinary tap water, Shimizu-yu (p115), in Aoyama, is a good spot on the west side of town.

Onsen Resorts

Outside Tokyo, but within reach of a day or overnight trip, are several onsen resorts – towns with famous springs. A worthwhile experience is a stay in an onsen ryokan, a traditional inn with hot-spring baths. Many such inns also open up their baths to day trippers in the afternoon; ask any tourist information centre where there are places offering *higaeri-onsen* (bathing without accommodation).

Less than two hours southwest of the city is Tokyo's favourite onsen getaway, Hakone. This centuries-old resort town with several distinct hot springs is set among forested peaks. There are many ryokan here, ranging from reasonable to lavish, as well as day spas.

Survival Guide

Transport

ARRIVING IN TOKYO

Narita Airport

Though modern and well-run, **Narita Airport** (NRT, 成田空港; ✆0476-34-8000; www.narita-airport.jp; 🛈) is inconveniently located 66km east of Tokyo. There are three terminals, with Terminal 3 handling low-cost carriers. All terminals have tourist information desks.

Only Terminals 1 and 2 have train stations; all terminals are accessible via coach lines.

A free shuttle bus runs between Terminal 2 and Terminal 3 approximately every five minutes (4.30am to 11.20pm); otherwise it is a 15-minute walk between the two terminals. Free shuttles also run between all terminals every 15 minutes (8am to 8pm) and every 30 minutes (7am to 8am and 8pm to 9.30pm).

When returning, note that there is a much better selection of shops and restaurants before security.

Bus

Access Narita (www.access narita.jp; ¥1000) Discount buses depart roughly every 20 minutes (7.30am to 10.45pm) for Tokyo Station and Ginza (one to 1¼ hours). There's no ticket counter at the airport;

just go directly to bus stop 31 at Terminal 1, or stops 2 or 19 at Terminal 2, and pay on board. Luggage is restricted to one suitcase of less than 20kg. For return trips to Narita, buses depart from platform 7 at the **JR Highway Bus Terminal** at Tokyo Station. You can reserve tickets online, but only in Japanese; departures are frequent, so if you leave yourself a little extra time, you should have no problem.

Friendly Airport Limousine (www.limousinebus.co.jp; adult/child ¥3100/1550) Coaches run to major hotels and train stations in central Tokyo. The journey takes 1½ to two hours depending on traffic. Travellers are allowed two bags up to 30kg each. No advance reservations are necessary but you must purchase a ticket before boarding. You can purchase tickets for the next available bus from one of the kiosks in any of the terminals' arrivals halls. At the time of research, discount round-trip tickets (¥4500), good for 14 days, were available for foreign tourists; ask at the airport ticket kiosk. From Tokyo, there's a ticket counter inside the Shinjuku Bus Terminal (p233); you can also reserve online up to the day before departure.

Train

Both Japan Railways (JR) and the independent Keisei line run between central Tokyo and Narita Airport Terminals 1 and 2. For Terminal 3, take a train to Terminal 2 and then walk or take the free shuttle bus to Terminal 3 (and budget an extra 15 minutes).

Tickets can be purchased upon arrival in the basement of either terminal, where the entrances to the train stations are located; you cannot buy tickets on the train. In general trains run slightly more frequently from the late morning to the late afternoon and less frequently earlier and later.

LIMITED EXPRESS TRAINS Seats on Narita Express and Skyliner trains are all reserved; purchase them at a ticket window or from the touch-screen machines. It's usually possible to get a seat on the next available train, though those with departure anxiety may want to book their outbound ticket in advance. Speed and comfort level are pretty much the same; both have space in the front of the cars to store luggage. Generally, the Skyliner is more convenient for destinations on the east side of Tokyo while the Narita Express gets you to the west side of the city faster.

Keisei Skyliner (www.keisei. co.jp) Nonstop direct trains to

Nippori (36 minutes) followed by Ueno (41 minutes) run approximately twice an hour between 7.30am and 10pm (adult/child ¥2470/1240). Transfer is available at Nippori Station for the JR Yamanote line and at Ueno for the JR Yamanote line and Ginza and Hibiya subway lines. Foreign nationals can purchase advance tickets online for slightly less (one-way/return ¥2200/4300).

Narita Express (N'EX; www.jreast.co.jp) Trains run between 7.45am and 9.45pm, departing Narita Airport for Tokyo Station (¥3020, 60 minutes) before splitting and heading out to other parts of the city. The most useful route runs approximately every half-hour to Shibuya (75 minutes) and Shinjuku (80 minutes); some trains stop first at Shinagawa (65 minutes) while others may continue to Ikebukuro (85 minutes). The price for all of the above destinations is the same: ¥3190. The ticket you purchase for your specific destination will ensure that you are in a seat in the right car – so it's pretty hard to mess this

up! At the time of research, foreign tourists could purchase return N'EX tickets for ¥4000 (¥2000 for under 12s), which are valid for 14 days and can be used on any route. Check online or enquire at the JR East Travel Service Centers at Narita Airport for the latest deals. Long-haul JR passes are valid on N'EX trains, but you must obtain a seat reservation (no extra charge) from a JR ticket office.

REGULAR TRAINS

Regular Keisei line trains run parallel to the Skyliner but make stops, and are a good budget option. There are no reserved seats on these trains; if you (and your bags) can squeeze in, you can ride. Purchase tickets from the touch-screen machines. These options can be a little bit more confusing, so pay attention to the signboards.

Keisei Main Line Rapid *tokkyū* (特急) trains run roughly every 20 minutes (from 6am to 10.30pm) to Nippori (¥1030; 66 minutes) and Ueno (¥1030; 71 minutes). There are also local trains that take significantly longer; make sure you get the *tokkyū*.

Keisei Access Express Approximately every 40 minutes (5.40am to 11pm) there are trains making limited stops on the same route until Aoto, after which they hook up with the Toei Asakusa line, running south to Asakusa (¥1290; 50 minutes), Nihombashi (¥1330; 59 minutes), Shimbashi (¥1330; 62 minutes) and Shinagawa (¥1520; 72 minutes).

Taxi

Fixed-fare taxis run ¥20,000 to ¥22,000 for most destinations in central Tokyo, plus tolls (about ¥2000 to ¥2500). There's a 20% surcharge between 10pm and 5am. Credit cards accepted.

Haneda Airport

Closer to central Tokyo, **Haneda Airport** (HND, 羽田空港; ✈ international airport 03-6428-0888; www.haneda-airport.jp; ☏) has two domestic terminals and one international terminal. Some international flights arrive at awkward night-time hours, between midnight and 5am, when the only public transport to central Tokyo will be infrequent night buses and taxis.

There's a **tourist information centre** (✆03-6428-0653; ⏰24hr; ☏) in the international terminal, on the 2nd floor of the arrivals lobby.

Bus

Purchase tickets at the kiosks at the arrivals hall. In Tokyo, there's a ticket counter inside the Shinjuku Bus Terminal (p233).

Friendly Airport Limousine (www.limousinebus.co.jp) Coaches connect Haneda with major train stations and hotels in Shibuya (¥1030), Shinjuku (¥1230), Roppongi (¥1130), Ginza (¥930) and others, taking anywhere from 30 to 90 minutes depending on traffic. Buses for Shinjuku depart every 30 to 40 minutes (5am

BAGGAGE SHIPMENT & STORAGE

Baggage couriers provide next-day delivery from Narita and Haneda airports to any address in Tokyo (around ¥2000 for a large suitcase) or beyond, which frees you from having to lug stuff on public transport. Look for kiosks in the arrival terminals. If you plan on taking advantage of this service, make sure to put the essentials you'll need for the next 24 hours in a small bag.

You can also have your bags shipped back to the airport, where you'll pick them up at a kiosk in the departures hall. Hotels can help you arrange this and some Tourist Information Centers (TICs) have baggage-forwarding counters. Many services also offer temporary baggage storage, which is useful if you want to take a detour to Mt Fuji or to an onsen resort without bringing all your stuff.

Courier services in Japan are very reliable. For more information and a list of courier counters, see www.jnto.go.jp/hands-free-travel.

to 11.30pm) and at 12.20am, 1am, 1.40am and 2.20am; departures for other areas are less frequent. Fares double between midnight and 5am.

Monorail

Tokyo Monorail (www. tokyo-monorail.co.jp) Leaves approximately every 10 minutes (5am to midnight) for Hamamatsuchō Station (¥490, 15 minutes), which is a stop on the JR Yamanote line. Good for travellers staying near Ginza or Roppongi.

Train

Keikyū Airport Express (www. haneda-tokyo-access.com) Trains depart several times an hour (5.30am to midnight) for Shinagawa (¥410, 12 minutes), where you can connect to the JR Yamanote line. From Shinagawa, some trains continue along the Asakusa subway line, which serves Higashi-Ginza, Nihombashi and Asakusa Stations.

Note that the international and domestic terminals have their own stations; when travelling to the airport, the international terminal is the second-last stop.

Taxi

Fixed fares from designated airport taxi stands include: Ginza (¥5900), Shibuya (¥6600), Shinjuku (¥7100), Ikebukuro (¥8900) and Asakusa (¥7200), plus highway tolls (around ¥800). There's a 20% surcharge between 10pm and 5am. Credit cards accepted.

GETTING AROUND

Bicycle

Tokyo is by no means a bicycle-friendly city. Bike lanes are almost nonexistent and you'll see no-parking signs for bicycles everywhere. (Ignore these at your peril: your bike could get impounded, requiring a half-day excursion to the pound and a ¥3000 fee.) Despite all this you'll see locals on bikes everywhere.

Cogi Cogi (www.cogicogi.jp; 24hr ¥2400) is a bike-sharing

system with ports around the city, including some hostels. There are instructions in English, but it's a little complicated to use. You'll need to download an app, register a credit card and have wi-fi connection on the go to sync with the ports.

Some accommodation has bikes to lend, sometimes for free or for a small fee. In Yurakuchō, Muji (p70) has bikes to rent.

Boat

Two operators run water buses up and down Sumidagawa (Sumida River). Tickets can be purchased subject to availability before departure at any pier.

Tokyo Cruise (水上バス, Suijō Bus; ☎0120-977-311; http:// suijobus.co.jp) Roughly twice an hour between 10am and 6pm, connecting Asakusa with Hama-rikyū Onshi-teien (¥980, 35 minutes) and Odaiba Kaihin-kōen (¥1260, 70 minutes); the latter may require a transfer at Hinode Pier. Advanced bookings are possible, up to one month, online.

Tokyo Mizube Cruising Line (東京水辺ライン; ☎03-5608-8869; www.tokyo-park.or.jp/ waterbus) Cheaper but less frequent trips from Asakusa to Hama-rikyū Onshi-teien (¥620, 40 minutes) and Odaiba Kaihin-kōen (¥1130, one hour) and back. The schedule is seasonal, with only a few boats daily in winter.

Bus

Toei (www.kotsu.metro.tokyo. jp/eng/services/bus.html) runs an extensive bus network, though it's rarely more convenient than the subway.
➡ Fares are ¥210/110 per adult/child; there are no transfer tickets. Pay by IC pass (prepaid rechargeable Suica

---

AIRPORT TRANSPORT & SUBWAY PASS PACKAGE DEALS

The following packages combine airport transport and an unlimited-ride Tokyo subway pass (good on Tokyo Metro and Toei lines, but not JR ones).

Limousine & Subway Pass (www.limousinebus.co.jp/ en/guide/ticket/subwaypass.html) One-way travel on the Friendly Airport Limousine from Narita or Haneda Airports to most (but not all) stations and hotels serviced by coach routes and a 24-hour subway pass; or round-trip travel and a 48- or 72-hour subway pass. Coming from Narita this package is cheaper than buying a regular return ticket. Any ticket packages can be purchased on arrival at the airport; one-way packages can also be purchased at Shinjuku Bus Terminal.

Skyliner & Tokyo Subway Ticket One-way or round-trip travel on the Skyliner between Narita Airport and Ueno plus a 24-, 48- or 72-hour subway pass. Purchase online in advance or on arrival at the ticketing counter for a saving of ¥540 to ¥2240 off the total combined price of the individual tickets included in the deal.

CLIMATE CHANGE & TRAVEL

Every form of transport that relies on carbon-based fuel generates CO_2, the main cause of human-induced climate change. Modern travel is dependent on aeroplanes, which might use less fuel per kilometre per person than most cars but travel much greater distances. The altitude at which aircraft emit gases (including CO_2) and particles also contributes to their climate change impact. Many websites offer 'carbon calculators' that allow people to estimate the carbon emissions generated by their journey and, for those who wish to do so, to offset the impact of the greenhouse gases emitted with contributions to portfolios of climate-friendly initiatives throughout the world. Lonely Planet offsets the carbon footprint of all staff and author travel.

and Pasmo cards) or deposit your fare into the box as you enter the bus; there's a change machine at the front of the bus that accepts ¥1000 notes.

➡ Most buses have digital signage that switches between Japanese and English (otherwise listen for your stop). Signal the bus to stop in advance of the approaching stop by pushing one of the buttons near the seats.

Car & Motorcycle

Considering the traffic, the confusing roads and the ridiculous cost of parking, we don't recommend using a car to get around Tokyo.

Day trips can easily be done by public transport, though having a car can expand your options.

You will need an International Driving Permit, which must be arranged in your own country before you leave. Play it safe by getting a copy of *Rules of the Road* (digital/print ¥864/1404) published by the Japan Automobile Federation (www.jaf.or.jp).

Rental companies with branches around the city include **Nippon Rent-a-Car** (www.nipponrentacar.co.jp/english) and **Toyota Rent-a-Car** (https://rent.toyota.co.jp/eng/). Expect to pay ¥8000 per day for a smallish rental car.

TRAVEL WITHIN JAPAN

Tokyo Station (p64) is the terminus for all *shinkansen*, the bullet trains that connect Tokyo to major cities all over Japan.

Shinkansen to/from points west (Kansai, Western Honshū and Kyūshū) will stop at Shinagawa (one stop before Tokyo Station for inbound trains), which may be more useful for destinations on the west or south side of the city.

Meanwhile, *shinkansen* from points east (Tōhoku and Hokkaidō) will stop at Ueno (one stop before Tokyo Station for inbound trains), which may be more useful for destinations on the east or north side of the city.

Shinjuku Bus Terminal (バスタ新宿, Busuta Shinjuku; Map p280; ☑03-6380-4794; www.shinjuku-busterminal. co.jp; 4th fl, 5-24-55 Sendagaya, Shibuya-ku; ☎; ℝJR Yamanote line to Shinjuku, new south exit), part of the JR Shinjuku train station complex, is Tokyo's biggest hub for highway coaches. Buses to both airports and Mt Fuji depart from here.

Taxi

Taxis only make economic sense for short distances or groups of four.

➡ Fares start at ¥410 for the first 1km, then rise by ¥80 for every 237m you travel or for every 90 seconds spent in traffic.

➡ There's a surcharge of 20% between 10pm and 5am.

➡ Drivers rarely speak English, though most taxis have navigation systems. Have your destination written down in Japanese, or better yet, a business card with an address.

➡ Taxis take credit cards and IC passes.

Ride-Sharing Apps

Tokyo strictly regulates ride-sharing apps: only licensed rivers can offer rides, meaning you're more likely to summon a town car that costs more than a regular taxi.

Train

Tokyo's extensive rail network includes JR lines, a subway system and private commuter lines that depart in every direction for the suburbs, like spokes on a wheel. Journeys that require transfers between lines run by different operators cost more than journeys that use only one operator's lines. Major transit hubs include Tokyo, Shinagawa, Shibuya, Shinjuku, Ikebukuro and

Ueno Stations. Trains arrive and depart precisely on time and are generally clean and pleasant, though they get uncomfortably crowded during rush hours.

Station vending machines sell single-journey paper tickets and rechargeable Suica and Pasmo train passes. The latter save a little money and a lot of hassle, as they work for all of the different train lines, subway and buses operating in the greater Tokyo area. See p25 for more information on tickets.

Japan Railways (JR) Lines

The JR network covers the whole country and includes the *shinkansen* (bullet train). In Tokyo, the above-ground Yamanote (loop) and the Chūō–Sōbu (central) lines are the most useful. Tickets start at ¥133 and go up depending on how far you travel.

Subway

Tokyo has 13 subway lines, nine of which are operated by **Tokyo Metro** (www.tokyo metro.jp) and four by **Toei** (www.kotsu.metro.tokyo.jp). The lines are colour-coded, making navigation fairly sim-

ple. Unfortunately a transfer ticket is required to change between the two; a Pasmo or Suica card makes this process seamless, but either way a journey involving more than one operator comes out costing slightly more. Rides on Tokyo Metro cost ¥170 to ¥240 (¥90 to ¥120 for children) and on Toei ¥180 to ¥320 (¥90 to ¥160 for children), depending on how far you travel.

Private Commuter Lines

Private commuter lines service some of the hipper residential neighbourhoods. Useful trains:

Keiō Inokashira line From Shibuya for Shimo-Kitazawa and Kichijōji.

Odakyū line From Shinjuku for Shimo-Kitazawa.

Tōkyū-Tōyoko line From Shibuya for Daikanyama and Naka-Meguro.

Note that the commuter lines run *tokkyū* (特急; limited-express services), *kyūkō* (急行; express) and *futsū* (普通; local) trains, which can be a little confusing.

Lockers

Hub stations have lockers in several sizes which cost from ¥200 to ¥600. Storage is good for 24 hours, after which your bags will be removed and taken to the station office.

Lost & Found

Larger stations have dedicated lost-and-found windows (labelled in English); otherwise lost items are left with the station attendant. Items not claimed on the same day will be handed over to the operator's lost-and-found centre. Items not claimed after several days are turned over to the police.

JR East Infoline (✆in English 050-2016-1603; ⊙10am-6pm)

Toei Transportation Lost & Found (✆03-3816-5700; www. kotsu.metro.tokyo.jp/eng/tips/ found.html; ⊙9am-8pm)

Tokyo Metro Lost & Found (Map p282;✆03-5227-5741; ⊙9am-8pm; ⊠JR Sōbu line to Iidabashi, west exit) Office located inside Iidabashi Station on the Namboku line.

TOURS

Bus tours are convenient for travellers who want to cover a lot of ground in one day (or want some respite from navigating). Walking tours offer insight into the history and culture of particular districts.

Bus Tours

Gray Line (Map p268;✆03-5275-6525; www.jgl.co.jp/ inbound/index.htm; half-/full day per person ¥4900/9800) Half-day and full-day tours with stops, covering key downtown sights and also day trips to Mt Fuji and Hakone. Pick-up service from major hotels is available, otherwise most tours leave from in front of the Dai-Ichi Hotel in Shimbashi (near Ginza).

FINDING AN ADDRESS IN TOKYO

Tokyo is difficult to navigate, even for locals. Only the biggest streets have official names, and they don't figure into addresses; instead, addresses are derived from districts, blocks and building numbers.

Central Tokyo is divided first into *ku* (wards; Tokyo has 23 of them), which in turn are divided into *chō* or *machi* (towns) and then into numbered districts called *chōme* (pronounced 'cho-may'). Subsequent numbers in an address refer to blocks within the *chōme* and buildings within each block.

It's near impossible to find your destination using the address alone. Smartphones with navigation apps have been a real boon. Many restaurants and venues have useful maps on their websites.

If you truly do get lost, police officers at *kōban* (police boxes) have maps and can help with directions (though few speak English). At the very least, they should be able to steer you back to the nearest train station from where you can try again.

DISCOUNT PASSES

City Passes

If you're planning a packed day, you might consider getting an unlimited-ride ticket.

Tokyo Subway Ticket Good for unlimited rides on both Tokyo Metro and Toei subway lines for 24 (¥800), 48 (¥1200) or 72 (¥1500) hours; half-price for children. This pass is only available to foreign travellers on a tourist visa; for more information and sales points see www.tokyometro.jp.

Tokyo Metro One-Day Open Ticket (adult/child ¥600/300) Unlimited rides over a 24-hour period on Tokyo Metro subway lines only. Purchase at any Tokyo Metro station; no restrictions apply.

Greater Tokyo Passes

Tokyo Wide Pass (adult/child ¥10,000/5000) Valid for three consecutive days of unlimited travel on JR limited-express trains between Tokyo, Nikkō, Kofu (near Mt Fuji), Ito and Narita Airport. From Ito, on the Izu Peninsula, you can continue on the Izu Kyūkō line free of charge to Shimoda, at the tip of the peninsula. The Tokyo Wide Pass is also good for the Jōetsu Shinkansen as far as Echigo-Yuzawa (and to ski resort Gala Yuzawa in winter) and the Tohoku Shinkansen as far as Nasu-Shiobara.

This is a great deal if you want to do a string of day trips. Purchase at any JR Travel Service Centre; this pass is restricted to foreign passport holders, but does not require you to be visiting on a tourist visa. For more details, see www.jreast.co.jp/e/tokyowide pass.

Hato Bus Tours (☎03-3435-6081; www.hatobus.com; tours ¥1500-12,000; [R]JR Yamanote line to Hamamatsuchō, south exit) This long-established bus-tour company offers hour-long, half-day and full-day bus tours of the city. Shorter tours cruise by the sights in an open-air double-decker bus; longer ones make stops. Tours leave from Hato Bus terminals in the annexe of the World Trade Centre in Hamamatsuchō, and Shinjuku and Tokyo train stations.

SkyBus (Map p266; ☎03-3215-0008; www.skybus.jp; 2-5-2 Marunouchi, Chiyoda-ku; tours adult/child from ¥1600/700, Sky Hop Bus ¥3500/1700; ⏰ticket office 9am-6pm; [R]JR Yamanote line to Tokyo, Marunouchi south exit) Open-top double-decker buses cruise through different neighbourhoods of the city for roughly 50 to 80 minutes. The Sky Hop Bus plan allows you to hop on and off buses on any of the three routes. English-language guidance is provided via earphones on board.

Walking Tours

Tokyo Metropolitan Government Tours (www.gotokyo.org/en/tourists/guideservice/guideservice/index.html; Ⓢ Ōedo line to Tochōmae, exit A4) Walking tours arranged by the Tokyo government tourism bureau in one of seven languages. There are several routes from which to choose, lasting around three hours each. Prices vary considerably based on group size (maximum five people) and destination, but include admission and transport for both participants and guides. Reserve online one month to three days in advance. Most depart from the TIC inside the Shinjuku Bus Terminal (p233).

To arrange more customised walking tours within Tokyo and beyond, contact the **Japan Guide Association** (☎03-3863-2895; www.jga21c.or.jp).

Free Tours

Free walking tours led by English-speaking volunteer guides take place regularly in a few neighbourhoods. No advance reservations are required – just show up (though places are limited). Tours last around 1½ hours. For more information see the homepage of the Tokyo Systemized Goodwill Guides Club (https://tokyosgg.jp/guide.html).

Asakusa Free Walking Tour Departs from the Asakusa Culture Tourist Information Center (p243) at 10.30am and 1.15pm daily except for Sundays.

Ueno Free Walking Tour Departs from in front of the Green Salon (グリーンサロン) cafe in Ueno-kōen (p148) at 10.30am and 1.30pm on Wednesdays, Fridays and Sundays.

Yanaka Free Walking Tour Departs from in front of the Asakura Museum of Sculpture, Taitō (p152) every Sunday at 10.30am and 1.30pm.

Directory A–Z

Accessible Travel

Tokyo is making steps to improve universal access – or *bariafurī* (barrier free; バリアフリー) in Japanese. It is a slow process, though one that has received a boost from the Olympics preparations. Newer buildings have wheelchair-access ramps, and more and more subway stations have elevators (look for signs on the platform, as not all exits have elevators); train station staff will help you on and off the train with a temporary slope.

A fair number of hotels – higher end of midrange and above – offer a barrier-free room or two (book well in advance); note that what constitutes barrier free is not always consistent, so check the details carefully. Larger attractions, train stations, department stores and shopping malls have wheelchair-accessible restrooms. Should you decide upon arrival that a wheelchair (車いす; *kuruma isu*) is necessary, hotel staff can help you rent one.

Accessible Japan (www.accessible-japan.com) is the best resource. Download Lonely Planet's free *Accessible Travel* guide from https://shop.lonely planet.com/categories/accessible-travel.com.

Customs Regulations

Japan has typical customs allowances for duty-free items; see Visit Japan Customs (www.customs.go.jp) for more information.

Stimulant drugs, which include ADHD medication Adderall, are strictly prohibited in Japan. Narcotics (such as codeine) are controlled substances; in order to bring them for personal medical use you need to prepare a *yakkan shōmei* – an import certificate for pharmaceuticals. See the Ministry of Health, Labour & Welfare's website (www.mhlw.go.jp/english/policy/health-medical/pharmaceuticals/01.html) for more details or contact the Tokyo office directly at tokyoncd@mhlw.go.jp.

Discount Cards

Grutto Pass (¥2200; www.rekibun.or.jp/grutto) Free or discounted admission to 90+ Tokyo attractions (mostly museums). This usually pays for itself after a few museum visits. All participating venues sell them.

International Student Identity Card (https://www.isic.org) Student discounts are common, but the International Student Identity Card is recognised inconsistently in Japan; a Japanese-university-issued student card will always work.

Seniors Many Tokyo attractions offer discounted admission to seniors (typically 65 years of age and over) – a passport is usually enough to prove eligibility.

Electricity

The Japanese electricity supply is an unusual 100V AC. Appliances with a two-pin plug made for use in North

---

PRACTICALITIES

Smoking From October 2019, smoking in Tokyo will be banned inside all bars and restaurants that employ staff (other than family) unless they can provide an air-tight smoking area – the strictest regulations in the country to date. For some time now, smoking has been banned in public spaces, including city streets and train stations, except for within designated smoking areas.

Weights & Measures The metric system is used along with some traditional Japanese measurements, especially for area (eg *jō* is the size of a tatami mat).

America will work without an adaptor, but may be a bit sluggish.

Type A
120V/60Hz

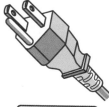

Type B
120V/60Hz

Embassies & Consulates

Australian Embassy (☎03-5232-4111; https://japan.embassy.gov.au; 2-1-14 Mita, Minato-ku; ⊘9am-12.30pm & 1.30-5pm Mon-Fri; ⓢNamboku line to Azabu-jūban, exit 2)

Canadian Embassy (カナダ大使館; Map p270; ☎03-5412-6200; www.canadainternational.gc.ca/japan-japon; 7-3-38 Akasaka, Minato-ku; ⊘9am-5.30pm Mon-Fri; ⓢGinza line to Aoyama-itchōme, exit 4)

Chinese Embassy (Map p270; ☎03-3403-3388; www.china-embassy.or.jp; 3-4-33 Moto-Azabu, Minato-ku; ⊘9am-noon Mon-Fri; ⓢHibya line to Hiro-o, exit 3)

Dutch Embassy (Map p270; ☎03-5776-5400; www.netherlandsandyou.nl; 3-6-3 Shiba-kōen, Minato-ku; ⊘9am-12.30pm Mon-Fri; ⓢHibiya line to Kamiyachō, exit 1)

French Embassy (☎03-5798-6000; www.ambafrance-jp.org; 4-11-44 Minami-Azabu, Minato-ku; ⊘9am-11.30am Mon-Fri; ⓢHibiya line to Hiro-o, exit 1)

German Embassy (☎03-5791-7700; https://japan.diplo.de; 4-5-10 Minami-Azabu, Minato-ku; ⊘8am-11am Mon-Fri; ⓢHibiya line to Hiro-o, exit 1)

Irish Embassy (Map p282; ☎03-3263-0695; www.dfa.ie/irish-embassy/japan; Ireland House, 2-10-7 Kōji-machi, Chiyoda-ku; ⊘10am-12.30pm & 2-4pm Mon-Fri; ⓢHanzōmon line to Hanzōmon, exit 4)

New Zealand Embassy (Map p272; ☎03-3467-2271; www.nzembassy.com/japan; 20-40 Kamiyama-chō, Shibuya-ku, Tokyo; ⊘9am-5.30pm Mon-Fri; ⓡJR Yamanote line to Shibuya, Hachikō exit)

Russian Embassy (Map p270; ☎03-3583-4445; https://tokyo.mid.ru/web/tokyo-en; 2-1-1 Azabudai, Minato-ku; 9am-12.30pm & 2-5.30pm Mon-Fri; ⓢHibiya line to Roppongi, exit 3)

South Korean Embassy (☎03-3452-7611, emergency 090-1693-5773; http://overseas.mofa.go.kr/jp-ko/index.do; 1-2-5 Minami-Azabu, Minato-ku; ⊘9am-noon & 1.30-6pm Mon-Fri; ⓢNamboku line to Azabu-Jūban, exit 1)

UK Embassy (Map p282; ☎03-5211-1100; www.gov.uk/government/world/organisations/british-embassy-tokyo; 1 Ichibanchō, Chiyoda-ku; ⊘9.30am-4.30pm Mon-Fri; ⓢHanzōmon line to Hanzōmon, exit 3A)

US Embassy (米国大使館; Map p270; ☎03-3224-5000; http://japan.usembassy.gov; 1-10-5 Akasaka, Minato-ku; ⊘8.30am-5.30pm Mon-Fri; ⓢGinza line to Tameike-sannō, exits 9, 12 & 13)

Emergency

Emergency operators typically won't speak English, but will immediately loop in a third-party translator.

INFORMATION HOTLINES

Japan Helpline (☎0570-000-911; ⊘24 hr) All purpose, English-language information hotline; for data users, contact them via the web form online at jhelp.com.

Police Consultation Hotline (☎03-3501-0110; ⊘24hr; translation services available 8.30am-5.15pm Mon-Fri) To report or ask for guidance on non-emergency, but nonetheless distressing situations.

Tokyo Medical Info Hotline (☎03-5285-8181; ⊘9am-8pm) English-speaking staff can recommend English-speaking doctors for specific ailments at municipal hospitals.

Ambulance & Fire	☑119
Police	☑110
Japan's country code	☑81
International access code	☑010

Insurance

Basic emergency coverage is adequate.

Internet Access

Decent wi-fi is standard in Tokyo accommodation (though exceptions exist). The city has an increasing number of free hot spots, which can be found on subway platforms, on the streets of some districts and at many convenience stores, major attractions and shopping centres. Look out for the sticker that says 'Japan Wi-Fi'.

This doesn't, however, mean staying connected while out and about is easy: public signals may be weak (and sometimes just nonexistent) or they might entail a clunky login process (requiring personal information, such as an email address) to access.

The Japan Connected (www.ntt-bp.net/jcfw/en.html) app simplifies the latter by allowing access to all partner networks without having to login to each one individually. Though travellers report hit-or-miss experiences with it.

If staying connected is a priority (and it can be very useful to have online-access navigation apps), consider renting a pocket internet device, which can be shared among multiple devices. Japan Wireless (www.japan-wireless.com) has reasonable prices and reliable service; and you can pre-order online.

Legal Matters

Japanese police have extraordinary powers compared with their Western counterparts: they have the right to detain a suspect without charging them for up to 48 hours. If the police can convince a judge of sufficient cause, they can detain you for a further 10 days (which can be extended for an additional 10 days). Bail is rarely granted.

You have the right to remain silent and the right to a lawyer. Note that police may begin questioning before a lawyer is present. If you do find yourself in police custody, you should first insist on speaking to your embassy and refuse to cooperate in any way until you are allowed to make such a call. Insist that a *tsuyakusha* (interpreter) be summoned (this is best, even if you can speak Japanese).

Japan takes a particularly hard-line approach to narcotics possession, with long sentences and fines even for first-time offenders.

Note that it is a legal requirement to have your passport (or, if you are staying longer than 90 days, your resident card) on you at all times. Though checks are not common, if you are stopped by police and caught without it, you could be hauled off to a police station to wait until someone fetches it for you.

LGBT+ Travellers

Gay and lesbian travellers are unlikely to encounter problems in Tokyo. There are no legal restraints on same-sex sexual activities in Japan, apart from the usual age restrictions.

Outright discrimination is unusual; however, travellers have reported being turned away or grossly overcharged when checking into love hotels with a partner of the same sex. Such discrimination is illegal, but is rarely litigated.

One thing to keep in mind: Japanese people, regardless of their sexual orientation, do not typically engage in public displays of affection.

Tokyo has made great strides in the past couple of years towards openness and acceptance; still, many LGBT people remain fearful of the potential social and economic ramifications of living publicly out – outside of safe spaces like Shinjuku-nichōme ('Nichōme' for short), the city's largest and liveliest gay quarter.

To keep up to date with issues concerning Tokyo's LGBT community, and to learn about events and meet-ups, follow the Nichōme Community Project (@NichomeComProj) and Nijiro News (@nijinews) on Twitter.

Akta Community Centre (Map p280;☑03-3226-8998; http://akta.jp; 301 Nakae Bldg No 2, 2-15-13 Shinjuku, Shinjuku-ku; ⏱6-10pm Thu-Mon; 🚃JR Yamanote line to Shinjuku, east exit) advocates for the health and safety of Tokyo's LGBT community. From the heart of Shinjuku-nichōme, Akta offers free AIDS tests, counselling

POLICE BOXES

Twenty-four-hour staffed *kōban* (交番; police boxes) are located near major train stations and intersections and also within commercial and entertainment districts. You can report crimes here – in which case they'll call in the nearest police station – and also fill out forms for lost items. *Kōban* officers rarely speak English, but are generally friendly and will try to help.

and any other information you might need.

Utopia Asia (www.utopia-asia.com) Lots of resources and recommendations for LGBT travellers.

Media

Asia & Japan Watch (www.asahi.com/ajw) Select news and commentary in English from Japanese newspaper the *Asahi Shimbun*.

Inter FM (76.1FM; www.interfm.co.jp) News broadcasts and public-service announcements in English.

Japan Times (www.japantimes.co.jp) Long-running, independent English-language daily and old-school expat lifeline.

NHK World (www3.nhk.or.jp/nhkworld) The English-language version of Japan's national broadcaster NHK has lots of shows on travel and food, in addition to local news.

Free Magazines By and for the expat community, Metropolis (https://metropolisjapan.com), Time Out Tokyo (www.timeout.com/tokyo) and Tokyo Weekender (www.tokyoweekender.com/) – all in English – are good sources of events listings and dining and drinking recommendations; look for them at Tourist Information Centers (TICs) and popular expat hang-outs.

Medical Services

The level of care in Tokyo is high, but English is only reliably spoken at certain clinics and hospitals. Your accommodation may be able to help; you can also use the city's emergency translation service.

The only insurance accepted at Japanese clinics and hospitals is Japan-issued health insurance; however, they cannot refuse treatment for lack of insurance. For any medical treatment you'll have to pay up front (credit cards are accepted at hospitals and may or may not be accepted at local clinics) and apply for reimbursement when you get home. Even paid in full, the cost of medical care in Japan is low compared to countries like the US.

Clinics, dentists and hospitals with a special interest in serving Tokyo's expat community may have arrangements with some of the larger, global providers; you will need to check with your provider in advance. These will also be able to provide claim forms in English.

Clinics

Every Tokyo neighbourhood has at least one primary care clinic. Called *naika* (内科), these are often small – sometimes run by just one doctor – and are considered the first point of contact for common, non-urgent complaints, like rashes, sinus infections, gastric upsets and the like. For additional care, the doctor can refer you to a specialist.

There is no requirement in the Japanese system to register with a particular primary care doctor or clinic. Most *naika* accept walk-ins; in fact, many do not take appointments. Be prepared to wait and note that most close for several hours during the early afternoon. Unfortunately, English can be hit-or-miss at neighbourhood *naika*.

Tokyo has a few clinics that cater to the expat community and thus have English-speaking (and often foreign-trained) doctors, nurses and staff. Bear in mind that the cost of healthcare at these facilities may be higher than that of a typical *naika*.

Reliable options include:

Primary Care Tokyo (プライマリーケア東京; Map p272; ☎03-5432-7177; http://pctclinic.com; 3rd fl, 2-1-16 Kitazawa, Setagaya-ku; consultation fee ¥8640; ⏲9am-12.30pm Mon-Sat, 2.30-6pm Mon-Fri, closed 1st & 3rd Wed; 🚉Keiō Inokashira line to Shimo-Kitazawa, south exit) Appointments accepted and recommended, but walk-ins will be seen.

Tokyo Medical & Surgical Clinic (東京メディカルアンドサージカルクリニック; Map p270; ☎03-3436-3028; www.tmsc.jp; 2nd fl, 32 Shiba-kōen Bldg, 3-4-30 Shiba-kōen, Minato-ku; consultations from ¥12,960; ⏲8.30am-5.30pm Mon-Fri, to noon Sat; [S]Hibiya line to Kamiyachō, exit 1) Appointments required; however, walk-ins needing urgent care will be accepted. Has in-house English-speaking specialists. Pricier than most.

For dental concerns, see English-speaking **Trust Dental Clinic** (トラスト歯科クリニック; Map p276; ☎03-3402-1501; www.trustdental.jp; 1-11-1 Jingūmae, Shibuya-ku; consultation ¥6480; ⏲9.30am-5.30pm, Sun-Fri; 🚉JR Yamanote line to Harajuku, Omote-sandō exit). They're very popular and often fully booked, but will try to accommodate those in need of urgent care.

Hospitals & Emergency Rooms

St Luke's International Hospital (聖路加国際病院; Sei-roka Kokusai Byōin; Map p268; ☎appointments 03-3527-9527, general 03-3541-5151, international department 03-5550-7166; http://hospital.luke.ac.jp; 9-1 Akashi-chō, Chūō-ku; ⏲international department 8.30am-5pm Mon-Fri; [S]Hibiya line to Tsukiji, exits 3 & 4) Tokyo's most foreigner-friendly hospital, with English-speaking doctors and translation services provided. Walk-ins accepted for primary care

(8.30am to 11am weekdays) and paediatric care (8.30am to 11am and 6.45pm to 9.45pm weekdays); appointments are required for specialist care. Has 24-hour emergency care.

Pharmacies

Common pharmacy chains include Matsumoto Kiyoshi (マツモトキヨシ), Tomod's (トモズ) and Tsuruha Drug (ツルハドラッグ). Almost every train station will have one nearby. Neighbourhood pharmacies are generally open 10am to 9pm but you can find 24-hour ones in big hubs like Shinjuku and Shibuya.

Pharmacies in Japan carry very few recognisable foreign brands (Tylenol, a brand of paracetamol, is an exception). Local substitutes of common medication such as ibuprofen and cough syrups are available, though the dosages may be less than what you're used to. For stronger doses, you'll need to see a doctor for a prescription. Packaging is often evocative, but double-check with the staff; some may speak some English, otherwise miming is usually effective.

Only some pharmacies carry clotrimazole (to treat yeast infections), which is kept behind the counter (you'll have to ask for it); better to pack your own.

Pharmacies are also the place to pick up condoms, pregnancy tests, feminine hygiene products and nappies.

Money

ATMs

Only a few branches of major Japanese banks – the big two are Sumitomo Mitsui (SMBC) and Tokyo-Mitsubishi UFJ (MUFG) – have ATMs that accept foreign-issued cards; there will be a sign in the window if the bank has an international

ATM. Otherwise, even bank ATMs that display Visa and MasterCard logos only work with Japan-issued versions of these cards.

The easiest place to get cash in Tokyo is at one of the city's ubiquitous 7-Eleven convenience stores. Their **Seven Bank** (www.seven bank.co.jp/english) ATMs consistently work with foreign-issued Visa, MasterCard, American Express, Plus, Cirrus, Maestro and Union Pay cards; have instructions in English; and are available 24 hours.

Other convenience store chains have international ATMs, but Seven Bank is the most user-friendly.

Japan Post Bank (ゆうちょ銀行; www.jp-bank.japan post.jp/en/ias/en_ias_index. html) has ATMs, found inside post offices and sometimes at train stations. They accept most foreign-issued cards and have English instructions. The downside is that they have opening hours that are only slightly longer than regular post-office hours.

There is a withdrawal limit of ¥100,000 per transaction at Seven Bank ATMs (and ¥50,000 at Japan Post Bank ATMs). Bear in mind that your bank or card company may impose an even stricter limit; if your card is rejected, this might be the reason why.

Cash

The currency in Japan is the yen (¥), and banknotes and coins are easily distinguishable. There are ¥1, ¥5, ¥10, ¥50, ¥100 and ¥500 coins; and ¥1000, ¥2000 (rare), ¥5000 and ¥10,000 banknotes. The ¥5 coin – bronze-coloured with a hole punched in the middle – is the only piece of currency not marked with Arabic numerals.

Note that prices are usually noted in Arabic numerals, but sometimes may be hand-written using the traditional kanji for numerals; you may also see the kanji for yen (円) used.

It's a good idea to keep at least several thousand yen on hand at all times (or more, to avoid ATM fees), to cover the odd shop that doesn't take cards.

Debit cards are just starting to become popular in Japan, but locals still tend to use cash for daily, sundry purchases. As such, many places require a minimum purchase to use a card. Some shops, and most convenience stores, allow you to pay with your Suica or Pasmo train pass.

Changing Money

Major banks and post office main branches can usually exchange US, Canadian and Australian dollars, pounds sterling, euros, Swiss francs, Chinese yuan and Korean won. MUFG also operates **World Currency Shop** (www.tokyo-card.co.jp/wcs/wcs-shop-e.php) foreign-exchange counters near major shopping centres that can handle a broader range of currencies, including Taiwan, Hong Kong, Singapore and New Zealand dollars. In all cases, you'll need to show your passport. Note that you receive a better exchange rate when withdrawing cash from ATMs than when exchanging cash or travellers cheques in Tokyo.

Credit Cards

Visa is the most widely accepted, followed by MasterCard, American Express and Diners Club. Foreign-issued cards should work fine. The standard in Japan is a chip card that requires a PIN for verification. Cards that require swiping and signing may confuse staff, but should still work; miming the required action usually does the trick.

Opening Hours

Note that some outdoor attractions (such as gardens) may close earlier in the winter. Standard opening hours:

Banks 9am to 3pm (some to 5pm) Monday to Friday

Bars 6pm to late, with no fixed closing hours

Boutiques Noon to 8pm, irregularly closed

Cafes Vary enormously; chains 7am to 10pm

Department stores 10am to 8pm

Museums 9am or 10am to 5pm; often closed Monday

Post offices 9am to 5pm Monday to Friday

Restaurants Lunch 11.30am to 2pm, dinner 6pm to 10pm; last orders taken about half an hour before closing

Post

Japan Post (JP) is reliable and efficient. Every Tokyo neighbourhood has a small post office (郵便局; *yūbinkyoku*). Every ward has a central office with extended hours; some of these have 24-hour 'Yu-Yu Madoguchi' (ゆうゆう窓口) that offer limited services – like mailing letters and small parcels, and purchasing stamps. For current rates, see www.post.japanpost.jp.

Useful post offices include the following:

Shibuya Post Office (渋谷郵便局; Map p272; 1-12-13 Shibuya, Shibuya-ku; ⊗9am-9pm Mon-Fri, to 7pm Sat & Sun, limited services 24hr; 🚉JR Yamanote line to Shibuya, east exit)

Shinjuku Post Office (新宿郵便局; Map p280; 1-8-8 Nishi-Shinjuku, Shinjuku-ku; ⊗9am-9pm, limited services 24hr; 🚉JR Yamanote line to Shinjuku, west exit)

Tokyo Central Post Office (東京中央郵便局; Map p266; ☎03-3217-5231; https://map.japanpost.jp/p/search/dtl/300101615000/; 2-7-2 Marunouchi, Chiyoda-ku; ⊗9am-9pm Mon-Fri, until 7pm Sat & Sun; 🚉JR lines to Tokyo, Marunouchi south exit)

Public Holidays

If a national holiday falls on a Monday, most museums and restaurants that normally close on Mondays will remain open and close the next day instead.

New Year's Day (Ganjitsu) 1 January

Coming-of-Age Day (Seijin-no-hi) Second Monday in January

National Foundation Day (Kenkoku Kinen-bi) 11 February

Emperor's Birthday (Tennō-no-Tanjōbi) 23 February

Spring Equinox (Shumbun-no-hi) 20 or 21 March

Shōwa Day (Shōwa-no-hi) 29 April

Constitution Day (Kempō Kinem-bi) 3 May

Green Day (Midori-no-hi) 4 May

Children's Day (Kodomo-no-hi) 5 May

Marine Day (Umi-no-hi) Third Monday in July

Mountain Day (Yama-no-hi) 11 August

Respect-for-the-Aged Day (Keirō-no-hi) Third Monday in September

Autumn Equinox (Shūbun-no-hi) 23 or 24 September

Health & Sports Day (Taiiku-no-hi) Second Monday in October

Culture Day (Bunka-no-hi) 3 November

Labour Thanksgiving Day (Kinrō Kansha-no-hi) 23 November

Responsible Travel

Tokyo being huge, the city has so far largely been able to absorb the rising number of tourists. Locals are less likely to grumble if visitors abide by established norms, such as queuing and refraining from loud conversations (especially on public transportation). One complaint that is common in the restaurant industry is no-shows; if you cannot make your reservation, do call (or have your accommodation call for you), or the restaurant takes the loss on the ingredients purchased specifically for your party – and may hesitate to accept reservations from overseas guests in the future.

Buy Local

Find accommodations through Japanese Guesthouses (www.japaneseguesthouses.com), which lists small, family-run inns.

Tread Lightly

➡ Refuse packaging by saying, 'Fukuro wa irimasen' (I don't need a bag), at the cash register, or just hold up a reusable shopping bag to show you've already got one.

➡ Limit your consumption of seafood threatened by overfishing, such as unagi (eel) and maguro (tuna) – including toro (fatty tuna belly).

➡ Skip vending machines, which use up a considerable amount of energy.

➡ Carry your own water bottle and find refilling stations via the app mymizu (www.mymizu.co).

Safe Travel

➡ Drink spiking continues to be a problem in Roppongi (resulting in robbery, extortion and, in extreme cases, physical assault). This is most often the case when touts are involved; never follow a tout into a bar, anywhere.

➡ Men are likely to be solicited in Roppongi and neighbourhoods that are considered

red-light districts, including Kabukichō (in Shinjuku) and Dōgenzaka (in Shibuya). Women – particularly solo women – are likely to be harassed in these districts.

➡ Groping does sometimes occur on crowded trains. Most Tokyo train lines have women-only carriages at peak times. These are marked with signs (usually pink) in Japanese and English. Children can ride in them, too.

➡ COVID-19 cases and casualties in Tokyo were low compared to many cities abroad; however, Japan's slow vaccine rollout has meant prolonged community transmission and a heightened chance for new variants to emerge. Travellers are advised to check the latest information before making travel plans; current border restrictions and quarantine protocols are posted on the Ministry of Foreign Affairs website (www.mofa.go.jp).

Taxes & Refunds

Some shops won't charge you consumption tax at the point of sale. Others – particularly department stores – will charge you and then require you to go to the store's tax refund counter to get the money back; a small service fee may be deducted for this process.

Airports in Japan do not handle tax refunds so you do need to sort it out at the time of purchase. A form will be affixed to your passport then, which you'll simply hand over to customs officials at the airport when you depart.

For details, see https://tax-freeshop.jnto.go.jp.

Telephone

Mobile Phones

Japan operates on the 3G network, so compatible phones should work in Tokyo.

Prepaid data-only SIM cards for unlocked smartphones are widely available and can be purchased at kiosks in the arrival halls at both Narita and Haneda airports and also from dedicated desks at major electronics retailers like Bic Camera and Yodobashi Camera.

Getting the SIM to work may require some fiddling with settings, so make sure you've got a connection before you leave the counter. Staff usually speak some English.

Currently only Mobal (www.mobal.com) offers SIMs that give you an actual phone number from which to make and receive calls; they offer English language support and can ship to your accommodation. Otherwise, the variety is huge, and which one to go with depends on the length of your stay and how much data you need.

Many mid- to high-end hotels in Tokyo offer complementary Handy phones, which you can use free of charge for data and calls. For a list of properties that provide this service, see www.handy.travel.

Phone Codes

Tokyo's area code is 03, although some outer suburbs have different area codes. Mobile phone numbers start with 090, 080 or 070; IP phone numbers with 050; and toll-free numbers with 0120, 0070, 0077, 0088 and 0800.

When dialling Tokyo from abroad, drop the first 0; dial 81-3 or 81-90.

Public Phones

Tokyo still has many public phones – a crucial lifeline when disasters wipe out the mobile network. Ordinary public phones are green; those that allow you to call abroad are grey and are usually marked 'International & Domestic Card/Coin Phone'. Public phones are most commonly located around train stations.

Local calls cost ¥10 per minute; note that you won't get change on a ¥100 coin. The minimum charge for international calls is ¥100, which buys you a fraction of a minute – good for a quick check-in but not economical for much more. Dial 001 010 (KDDI), 0061 010 (SoftBank Telecom) or 0033 010 (NTT), followed by the country code, area code and local number.

There's very little difference in the rates from the different providers; all offer better rates at night. Reverse-charge (collect) international calls can be made by dialling 0051.

Time

Tokyo local time is nine hours ahead of Greenwich Mean Time (GMT). Japan does not observe daylight saving time.

JAPANESE YEARS

Japan uses the near-universal Gregorian calendar, but also counts years in terms of the reigns of its emperors, using the ceremonial names bestowed upon them (such as Meiji, Shōwa and Heisei). So for example, the first year of Emperor Akihito's reign (1989) is known as Heisei 1. Because the transition often happens mid-year, some 'years' are shorter than normal. For example, the year Heisei 31 ended on 30 April 2019 with Akihito's abdication, and the current era, Reiwa, began the following day, when Emperor Naruhito ascended the throne.

Toilets

➡ The word for toilet in Japanese is *toire* (トイレ, pronounced 'to-ee-rey') but many prefer to use the more politely evasive *o-te-arai* (お手洗い; wash room) or *keshōshitsu* (化粧室; powder room).

➡ Tokyo has few actual public toilets; most people prefer the privately maintained ones provided by train stations, tourist attractions, department stores and malls, which tend to be nicer. Some convenience stores have toilets, too.

➡ Toilets are typically marked with generic gendered pictograms; but just in case, note the characters for female (女) and male (男).

➡ Newer or recently redeveloped buildings may have 'multi-functional' (多機能; *takinō*) restrooms; these large, separate rooms are wheelchair accessible, may have nappy changing or ostomate facilities, and are gender-neutral.

➡ Most of Tokyo's old-style squat toilets (called *washiki*; 和式) have been phased out in favour of Western-style toilets (*yōshiki*; 洋式), often with fancy bidet features (these are called washlets). If you do use a squat toilet, the correct position is facing the hood.

➡ Toilet paper is usually present, but it's a good idea to carry a packet of tissues.

➡ Paper towels and hand dryers may or may not be present; most Japanese carry a handkerchief for use after washing their hands.

➡ Separate toilet slippers will be provided in establishments where you take off your shoes at the entrance; they are typically just inside the toilet door. These are for use in the toilet area only, so remember to shuffle out of them when you leave.

Tourist Information

Tokyo Metropolitan Government Building Tourist Information Center (Map p280;☎03-5321-3077; info@tokyo-tourism.jp; 1st fl, Tokyo Metropolitan Government Bldg 1, 2-8-1 Nishi-Shinjuku, Shinjuku-ku; ⊗9.30am-6.30pm; ⓈŌedo line to Tochōmae, exit A4) is the main municipal tourist information centre with a huge amount of English-language information and English-speaking staff.

Additional branches include the following:

Haneda Airport Tourist Information Center (☎03-6428-0653; ⊗24hr; 🖥)

Keisei Ueno Tourist Information Center (Map p284;☎03-3836-3471; 1-60 Ueno-kōen, Taitō-ku; ⊗9.30am-6.30pm; 🖥; ℝJR & Keisei lines to Ueno, Ikenohata exit)

Shinjuku Bus Terminal Tourist Information Center (Map p280; ☎03-6274-8192; 3rd fl, Shinjuku Bus Station, 5-24-55 Sendagaya, Shibuya-ku; ⊗6.30am-11pm; ℝJR Yamanote line to Shinjuku, new south exit) Nearly paper-free, with iPads you can use to browse the city's official app and English-speaking staff.

There's also a luggage-forwarding counter.

JNTO Tourist Information Center (Map p266;☎03-3201-3331; www.jnto.go.jp; 1st fl, Shin-Tokyo Bldg, 3-3-1 Marunouchi, Chiyoda-ku; ⊗9am-5pm; 🖥; ⓈChiyoda line to Nijūbashimae, exit 1) Run by the Japan National Tourism Organisation (JNTO), this TIC has information on Tokyo and beyond. Staff speak English.

In addition to the nationally and municipally run Tourist Information Centers, there are many others around the city, run by individual wards, neighbourhood revitalisation NPOs (nonprofits) and private enterprises.

Beyond general information in English, some offer luggage storage and shipping services, neighbourhood tours and cultural activities. Note that TICs cannot make accommodation bookings.

Asakusa Culture Tourist Information Center (浅草文化観光センター; Map p286; ☎03-3842-5566; www.city.taito.lg.jp; 2-18-9 Kaminarimon, Taitō-ku; ⊗9am-8pm; 🖥; ⓈGinza line to Asakusa, exit 2) A ward-run TIC, has lots of info on Asakusa and Ueno, and a Pia ticket counter (for purchasing tickets to concerts

JR EAST TRAVEL SERVICE CENTERS

At all JR East Travel Service Centers, located at both airports and at JR Tokyo, Shinjuku, Shibuya, Ikebukuro, Ueno and Hamamatsuchō Stations, you can book *shinkansen* (bullet-train) tickets, purchase rail passes or exchange rail-pass vouchers and get tourist information in English. The main branch, at **Tokyo Station** (JR東日本トラベルサービスセンター; Map p266; ☎03-5221-8123; www.jreast.co.jp; Tokyo Station, 1-9-1 Marunouchi, Chiyoda-ku; ⊗7.30am-8.30pm; 🖥; ℝJR Yamanote line to Tokyo, Marunouchi north exit), also offers currency exchange, same-day baggage storage (¥600), luggage forwarding, and booking services for ski and onsen getaways that are accessed via JR lines (and with lodgings at partner hotels); bookings can also be made at the Shinjuku branch.

and shows), near the entrance to Sensō-ji.

G Info (Map p268; www.ginza.jp; 5-2-1 Ginza, Chūō-ku; ⏰11am-6pm; ⓈGinza line to Ginza, exits C2 & C3) English-speaking staff are available to help at this official Ginza information point outside of Tōkyū Plaza Ginza.

Shibuya Station Tourist Information Centre (⏰10am-7pm) In the basement of Shibuya Station, in the passageway between exits 8 and 9, this counter has English-speaking staff, a useful map of the area and free city magazines in English.

Tōbu Sightseeing Service Center (Map p286;✆03-3841-2871; www.tobu.co.jp/foreign; Tōbu Asakusa Station, 1-4-1 Hanakawado, Taitō-ku; ⏰7.20am-7pm; ⓈGinza line to Asakusa, exit 1) Sells passes for Tōbu rail transport from Asakusa to Nikkō and unlimited hop-on, hop-off bus services around Nikkō.

Visas

Temporary Visas

Citizens of 68 countries/regions, including Australia, Canada, Korea, New Zealand, Singapore, USA, UK and almost all European nations, will be automatically issued a *tanki-taizai* (temporary visitor visa) on arrival. Typically this visa is good for 90 days. For a complete list of visa-exempt countries and durations, consult www.mofa.go.jp/j_info/visit/visa/short/novisa.html#list.

Citizens of Austria, Germany, Ireland, Lichtenstein, Mexico, Switzerland and the UK can extend this visa once, for another 90 days. To do so, you need to apply at the **Tokyo Regional Immigration Bureau** (東京入国管理局, Tokyo Nyūkoku Kanrikyoku; ✆03-5796-7111; www.immi-moj.go.jp; 5-5-30 Kōnan, Minato-ku; ⏰9am-noon & 1-4pm Mon-Fri; 🚉99 from Shinagawa Station, east exit to Tokyo Nyūkoku Kanrikyokumae, 🚃Rinkai line to Tennōzu Isle) before the initial visa expires.

Resident Cards

Anyone entering Japan on a visa for longer than the standard 90 days for tourists will be issued a resident card (在留カード; *zairyū kādo*); these are given out at Narita or Haneda airports (show your visa to airport staff to be directed to the correct counter). The resident card works in lieu of a passport for identification and must be carried at all times.

Work Visas

It is difficult these days to find jobs, even English-teaching ones, that offer visa sponsorship. If you do find one, know that the sponsorship process can be a lengthy one – typically taking at least three months.

The first step is to apply for a Certificate of Eligibility, which requires handing over any number of documents (depending on the desired visa status), at your nearest Japanese immigration office. Once this certificate has been issued, you can then apply for a visa. Some companies may handle some or all of this process for you.

Given the high cost of living in Tokyo, it makes sense to secure employment and, at the very least, the Certificate of Eligibility while still in your home country.

Working-Holiday Visas

Citizens of 20 countries/regions are eligible for working-holiday visas: Argentina, Australia, Austria, Canada, Chile, Denmark, France, Germany, Ireland, Hungary, Korea, New Zealand, Norway, Poland, Portugal, Slovakia, Spain and the UK.

To qualify you must be between the ages of 18 and 30 (or 18 and 25 for Australians, Canadians and Koreans) with no accompanying dependants. With few exceptions, the visa is valid for one year and you must apply from a Japanese embassy or consulate abroad.

The visa is designed to enable young people to travel during their stay, and there are legal restrictions about how long and where you can work; you may also be required to show proof of adequate funds.

For more details, see www.mofa.go.jp/j_info/visit/w_holiday.

Language

Japanese is spoken by more than 125 million people. While it bears some resemblance to Altaic languages such as Mongolian and Turkish and has grammatical similarities to Korean, its origins are unclear. Chinese is responsible for the existence of many Sino-Japanese words in Japanese, and for the originally Chinese kanji characters which the Japanese use in combination with the homegrown hiragana and katakana scripts.

Japanese pronunciation is easy to master for English speakers, as most of its sounds are also found in English. If you read our coloured pronunciation guides as if they were English, you'll be understood. In Japanese, it's important to make the distinction between short and long vowels, as vowel length can change the meaning of a word. The long vowels, shown in our pronunciation guides with a horizontal line on top of them (ā, ē, ī, ō, ū), should be held twice as long as the short ones. It's also important to make the distinction between single and double consonants, as this can produce a difference in meaning. Pronounce the double consonants with a slight pause between them, eg sak·ka (writer).

Note also that the vowel sound ai is pronounced as in 'aisle', air as in 'pair' and ow as in 'how'. As for the consonants, ts is pronounced as in 'hats', f sounds almost like 'fw' (with rounded lips), and r is halfway between 'r' and 'l'. All syllables in a word are pronounced fairly evenly in Japanese.

WANT MORE?

For in-depth language information and handy phrases, check out Lonely Planet's *Japanese Phrasebook*. You'll find it at **shop. lonelyplanet.com**, or you can buy Lonely Planet's iPhone phrasebooks at the Apple App Store.

BASICS

Japanese uses an array of registers of speech to reflect social and contextual hierarchy, but these can be simplified to the form most appropriate for the situation, which is what we've done in this language guide too.

Hello.	こんにちは。	kon·ni·chi·wa
Goodbye.	さようなら。	sa·yō·na·ra
Yes.	はい。	hai
No.	いいえ。	ī·e
Please. (when asking)	ください。	ku·da·sai
Please. (when offering)	どうぞ。	dō·zo
Thank you.	ありがとう。	a·ri·ga·tō
Excuse me. (to get attention)	すみません。	su·mi·ma·sen
Sorry.	ごめんなさい。	go·men·na·sai

You're welcome.
どういたしまして。　　　dō i·ta·shi·mash·te

How are you?
お元気ですか?　　　o·gen·ki des ka

Fine. And you?
はい、元気です。　　　hai, gen·ki des
あなたは?　　　a·na·ta wa

What's your name?
お名前は何ですか?　　　o·na·ma·e wa nan des ka

My name is ...
私の名前は　　　wa·ta·shi no na·ma·e wa
…です。　　　... des

Do you speak English?
英語が話せますか?　　　ē·go ga ha·na·se·mas ka

I don't understand.
わかりません。　　　wa·ka·ri·ma·sen

Does anyone speak English?
どなたか英語を　　　do·na·ta ka ē·go o
話せますか?　　　ha·na·se·mas ka

ACCOMMODATION

Where's a ...?	…はどこですか?	... wa do·ko des ka
campsite	キャンプ場	kyam·pu·jō
guesthouse	民宿	min·shu·ku
hotel	ホテル	ho·te·ru
inn	旅館	ryo·kan
youth hostel	ユースホステル	yū·su·ho·su·te·ru

Do you have a ... room?	…ルームはありますか?	...rū·mu wa a·ri·mas ka
single	シングル	shin·gu·ru
double	ダブル	da·bu·ru

How much is it per ...?	…いくらですか?	... i·ku·ra des ka
night	1泊	ip·pa·ku
person	1人	hi·to·ri

air-con	エアコン	air·kon
bathroom	風呂場	fu·ro·ba
window	窓	ma·do

DIRECTIONS

Where's the ...?
…はどこですか? ... wa do·ko des ka

Can you show me (on the map)?
(地図で)教えて (chi·zu de) o·shi·e·te
くれませんか? ku·re·ma·sen ka

What's the address?
住所は何ですか? jū·sho wa nan des ka

Could you please write it down?
書いてくれませんか? kai·te ku·re·ma·sen ka

behind ...	…の後ろ	... no u·shi·ro
in front of ...	…の前	... no ma·e
near ...	…の近く	... no chi·ka·ku
next to ...	…のとなり	... no to·na·ri
opposite ...	…の向かい側	... no mu·kai·ga·wa
straight ahead	この先	ko·no sa·ki

Turn ...	…まがってください。	... ma·gat·te ku·da·sai
at the corner	その角を	so·no ka·do o
at the traffic lights	その信号を	so·no shin·gō o
left	左へ	hi·da·ri e
right	右へ	mi·gi e

KEY PATTERNS

To get by in Japanese, mix and match these simple patterns with words of your choice:

When's (the next bus)?
(次のバスは) (tsu·gi no bas wa)
何時ですか? nan·ji des ka

Where's (the station)?
(駅は)どこですか? (e·ki wa) do·ko des ka

Do you have (a map)?
(地図) (chi·zu)
がありますか? ga a·ri·mas ka

Is there (a toilet)?
(トイレ) (toy·re)
がありますか? ga a·ri·mas ka

I'd like (the menu).
(メニュー) (me·nyū)
をお願いします。 o o·ne·gai shi·mas

Can I (sit here)?
(ここに座って) (ko·ko ni su·wat·te)
もいいですか? mo ī des ka

I need (a can opener).
(缶切り) (kan·ki·ri)
が必要です。 ga hi·tsu·yō des

Do I need (a visa)?
(ビザ) (bi·za)
が必要ですか? ga hi·tsu·yō des ka

I have (a reservation).
(予約)があります。 (yo·ya·ku) ga a·ri·mas

I'm (a teacher).
私は(教師) wa·ta·shi wa (kyō·shi)
です。 des

EATING & DRINKING

I'd like to reserve a table for (two people).
(2人)の予約を (fu·ta·ri) no yo·ya·ku o
お願いします。 o·ne·gai shi·mas

What would you recommend?
なにが na·ni ga
おすすめですか? o·su·su·me des ka

What's in that dish?
あの料理に何 a·no ryō·ri ni na·ni
が入っていますか? ga hait·te i·mas ka

Do you have any vegetarian dishes?
ベジタリアン料理 be·ji·ta·ri·an ryō·ri
がありますか? ga a·ri·mas ka

I'm a vegetarian.
私は wa·ta·shi wa
ベジタリアンです。 be·ji·ta·ri·an des

I'm a vegan.
私は厳格な wa·ta·shi wa gen·ka·ku na
菜食主義者 sai·sho·ku·shu·gi·sha
です。 des

I don't eat ...	…は 食べません。	... wa ta·be·ma·sen
dairy products	乳製品	nyū·sē·hin
(red) meat	(赤身の) 肉	(a·ka·mi no) ni·ku
meat or dairy products	肉や 乳製品は	ni·ku ya nyū·sē·hin
pork	豚肉	bu·ta·ni·ku
seafood	シーフード 海産物	shī·fū·do/ kai·sam·bu·tsu

Is it cooked with pork lard or chicken stock?

これはラードか鶏の だしを使って いますか?	ko·re wa rā·do ka to·ri no da·shi o tsu·kat·te i·mas ka

I'm allergic to (peanuts).

私は (ピーナッツ)に アレルギーが あります。	wa·ta·shi wa (pī·nat·tsu) ni a·re·ru·gī ga a·ri·mas

That was delicious!

おいしかった。	oy·shi·kat·ta

Cheers!

乾杯!	kam·pai

Please bring the bill.

お勘定をください。	o·kan·jō o ku·da·sai

Key Words

appetisers	前菜	zen·sai
bottle	ビン	bin
bowl	ボール	bō·ru
breakfast	朝食	chō·sho·ku
cold	冷たい	tsu·me·ta·i
dinner	夕食	yū·sho·ku
fork	フォーク	fō·ku
glass	グラス	gu·ra·su

SIGNS

入口	**Entrance**
出口	**Exit**
営業中/開館	**Open**
閉店/閉館	**Closed**
インフォメーション	**Information**
危険	**Danger**
トイレ	**Toilets**
男	**Men**
女	**Women**

grocery	食料品	sho·ku·ryō·hin
hot (warm)	熱い	a·tsu·i
knife	ナイフ	nai·fu
lunch	昼食	chū·sho·ku
market	市場	i·chi·ba
menu	メニュー	me·nyū
plate	皿	sa·ra
spicy	スパイシー	spai·shī
spoon	スプーン	spūn
vegetarian	ベジタリアン	be·ji·ta·ri·an
with	いっしょに	is·sho ni
without	なしで	na·shi de

Meat & Fish

beef	牛肉	gyū·ni·ku
chicken	鶏肉	to·ri·ni·ku
duck	アヒル	a·hi·ru
eel	うなぎ	u·na·gi
fish	魚	sa·ka·na
lamb	子羊	ko·hi·tsu·ji
lobster	ロブスター	ro·bus·tā
meat	肉	ni·ku
pork	豚肉	bu·ta·ni·ku
prawn	エビ	e·bi
salmon	サケ	sa·ke
seafood	シーフード 海産物	shī·fū·do/ kai·sam·bu·tsu
shrimp	小エビ	ko·e·bi
tuna	マグロ	ma·gu·ro
turkey	七面鳥	shi·chi·men·chō
veal	子牛	ko·u·shi

Fruit & Vegetables

apple	りんご	rin·go
banana	バナナ	ba·na·na
beans	豆	ma·me
capsicum	ピーマン	pī·man
carrot	ニンジン	nin·jin
cherry	さくらんぼ	sa·ku·ram·bo
cucumber	キュウリ	kyū·ri
fruit	果物	ku·da·mo·no
grapes	ブドウ	bu·dō
lettuce	レタス	re·tas
nut	ナッツ	nat·tsu
orange	オレンジ	o·ren·ji
peach	桃	mo·mo

peas	豆	ma·me
pineapple	パイナップル	pai·nap·pu·ru
potato	ジャガイモ	ja·ga·i·mo
pumpkin	カボチャ	ka·bo·cha
spinach	ホウレンソウ	hō·ren·sō
strawberry	イチゴ	i·chi·go
tomato	トマト	to·ma·to
vegetables	野菜	ya·sai
watermelon	スイカ	su·i·ka

Other

bread	パン	pan
butter	バター	ba·tā
cheese	チーズ	chī·zu
chilli	唐辛子	tō·ga·ra·shi
egg	卵	ta·ma·go
honey	蜂蜜	ha·chi·mi·tsu
horseradish	わさび	wa·sa·bi
jam	ジャム	ja·mu
noodles	麺	men
pepper	コショウ	koshō
rice (cooked)	ごはん	go·han
salt	塩	shi·o
seaweed	のり	no·ri
soy sauce	しょう油	shō·yu
sugar	砂糖	sa·tō

Drinks

beer	ビール	bī·ru
coffee	コーヒー	kō·hī
(orange) juice	(オレンジ)ジュース	(o·ren·ji·)jū·su
lemonade	レモネード	re·mo·nē·do
milk	ミルク	mi·ru·ku
mineral water	ミネラルウォーター	mi·ne·ra·ru·wō·tā

QUESTION WORDS

How?	どのように?	do·no yō ni
What?	なに?	na·ni
When?	いつ?	i·tsu
Where?	どこ?	do·ko
Which?	どちら?	do·chi·ra
Who?	だれ?	da·re
Why?	なぜ?	na·ze

red wine	赤ワイン	a·ka wain
sake	酒	sa·ke
tea	紅茶	kō·cha
water	水	mi·zu
white wine	白ワイン	shi·ro wain
yoghurt	ヨーグルト	yō·gu·ru·to

EMERGENCIES

Help!
たすけて! — tas·ke·te

Go away!
離れろ! — ha·na·re·ro

I'm lost.
迷いました。 — ma·yoy·mash·ta

Call the police.
警察を呼んで。 — kē·sa·tsu o yon·de

Call a doctor.
医者を呼んで。 — i·sha o yon·de

Where are the toilets?
トイレはどこですか? — toy·re wa do·ko des ka

I'm ill.
私は病気です。 — wa·ta·shi wa byō·ki des

It hurts here.
ここが痛いです。 — ko·ko ga i·tai des

I'm allergic to ...
私は…
アレルギーです。 — wa·ta·shi wa ...
a·re·ru·gī des

SHOPPING & SERVICES

I'd like to buy ...
…をください。 — ... o ku·da·sai

I'm just looking.
見ているだけです。 — mi·te i·ru da·ke des

Can I look at it?
それを見ても
いいですか? — so·re o mi·te mo
ī des ka

How much is it?
いくらですか? — i·ku·ra des ka

That's too expensive.
高すぎます。 — ta·ka·su·gi·mas

Can you give me a discount?
ディスカウント
できますか? — dis·kown·to
de·ki·mas ka

There's a mistake in the bill.
請求書に間違いが
あります。 — sē·kyū·sho ni ma·chi·gai ga
a·ri·mas

ATM	ATM	ē·tī·e·mu
credit card	クレジットカード	ku·re·jit·to·kā·do
post office	郵便局	yū·bin·kyo·ku
public phone	公衆電話	kō·shū·den·wa
tourist office	観光案内所	kan·kō·an·nai·jo

TIME & DATES

What time is it?
何時ですか？ — nan·ji des ka

It's (10) o'clock.
(10)時です。 — (jū)·ji des

Half past (10).
(10)時半です。 — (jū)·ji han des

am	午前	go·zen
pm	午後	go·go

Monday	月曜日	ge·tsu·yō·bi
Tuesday	火曜日	ka·yō·bi
Wednesday	水曜日	su·i·yō·bi
Thursday	木曜日	mo·ku·yō·bi
Friday	金曜日	kin·yō·bi
Saturday	土曜日	do·yō·bi
Sunday	日曜日	ni·chi·yō·bi

January	1月	i·chi·ga·tsu
February	2月	ni·ga·tsu
March	3月	san·ga·tsu
April	4月	shi·ga·tsu
May	5月	go·ga·tsu
June	6月	ro·ku·ga·tsu
July	7月	shi·chi·ga·tsu
August	8月	ha·chi·ga·tsu
September	9月	ku·ga·tsu
October	10月	jū·ga·tsu
November	11月	jū·i·chi·ga·tsu
December	12月	jū·ni·ga·tsu

TRANSPORT

boat	船	fu·ne
bus	バス	bas
metro	地下鉄	chi·ka·te·tsu
plane	飛行機	hi·kō·ki
train	電車	den·sha
tram	市電	shi·den

What time does it leave?
これは何時に — ko·re wa nan·ji ni
出ますか？ — de·mas ka

Does it stop at (...)?
(…)に — (...) ni
停まりますか？ — to·ma·ri·mas ka

Please tell me when we get to (...).
(…)に着いたら — (...) ni tsu·i·ta·ra
教えてください。 — o·shi·e·te ku·da·sai

NUMBERS

1	一	i·chi
2	二	ni
3	三	san
4	四	shi/yon
5	五	go
6	六	ro·ku
7	七	shi·chi/na·na
8	八	ha·chi
9	九	ku/kyū
10	十	jū
20	二十	ni·jū
30	三十	san·jū
40	四十	yon·jū
50	五十	go·jū
60	六十	ro·ku·jū
70	七十	na·na·jū
80	八十	ha·chi·jū
90	九十	kyū·jū
100	百	hya·ku
1000	千	sen

A one-way/return ticket (to ...).
(... 行きの) — (...·yu·ki no)
片道/往復 — ka·ta·mi·chi/ō·fu·ku
切符。 — kip·pu

first	始発の	shi·ha·tsu no
last	最終の	sai·shū no
next	次の	tsu·gi no

aisle	通路側	tsū·ro·ga·wa
bus stop	バス停	bas·tē
cancelled	キャンセル	kyan·se·ru
delayed	遅れ	o·ku·re
ticket window	窓口	ma·do·gu·chi
timetable	時刻表	ji·ko·ku·hyō
train station	駅	e·ki
window	窓側	ma·do·ga·wa

I'd like to hire a ...	…を借りたい のですが。	... o ka·ri·tai no des ga
bicycle	自転車	ji·ten·sha
car	自動車	ji·dō·sha
motorbike	オートバイ	ō·to·bai

GLOSSARY

Amida Nyorai – Buddha of the Western Paradise

ANA – All Nippon Airways

-bashi – bridge (also *hashi*)

bashō – sumo tournament

bentō – boxed lunch or dinner, usually containing rice, vegetables and fish or meat

bosatsu – a bodhisattva, or Buddha attendant, who assists others to attain enlightenment

bugaku – dance pieces played by court orchestras in ancient Japan

bunraku – classical puppet theatre that uses life-size puppets to enact dramas similar to those of *kabuki*

chō – city area (for large cities) sized between a *ku* and *chōme*

chōme – city area of a few blocks

Daibutsu – Great Buddha

daimyō – domain lords under the *shōgun*

dōri – street

fugu – poisonous pufferfish, elevated to haute cuisine

futon – cushion-like mattress that is rolled up and stored away during the day

futsū – local train; literally 'ordinary'

gagaku – music of the imperial court

gaijin – foreigner; the contracted form of *gaikokujin* (literally, 'outside country person')

-gawa – river (also *kawa*)

geisha – a woman versed in the arts and other cultivated pursuits who entertains guests

-gū – shrine (also *-jingū* or *-jinja*)

haiden – hall of worship in a shrine

haiku – seventeen-syllable poem

hakubutsukan – museum

hanami – cherry-blossom viewing

hashi – bridge (also *-bashi*); chopsticks

higashi – east

hiragana – phonetic syllabary used to write Japanese words

honden – main building of a shrine

hondō – main building of a temple

ikebana – art of flower arrangement

irori – open hearth found in traditional Japanese homes

izakaya – Japanese pub/eatery

-ji – temple (also *tera* or *dera*)

-jingū – shrine (also *-jinja* or *-gū*)

-jinja – shrine (also *-gū* or *-jingū*)

jizō – bodhisattva who watches over children

JNTO – Japan National Tourist Organization

-jō – castle (also *shiro*)

JR – Japan Railways

kabuki – form of Japanese theatre that draws on popular tales and is characterised by elaborate costumes, stylised acting and the use of male actors for all roles

kaiseki – Buddhist-inspired, Japanese haute cuisine; called *cha-kaiseki* when served as part of a tea ceremony

kaisoku – rapid train

kaiten-sushi – conveyor-belt sushi

kamikaze – literally, 'wind of the gods'; originally the typhoon that sank Kublai Khan's 13th-century invasion fleet and the name adopted by Japanese suicide bombers in the waning days of WWII

kampai – cheers, as in a drinking toast

kanji – literally, 'Chinese writing'; Chinese ideographic script used for writing Japanese

Kannon – Buddhist goddess of mercy

karaoke – a now-famous export where revellers sing along to recorded music, minus the vocals

kawa – river

-ken – prefecture, eg Shiga-ken

kimono – traditional outer garment that is similar to a robe

kita – north

-ko – lake

kōban – local police box

kōen – park

ku – ward

kyōgen – drama performed as comic relief between *nō* plays, or as separate events

kyūkō – ordinary express train (faster than a *futsū*, only stopping at certain stations)

live house – a small concert hall where live music is performed

machi – city area (for large cities) sized between a *ku* and *chōme*

mama-san – older women who run drinking, dining and entertainment venues

maneki-neko – beckoning or welcoming cat figure frequently seen in restaurants and bars; it's supposed to attract customers and trade

matcha – powdered green tea served in tea ceremonies

matsuri – festival

midori-no-madoguchi – ticket counter in large Japan Rail stations, where you can make more complicated bookings (look for the green band across the glass)

mikoshi – portable shrine carried during festivals

minami – south

minshuku – Japanese equivalent of a B&B

mon – temple gate

mura – village

N'EX – Narita Express

Nihon – Japanese word for Japan; literally, 'source of the sun' (also known as *Nippon*)

Nippon – see *Nihon*

nishi – west

nō – classical Japanese drama performed on a bare stage

noren – door curtain for restaurants, usually labelled with the name of the establishment

NTT – Nippon Telegraph & Telephone Corporation

o- prefix used as a sign of respect (usually applied to objects)

obi – sash or belt worn with *kimono*

O-bon – mid-August festivals and ceremonies for deceased ancestors

o-furo – traditional Japanese bath

onsen – mineral hot spring with bathing areas and accommodation

o-shibori – hot towels given in restaurants

pachinko – vertical pinball game that is a Japanese craze

Raijin – god of thunder

ryokan – traditional Japanese inn

ryōri – cooking; cuisine

ryōtei – traditional-style, high-class restaurant; *kaiseki* is typical fare

sabi – a poetic ideal of finding beauty and pleasure in imperfection; often used in conjunction with *wabi*

sakura – cherry trees

salaryman – male employee of a large firm

-sama – a suffix even more respectful than *san*

samurai – Japan's traditional warrior class

-san – a respectful suffix applied to personal names, similar to Mr, Mrs or Ms but more widely used

sentō – public bath

setto – set meal; see also *teishoku*

Shaka Nyorai – Historical Buddha

shakkei – borrowed scenery; technique where features outside a garden are incorporated into its design

shamisen – three-stringed, banjo-like instrument

-shi – city (to distinguish cities with prefectures of the same name)

shinkansen – bullet train (literally, 'new trunk line')

Shintō – indigenous Japanese religion

Shitamachi – traditionally the low-lying, less-affluent parts of Tokyo

shōgun – military ruler of pre-Meiji Japan

shōjin ryōri – Buddhist vegetarian cuisine

shokudō – Japanese-style cafeteria/cheap restaurant

soba – thin brown buckwheat noodles

tatami – tightly woven floor matting on which shoes should not be worn

teishoku – set meal in a restaurant

tokkyū – limited express train

torii – entrance gate to a *Shintō* shrine

tsukemono – Japanese pickles

udon – thick, white, wheat noodles

ukiyo-e – woodblock prints; literally, 'pictures of the floating world'

wabi – a Zen-inspired aesthetic of rustic simplicity

wasabi – spicy Japanese horseradish

washi – Japanese paper

yakuza – Japanese mafia

Zen – a form of Buddhism

FOOD GLOSSARY

Rice Dishes

katsu-don (かつ丼) – rice topped with a fried pork cutlet

niku-don (牛丼) – rice topped with thin slices of cooked beef

oyako-don (親子丼) – rice topped with egg and chicken

ten-don (天丼) – rice topped with tempura shrimp and vegetables

Izakaya Fare

agedashi-dōfu (揚げだし豆腐) – deep-fried tofu in a dashi broth

jaga-batā (ジャガバター) – baked potatoes with butter

niku-jaga (肉ジャガ) – beef and potato stew

shio-yaki-zakana (塩焼魚) – a whole fish grilled with salt

poteto furai (ポテトフライ) – French fries

chiizu-age (チーズ揚げ) – deep-fried cheese

hiya-yakko (冷奴) – cold tofu with soy sauce and spring onions

tsuna sarada (ツナサラダ) – tuna salad over cabbage

Sushi & Sashimi

ama-ebi (甘海老) – shrimp

awabi (あわび) – abalone

hamachi (はまち) – yellowtail

ika (いか) – squid

ikura (イクラ) – salmon roe

kai-bashira (貝柱) – scallop

kani (かに) – crab

katsuo (かつお) – bonito

sashimi mori-awase (刺身盛り合わせ) – a selection of sliced sashimi

tai (鯛) – sea bream

toro (とろ) – the choicest cut of fatty tuna belly

uni (うに) – sea-urchin roe

Yakitori

yakitori (焼き鳥) – plain, grilled white meat

hasami/negima (はさみ/ねぎま) – pieces of white meat alternating with leek

sasami (ささみ) – skinless chicken-breast pieces

kawa (皮) – chicken skin

tsukune (つくね) – chicken meatballs

gyū-niku (牛肉) – pieces of beef

tebasaki (手羽先) – chicken wings

shiitake (しいたけ) – Japanese mushrooms

piiman (ピーマン) – small green peppers

tama-negi (玉ねぎ) – round white onions

yaki-onigiri (焼きおにぎり) – a triangle of rice grilled with *yakitori* sauce

Rāmen

rāmen (ラーメン) – soup and noodles with a sprinkling of meat and vegetables

chāshū-men (チャーシュー麺) – *rāmen* topped with slices of roasted pork

wantan-men (ワンタン麺) – *rāmen* with meat dumplings

miso-rāmen (みそラーメン) – *rāmen* with miso-flavoured broth

chānpon-men (ちゃんぽん麺) – Nagasaki-style *rāmen*

Soba & Udon

soba (そば) – thin brown buckwheat noodles

udon (うどん) – thick white wheat noodles

kake soba/udon (かけそば/うどん) – *soba/udon* noodles in broth

kata yaki-soba (固焼きそば) – crispy noodles with meat and vegetables

kitsune soba/udon (きつねそば/うどん) – *soba/udon* noodles with fried tofu

tempura soba/udon (天ぷらそば/うどん) – *soba/udon* noodles with tempura shrimp

tsukimi soba/udon (月見そば/うどん) – *soba/udon* noodles with raw egg on top

yaki-soba (焼きそば) – fried noodles with meat and vegetables

zaru soba (ざるそば) – cold noodles with seaweed strips served on a bamboo tray

Tempura

tempura moriawase (天ぷら盛り合わせ) – a selection of tempura

shōjin age (精進揚げ) – vegetarian tempura

kaki age (かき揚げ) – tempura with shredded vegetables or fish

Kushiage & Kushikatsu

ika (いか) – squid

renkon (れんこん) – lotus root

tama-negi (玉ねぎ) – white onion

gyū-niku (牛肉) – beef pieces

shiitake (しいたけ) – Japanese mushrooms

ginnan (銀杏) – ginkgo nuts

imo (いも) – potato

Okonomiyaki

mikkusu (ミックスお好み焼き) – mixed fillings of seafood, meat and vegetables

modan-yaki (モダン焼き) – *okonomiyaki* with *yaki-soba* and a fried egg

ika okonomiyaki (いかお好み焼き) – squid *okonomiyaki*

gyū okonomiyaki (牛お好み焼き) – beef *okonomiyaki*

negi okonomiyaki (ネギお好み焼き) – thin *okonomiyaki* with spring onions

Kaiseki

bentō (弁当) – boxed lunch

ume (梅) – regular course

take (竹) – special course

matsu (松) – extra-special course

Unagi

kabayaki (蒲焼き) – skewers of grilled eel without rice

unagi teishoku (うなぎ定食) – full-set *unagi* meal with rice, grilled eel, eel-liver soup and pickles

una-don (うな丼) – grilled eel over a bowl of rice

unajū (うな重) – grilled eel over a flat tray of rice

Alcoholic Drinks

nama biiru (生ビール) – draught beer

shōchū (焼酎) – distilled grain liquor

oyu-wari (お湯割り) – *shōchū* with hot water

chūhai (チューハイ) – *shōchū* with soda and lemon

whisky (ウィスキー) – whisky

mizu-wari (水割り) – whisky, ice and water

Coffee & Tea

kōhii (コーヒー) – regular coffee

burendo kōhii (ブレンドコーヒー) – blended coffee, fairly strong

american kōhii (アメリカンコーヒー) – weak coffee

kōcha (紅茶) – black, British-style tea

kafe ōre (カフェオレ) – cafe au lait, hot or cold

Japanese Tea

o-cha (お茶) – green tea

sencha (煎茶) – medium-grade green tea

matcha (抹茶) – powdered green tea used in the tea ceremony

bancha (番茶) – ordinary-grade green tea, brownish in colour

mugicha (麦茶) – roasted barley tea

Behind the Scenes

SEND US YOUR FEEDBACK

We love to hear from travellers – your comments keep us on our toes and help make our books better. Our well-travelled team reads every word on what you loved or loathed about this book. Although we cannot reply individually to your submissions, we always guarantee that your feedback goes straight to the appropriate authors, in time for the next edition. Each person who sends us information is thanked in the next edition – the most useful submissions are rewarded with a selection of digital PDF chapters.

Visit **lonelyplanet.com/contact** to submit your updates and suggestions or to ask for help. Our award-winning website also features inspirational travel stories, news and discussions.

Note: We may edit, reproduce and incorporate your comments in Lonely Planet products such as guidebooks, websites and digital products, so let us know if you don't want your comments reproduced or your name acknowledged. For a copy of our privacy policy visit lonelyplanet.com/privacy.

WRITER THANKS

Rebecca Milner

Thank you to my family and friends, who are there for me through all the ups and downs and late nights; to my indefatigable co-author Simon, for his inspiration and guidance; to LP for standing by me; and to all the chefs, curators, professors, baristas and total strangers who knowingly or unknowingly provided me with new insight into this city, which I must also thank, for always keeping me on my toes.

Simon Richmond

Many thanks to co-writer Rebecca and to the following: Will Andrews, Toshiko Ishii, Kenichi, Giles Murray, Chris Kirkland, Shoji Kobayashi, Jun Onuma, Sabrina Suljevic, Ken Gail Kato, Toyokuni Honda, Tim Hornyak and Tomoko Yoshizawa.

ACKNOWLEDGEMENTS

Illustration pp146–7 by Michael Weldon.
Cover photograph: Sensō-ji, Asakusa, coward_lion/Getty Images ©

Tokyo Metro map used with permission of Tokyo Metro and TBTMG. All rights reserved.

Climate map data adapted from Peel MC, Finlayson BL & McMahon TA (2007) 'Updated World Map of the Köppen-Geiger Climate Classification'; _Hydrology and Earth System Sciences_, 11, 1633–44.

THIS BOOK

This 13th edition of Lonely Planet's *Tokyo* guidebook was researched and written by Rebecca Milner and Simon Richmond. The 11th and 12th editions were also written by Rebecca and Simon. This guidebook was produced by the following:

Destination Editors Laura Crawford, James Smart

Senior Product Editors Kate Chapman, Sandie Kestell

Regional Senior Cartographer Julie Sheridan

Product Editor Pete Cruttenden

Book Designer Ania Bartoszek

Assisting Editors Bridget Blair, Victoria Harrison, Anne Mulvaney, Lauren O'Connell, Kristin Odijk

Assisting Cartographers Hunor Csutoros

Assisting Book Designer Clara Monitto

Cover Researcher Fergal Condon

Thanks to Naoko Akamatsu, Graham Holey, Elizabeth Jones, David Lurie, Matteo Pianca, Ed Schlenk, Victoria Smith, Saralinda Turner, Lim Chee Wah, Amanda Williamson

See also separate subindexes for:

✗ **EATING P260**

🍷 **DRINKING & NIGHTLIFE P260**

☆ **ENTERTAINMENT P261**

🛍 **SHOPPING P261**

🏃 **SPORTS & ACTIVITIES P262**

🛏 **SLEEPING P262**

Index

Tokyo Maps

Sights

- Beach
- Bird Sanctuary
- Buddhist
- Castle/Palace
- Christian
- Confucian
- Hindu
- Islamic
- Jain
- Jewish
- Monument
- Museum/Gallery/Historic Building
- Ruin
- Shinto
- Sikh
- Taoist
- Winery/Vineyard
- Zoo/Wildlife Sanctuary
- Other Sight

Activities, Courses & Tours

- Bodysurfing
- Diving
- Canoeing/Kayaking
- Course/Tour
- Sento Hot Baths/Onsen
- Skiing
- Snorkelling
- Surfing
- Swimming/Pool
- Walking
- Windsurfing
- Other Activity

Sleeping

- Sleeping
- Camping
- Hut/Shelter

Eating

- Eating

Drinking & Nightlife

- Drinking & Nightlife
- Cafe

Entertainment

- Entertainment

Shopping

- Shopping

Information

- Bank
- Embassy/Consulate
- Hospital/Medical
- Internet
- Police
- Post Office
- Telephone
- Toilet
- Tourist Information
- Other Information

Geographic

- Beach
- Gate
- Hut/Shelter
- Lighthouse
- Lookout
- Mountain/Volcano
- Oasis
- Park
- Pass
- Picnic Area
- Waterfall

Population

- Capital (National)
- Capital (State/Province)
- City/Large Town
- Town/Village

Transport

- Airport
- Border crossing
- Bus
- Cable car/Funicular
- Cycling
- Ferry
- Metro/MTR/MRT station
- Monorail
- Parking
- Petrol station
- Skytrain/Subway station
- Taxi
- Train station/Railway
- Tram
- Underground station
- Other Transport

Routes

- Tollway
- Freeway
- Primary
- Secondary
- Tertiary
- Lane
- Unsealed road
- Road under construction
- Plaza/Mall
- Steps
- Tunnel
- Pedestrian overpass
- Walking Tour
- Walking Tour detour
- Path/Walking Trail

Boundaries

- International
- State/Province
- Disputed
- Regional/Suburb
- Marine Park
- Cliff
- Wall

Hydrography

- River, Creek
- Intermittent River
- Canal
- Water
- Dry/Salt/Intermittent Lake
- Reef

Areas

- Airport/Runway
- Beach/Desert
- Cemetery (Christian)
- Cemetery (Other)
- Glacier
- Mudflat
- Park/Forest
- Sight (Building)
- Sportsground
- Swamp/Mangrove

Note: Not all symbols displayed above appear on the maps in this book

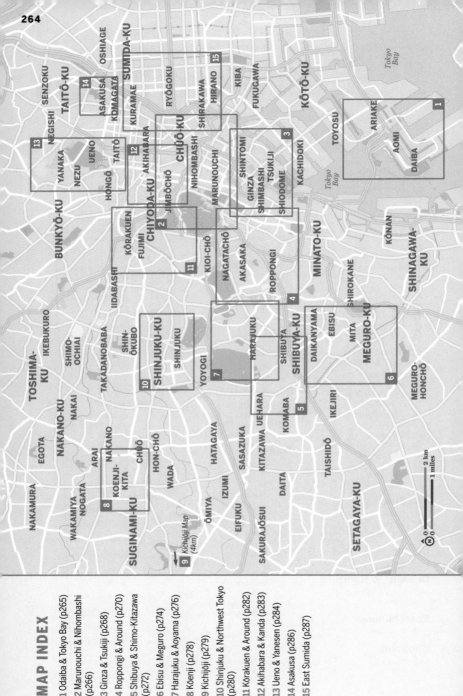

264

MAP INDEX

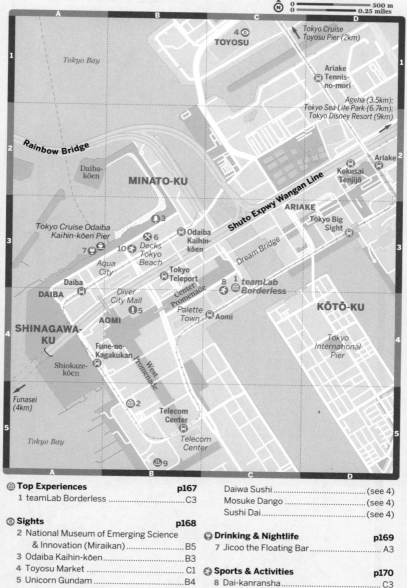

MARUNOUCHI & NIHOMBASHI

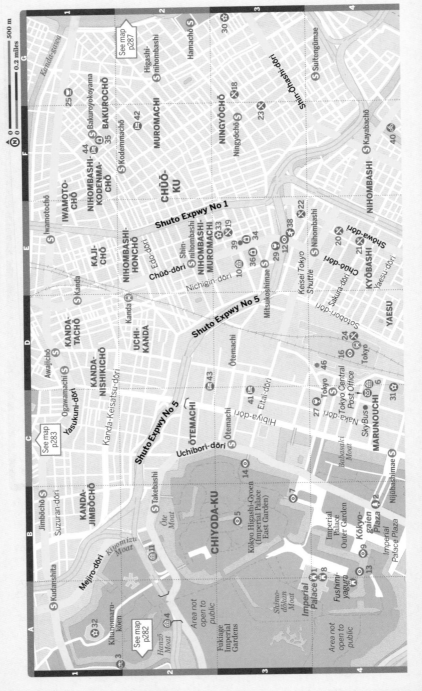

N

500 m
0.2 miles

See map p287

See map p283

See map p282

CHIYODA-KU

CHŪŌ-KU

Kanda-zawa

Hamachō Ⓢ

Higashi-nihombashi Ⓢ

Suitengūmae Ⓢ

BAKUROCHŌ

Bakuroyokoyama Ⓢ

MUROMACHI

NINGYŌCHŌ

Shin-Ōhashi-dōri

Ningyōchō Ⓢ

Kayabachō Ⓢ

NIHOMBASHI

Ⓢ Kodemmachō

IWAMOTO-CHŌ

NIHOMBASHI-KODENMA-CHŌ

Ⓢ Iwamotochō

Shuto Expwy No 1

KAJI-CHŌ

NIHOMBASHI-HONCHŌ

Shin-nihombashi Ⓢ

NIHOMBASHI-MUROMACHI

Edo-dōri

Chūō-dōri

Nichigin-dōri

Ⓢ Nihombashi

Ⓢ Kanda

Kanda Ⓢ

KANDA-TACHŌ

UCHI-KANDA

Shuto Expwy No 5

Mitsukoshimae Ⓢ

KYŌBASHI

Snowa-dōri

Yaesu-dōri

YAESU

Awajichō Ⓢ

KANDA-NISHIKICHŌ

Ⓢ Ogawamachi

Yasukuni-dōri

Kanda-Keisatsu-dōri

Keisei Tokyo Shuttle

Sakura-dōri

Sotobori-dōri

Chūō-dōri

Ōtemachi

Ōtemachi

Ⓢ Ōtemachi

Eitai-dōri

Tokyo Ⓢ

Tokyo Central Post Office

MARUNOUCHI

Shuto Expwy No 5

Jimbōchō Ⓢ

KANDA-JIMBŌCHŌ

Suzuran-dōri

Meijiro-dōri

Ⓢ Kudanshita

Ⓢ Takebashi

Uchibori-dōri

Hibiya-dōri

Naka-dōri

SkyBus

Babasaki Moat

Nijūbashimae Ⓢ

Kitanomaru-kōen

Ōte Moat

Kiyomizu Moat

Hanzō Moat

Shimo-dōkan Moat

Kōkyo Higashi-Gyoen (Imperial Palace East Garden)

Fukiage Imperial Gardens

Area not open to public

Imperial Palace

Fushimi-yagura

Imperial Palace Outer Garden

Kōkyo-gaien Plaza

Imperial Palace Plaza

Area not open to public

3 ☆

32 ☆

4 🏛

11 🏛

5 ◉

14 ◉

7 ◉

8 ✕

1 ✕

9 ◉

13 ◉

2 ◉

12 ◉

31 ☆

6 🏛

21 ◉

27 ◉

16 ◉

24 ✕

46 ◉

43 🏛

41 🏛

20 ✕

22 ✕

38 ★

12 ◉

29 ◉

34

36 🏛

39

10 🏛

33 ✕

19

23 ✕

18 ✕

42 🏛

35

44 🏛

25 🏛

30 ☆

40 ◉

45

See map p270

Sakuradamon Ⓢ

Kokkai-gijidōmae Ⓢ

Ⓢ Kasumigaseki

SHINKAWA

Sumida-gawa (Sumida River)

Hibiya Moat

Harumi-dōri

Hibiya-kōen

Hibiya Ⓢ

Kajibashi-dōri

YŪRAKUCHŌ Ⓢ 15 🚹 45

26

Yūrakuchō Ⓢ

Yūrakuchō Ⓡ 28

17

Sakura-dōri

Ginza-itchōme Ⓢ

GINZA

Ⓢ Ginza

37

Kyōbashi Ⓢ

Takaramachi Ⓢ

CHŪŌ-KU

Shin-Ōhashi-dōri

See map p268

Hatchōbori Ⓢ

HATCHŌBORI

Hatchōbori Ⓡ

Ⓢ Kyōbashi

◎ Top Experiences   p62
1 Imperial Palace..B4
2 Kōkyo-gaien Plaza................................B4

◎ Sights   p64
3 Chidori-ga-fuchi....................................A1
4 Crafts Gallery..A2
5 Imperial Palace East Garden.............B3
6 Intermediatheque.................................D4
7 Kikyō-mon...B3
8 Kyūden..B4
9 Megane-bashi..B4
10 Mitsui Memorial Museum....................E3
11 National Museum of Modern
    Art (MOMAT).......................................B2
12 Nihombashi...E3
13 Niju-bashi..B4
14 Ōte-mon...C3
15 Tokyo International Forum...................C5
16 Tokyo Station..D4

◎ Eating   p65
17 Dhaba India..D5
18 Kizushi..G3
    Meal MUJI Yūrakuchō...................(see 37)
    Nemuro Hanamaru.........................(see 6)
19 Nihombashi Dashi Bar
    Hanare...E3
20 Nihombashi Tamai................................E4
21 Pokémon Cafe.......................................E4
22 Taimeiken...E3
23 Tamahide..F3
24 Tokyo Ramen Street............................D4

◎ Drinking & Nightlife   p68
25 Bridge Coffee & Icecream.................G1
26 Chashitsu Kaboku.................................C5
27 (marunouchi) House.............................C4

28 Peter: the Bar...C5
29 Toyama Bar..E3

◎ Entertainment   p69
30 Arashio Stable...G3
31 Cotton Club..C4
32 Nippon Budōkan.....................................A1
33 Suigian...E3

◎ Shopping   p69
34 Coredo Muromachi................................E3
35 Gallery aM..F1
    Good Design Store Tokyo
    by Nohara.....................................(see 6)
    KITTE...(see 6)
36 Mitsukoshi...E3
37 Muji..C5
    Ōedo Antique Market...................(see 15)

◎ Sports & Activities   p70
38 Nihombashi Cruise................................E3
39 Time to Geisha.......................................E3
40 Tokyo Great Cycling
    Tour..F4

◎ Sleeping   p189
41 Aman Tokyo..C3
42 Citan...F2
43 Hoshinoya Tokyo....................................D2
44 Kikka..F1
    Peninsula Tokyo.............................(see 28)

◎ Information   p243
45 JNTO Tourist
    Information Center..........................C5
46 JR East Travel Service
    Center..D4

GINZA & TSUKIJI

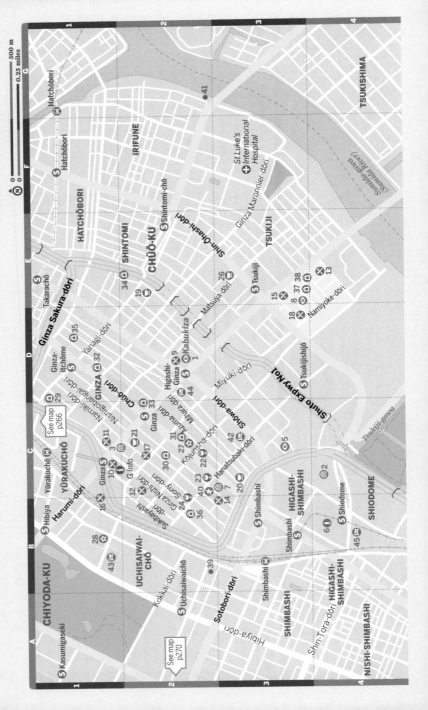

0   500 m
0   0.25 miles

CHIYODA-KU

YŪRAKUCHŌ

UCHISAIWAI-CHŌ

HATCHŌBORI

IRIFUNE

SHINTOMI

CHŪŌ-KU

GINZA

TSUKIJI

TSUKISHIMA

SHIMBASHI

HIGASHI-SHIMBASHI

SHIODOME

NISHI-SHIMBASHI

Kasumigaseki

Hibiya

Yūrakuchō

Ginza-itchōme

Takarachō

Hatchōbori

Hatchōbori

Hatchōbori

Shintomi-chō

Tsukiji

Kabukiza

Higashi-Ginza

Tsukijishijō

Shimbashi

Shimbashi

Shimbashi

Shiodome

Uchisaiwaichō

St Luke's International Hospital

Ginza Sakura-dōri

Ginza-dōri

Chūō-dōri

Namiki-dōri

Nishigobankei-dōri

Yanagi-dōri

Matsuya-dōri

Azuma-dōri

Minato-dōri

Miyuki-dōri

Showa-dōri

Kojunsha-dōri

Hanatsubaki-dōri

Ginza Nishi-dōri

Sony-dōri

Suzuki-dōri

Harumi-dōri

Sotobori-dōri

Hibiya-dōri

Kokkai-dōri

Shin-Tora-dōri

Shin-Ōhashi-dōri

Ginza Maronnier-dōri

Namiyoke-dōri

Shuto Expwy No.1

Sumida-gawa (Sumida River)

Tsukiji-gawa

See map p266

See map p270

G Info

41

34

19

26

15

13

37 38

8

18

35

29

32

9

1

44

33

31

27

30

3

11

21

17

22

42

5

2

45

6

28

43

16

10

12

36

24

40

23

14 7

20

39

GINZA & TSUKIJI

SHIBA-KŌEN

MINATO-KU

KŌTŌ-KU

KACHIDOKI

Tokyo Cruise Pier

Hama-rikyū Onshi-teien

Hato Bus Tours (300m)

Kaigan-dōri

Kiyosumi-dōri

Harumi-dōri

Kachidoki

Shiori-no-Ike

◎ **Top Experiences** p74
1 Kabukiza....................................D2

◎ **Sights** p73
2 Advertising Museum Tokyo......C4
3 Ginza Maison Hermès Le
   Forum..................................C1
4 Hama-rikyū Onshi-teien...........C5
5 Nakagin Capsule Tower...........C3
6 Ni-Tele Really Big Clock..........B4
7 Shiseido Gallery.....................C3
8 Tsukiji Market.......................E3

✖ **Eating** p74
9 Ain Soph...............................D2
10 Apollo...................................C1
11 Bird Land...............................C1
12 Ginza Sato Yosuke.................C2
13 Kimagure-ya.........................E4
14 Kyūbey.................................B3
15 Sanokiya..............................E3
16 Shimanto-gawa.....................B1
17 Tempura Kondō......................C2
18 Yamachō...............................D3

◎ **Drinking & Nightlife** p75
19 Bongen Coffee.......................E2
20 Cafe de l'Ambre....................C3
21 Cha Ginza.............................C2
22 Ginza Lion............................C2
23 Ginza Music Bar....................C2
24 Karat...................................(see 1)
25 Nakajima no Ochaya..............C5

Jugetsudo..............................B2
Karat....................................B2
Nakajima no Ochaya...............C5

Old Imperial Bar....................(see 43)
26 Turret Coffee........................E3

◎ **Entertainment** p76
27 Kanze Nōgakudō....................C2
28 Tokyo Takarazuka Theatre.....B1

🛍 **Shopping** p77
29 Akomeya...............................D1
30 Dover Street Market Ginza......C2
31 Ginza Six..............................C2
32 Itoya...................................(see 31)
33 Mitsukoshi............................D1
34 Morioka Shoten & Co.............E2
35 Okuno Building......................D1
36 Takumi.................................B2

37 Tsukiji Hitachiya...................E3
38 Tsukiji Uogashi.....................E3
   Uniqlo................................(see 30)

◎ **Sports & Activities** p78
39 Gray Line..............................B2
40 Komparu-yu...........................C2
41 Tsukiji Soba Academy.............G2

🛏 **Sleeping** p189
42 Bay Hotel Ginza.....................C3
43 Imperial Hotel.......................B1
44 Millennium Mitsui Garden Hotel
   Tokyo.................................D2
45 Park Hotel Tokyo...................B4

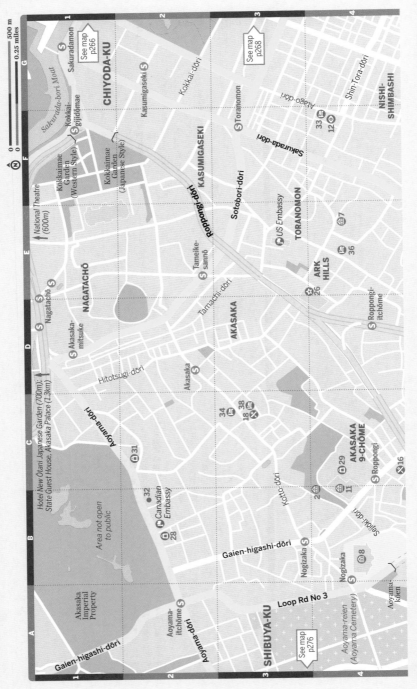

ROPPONGI & AROUND

270

500 m
0.25 miles

See map p266

CHIYODA-KU

See map p268

Sakuradamon Ⓢ

Kokkai-gijidōmae Ⓢ

Kokkai Ⓢ

Kasumigaseki Ⓢ

Sakurada-bori Moat

Kokkaimae Garden (Western Style)

Kokkaimae Garden (Japanese Style)

National Theatre (600m)

Hotel New Ōtani Japanese Garden (700m);
State Guest House, Akasaka Palace (1.3km)

NAGATACHŌ

Nagatachō Ⓢ

Akasaka-mitsuke Ⓢ

Tameike-sannō Ⓢ

KASUMIGASEKI

Kasumigaseki Ⓢ

Toranomon Ⓢ

Atago-dōri

Shin-Tora-dōri

NISHI-SHIMBASHI

Sakurada-dōri

33 🏛
12 ◎

US Embassy

TORANOMON

🏛 7

ARK HILLS

36 🏛

26 ✦

Roppongi-itchōme Ⓢ

Sotobori-dōri

Roppongi-dōri

Tamachi-dōri

AKASAKA

Akasaka Ⓢ

Hitotsugi-dōri

Aoyama-dōri

31 🏛

32 ●

Canadian Embassy

28 🏛

34 ●
18 ✕ 38 🏛

AKASAKA 9-CHŌME

29 🏛
11 🏛
2 🏛

Roppongi Ⓢ

16 ✕

Kotto-dōri

Gaien-higashi-dōri

Nogizaka Ⓢ

Nogizaka

🏛 8

Seijōki-dōri

Akasaka Imperial Property

Area not open to public

Aoyama-itchōme Ⓢ

Aoyama-dōri

SHIBUYA-KU

See map p276

Loop Rd No 3

Aoyama-reien (Aoyama Cemetery)

Aoyama-kōen

Gaien-higashi-dōri

ROPPONGI & AROUND

SHIBUYA & SHIMO-KITAZAWA

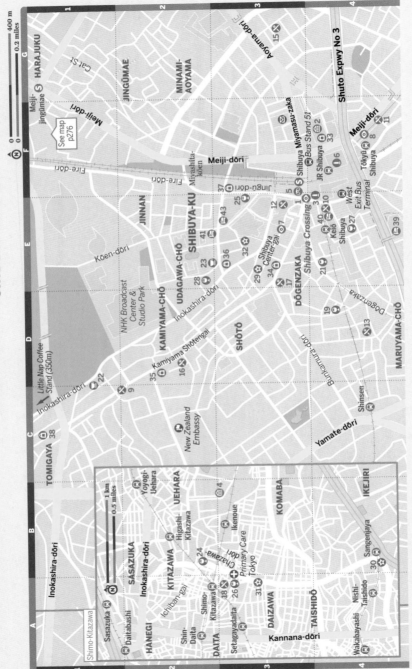

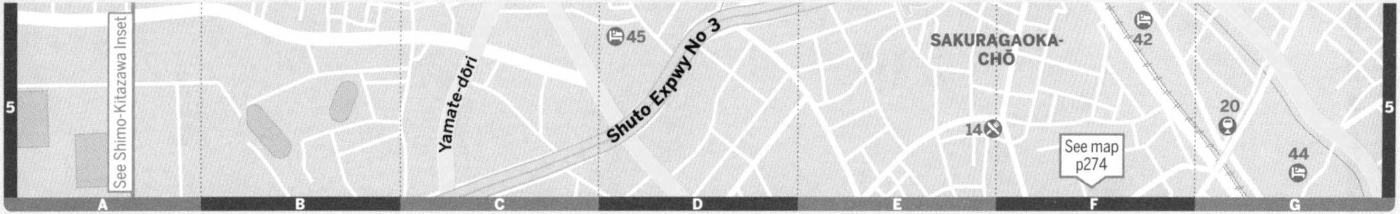

See Shimo-Kitazawa Inset
Yamate-dōri
Shuto Expwy No 3
SAKURAGAOKA-CHŌ
See map p274
45
42
20
14
44
A
B
C
D
E
F
G
5
5

Top Experiences p98
1 Shibuya Crossing E3

Sights p99
2 d47 Museum F4
3 Hachikō Statue E4
4 Japan Folk Crafts Museum B3
5 Mag's Park F3
6 Myth of Tomorrow F4
7 Shibuya Center-gai E3
8 Shibuya Stream F4

Eating p99
9 Camelback C2
d47 Shokudō (see 2)
10 Food Show E4
11 Gyūkatsu Motomura F4
12 Katsu Midori E3
Maru Bengara (see 8)
13 Matsukiya D4
14 Nagi Shokudō E5
15 Narukiyo G3
16 Pignon D2
17 Sagatani E3
18 Shirube A3

Drinking & Nightlife p101
19 Beat Cafe D4
20 Circus Tokyo G5
21 Contact E4
22 Fuglen Tokyo D1
23 Gen Gen An E2
24 Ghetto B2
25 Karaoke Rainbow E3
26 Mother A3
27 Oath E4
28 Rhythm Cafe E2

Entertainment p103
29 Club Quattro E3
30 Setagaya Public Theatre B4
31 Shimo-Kitazawa Three A3
32 WWW E3

Shopping p104
33 d47 design travel store F4
34 Mega Donki E3
Shibuya Hikarie (see 2)
35 Shibuya Publishing & Booksellers D2
36 Tokyu Hands E3
37 Tower Records F3
38 Tsukikageya C1

Sleeping p191
39 Cerulean Tower Tōkyū Hotel E4
40 Excel Hotel Tokyu E4
41 Hotel Koé Tokyo E2
42 Hotel Mets Shibuya F5
43 Millennials E3
44 Mustard Hotel G5
Shibuya Stream Excel Hotel Tokyu (see 8)
45 Turntable D5

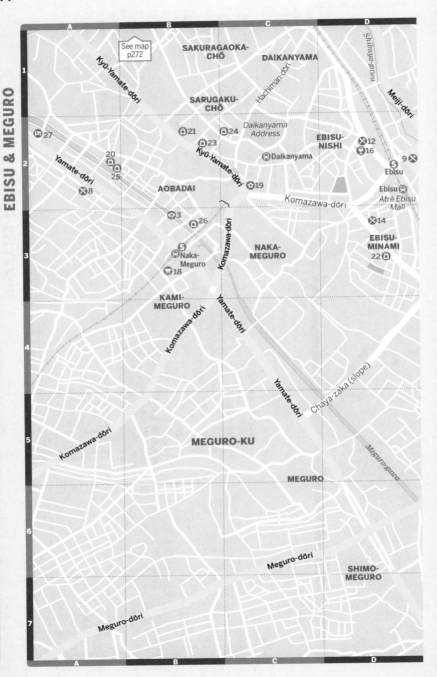

See map p272

SAKURAGAOKA-CHŌ

DAIKANYAMA

Hachiman-dōri

SARUGAKU-CHŌ

Kyū-Yamate-dōri

27

Daikanyama Address

EBISU-NISHI

21

24

23

Daikanyama

12

16

9

Ebisu

Yamate-dōri

20

25

8

Kyū-Yamate-dōri

19

AOBADAI

Komazawa-dōri

Ebisu Atré Ebisu Mall

3

26

14

EBISU-MINAMI

Komazawa-dōri

NAKA-MEGURO

22

Naka-Meguro

18

KAMI-MEGURO

Komazawa-dōri

Yamate-dōri

Chaya-zaka (slope)

Yamate-dōri

MEGURO-KU

Meguro-gawa

Komazawa-dōri

MEGURO

6

Meguro-dōri

SHIMO-MEGURO

Meguro-dōri

Meiji-dōri

Shibuya-gawa

HARAJUKU & AOYAMA

0 — 500 m
0 — 0.25 miles

Gaien-higashi-dōri

Ichō-Namiki

Aoyama-dōri

Gaienmae Ⓢ

Gaien-nishi-dōri

28 ⚽

Meiji-kōen

Gaien-nishi-dōri

JINGŪMAE

25 ❌ 21 ❌

URA-HARA

35 🏛 22 ❌

29 ⭐ SENDAGAYA

Kita-sandō Ⓢ

Meiji-dōri

14 ❌ 📍 Meiji-dōri

2 🏛

6 ◎

19 ❌ Cat St

10 ◎ 34 Meiji-jingūmae

33 Ⓢ 20

Meiji-jingū Kaikan

Kita-sandō

HARAJUKU 11 🏛 Trust Dental Clinic

Takeshita-dōri

36

Harajuku 🚉

Minami-sandō

7 ◎ 17 ❌ Meiji-jingūmae Ⓢ

SHIBUYA-KU

Meiji-jingū 🛕 1

12 ◎

3 ◎

Yoyogi-kōen 🌳 13

Sangūbashi 🚉

See map p270

HARAJUKU & AOYAMA

KŌENJI

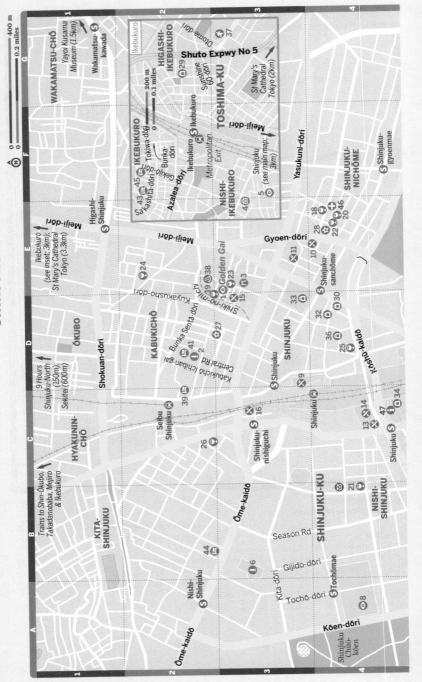

SHINJUKU & NORTHWEST TOKYO

0 400 m
0 0.2 miles

WAKAMATSU-CHŌ

Yayoi Kusama
Museum (1.5km)

Wakamatsu-
kawada Ⓢ

Ikebukuro
(see inset: 3km);
St Mary's Cathedral
Tokyo (3.3km)

Meiji-dōri

Higashi-
Shinjuku Ⓢ

ŌKUBO

Shokuan-dōri

KABUKICHŌ

Kuyakusho-dōri

Bunka Senta-dōri

Kabukichō Ichiban-gai

Central Rd

Shiki-no-michi

Shinjuku-dōri

Golden Gai

Meiji-dōri

HYAKUNIN-
CHŌ

Trains to Shin-Ōkubo,
Takadanobaba, Mejiro
& Ikebukuro

9 Hours
Shinjuku-North
(150m);
Sekitei (600m)

KITA-
SHINJUKU

Nishi-
Shinjuku Ⓢ

Seibu
Shinjuku Ⓢ

Shinjuku-
nishiguchi Ⓢ

Shinjuku Ⓢ

SHINJUKU

Shinjuku-
sanchōme Ⓢ

Gyoen-dōri

Yasukuni-dōri

SHINJUKU-
NICHŌME

Shinjuku-
gyoenmae Ⓢ

Ōme-kaidō

Season Rd

SHINJUKU-KU

Kita-dōri

Gijido-dōri

Tochō-dōri

Kōen-dōri

Tochōmae Ⓢ

Ōme-kaidō

NISHI-
SHINJUKU

Kōshū-kaidō

Shinjuku
Chūō-
Kōen

Inset: Ikebukuro

Shuto Expwy No 5

HIGASHI-
IKEBUKURO

Otome-dōri

TOSHIMA-KU

Sunshine
60-dōri

St Mary's
Cathedral
Tokyo (2km)

Meiji-dōri

IKEBUKURO

Ikebukuro Ⓢ Ikebukuro

Metropolitan
Exit

Bunka-
dōri

Gekijo-dōri

Azalea-dōri

Top-dōri

Kashita-dōri

Sa

NISHI-
IKEBUKURO

Shinjuku
(see main map:
3km)

200 m
0.1 miles

SHINJUKU & NORTHWEST TOKYO

UENO & YANESEN

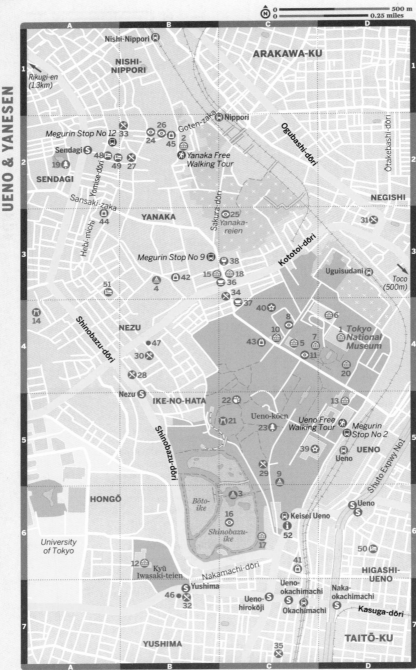

Nishi-Nippori

ARAKAWA-KU

NISHI-NIPPORI

Rikugi-en
(1.3km)

Nippori

Goten-zaka

Ogubashi-dōri

Ōtakebashi-dōri

Megurin Stop No 12   33
26
24   45
2

Sendagi   48
19   49   27

Yanaka Free
Walking Tour

NEGISHI

SENDAGI

Sansaki-zaka

Sakura-dōri

31

YANAKA

25
Yanaka-
reien

Kototoi-dōri

44

Hebi-michi

Yomise-dōri

Megurin Stop No 9   38

Uguisudani

Toco
(500m)

Shinobazu-dōri

42
4

15   18
36

51

34
37

14

40

NEZU

10

8
6

1 Tokyo
National
Museum

47

43

7
5

30

11

28

20

Nezu

IKE-NO-HATA

22

13

21

Ueno-kōen

23

Ueno Free
Walking Tour

Megurin
Stop No 2

39

UENO

Ueno

29
9

Shinobazu-dōri

Shuto Expwy No 1

Ueno

HONGŌ

Bōto-
ike

3

16
Shinobazu-
ike

Keisei Ueno
52

Ueno

University
of Tokyo

17

50

41

HIGASHI-
UENO

12   Kyū
Iwasaki-teien

Nakamachi-dōri

Ueno-
okachimachi

Naka-
okachimachi

46   Yushima
32

Ueno-
hirokōji

Okachimachi

Kasuga-dōri

YUSHIMA

35

TAITŌ-KU

UENO & YANESEN

Tokyo Sky Tree

0 ——— 200 m
0 ——— 0.1 miles

TAITŌ-KU

ASAKUSA

OSHIAGE

Tokyo Sky Tree Station

Oshiage

NARIHIRA

Main Map (1km) 0 ——— 200 m

↑ *Andon Ryokan (1.5km)*

Kototoi-dōri

MATSUGAYA

NISHI-ASAKUSA

Kappabashi Hon-dōri

Hisago-dōri

Hoppy-dōri

Senso-ji

Asakusa-kōen

Umamichi-dōri

HANAKAWADO

Sumida-kōen

Edo-dōri

Tsukuba Express Asakusa

Sushiya-dōri

Shin-Nakamise-dōri

KOMAGATA

Dembo-in-dōri

Tōbu Asakusa

Tokyo Mizube Cruising Line Niten-mon Pier

ASAKUSA

Orange-dōri

Chinyoko-dōri

Nakamise-dōri

Metro-dōri

Kaminari-mon-dōri

Asakusa Free Walking Tour

Asakusa

Tokyo Cruise Asakusa Pier

Tawaramachi

KAMINARI-MON

Kokusai-dōri

Asakusa-dōri

Asakusa

Sumida-gawa *(Sumida River)*

Shuto Expwy No 6

AZUMABASHI

KOTOBUKI

KOMAGATA

Dembōin-dōri

Komagata-bashi

Tokyo Sky Tree (see inset) (1km)